D1420523

SCOTTISH HISTORY SOCIETY

SIXTH SERIES

VOLUME 3

———

Records of
the Convention of Royal Burghs
1555; 1631–1648

Records of
the Convention of Royal Burghs
1555; 1631–1648

Edited by
Alan R. MacDonald
Mary Verschuur

COLLIGITE FRAGMENTA NE PEREANT

SCOTTISH HISTORY SOCIETY
2009

THE BOYDELL PRESS

First published 2013

A Scottish History Society publication
in association with The Boydell Press
an imprint of Boydell & Brewer Ltd
PO Box 9, Woodbridge, Suffolk IP12 3DF, UK
and of Boydell & Brewer Inc.
668 Mt Hope Avenue, Rochester, NY 14620–2731, USA
website: www.boydellandbrewer.com

ISBN 978–0–906245–34–7

A CIP catalogue record for this book is available
from the British Library

The publisher has no responsibility for the continued existence or accuracy
of URLs for external or third-party internet websites referred to in this
book, and does not guarantee that any content on such websites is,
or will remain, accurate or appropriate.

Papers used by Boydell & Brewer Ltd are natural, recyclable products
made from wood grown in sustainable forests

MIX
Paper from
responsible sources
FSC® C013604

Printed and bound in Great Britain by
CPI Group (UK) Ltd, Croydon, CR0 4YY

CONTENTS

ACKNOWLEDGEMENTS

The editors would like to thank the staff of the National Library of Scotland, the National Archives of Scotland and Aberdeen City Archives for their courteous and efficient service and advice. We should also like to acknowledge the kind permission of Fife Council Archives for the publication of the Burntisland material. Citation from the Fort Augustus manuscript has been granted with the permission and approval of the Trustees of the National Library of Scotland. Aberdeen City Archives are to be thanked for granting permission to reproduce the records in their care and for allowing digital images of the manuscripts to be taken, significantly speeding up the task of transcription. Particular debts of thanks are also owed to a number of individuals, notably Professor Archie Duncan for bringing the record of the 1555 convention to our attention and Judith Cripps, former archivist at Aberdeen City Archives, who provided considerable help and encouragement with the main body of the records in this volume and whose discovery in the 1980s of Aberdeen's copies of convention minutes has at last borne fruit. A number of others had a more or less unwitting hand in this and we thank them all: John Toller helped with the development of the project and some preliminary work in Aberdeen City Archives; Céline Foggie provided advice on French; Steve Murdoch answered questions and provided references on Robert Buchan, the pearl patentee; Roy Pinkerton on Latin; Siobhan Talbott on trade with France; Martine Van Ittersum and Peter Blom on Dutch placenames, currency and shipping; Chris Whatley on coal; and Kathrin Zickerman on German trade. Any errors which remain are, of course, the fault of the editors rather than these very obliging helpers to whom we are very grateful indeed.

Alan R. MacDonald, Mary Verschuur

ABBREVIATIONS

ACA	Aberdeen City Archives
GCA	Glasgow City Archives
MacDonald, *Burghs and Parliament*	A.R. MacDonald, *The Burghs and Parliament in Scotland, c.1550–1651* (Aldershot, 2007)
NAS	National Archives of Scotland
NLS	National Library of Scotland
Pryde, *The Burghs of Scotland*	G.S. Pryde, *The Burghs of Scotland: A Critical List* (Oxford, 1965)
RCRBS	J.D. Marwick et al. (eds.), *Records of the Convention of the Royal Burghs of Scotland*, 7 vols. (Edinburgh, 1866–1918)
RPC	J.H. Burton et al. (eds.), *Register of the Privy Council of Scotland*, 37 vols. (Edinburgh, 1877)
RPS	K.M. Brown et al. (eds.), *Records of the Parliaments of Scotland to 1707* (St Andrews, 2007–2010), www.rps.ac.uk
Young, *The Parliaments of Scotland*	M.Young (ed.), *The Parliaments of Scotland: Burgh and Shire Commissioners*, 2 vols. (Edinburgh, 1992–3)

INTRODUCTION

The Convention of Burghs

Although the early history of the body that was to develop into the convention of the royal burghs of Scotland remains somewhat obscure, there is sufficient material in print on the subject for it to be unnecessary to discuss its nature and development at length here.[1] Its origins lie in the thirteenth-century court of the four burghs, presided over by the king's chamberlain. This court, originally consisting of representatives from Berwick, Roxburgh, Edinburgh and Stirling, had jurisdiction over all of the king's burghs. This was possible because of the convenient fact that, when twelfth-century kings founded Scotland's first incorporated towns, a corpus of laws which were to obtain in every burgh, the *leges burgorum*, was drawn up. This gave Scotland's towns a legal and administrative uniformity virtually unknown elsewhere in western Europe and goes a long way to explaining why there was nothing like the convention of royal burghs in other European states. By the beginning of the fifteenth century, clear efforts were being made to enhance the representative nature of the court by commissioners being sought from all but the most northerly burghs. The court was occasionally referred to as a 'parliament', implying representative and deliberative as well as judicial functions. Although the earliest surviving official records date from 1552, evidence from other sources suggests that, by no later than the 1520s, it had developed into a fairly regular, if not yet annual, meeting.

The convention was an assembly of representatives from all those towns which received a parliamentary summons and whose merchants were permitted to engage in overseas trade. The representatives were known as 'commissioners', in common with the elected members of all representative assemblies in early modern Scotland. Commissioners were elected by the councils of the burghs that they represented and, with the exception of Edinburgh's right to elect both a merchant and a craftsman, they consisted entirely of 'trafficking merchant burgesses'. Indeed, strenuous efforts were

---

[1]   T. Pagan, *The Convention of the Royal Burghs of Scotland* (Glasgow, 1926), ch. 1; A.R. MacDonald, *The Burghs and Parliament in Scotland, c.1550–1651* (Aldershot, 2007), esp. 5–8. What follows is largely drawn from these sources.

made to ensure that this regulation was adhered to, one instance of which is recorded in this volume, when a commissioner from Glasgow at the general convention of 1632 was forbidden to sit because he was 'ane craftis man'.[2]

As the records published here show, the convention had a wide range of responsibilities, including the defence of the burghs' collective and individual trading privileges, lobbying central government, promoting manufactures and trade (both internal and international), arbitrating in disputes between burghs, co-ordinating the raising of money for public building projects within burghs, and maintaining and regulating the Scottish staple port at Veere (usually called Campvere in this period) on what was then the island of Walcheren in the province of Zeeland in the Netherlands but is now part of the mainland as the result of land reclamation.

The annual general convention usually met in early July, although it might be moved to avoid clashing with a parliamentary session: for example in 1633, because parliament met towards the end of June, the general convention at St Andrews was postponed until August to allow commissioners to report back on their parliamentary activities before the convention of burghs met. Attendance by representatives from all burghs was expected and fines were imposed upon those failing to send commissioners. Absence was permitted only if a burgh had obtained explicit permission from a previous convention, in which case, an absent burgh had to undertake to pay its normal dues and its proportionate share of any general contributions that were agreed upon, to promise to respect all decisions made by the conventions at which it was not represented, and to spend on public works any expenses that would have been incurred had a commissioner been sent.[3] 'Particular' conventions were also held at other times, with as many as four of these additional meetings sometimes taking place in one calendar year. They consisted of representatives from a smaller number of burghs, usually selected in advance at the preceding general convention. Their purpose was to handle business delegated to them by the general convention or, occasionally, to deal with matters arising between conventions, in which case the council of Edinburgh was empowered to choose which burghs to summon.[4] In addition, what effectively amounted to extraordinary general conventions commonly met immediately before parliamentary sessions, an example of which appears in this volume, with the convention that met at Edinburgh in June 1633.[5]

---

2   See below, 82; MacDonald, *Burghs and Parliament*, ch. 2.
3   See, for example, the sederunt for the general convention of 1636 which lists five burghs that were exempt in this way (251–2 below), and the 44th act of that convention which issued exemptions to four burghs (271 below).
4   See below, 56.
5   MacDonald, *Burghs and Parliament*, 58–62.

The Records of the Convention of Royal Burghs

Before the 1580s, the convention's records were not kept systematically, the convention having neither any permanent officers until 1584 nor a fixed location.[6] It is not difficult to see how this must have interfered with the efficient conduct of business and, in 1580 at a convention at Aberdeen, it was lamented that the burghs were 'greitlie prejugit be the inlaik [i.e. lack] of ane generall buke quhilk suld contene the haill lawis and constitution of burrowis'. It was therefore resolved that the burgh council of Edinburgh would 'cause the said buke be maid' and request all the other burghs to send in copies of any 'lawis, actis, and constitutionis' passed by conventions of burghs that were preserved in their own records. They were given until the next general convention in 1580 to carry this out.[7] It was a further two years, however, before the task was complete and the book was presented to the convention by John Guthrie, burgh clerk of Edinburgh, and subsequently the first official clerk to the convention. It was agreed that the council of Edinburgh would retain custody of the records and that any burgh wanting a copy for its own use might have one made for ten merks ($£6$ 13s. 4d.). This was confirmed in 1584 when Guthrie was explicitly appointed as 'thair commoun clark and kepar of thair generall buke'.[8]

As a result of the burghs' failure to begin the systematic compilation of the records of their convention until 1580, the records from before that date are incomplete, consisting only of those acts which were found in the process of commencing the official register. The oldest material in the first manuscript volume is the minute of a convention at Edinburgh in April 1552.[9] It is tempting to see in the first act of that meeting a genuine beginning, for it was a resolution that the burghs should meet annually thereafter. On closer inspection, however, this illusion dissolves, for the act notes that it had long been intended to convene annual meetings, the implication being that, while meetings of the burghs had occurred, the aspiration of regularity had not been realised, so efforts to achieve this were being renewed. There had been previous acts for annual conventions and it is not clear whether this one had any more immediate success. Therefore the only reason that the official records of the convention of burghs commence in 1552 is that these were the earliest minutes that were unearthed as a result of the investigations

---

6 John Guthrie was appointed permanent clerk in 1584, having acted as clerk since 1581 (see *RCRBS*, i, 120, 168, 185). Six years later, the convention appointed James Winram as its legal agent (see *RCRBS*, i, 348). Not until the later 1670s did the convention begin to meet almost invariably at Edinburgh, although the itinerant nature of general conventions had been in decline since 1660.

7 *RCRBS*, i, 103.

8 *RCRBS*, i, 128–9, 185–6.

9 *RCRBS*, i, 1–5.

initiated at Aberdeen in 1580. The records from between 1552 and 1580 are patchy, for individual burgh records reveal that a number of conventions met during that period for which no records survive. The Victorian published edition of the convention's records includes various acts from and evidence of additional meetings of burghs from as early as the late thirteenth century, while the record of a convention at Perth in 1555 that is published here for the first time reveals yet another previously lost meeting.[10]

From the early 1580s until 1631 the official manuscript record is virtually complete and so, therefore, is the Victorian edition of the convention's records. At the foot of page 330 of the third volume of *Extracts from the Records of the Convention of the Royal Burghs of Scotland* there is a short note to the reader in square brackets, following the last entry in the minute of a particular convention of burghs at Edinburgh on 3 March 1631. It states simply that 'The Convention Records are wanting from 3d March 1631 to 3d July 1649'.[11] The record then skips to the general convention of burghs at South Queensferry in July 1649. Much had happened over those eighteen years. Indeed, South Queensferry had not even been a royal burgh in 1631, not being enrolled until 1642, after years of resistance from Linlithgow.[12] When the venture to gather and publish the surviving records of the convention of royal burghs began in the middle of the nineteenth century, a whole volume of records, covering those eighteen years, was missing. The editors made valiant efforts to trace material which might fill that gap, hunting through the municipal archives of Scotland, but to no avail.[13] All that could be done was to provide brief summaries of some acts from some of those conventions that met in that period from a digest of acts of the convention that had been compiled at its behest in the later seventeenth century, a venture which appears to have been intended to update a similar digest of 1632, although the earlier one is no longer extant.[14] It would seem, from the records of the creation of that digest, and of further revisions of it that were begun in the later 1690s, that the volume covering the years 1631–1649 was still in existence at the beginning of the eighteenth century.[15] How and when it went missing between that date and the middle of the nineteenth century may never be known, although it remains possible that it will yet come to light, mis-shelved in an archive or having found its way into the obscurity of a private collection.

---

[10]   *RCRBS*, i, pp. xxi–xxv, 510–33.
[11]   *RCRBS*, iii, 330.
[12]   MacDonald, *Burghs and Parliament*, 22–3.
[13]   *RCRBS*, i, pp. xiii–xvi. See also n. 4 on p. viii where it mentions the missing volume of records from 1631–1649.
[14]   See below, 98.
[15]   *RCRBS*, iii, 628, iv, 210, 241, 306, 319, 466, 525–8.

It has, however, proved possible to recover the records of many of the conventions, both general and particular, from seven years of the period covered by that missing volume. It is a tragedy that the minutes of the convention of royal burghs that cover the later 1630s, the prelude to the Covenanting revolution of 1638, the revolution itself, and the bulk of the period of Covenanting rule remain lost. Yet it is a pleasure to be able to present here, for the first time in print, the full record of most of the conventions of burghs from July 1631 until July 1636, and of the general convention of July 1647. No claim is being made for the dramatic rediscovery of the bulk of these records, although those from 1647 were genuinely chanced upon in the course of personal research. The minutes of the conventions between 1631 and 1636 have been known about for some time already, albeit they have been neither widely publicised nor much used. In 1980, Judith Cripps, then city archivist with Aberdeen District Council, on discovering that her archive contained unpublished records of the convention of royal burghs, wrote to her counterpart in Edinburgh, Walter Makey, informing him of this. She enquired as to whether they were unique, since they were not included in the printed *Extracts*.[16] Makey replied promptly, expressing interest and describing the material from the 1630s as 'of the greatest interest'. Nothing further appears to have come of this exchange, however, and it was not until more recent research on the parliamentary activities of the burghs was being carried out that they were uncovered once again.

Aberdeen appears to be unique among Scotland's parliamentary burghs in retaining such an extensive body of convention records. From the later sixteenth century, in the wake of the decision by the convention of burghs to create and maintain an official register of its own records and to employ a permanent clerk, the burgh council of Aberdeen took the prudent decision to ensure that every returning commissioner brought a full minute of the convention home with him. The first recorded instance of this occurred in November 1589 when Mr David Rutherford 'producit the haill actis and proceidingis' of a particular convention which had recently met at Edinburgh.[17] In the following year, the council passed an 'Ordinance anent the diligence to be reportit be commissionaris to conventiounis'.[18] It included the stipulation that every returning commissioner must 'produce befoir the counsale the extract of the haill acts set doun, maid and concludit at

16 Edinburgh City Archives, Correspondence relating to the records of the convention of burghs preserved in ACA, SL30/8/16, consisting of a letter from Judith Cripps to Walter Makey and his reply.
17 ACA, Council Minutes, CR1/32, p. 574. Oddly, the record of this convention is not contained in the first volume of convention minutes held at Aberdeen, nor in the printed volumes of the nineteenth century.
18 ACA, Council Minutes, CR1/33/1, p. 656.

that conventioun to the quhilk he salbe chosin within aucht dais eftir his returnyng', or face a hefty fine of £20. Thereafter, it was common for the council minutes to record the return of the commissioner and his produc-tion of the minutes of the convention.[19] At some point, although it was not recorded in Aberdeen's council minutes, the burgh also acquired a copy of the older acts and thus the first volume of convention records held in Aberdeen includes those dating back to 1552 which were compiled between 1580 and 1582 by John Guthrie.[20] It is therefore by design, not by accident, that Aber-deen City Archives has the missing records from the 1630s. It is testament to the diligence with which that burgh's archives have been kept over the centuries that many of Aberdeen's copies survive while those which were acquired by other burghs do not. It was not uncommon for commissioners from other burghs to return from conventions with a copy of the full minute of the meeting but only in Aberdeen do they appear to have survived.[21] Even there, only those records from before 1637 were bound, while most of those dating from after 1636 appear to have perished or been lost. It is ironic that the first year after Aberdeen's virtually continuous sequence of bound convention minutes fails is 1637, a year in which Aberdeen itself hosted the general convention of burghs.[22] There is, however, a clue as to the fate of some of them. The verso of the third-from-last (unnumbered) folio of the first volume of convention records held in Aberdeen contains a note that 'The towne wants the actis of borrows from 1607 to 1617, as lykways they want the acts 1633, as also the acts 1637 and 1638. George Moriesone at Michaelmas 1650 did resave certane actis quhilk he hes not redelyvered.' This is probably the same George Morrison who was provost in the 1650s and possibly also dean of gild in 1631 and a bailie in 1637.[23] Of those listed, only the records from 1637 and 1638 appear not to have been returned, for those of 1607, 1617 and 1633 are all bound in the second volume. The note in the first volume also indicates that the records must have been bound for

---

[19] See, for example, ACA, Council Minutes, CR1/34/2, p. 865.

[20] ACA, 'Acts of Convention', SRO 25/3/1.

[21] See, for example, NAS, Burntisland Council Minutes, B9/12/2, fo. 64v; Linlithgow Town Council Minutes, B48/9/1, 324–5.

[22] NAS, Linlithgow Town Council Minute Book 1620–1640, B48/9/1, pp. 377–9. See ACA, CR1/52/1, pp. 342–3, recording the election of the burgh's commissioner and his report to the council after the convention. He was deemed to have 'done ane sufficient diligence in the said commissioun' but there was no mention of his presenting of the minutes of the convention.

[23] A.M. Munro, *Memorials of the Aldermen, Provost and Lord Provosts of Aberdeen, 1272–1893* (Aberdeen, 1897), 165–7; J. Stuart (ed.), *Extracts from the Council Register of Aberdeen, 1625–1642* (Edinburgh, 1871), 39; ACA, CR1/52/1, p. 356. There are no similar notes in the second volume of convention records.

the first time at some point after 1650, otherwise Morrison would not have been able to remove the records of individual conventions.

The Manuscripts

The records of the convention of royal burghs in this volume come from three different sources: the earliest, the record of a convention at Perth in 1555, was unearthed among the Fort Augustus Manuscripts held in the National Library of Scotland; the records of conventions between 1631 and 1636, along with some other papers from the 1640s, are held in Aberdeen City Archives; while the records of a convention at Edinburgh in 1647 are preserved among the burgh records of Burntisland, held in the National Archives of Scotland, Edinburgh.

Fort Augustus Manuscripts, National Library of Scotland, and the Pittenweem Writ, National Archives of Scotland

James D. Marwick's edition of the *Records of the Convention of the Royal Burghs of Scotland* opens with the records of a convention at Edinburgh in 1552.[24] These are followed immediately by those of another convention at the same burgh in May 1555. Due to the pressure of other business, the Edinburgh meeting was prorogued and the delegates were ordered to re-convene at Perth at the end of July. The minutes of the Perth gathering eluded Marwick, yet it was clear that the meeting had been held for the minutes of a later meeting, in September at Dundee, refer to the previous one at Perth.[25]

The minutes of the convention at Perth on 4 and 5 of August 1555 have recently come to light, engrossed in a sixteenth-century volume containing a copy of *Regiam Majestatem* and other legal documents that had been kept at Fort Augustus Abbey but is now in the National Library of Scotland.[26] There is nothing to distinguish the minutes amongst the miscellaneous entries in this bulky volume. They simply appear eight lines from the bottom of folio 330v and continue to the end of folio 333v. The Perth minutes are preceded by copies of the five statutes that were approved by the convention at Edinburgh in April 1552 noted above.[27] These are followed immediately by the heading 'At Perth 4 August 1555'. In contrast to the preceding entry, the record of the Perth meeting is transcribed in full from the sederunt to the final signatures. This appears to be a final copy of the business dealt with by

---

24 *RCRBS*, i, 1–5.
25 *RCRBS*, i, 10–15.
26 NLS, The Fort Augustus Collection, Acc. 11218/5. The existence of this document was brought to the editors' attention by Professor A.A.M. Duncan.
27 *RCRBS*, i, 2–4.

the commissioners at Perth, compiled and attested to by sir Henry Elder, notary and burgh clerk of Perth on 4 and 5 August 1555.[28] This material from the conventions of 1552 and 1555 has no obvious connection with either the previous or subsequent entries in what is a rather eclectic volume.

One of the acts of this convention is also preserved in the Pittenweem Writs, held in the National Archives of Scotland.[29] It covers two sides of one folio; the first 20 lines comprise a copy of the heading, the sederunt and the ninth statute passed at Perth in August 1555. The remaining 53 lines are a transcription of an act of parliament of 22 May 1584.[30] This act, 'Anent the gaige and standart of salmondis heringis and quhite fische and principall stapillis thairof', does not appear to have any obvious connection with the preceding Perth extract. The two simply seem to have ended up being copied on the same piece of paper.

Records held in Aberdeen City Archives

Aberdeen City Archives holds a substantial collection of manuscripts relating to the convention of royal burghs. The bulk of the material reproduced here comes from the second of three manuscript volumes, the first two of which contain full transcripts of the minutes of most conventions of royal burghs from 1552 to 1636, while the third contains abstracts of the acts of the convention from 1552 to 1669.[31] The material in the first two volumes, up to and including a particular convention of burghs at Edinburgh in March 1631, is identical to that contained in the first two printed volumes of convention records which were taken from the official minutes now held by Edinburgh City Archives.[32] The last six years of records in the second Aberdeen volume are unique and have not previously been published. The abstracts in the third volume are identical to those that were published in the fourth printed volume of convention records.[33] The first two Aberdeen volumes are foliated throughout, with numbers which are clearly in a seventeenth-century hand, suggesting that the records of individual conventions, which were brought back to Aberdeen by returning commissioners were bound within no more than a few decades of their creation. However, there are gaps and inconsistencies in the numbering of the folios. This may indicate that foliation occurred prior to binding and that some records were lost in that process, or that because the records have been bound more than once

28 NLS, The Fort Augustus Collection, Acc. 11218/5, fos. 330r–333v.
29 NAS, Pittenweem Writs, GD62/6/1.
30 *RPS*, 1584/5/25.
31 ACA, Acts of Convention, SRO 25/3/1–3.
32 *RCRBS*, i, passim, ii, 1–330.
33 *RCRBS*, iv, 525–58.

(most recently in the first half of the nineteenth century), some folios were lost during their disbinding and rebinding.

In addition to the bound material, Aberdeen City Archives holds a number of bundles of papers relating to the convention of royal burghs.[34] These include some copies of minutes of conventions from the later seventeenth century (all of which are already in print), and from the eighteenth and nineteenth centuries, as well as letters of instruction to the burgh's commissioners to the convention, and copies of the missives which were despatched to each burgh, requesting the election of the burgh's commissioner and containing a detailed agenda for the forthcoming convention. It was important to the convention that each burgh was an active participant in this representative system and, as can be seen from the records in this volume, it was common for an act to end with the statement that an unresolved matter should be a 'heid of the nixt missive', that is, an item on the agenda of the next convention. This ensured that each burgh council could send its commissioner 'sufficientlie instructed' on these matters and thus able to contribute fully to the discussion.[35] The representative theory was firmly one of delegation, whereby commissioners were directly representing the views of their electors, so much so that if a matter arose which had not been on that year's missive, it was customary to carry it over to the following year. Some of the missives from the period before 1644 have been published in *Aberdeen Council Letters*; not all of those held by Aberdeen City Archives appear in those volumes.[36] Those from the periods for which full minutes of conventions do not survive are an invaluable source of information on the business of those conventions and therefore the previously unpublished missives for 1641, 1643 and 1648 are included in this volume, having been omitted from the published council letters apparently because they were filed as papers relating to the convention of burghs, rather than as correspondence. There is therefore considerable value in reproducing these missives because their publication helps, at least partially, to fill some of the voids that remain in the surviving minutes of the convention of burghs between 1631 and 1649. These documents (along with the missives for 1638, 1639 and 1642 already published in *Aberdeen Council Letters*) reveal what

---

[34] ACA, Press 18, Bundles 69–71, 88. Only in bundles 70 and 88 is there any material that merits inclusion in this volume.

[35] The minutes of conventions are littered with this phrase, but see for example the 36th and 37th acts of the general convention of 1632, 99 below (fo. 411v).

[36] L.B. Taylor (ed.), *Aberdeen Council Letters*, 6 vols. (Aberdeen, 1942–61). The published missives are as follows: vol. i, 96–100 (1604), 153–7 (1617), 212–17 (1623), 238–43 (1626), 281–6 (1628), 298–304 (1629), 344–51 (1632), vol. ii, 89–98 (1638), 117–26 (1639), 300–307 (1642). The official records of the convention in the possession of Edinburgh City Archives include no missives from before the 1730s: ECA, SL30/4/8, Annual missives, 1733–1855.

business was to be handled at each convention and what had been carried over from previous years.

Burntisland Council Minutes, National Archives of Scotland
Burntisland hosted the general convention of royal burghs in the summer of 1648, as the missive for that year, reproduced here, shows.[37] The council of Burntisland was therefore responsible for sending the missives to all burghs that were entitled to elect commissioners. To ensure the accuracy of these missives, when Burntisland's commissioner returned from the general convention of 1647 at Edinburgh, the council exceptionally had the whole minute of that convention, including the sederunt, copied into its own minute book. The minute is preceded by a sederunt of the burgh council and a single act of the council, recording the return of the burgh's commissioner: 'Compeirit Captane Andro Watsone commissioner at the last generall conventioun of burrouis hauldin at Edinburgh the fyft day of Julij last and maid report of his commissioun and producit the extract of the whole actis quhairof the tennor followis'.[38] The record then takes up twenty-five pages of the council minute book, with the council minutes recommencing immediately thereafter, without even a new page being taken, either at the start or the end of the minutes of the convention. These minutes are not, however, quite as full as those that are preserved at Aberdeen. Aberdeen's convention minutes are verbatim copies of the official minutes, give or take a few inevitable scribal errors and variations in spelling made by the clerk to the convention in copying the record for Aberdeen's commissioner to take home with him. Those in the Burntisland council book, on the other hand, are a copy of a copy, having been taken by the burgh clerk from a full official copy that had been brought back by the burgh's commissioner. The clerk summarised some of the more routine acts and those that related to matters that were not to be raised again at the convention of 1648.[39]

The Records and their Significance

This volume contains much material for historians on a wide range of themes including economic affairs, national and local government, internal and international trade, parliamentary affairs, relations between the burghs and the crown, fishing, manufacturing, monopolies, education, and taxation.

---

37 See below, 322–8.
38 NAS, Burntisland Council Minutes, B9/12/9, p. 63.
39 See below, 289–96 (Burntisland, pp. 78–84), which indicates that three of these abbreviated acts (nos. 42, 47 and 57) were to be heads of the 1648 missive.

The convention at Perth in 1555

In May 1555 a convention of burghs assembled at Edinburgh. It was scheduled at the same time as a parliament called by the regent, Mary of Guise.
In their work on parliaments and other meetings of the estates, Mackie
and Pryde noted that meetings of parliaments and conventions of burghs
were not regularly synchronised until after May 1567, yet these two bodies
certainly met at the same time and in the same burgh on 29 May 1555.[40]

As the printed record indicates, the convention opened as scheduled
and immediately put into action a plan to alter the taxes assessed on all of
the member burghs. It was remarked at the time that while some burghs
had prospered and grown, others had shrunk. A new tax roll was required
to reflect this. Consequently, twelve individuals from six burghs, three from
north and three from south of the Forth, were nominated to undertake the
'alteratioun of the extent'.[41] However, by 3 June it was clear that, 'becaus
the maist pairt of the provestes forsaidis wer chosin Lordis of Articilis of
Parliament' and were pre-occupied with that role, the convention could not
carry out its business. The meeting was prorogued and the delegates warned
to convene at Perth at the end of July.[42] Those chosen to alter the tax roll
were advised to be prepared to present the revised roll at the Perth meeting.
Although the records of that convention eluded the editors of the published
convention records, the minutes of the convention at Dundee in September
of that year note that the Perth convention had taken place.[43]

The discovery of the Perth minutes thus fills an important gap in the
record.[44] The convention comprised twenty commissioners from ten burghs.[45]
They met over a period of two days, passed eleven acts and approved the
new tax roll.[46] The acts echo many of the themes most commonly addressed
by conventions throughout the sixteenth and seventeenth centuries. Issues
like unfreemen using merchandise, non-resident merchants, and the stand-
ardisation of weights and measures were repeatedly expressed at conventions
just as they were at Perth in 1555. The Perth minutes thus add little that is
new to our knowledge of the workings of the organisation. However, the
survival in this manuscript of the complete tax roll compiled in 1555 is

[40] J.D. Mackie & G.S. Pryde, *The Estate of burgesses in the Scots Parliament and its relation to the Convention of Royal Burghs* (St Andrews, 1923), 12. See also, MacDonald, *Burghs and Parliament*, ch. 3.

[41] *RCRBS*, i, 6–7.

[42] *RCRBS*, i, 9.

[43] *RCRBS*, i, 13.

[44] See above, 7–8.

[45] Compared with twenty burghs being represented at Edinburgh in July and sixteen at Dundee in Sept.

[46] See below, 33–40.

unique; although the convention at Dundee in September ratified it, the roll is not incorporated into the minutes of that meeting.[47]

This copy of a complete tax table provides a benchmark for the middle of the sixteenth century. A partial tax roll on burghs north of the Forth, compiled in 1483, was printed by Marwick in the first volume of the Convention records.[48] Seventeen burghs were listed in 1483, two of which had disappeared from the list by 1555. Five, identified in 1555 were not on the list in 1483. A lapse of 72 years makes comparison hypothetical if one takes into account inflation and devaluation of the currency but it is interesting to note that Aberdeen and Dundee were assessed at the same rate in 1483 but by 1555 Dundee was asked to pay £100 more than Aberdeen. In his appendix to volume one, Marwick printed four sixteenth-century assessments imposed on the burghs between 1535 and 1556. All of these represent the burghs' portions of taxes authorised by parliament or the governor or regent.[49] Further sixteenth-century alterations of the tax roll, a process undertaken every four years between 1579 and 1594, are increased assessments based upon every £100 of all taxations on each burgh rather than being full, new tables as was the one compiled at Perth in August 1555.[50]

One other curiosity about the Perth convention is that only nine signatures appear at the end of the tax roll, although twelve assessors were appointed at the Edinburgh meeting.[51] The absence of John Erskine of Dun might be explained by his having been drawn away on some official state business since he was a trusted servant of the regent. Although he is named with the nine others in the minute introducing the tax roll, he did not sign it, nor is he included in the sederunt at the opening of the convention.[52] He was certainly appointed along with his fellow townsman William Panter but only the latter witnessed the new roll. Erskine may have been present briefly on 5 August, but it seems more likely that the notary simply copied his name from the Edinburgh minutes. The other two absentees, the commissioners from Edinburgh, receive no mention of having been present at Perth at any time during the convention. Furthermore, there is no record of any altercations among the commissioners, yet the Dundee minutes state that Edinburgh's commissioners travelled to Perth but 'departed fra the samyn conventioun, and wald nocht apply thameselffis to this effect, quhairunto

---

47   *RCRBS*, i, 12–13.
48   Ibid., 543.
49   Ibid., 514–522. A fifth table, dated Sept. 1556, asking the burghs to finance Convention business also appears here, 523–4.
50   Ibid., passim. See below 37–40.
51   See below, 40.
52   See below, 37.

thai wer oblist of befoir'.[53] There is, however, no indication of the nature of the dispute that led to their departure.

The Pittenweem writ

The Pittenweem writ is a curious document. It opens with a heading that indicates that what will follow is a copy of the minutes of the Perth convention of 1555. The sederunt is identical to that in the Fort Augustus manuscript, except that 'George' Lowell, commissioner for Dundee, is listed as 'James'.[54] The sederunt is followed by a copy of the ninth statute in the Perth agenda. The statute is not copied verbatim, the writer using fewer contractions than the Perth copyist and in places substituting synonyms for a word so that, for example, 'limits' in the Perth copy became 'bounds and liberty' in the Pittenweem document. The ninth statute deals with the regulation of staple goods and makes mention of red and white fish, which surely would have been landed at Pittenweem but was this why it was singled out? Had it been the first or the last item on the agenda that was copied here, one might conclude that the following or preceding pages had gone missing but that cannot have been the case in light of the ensuing item on the same sheet of paper.

The twenty lines devoted to the Perth convention are immediately followed by the text of an act of parliament, with a title but no context or date. This is not, as one might expect, an act passed by the 1555 parliament, but one from May 1584.[55] There is no obvious connection between the two extracts. The content of the second, like the first, refers to the regulation of the fishing trade, though in greater detail. This might explain why they were copied on to the same page but it might be equally plausible that the two were transcribed together simply in an attempt to conserve paper. One might wish for something more from this find. The most that it offers is evidence that the burghs either received or made and saved copies of the statutes of conventions of royal burghs and other relevant documents for their own use and reference.[56]

Conventions from 1631 to 1648

To anyone who has read the records of the convention of burghs in the period before 1631 or after 1648, much of the seventeenth century material in this volume will appear very familiar. Persistent and effective action

53 RCRBS, i, 13.
54 Young, The Parliaments of Scotland, ii, 438–9, suggests that James is the correct name.
55 For the act of parliament, see RPS, 1584/5/25.
56 For a discussion of copies, see above, 6. That Pittenweem had a copy of an act from 1555 is intriguing, given that it did not begin to send commissioners to conventions until 1575, suggesting that the records of the Perth convention were still extant in the 1570s.

continued against 'unfree traders', that is those from outwith royal burghs who did not share in their trading privileges. Like many campaigns against many aspects of law-breaking, it was a battle that was never going to be won. Yet the efforts of the convention to ensure that its members took action against unfree traders demonstrate its continued determination to defend the privileges of the royal burghs. Wherever unfree traders were found to be operating, the convention sought to ensure that individual burghs gave undertakings to carry out decisive action against them, and it followed up those undertakings to ensure that they had been fulfilled.[57] Similarly, the willingness of the convention to organise aid to impecunious burghs in carrying out public works, including repairs to harbours, bridges, churches and tolbooths, and the paving of streets continued as before, however difficult that may have become during the straitened times of the 1640s.[58] The range of responsibilities that were taken on by the convention went beyond issues that related directly to trade and urban administration to include education, as can be seen in the continuing efforts to ensure that burgh schools all over Scotland adhered to the same Latin grammar, perhaps one of the earliest instances of such a thing on a national scale.[59] So voluminous are the records from this period that what follows does not seek to be a comprehensive analysis of the material. It would be impossible here to provide an exhaustive account of any, let alone all, of these things. Instead, it seeks to examine a number of significant themes to illustrate the wide range of matters with which the convention of burghs concerned itself in the second quarter of the seventeenth century and therefore its prominent role in national affairs.

The Scots staple port at Veere[60]
From the middle of the sixteenth century, the merchants of Scotland had their 'staple port' situated at Veere (which they usually referred to as 'Campheir' or 'Campvere'), a small port on what was then the island of Walcheren in the province of Zeeland in the Netherlands. Previously the staple had been sited at Bruges in Flanders and Middelburg which was situated, like Veere, on Walcheren. All staple goods that were to be exported to the Netherlands (skins, hides, woollen cloth, salmon, tallow and beef)

57 See below, 135–7.
58 See below, 138, 284.
59 See below, 56–7.
60 Most of the background on the Scottish staple comes from the following sources: J. Davidson & A. Gray, *The Scottish Staple at Veere: a study in the economic history of Scotland* (London, 1909); and M.P. Rooseboom, *The Scottish Staple in the Netherlands: an account of the trade relations between Scotland and the Low Countries from 1292 till 1676* (The Hague, 1910); V. Enthoven, 'Thomas Cunningham (1604–1669): conservator of the Scottish court at Veere', in D. Dickson, J. Parmentier & J. Ohlmeyer (eds.), *Irish and Scottish Mercantile Networks in Europe and Overseas in the Seventeenth and Eighteenth Centuries* (Ghent, 2007).

were to be exported exclusively through that port. The advantage to the Scots was that the staple arrangement consisted of an agreement between the royal burghs and the magistrates and council of Veere: neither tolls nor customs were levied on Scottish imports; the Scots were allowed to establish a 'conciergerie house' in which their merchants would obtain bed and board; there was an independent court, presided over by the 'conservator of the Scottish privileges', with jurisdiction over disputes involving Scottish merchants. After the Reformation, a separate Scots church was established with its own minister and reader, funded by levies on Scottish trade which were collected by 'factors' who, like the conservator, were normally expatriate Scots and who acted as agents for Scottish merchants, selling their goods on commission, collecting dues to maintain the church, and pay the stipends of the minister and reader, and returning any balance to Scotland.

As can be seen from the records in this volume, the administration of the staple was one of the most prominent items of business on the agenda of most general conventions. Indeed, it seems to have been a constant headache for the convention, posing all sorts of problems relating to the upkeep of the church, ensuring that the conservator and factors did their jobs properly, and trying to maintain the agreed relationship between the council of Veere and the Scots merchants there. This relationship was not always a happy one, becoming so strained at one point that the convention considered relocating the staple to Middelburg.[61] One of the main problems was ensuring that Scots merchants exporting to the Netherlands paid the dues that were required of them.[62] However, the problems evident in the 1630s were nothing new, similar difficulties having occurred in the 1620s when relations between the convention and the Veere authorities had reached such a low point that the convention had already considered moving the staple elsewhere, a plan which was again being entertained in the 1660s when Rotterdam was the mooted alternative.[63]

In many ways it seems puzzling that the convention persisted with the maintenance of the staple at Veere, given the chronic problems of administering the agreement with the magistrates and council of the port and of the upkeep of the minister, reader, conservator, factors and conciergerie house. It is equally bamboozling that there was any enthusiasm for the maintenance of the staple arrangements among the membership of the convention, given the size of the Scottish community at Rotterdam and the fact that so many

---

61 For examples of these problems (all from 1634, but similar examples can be found in the minutes of other conventions), see below, 175–6; for problems with payments of dues see 176–77 (fos. 465v–466r). For the proposal to move to Middelburg, see 90–92.
62 See below, 176–7
63 *RCRBS*, iii, 270, 561.

Scottish merchants were evidently bypassing Veere in spite of the facility that the factors provided.[64] Why, since it appears to have proved so difficult to maintain meaningful oversight of the activities of Scottish merchants in the Low Countries, was the most drastic solution that they seemed to be willing to entertain the shifting of the staple to another nearby port in Zeeland or to Rotterdam? Scots merchants traded to France, Spain, Germany, England, Ireland, the Scandinavian kingdoms and the other states that fringed the Baltic Sea without the need for a single entrepot in any of those places, while many used the services of agents in the ports to which they traded, rather than travelling in person with their goods. Many Scottish merchants were evidently unwilling to use the staple at Veere, as the numbers known to have evaded payment of their dues is likely to have been only a fraction of the total. In spite of all this, throughout the frequent discussions of the difficulties with the staple, not once did anyone suggest that the institution be disbanded.

The parliament of 1633

The records of the conventions in the summer of 1633 are some of the most interesting and most frustrating in this volume. In that year, Charles I returned to Scotland for the first time since he had left to join the rest of the royal family in England early in 1604 at the age of three. He came north for his Scottish coronation and to hold his first parliament, which would prove to be the only parliament of his reign over which he had any meaningful control. The visit was not a political success. Highly ritualised liturgies were used in the coronation service and other religious services attended by the monarch, breeding what proved to be well-founded fears of a royal desire for radical reforms of Scottish worship along Laudian lines. The parliamentary session was tightly controlled, dissent was silenced and members were intimidated by the king in casting their votes.[65] Indeed, the parliament appears to have focused opposition to the kingship of Charles I in general as well as to specific aspects of it. It is clear from the minutes of the conventions of burghs that met around the time of parliament that something went wrong and that a number of burgh commissioners did not conduct themselves as they ought to have during this parliamentary session.

---

64 For the Scots in Rotterdam, see D. Catterall, 'Scots along the Maas, c.1570–1750', in A. Grosjean & S. Murdoch (eds.), *Scottish Communities Abroad in the Early Modern Period* (Leiden, 2005).

65 For details of the king's visit, see M. Lee, *The Road to Revolution: Scotland under Charles I* (Urbana, 1985), ch. 4, esp. 126–36; A.I. Macinnes, *Charles I and the Making of the Covenanting Movement 1625–1641* (Edinburgh, 1991); and for detailed analysis of the parliamentary session in particular, see J.R. Young, 'Charles I and the 1633 Parliament', in K.M. Brown & A.J. Mann (eds.), *The History of the Scottish Parliament, Volume 2: Parliament and Politics in Scotland 1567–1707* (Edinburgh, 2005).

On 13 June 1633, as had been customary since at least the middle of the sixteenth century, a convention of burghs met at Edinburgh in preparation for the parliamentary session, which began five days later. As the burgh commissioners were almost certainly occupied largely with parliamentary business, the record for that day consists merely of the sederunt and the election of the moderator, for the deliberations of the burghs as a parliamentary estate (rather than as the convention *per se*) tended not to be recorded in the convention's minutes. Yet it is common to find rather more in the minutes of similar preparatory conventions and it might be surmised that the brevity of the record of this convention indicates a desire to err on the side of caution in recording the burghs' views.[66] The next entry after the election of the moderator is dated Saturday 29 June, the day after parliament had ended. It contains a laconic reference to the need for 'takeing ordour with disordoures in this present conventioun and parliament'.[67] No details of the nature of these 'disordoures' were provided, perhaps because it was deemed expedient not to minute them.

When the general convention met at St Andrews in August, having been postponed from its usual date of early July because of the parliament, the issue was addressed at some length, although the record still gives no specific details.[68] The problem appears to have been one of some burghs breaking with the tactic of voting *en bloc* on issues of common concern, something which had been a key element of the burghs' parliamentary strategy since the 1570s.[69] The general convention at St Andrews noted that there had been an 'inlaike of lauchfull and uniforme concurrence as is requisit and expedient in the members of ane body' and various acts of convention relating to this were cited and ratified.[70] It is, however, unclear to what particular issue in the parliament of 1633 the problem relates, as there is no evidence that the burghs failed to secure any act which they had sought. Indeed, they were delighted to have obtained the passage of a detailed ratification of numerous former statutes in their favour, which they not only inserted in their own records but ordered to be copied into the court records of every burgh.[71] It may be that pressure had been applied by the crown to persuade the burghs to extend their whip system beyond legislation relating to the interests of the burghs into more political matters, voting on which had previously been explicitly reserved to the conscience of the individual commissioner.[72]

66   See, for example, *RCRBS*, ii, 269–71; MacDonald, *Burghs and Parliament*, 61–2.
67   See below, 124–7.
68   See below, 143–4.
69   MacDonald, *Burghs and Parliament*, 62–4.
70   See below, 143.
71   See below, 141–2.
72   *RCRBS*, i, 25.

Certainly, something untoward occurred involving the burghs' votes on 28 June, although the only controversy which has been identified in other sources involved the two commissioners from Aberdeen. The burgh's principal commissioner, its provost Sir Paul Menzies of Kinmundy, had been one of the lords of the articles and therefore probably sympathetic to the king's programme in parliament. For reasons unknown, although most probably illness, he was unable to attend on the final day when the legislation was to be voted on. As was customary, his 'assessor' (a named deputy in the burgh's parliamentary commission), Sir Patrick Leslie of Iden, took his place but voted against some of the crown's acts. This probably included that which notoriously combined a confirmation of the royal prerogative with the power to dictate clerical apparel, which caused widespread unease among parliamentarians. They felt torn between denying the king's prerogative and denying their consciences, as they feared that the king would use the act to prescribe Anglican vestments in Scotland. Charles I was a king who bore grudges and when Aberdeen elected Leslie as its provost two years later, the furious monarch not only overturned the election but debarred Leslie from ever holding office in Aberdeen again.[73]

The royal visit of 1633 also provided what was potentially a precious opportunity for the burghs' representatives to lobby the king directly on a number of issues of particular concern. Before 1603, this sort of thing had been commonplace, with conventions of burghs regularly sending delegations to James VI on a whole range of issues. Since the king's departure for England, however, contact had been much more indirect and difficult, in spite of the establishment of an agent for the burghs at court in 1613.[74] Determined to make the most of the opportunity presented by the king's visit, the particular convention meeting at the time of parliament commissioned the representatives of ten burghs to try to meet him 'before his Majestie pas in to England' to discuss the most pressing issues that concerned them, namely fishing, the exclusion of Scottish merchants from English trading privileges, the two 'extraordinarie' taxes just voted by parliament, the depredations of Dunkirk pirates, and a number of matters that parliament had remitted to the privy council.[75] They met at Edinburgh on 1 July, noted that they had been unable to speak to the king because he was out of town but that he would return in nine days and therefore delegated two of their number, along with the clerk of the convention, to try to meet him then.[76] When the general convention

73 ACA, CR1/52/1, pp. 198, 203, 227, 239–40; *Aberdeen Council Letters*, ii, 28–31; Young, *The Parliaments of Scotland*, ii, 421–2; MacDonald, *Burghs and Parliament*, 53; Lee, *Road to Revolution*, 132–3, 175.
74 *RCRBS*, ii, 353, 406.
75 See below, 126–7.
76 See below, 128.

met at St Andrews in August, it transpired that no meeting had taken place. It has been observed that, before his return to England, Charles 'persistently snubbed those who had voted against him in parliament'.[77] Could it be that opposition in parliament by some of the burgesses prevented them from putting their case to the king? At St Andrews, it was resolved that a further particular convention of commissioners from nineteen burghs would meet in October to devise means of dealing with the crown, by direct contact with the privy council and indirectly with the king.[78] That convention made no more progress, finding that, in spite of an agreement on fishing having been achieved, English fishermen continued to operate in Scottish waters and to encroach upon fishing grounds that the Scots believed were reserved to themselves.[79] The matter was, once more, remitted to another particular convention in the following January. Although the failure of the burghs to obtain from the crown a satisfactory response to their grievances was no novelty, it is difficult to avoid the conclusion that they had a strong sense of a missed opportunity in the summer of 1633. They had tried to deal directly with Charles I but had failed to attract his attention and the issues which concerned them remained unresolved.

Trade with England and Ireland

While frustration with the events of the summer of 1633 may mark a peak in the burghs' difficult relationship with Charles I, tensions are evident throughout the records in this volume. In 1638, many burgh councils were happy to describe the efforts of the Covenanters against their king as the 'common cause' and, although religious and constitutional issues were to the fore in the Covenanters' struggle, there was a wider range of reasons for underlying discontent with Charles I, many of which were shared by different social groups, but some were peculiar to one group or another.[80] Exclusion from the decision-making process at the heart of government, for example, was keenly felt by many peers but it was not something that particularly exercised the burghs. Their enthusiastic support for the Covenanting revolution is already well-known, but these records provide evidence that their discontent was grounded upon a much wider range of issues than their heightened tax burden, upon which historians have tended to concentrate in the past.[81]

---

[77] Lee, *Road to Revolution*, 136.
[78] See below, 145–6.
[79] See below, 153–6.
[80] The phrase is common and can be found, for example, in Glasgow's council minutes, GCA, C1/1/10, 25 Aug. 1638.
[81] Stevenson, *The Scottish Revolution*, 51; D. Stevenson, 'The burghs and the Scottish revolution', in M. Lynch (ed.), *The Early Modern Town in Scotland* (Edinburgh, 1987), 176–7; M. Lynch, *Scotland: A New History* (London, 1991), 267; J.R. Young, 'The Scottish parliament and the

One striking feature of the records from the 1630s is the evidence of a strong sense of grievance within the merchant community over what they perceived as the unequal treatment given to merchants from the different kingdoms ruled by Charles I. While the English navigation laws which excluded non-English ships from trade with England's colonies would not be passed until the Cromwellian era, the failure of a British customs union under James VI (abandoned in 1610 only a few years after it had begun) meant that there was no freedom of trade within the king's dominions.[82] In 1632 the 'equalitie of custome in Ingland, Scotland and Irland' was discussed with what appears to have been a positive outcome, the burghs' agent at court having obtained a 'new gift' of the equality of customs throughout the three kingdoms. However, it transpired that, in spite of a royal command, this had not been proclaimed in Ireland, where a levy of 10s. continued to be demanded for every tun of wine imported in Scottish (but not English) ships.[83] By the summer of 1633, the problem was being described in broader terms as the 'inequalitie of the liberties betuix this kingdome and the king-dome of England', because English merchants were able to trade freely with Ireland, whereas Scottish merchants were not.[84] It was just one of a list of disadvantages that the burghs claimed to be suffering, the other prominent ones being the degree to which English fishing boats (as well as Dutch ones) had the right to fish in Scottish waters, the granting of patents and monopolies by the crown, the depredations of Dunkirk pirates and reform of the coinage.[85] Apparently favourable responses were received from the king on all of these issues and specific undertakings were given to put an end to certain patents and monopolies. However, no positive action appears to have been taken relating to the two key matters of 'restraint in Ireland and mutuall participatioun of all native comodities betuixt his Majesties thrie kingdomes'.[86]

Many of these issues remained unresolved by the time of the revolution of 1638 and can be added to the growing levels of crown interference in urban government and the economic pressures of the heightened tax burden as reasons for discontent among Scotland's merchant elite.[87] It thus becomes

covenanting revolution: the emergence of a Scottish commons', in J.R. Young (ed.), *Celtic Dimensions of the British Civil Wars* (Edinburgh, 1997).

82   B. Galloway, *The Union of England and Scotland, 1603–1608* (Edinburgh, 1986), 141–2.

83   See below, 107–8, 110–11, 119.

84   See below, 126.

85   See, for example, below, 157–61. For further details on the fisheries, coinage and monopolies, see Lee, *Road to Revolution*, 103–7; Macinnes, *Charles I and the Making of the Covenanting Movement*, 106–13, 119–22; B. Harris, 'Scotland's herring fisheries and the prosperity of the nation, c.1660–1760', *SHR*, lxxix (2000), 39–60.

86   See below, 178–80.

87   Stevenson, 'The burghs and the Scottish revolution', 174–7; MacDonald, *Burghs and Parliament*, 79–80.

even easier to see why the burghs were so willing to join the revolution against Charles I when it broke out in the winter of 1637–8. Ironically, under the Covenanting regime the burghs would find themselves paying levels of taxation and experiencing economic disruption and central interference that would have made the policies of Charles I appear moderate in comparison, but they could not have known that when they backed the Covenant with such enthusiasm in 1638.[88]

Privileges in France

While Charles I seems to have had little care to address some of the grievances of his Scottish mercantile subjects as far as their rights in the rest of his dominions were concerned, he was more willing to help them in their trade with France. It has often been assumed that all Franco-Scottish connections, including Scotland's special economic privileges, were severed in 1560 when Scotland adopted Protestantism and began to realign its foreign policy as a result, and that they certainly vanished in 1603. Current research is demonstrating that this was certainly not the case, a view that is clearly supported in this volume.[89]

The references to France, specifically Normandy and Picardy, in the minutes of the convention of royal burghs are interesting for a number of reasons. Their principal significance lies in the fact that they demonstrate an undiminished belief among Scots merchants that their ancient trading privileges in France ought to be unaffected by the political and religious changes of the previous seventy years or so. There were even attempts to establish and oversee factors in France to monitor and facilitate Scottish trade, as was the policy in Veere. In spite of the fact that Scottish trade in northern France appears to have been concentrated on only two ports (Dieppe and Le Havre), just as with Veere, it proved difficult to operate such a system. Problems with factors abusing their positions during the later 1620s led to efforts to replace them with people who would swear to be subject to Scots law and to relinquish their own mercantile activities. Persistent efforts by the convention of burghs during the early 1630s were in vain, as it proved impossible to find anyone willing to serve under the direction and authority of the convention of royal burghs in such a capacity.[90] There may have been too few Scots in these ports, or perhaps those who were operating as factors were unwilling to cease trading as merchants themselves. It seems

[88] Stevenson, 'The burghs and the Scottish revolution', 179–82, 185–7; MacDonald, *Burghs and Parliament*, 41–3, 96–8.

[89] For a review of the historiography on this subject, see S. Talbot, 'Introduction', in 'An Alliance Ended? Franco-Scottish Commercial Relations c.1560–1713' (University of St Andrews, PhD thesis, 2010).

[90] *RCRBS*, iii, 203, 221, 285, 312; and see below, 45–6, 69–70, 85–6, 114–15, 134, 164–5.

that the root of the problem with the Scottish factors in France was that they had been profiting by abusing their position. Unlike those in Veere, who were under the jurisdiction of the convention and were forbidden to trade personally so that the interests of the merchants whom they represented would be safeguarded, those in France would sell their own goods first, thus obtaining the best price, before selling the wares of their compatriots.

The convention also discussed the alleged 'new and heavie impositiounes in France', whereby customs were being levied on Scottish goods in spite of the Scots' belief that they had the right to trade freely with France as part of 'thair ancient libertyes in the said kingdome'.[91] It was resolved in 1634 to negotiate directly with Louis XIII by sending and funding an ambassador of their own. This approach was unusual, for it bypassed the normal diplomatic channels, but it had numerous precedents in the history of the convention of burghs.[92] Although the initiative came from the burghs, out of respect for Charles I and to improve the chance of success, the burghs' ambassador was instructed to go via court and obtain a letter of recommendation from the king, which he duly did.[93] The mission cost 8,000 merks (£5,333 6s. 8d.) and the burghs' ambassador obtained a 50 per cent reduction in the impositions upon Scottish goods going to France. Unfortunately, the precise nature of the 'ancient libertyes' remained undefined but it seems safe to say that, whatever the Scots thought they were, the French were not keen to concede too much. In spite of what was agreed in the 1630s, there were still problems in 1647, when the convention received a complaint from 'severall merchandis of the great prejudice they sustein throw the great infringment of breaking of our ancient priviledges and liberties within the kingdome of France by augmenting of our customes and laying of heavie impositionis upoun our countriemen in the name of strangeris'.[94] In the 1630s, Edinburgh had advanced the ambassador's expenses to him and, to refund them, with interest, the convention agreed on an imposition on all Scottish trade with Normandy and Picardy. As a result, the convention then required the burghs to monitor trade through those regions of France so that a levy could be taken to reimburse the costs of the embassy, and this appears to have continued through the 1640s, demonstrating the great expense to which their ambassador went, or the limited nature of Franco-Scottish trade, or perhaps the difficulty of collecting the levy. Another possibility is that a second levy was required to defray further costs incurred at some point after 1636. The French trade of Edinburgh, Dundee and Aberdeen alone raised £1,181 14s. in the first year of the levy, amounting to more than 20 per cent

---

91   See below, 181, 194–5.
92   *RCRBS*, i, 182, 186, 211, 249–51.
93   See below, 194.
94   See below, 297.

of the total cost of the ambassador's trip in 1634, while the act from 1647 that related to the levies on trade with Picardy and Normandy appears to refer to a second set of payments beginning in 1642.[95] Unfortunately, only the fact that the monitoring was carried out was recorded, for the papers containing the details of that trade do not appear to have survived.

Revision of the burghs' tax roll, 1635

The 'taxt roll', sometimes called the 'stent roll', of the burghs consisted of a list of the burghs and the proportion of every £100 of taxes which was due from each of them. Parliaments voted taxes, but the burghs reserved the right to apportion their share of those taxes among themselves. The tax roll was also used by the convention to divide up any sums which the burghs agreed to collect on their own initiative, such as the collection of £800 in 1636 to aid Pittenweem in the repair of its harbour.[96] It was believed that in 1635 Charles I ordered that the existing stent roll, which had pertained since 1612, be recalculated. It has been assumed that nothing was actually done in response to this demand and that the roll remained unaltered between 1612 and 1649, in spite of the remarkably long duration of this period, the enrolment of six new members into the convention and the significant economic upheavals of the 1630s and 1640s.[97] The records in this volume not only suggest that this was not the case, they also indicate that the initiative in the 1630s may not have come from the king at all but from the burghs themselves. They also indicate that not only was the roll altered in 1635, it appears to have been revised on at least two further occasions thereafter.

The issue was first raised as early as 1633, at the general convention at St Andrews (with no indication that the king had initiated discussion), when it was agreed that commissioners to the next general convention should be sent 'sufficientlie instructed ... whither it salbe expedient to alter the taxt roll [of 1612] or not'.[98] It was then agreed in 1634 that the roll should be recalculated because it 'hes not bein this long tyme alterit' and, as a result, the fortunes of many burghs had changed, a process described in the convention minutes as the 'manifest decay of sum borrowes and increase of utheres'. The cumbersome system by which the convention operated meant that, once this decision had been made, it was necessary to ask every burgh to send its commissioners to the next general convention 'suficientlie instructid

---

95 See below, 237–8, 267–8, 303–11, 312–21, 296, 322–8.
96 See below, 261–2.
97 M. Lynch, 'Introduction: Scottish towns 1500–1700', in Lynch (ed.), *The Early Modern Town*, 6; Stevenson, 'The burghs and the Scottish revolution', 173.
98 See below, 148–9.

... anent the alteratioun of the taxt rooll, forme and maner thairof'.[99] At the next general convention, at Perth in 1635, eleven burghs were commissioned to meet at Edinburgh in the following November to recalculate the tax roll.[100] Frustratingly, the volume of convention records in Aberdeen contains no minutes of a meeting at Edinburgh in November. A particular convention did meet in October but its records are not preserved in the Aberdeen volume either, although there are numerous references to its acts in the minutes of the general convention at Glasgow in 1636. The council minutes of Edinburgh did describe the October convention as a committee of burghs for revising the burghs' stent roll but made no subsequent reference to it.[101] While the minutes of the general convention of 1636 contain references to the tax roll (when sums of money were to be apportioned among the burghs) they make no mention of its recent revision.[102] However, the council minutes of Burntisland record the return of its commissioner from the meeting at Edinburgh in October. He reported that the tax roll had been altered but that Burntisland 'was not alterit in the taxt roll bot was continuit in the auld estait as it payit of befor'.[103] It is unclear how long the revised roll of 1635 endured, but it seems to have been revised at least twice before 1649. The records of the general convention of 1647 reveal that the previous general convention, in 1646, had adopted an altered tax roll, while the missive for 1643 suggests that another alteration may have been made in that year, the general convention of 1642 having initiated the process.[104] It would be surprising, given the economic upheavals of the period, had there not been continual pressure for revision of the roll, and 1643 is a likely candidate since complaints arising in 1647 from the alteration of the roll in 1646 were met with the response that the roll had to stand for three years, hence the next alteration occurred in 1649.[105] Given the extent to which tax rolls have been used as a proxy for the fortunes of the burghs relative to each other, it is a matter of some frustration that none of the rolls compiled between 1612 and 1649 survives.[106] Yet it might still be possible, through extensive research in surviving burgh council minutes and accounts, to reconstruct at least some of those lost tax rolls and thus

---

99   See below, 171,
100   See below, 225–6.
101   M. Wood (ed.), *Extracts from the Records of the Burgh of Edinburgh* [*Edin. Extracts*] *1626–1641* (Edinburgh, 1936), 168.
102   See below, 257–8, 269–70. In 1649, the general convention ratified the recently adjusted tax roll: see *RCRBS*, iii, 332–3.
103   NAS, Burntisland Council Minutes, B9/12/6, fo. 100v.
104   See below, 287, 320.
105   See below, 287.
106   See Lynch, 'Introduction', 4–8 for a discussion of the use of tax rolls to analyse the relative prosperity of burghs.

elucidate the relative economic fortunes of Scotland's towns between 1612 and 1649. Much more might then be understood about the effects of the economic upswing of the 1620s and the turmoil and disruption brought about by the Covenanting revolution and wars of the 1640s. It might even prove possible to pin down the timing of the rise of Glasgow more precisely.

Constant councils

Another issue which may well have been a significant new source of contention between the burghs and the crown in the later 1630s, was 'constant councils'. This was a system by which councillors would not be elected annually but new councillors would be chosen only on the death or incapacity of an existing member, as was the case in some other parts of Europe, notably Castile. After an act of parliament of 1469 that lamented the 'gret truble and contensione yeirly for the chesing of the samyne throw multitud and clamor of commonis sympil personis', burgh councils had ceased to be elected by all burgesses.[107] Instead a rotational system was introduced, whereby a proportion of councillors demitted office each year and their replacements were chosen by the old council (both those demitting and those continuing). The magistrates were then elected by a combination of the old and new councillors.

The issue of the manner of election of magistrates and councils was first raised at a particular convention at Edinburgh in October 1635. The records for that convention do not survive, so the terms of the changes discussed at that time are unknown. It is likely, however, that the behaviour of some burgh commissioners at the parliament of 1633 and the subsequent wrangle between Aberdeen and the king over their elections had a part to play in prompting these discussions and may also have been a significant factor in prompting the king to intervene.[108] The first explicit mention of 'constant councils' came in a royal letter that took to new levels the sort of interference in elections that had been common under both Charles I and his father.[109] Charles wrote to the council of Edinburgh in May 1636, intimating that 'we by oure experience doe find that the frequent chainge of persounes in publict effaires does breid inconstancie in government'. Out of what was described as his zeal for the weal of the burgh, he was 'pleased to recommend unto yow a constant counsall', and to 'will you to order the same

107 RPS, 1469/19.
108 See below, 260–61. For the controversies surrounding the election of Aberdeen's council in the 1630s, see G. DesBrisay, '"The civill warrs did overrun all": Aberdeen, 1630–1690', in E.P. Dennion, D. Ditchburn & M. Lynch (eds.), *Aberdeen Before 1800: A New History* (East Linton, 2002), 240–43.
109 MacDonald, *Burghs and Parliament*, 39–41; Lynch, 'The crown and the burghs', in Lynch (ed.), *The Early Modern Town*, 56–8.

among yourselffis'.[110] Other burghs probably received similar letters, for the records of the general convention in 1636 reveal that the issue was whether there should be 'ane constant counsell in ilk burght [or] ane yeirlie chaynge of magistratts', which was to be considered at a particular convention at Edinburgh in the following October.[111] Again, the minutes of that meeting do not survive, for those of the general convention of 1636 are the last of those preserved in the second volume of Aberdeen's convention records. There is evidence, however, that it was to be discussed again at the general convention at Aberdeen in July 1637, for Glasgow specifically instructed its commissioner to vote in favour of constant councils.[112] That should come as no great surprise, and cannot be taken as representative of urban opinion in general, since the archbishop of Glasgow had the right to appoint that burgh's magistrates and, as a result, Glasgow tended to be politically conservative in this period. Whatever was agreed at that convention with regard to constant councils, only days after it ended, a new prayerbook was introduced for public worship, sparking the emergence of open defiance to the government of Charles I which, in turn, led to the drawing up of the National Covenant, revolution and war. Plans for municipal reform were one of the less prominent casualties of these events.

The burghs and the Covenanting revolution

In March 1638, an extraordinary convention of burghs adopted the National Covenant and enjoined all burghs to endorse it. In spite of its tussles with the crown over the previous few years, the only burgh to make a determined stand against subscription of the Covenant was Aberdeen. The burgh thus achieved the dubious honour of being the first town to be occupied in the course of the wars which would rage across Britain and Ireland for the next twelve years, having held out against subscribing the Covenant until May 1639.[113] In spite of the burghs' apparent enthusiasm for the Covenant, the surviving records of the convention from the 1640s are not strikingly different from those of the previous decade, as the merchants of Scotland, perhaps unsurprisingly, remained focused on trade. If the full minutes of more than one convention from the period between 1636 and 1649 were to be unearthed, a different picture might emerge, but as it is the impression is one of business as usual.

The caution with which the convention of burghs tended to proceed is epitomised in the changes that were made to the qualifications for commissioners to the convention. The missives for the general conventions

---

110   *Edin. Extracts, 1626–1641*, 179.
111   See below, 260–61.
112   GCA, C1/1/10, 24 June 1637.
113   DesBrisay, 'The civill warrs did overrun all', 243.

of 1641 and 1643 continue to adhere to the traditional requirements that commissioners had to be men fearing God, adhering to the true religion and resident, taxpaying burgesses of the burghs that they represented, just as had been the case before the revolution.[114] The missive for the general convention of 1648, the next that survives after 1643, as well as stating that commissioners must be of the true religion, added that there must be no 'suspitioun in the contrair' and that commissioners must be 'subscryveris of the Covenant'.[115] These additional requirements were probably introduced in 1645 or soon afterwards as a result of the royalist rebellion led by James Graham, marquis of Montrose. As well as undermining the confident unity of the Covenanting movement, Montrose had persuaded the council of at least one burgh, Glasgow, to support him.[116] The stricter conditions for commissioners to the convention of burghs was part of a wider trend of excluding from public office any whose loyalty to the Covenants was in doubt. It would reach its fullest extent in the parliamentary Acts of Classes of 1646 and 1649.[117]

There are, not surprisingly, signs in the records of the dislocation and disruption caused by war. One is an apparent increase in absenteeism from conventions. In 1641, more than twenty burghs were to be fined for failing to send commissioners to recent conventions or for their commissioners having departed from conventions before they were over.[118] Another is what appears to have been an increase in burghs seeking help for repairs to harbours and public buildings. Although it had been a common occurrence in conventions before the 1640s, it features more prominently in this period, which perhaps indicates both the direct destructive effects of war and its indirect effects as the burden of taxation to support the army and the general economic dislocation resulting from conflict took their toll. The clearest possible indication of 'the heavie conditioun of all the ... burghis' as a result of the wars can be found in the forty-first act of the general convention of burghs in 1647, where it is recorded that £35,000 sterling (£420,000 Scots) was promised 'towardis the reparatioun of the burrowis losses be sea and land'.[119] That parliament agreed to grant such sums to the burghs is compelling evidence that complaints about their miserable state were taken seriously. However, it seems unlikely that very much of that money was ever forthcoming, given the failure of the English to pay most of the 'brotherly assistance' of £300,000 sterling promised in the treaty

---

114   See below, 303, 312.
115   See below, 322.
116   GCA, C1/1/11, 30 Sept. 1645.
117   *RPS*, 1645/11/110, 1649/1/43.
118   See below, 309–10.
119   See below, 293–4.

of London of 1641 and the priority given by the Covenanting regime to military expenditure.[120] Parliament was often willing to grant payments to impecunious individuals and burghs out of the 'first and reddiest moneyes' that the government would receive.[121] However, there was rarely anything left over after the army had been paid, and there were often insufficient funds even to pay the army. The missive for 1648 shows that the convention was responding to the economic crisis by seeking to ensure that every burgh was utilising its common lands to the full. Ratification of an act of parliament against dilapidation of common lands was being sought, and five burghs were asked to demonstrate that they were putting that resource to good use.[122] It was neither a creative nor an innovative way of raising funds and the relatively small sums that could be generated in this way reveal the desperate state of many burghs by the end of the 1640s.

David Wedderburn's grammar

The *de facto* authority which the convention expected to exercise over its members is demonstrated in the story of the approval of what was one of Scotland's first national school textbooks, *A Short Introduction to Grammar* by Mr David Wedderburn, master of the grammar school of Aberdeen.[123] Until these records were unearthed, it had been assumed that the direction came principally, if not solely, from the privy council, which licensed Wedderburn's grammar, giving him exclusive copyright for twenty-one years.[124] The privy council actively sought the approval of the convention of burghs which, in spite of the fact that the opinions of 'the univerities and colledgis of this kingdome and uther learnit men' had already been canvassed, was determined to take its own measures to ensure the book's quality. The convention therefore resolved to pay for 200 copies of the book to be printed for distribution once again to the learned men of the kingdom and that, thereafter, a committee be formed under the authority of the privy council to revise

120 Stevenson, *The Scottish Revolution*, 240, 267, 269, 281, 282, 293.
121 See, for example, *RPS*, 1644/6/122 promising payment of money to Dundee.
122 See below, 323, 324.
123 Wedderburn's grammar replaced the first single-volume national grammar textbook, *Grammaticae Nova* (1612) by Alexander Hume. For an account of the difficulties surrounding the adoption of standard grammars in Scotland, see J. Durkan, ed. and rev. J. Reid Baxter, *Scottish Schools and Schoolmasters 1560–1633* (Scottish History Society, forthcoming), 'Introduction' (I am very grateful to John McCallum for allowing me access to this material prior to publication); see also A.J. Mann, *The Scottish Book Trade 1500–1720: Print Commerce and Print Control in Early Modern Scotland* (East Linton, 2000), 153–4; and *RPC*, 2nd series, ii, pp. xxxi–ii. For details of Wedderburn's life, see A.S. Wayne Pearce, 'Wedderburn, David (bap. 1580, d. 1646)', *Oxford Dictionary of National Biography*, Oxford University Press, Sept. 2004; online edn, May 2007 [http://www.oxforddnb.com/view/article/28955, accessed 19 Aug. 2010].
124 Mann, *The Scottish Book Trade*, 100–101, 105–7, 110, 153–4.

the book along with Wedderburn before its final approval.[125] The minutes of a particular convention of burghs immediately after the general convention record that the privy council had approved the convention's proposal, although intriguingly this was on 31 July while the privy council's decision was actually dated 2 August.[126] The proposal was duly carried out, and the general convention of burghs in 1632 noted that a new, revised impression of the grammar was to be printed. The convention agreed that it should be used exclusively by all burgh schoolmasters from Martinmas 1632 (11 November), requiring every burgh to report to the next general convention on its diligence in seeing that this was carried out. In setting the price, the convention's act reveals that the work consisted of two different books, a basic book of 'rudimentis' to be sold at two shillings and the 'grammer ... conteining thairin the etimologie, syntax, orthographie and prosodie', at four shillings.[127] The privy council did not seek to enforce Wedderburn's grammar as the only one to be used in Scotland, approving it but allowing the use of others.[128] However, the convention of royal burghs took a different view, insisting in July 1631 that, once it was approved, Wedderburn's grammar 'and no uther' should be used in the kingdom's schools.[129] It does not seem, however, that the book was taken up with the hoped-for enthusiasm. In 1633, 1634 and 1635, the convention repeatedly enjoined the universal use of the grammar, and required commissioners to the following year's general convention to report their burghs' use of it in their schools.[130] By 1636, the convention was increasing the pressure on its members, requiring them to 'conveyne thair scoolmaisteris befor theme and to injoyne theme the teatching of the said grammer under the payne of depryveatioune'.[131]

The convention's minutes show that there was frequent interaction between it and the privy council, but the records of the latter mention the burghs' involvement only once. Perhaps this indicates the low esteem in which the aristocratically-dominated council held the merchants. Taking a view more sympathetic to the burghs, however, it may be evidence that the privy council conducted considerably more business than is recorded in its official minutes.[132] The convention was not an organ of the state, for it met without royal summons and was not part of the apparatus of central government. Its involvement in the approval and implementation of the

125 See below, 56–7.
126 See below, 65; RPC, 2nd series, iv, 310.
127 For the process of gathering and considering the comments of the learned men, see RPC, 2nd series, iv, 432, 436–7, 451, 454–5, 500.
128 Mann, The Scottish Book Trade, 154.
129 See below, 56.
130 See below, 133, 179–80, 215–16.
131 See below, 253–4.
132 RPC, 2nd series, iv, 310.

educational policy of the crown demonstrates its capacity to co-operate with government and at least its potential for linking the centre and the localities more effectively than the state could do on its own. It is an illustration of the extent to which Scotland remained, in the first half of the seventeenth century, a highly decentralised state. It also reveals that, in contrast to the crown's attempt to introduce another book to Scotland, the prayerbook of 1637, engaging in consultation and obtaining consent were not entirely alien to the Scottish regime of Charles I.

EDITORIAL CONVENTIONS

Editorial interventions have been kept to a minimum, but the following conventions have been adopted. Capitalisation has been regularised according to modern usage and some punctuation has been introduced to aid the reader's understanding of the text. The letters *i* and *j*, and the letters *u*, *v* and *w* have generally been altered to accord with modern expectations, except in some cases (words such as 'toun') where original spelling has been retained. The letters 'thorn' and 'yogh' have been transcribed as 'th' and 'y' respectively to accord with their pronunciation and to avoid confusion with 'y' and 'z' respectively. Scribal abbreviations (including the ampersand) have been silently extended. Where an unusual or apparently erroneous spelling might be taken to be a mistake by the editors '[sic]' has been inserted. Less common words are explained in footnotes where possible, as are older, less familiar or less obvious spellings of placenames. Where a placename is not that of a royal burgh, the county in which it lies is also given. Errors made by the original copyist mean that single words or short phrases were often repeated in the MS and this repetition has been removed, but noted in footnotes, as has the deliberate repetition of words inserted at the end of a page to indicate the word with which the next page commences. Straightforward editorial interpolations have been inserted in square brackets without explanation, for example when it is virtually certain that a letter or single word has been omitted in error by the copyist or where there is damage to the manuscript but it is fairly clear what would have been in the original. Longer interpolations and those which might be regarded as more speculative have the addition of explanatory material in footnotes. In some instances, it has not proved possible to identify missing text. In a number of places, the manuscripts contain a blank space where the copyist has actually omitted something, for example if he had difficulty reading unfamiliar place and personal names. Where it has not proved possible to determine what has been omitted, an ellipsis has been inserted in square brackets thus '[…]'. Where there are numbered folios (as in the case of the records from the National Library of Scotland and Aberdeen City Archives) or pages (as in the case of the material from Burntisland Council Minutes), folio numbers (including recto and verso) or page numbers have been inserted in square brackets within the text. The acts of conventions were normally numbered and referred to in subsequent conventions by these numbers. Where act numbers have been omitted by the copyist, to aid cross-referencing they have been inserted in square brackets. Marginalia (notably the short titles which were inserted to facilitate quick identification of individual acts) have been put within braces (curly brackets) at the beginning of the acts to which they relate.

All currency, unless otherwise stated in the text, is given in pounds Scots. The abbreviations for pounds, shillings and pence vary (for example, pounds are represented by 'lb', 'lib', 'libs' and 'ls'), so they are presented here as they are found in the manuscript, with the addition of a full stop. The most common foreign currencies to be mentioned in these records are those of the Low Countries (the United Provinces of the Netherlands, also known as the Dutch Republic, and Flanders, which was under Spanish rule). The currencies of these two countries were closely related to each other. As with sterling and pounds Scots, the Flemish pound was divided into 240 units called 'grooten', with twelve 'grooten' to a shilling. The Dutch guilder was one sixth of a pound, or 40 'grooten'. The guilder was also divided into twenty 'stuivers', each worth two 'grooten'. The smallest coin in circulation was the 'doit', of which there were eight to one 'stuiver' and therefore 160 to one guilder. References to French currency were also common. The French pound (*livre*, but also called a *franc*) was divided, as with the other currencies, into twenty shillings (*sous*), each of twelve pence (*deniers*).

RECORDS OF
THE CONVENTION OF ROYAL BURGHS

Particular Convention at Perth, August 1555[1]

[fo. 330v]

Apud Perth quarto die mensis Augustii anno Domini 155quinto

Convenit wythin the burgh of Pertht, Patrik lord Rewen provest, Patrik Murray and Thomas Flemyng commissionaris thairof, Thomas Menyeis provest and David Mar commissionaris of Abirdeyne, Hendre Levyngtowne provest and Willyeam Norwall commissionaris of Sterlyng, Robert Widderspout provest, Hendre Fowles commissionaris of Lynlythquhow,[2] James Olephant provest and Johne Forres commissionaris of Haldingtowne,[3] James Rollok and George Lyvell[4] commissionaris of [fo. 331r] Dunde, Androw Dunlap and William Donaldson commissionaris of Glasgow, Charlis Guthre and Thomas Martin commissionaris of Santandrois,[5] Thomas Panther[6] commissioner of Montross, Thomas Flescher and Robart Williamson commissionaris of Cowpar,[7] for the weill and effaris of all burrowis conforme to the act maid in Edinburgh at the last conventioun of burrowis the thrid day of Junii the yeir of God 155fyf yeris. It is concludit be the saidis provestis and commissionaris in the actis and ordinencis following for the weill of all burrowis be observit and kepit in all burrowis in tyme to cum as followis.

---

[1] NLS, Acc. 11218/5, 'The Fort Augustus Collection'. This record is immediately preceded by the acts of the Convention of Royal Burghs held at Edinburgh in April 1552, printed in *RCRBS*, i, 2–4.

[2] Linlithgow.

[3] Haddington.

[4] In the Pittenweem writs (NAS, GD62/6) he is identified as James Lowell/Lovell.

[5] St Andrews.

[6] This is probably a scribal error as the convention in May appointed William Painter to serve as one of the auditors (*RCRBS*, i, 4) and he appears as William elsewhere in this record.

[7] Cupar. There is another version of this sederunt in NAS, Pittenweem Writs, GD62/6 but it ends at this point.

[1]

Item in the first it is ordanit that all denis of gild of burrowis sall vesye[8] and tak cognitioun of all weychtis and elwandis within the burgh four tymes ilk yeir and oftir gif neid beis as salbe thocht expedient and neidfull be the saidis dene of gild that the samyn be of just weycht and messour conforme to the act of parliament and deliverance of the lordis commissioneris direct thairupon. And gif the denis of gild be necligent heirin to pay x lib. mone to the commoun weill and warkis of ilk burgh and upliftit be the provest and baillyeis of ilk burgh and plyit to the commoun weil. And all personis quhom ilk dene of gild hapynnis to fynd wyth insufficient weychtis and elwandis at the first veseing and cognitioun tane beand convict to pay xl s. to the commoun weill and warkis of the samyn burgh. And at the secund veseing the personis convict as said is to be dischergit of toppin[9] and selling of ony sic merchandreis for yeir and day thaireftyr without ony dispensatioun to be giffin to thame be the provest or baillies of the burgh thairupon. And quhat weycht ony persoun within burgh happynnis to by merchandreis sic as buttyr and cheis that the byar sall sell the samyn merchandreis with the samyn weycht. And quha that dois the contrar beand convict to underly the pane forsaid in maner forsaid.[10]

[2]

Item that na freman travellouris beand fre of ony towne passand and traveland passand betuix bruchis wyth hors laidis or cartis be land bringand and producand wyth thame ane extract quhar thai ar maid fre of the towne tha dwell in and subscrivit be the clark thairof that thai salbe fre of all small custummes in the burgh thai travell to. Quhilk extract thai sall schaw to the clerk of the burgh tha cum to that the samyn ma be insert in the bukis of that burgh for verefeing tharof in tyme cumyng.

[3]

Item that na gildbrodyr sonnis nor wyvis jois nor bruke the fredome and libertie of gildbroderschip nor be entrit thairto bot conforme to the burrow lawis that is to say ane burges son als lang as he is at his fatheris burd he sall haif that ilk fredome to by and sell that his father hes bot quhat tyme that he passis fra his fatheris burd to his awin finding he sall nocht be fre bot gif he by it, excep[t]and the eldest son to be fre conforme to the auld use of burrowis.

---

8 vesy = visit/inspect.
9 Top/tap = buy.
10 Parliament had issued a new metrological act in June 1555, see RPS, A1555/6/21. The full text is also printed in R.D. Connor, A.D.C. Simpson & A.D. Morrison-Low (eds.), *Weights and Measures in Scotland: A European Perspective* (Edinburgh, 2004), appendix A.6, 622.

[fo. 331v]

[4]

Item that ony woman mareand ane burgess and gild [brothir] eftyr hir husbandis deceiss, sa lang as scho remanis wedo to bruke hir fredome and be fre to by and sell as he dyd in his lyftime. And gif scho mareis to tyne hir fredome and previlege and he that happynnis to mare her beand nocht gildbrodyr of befoir to by his fredome.

[5]

Item that na burges and gildbroder that dwellis without the burgh top or sell ony stapill gudis without the burgh nor jois nor bruke the previlege tharof without thai cum and remane, hald stob and staik within the burgh, scat and loyt wyth the nychtbouris thairof thai beand requirit tharto be[11] proclamatioun at the mercat croce at the burgh quhar thai ar maid gildbrodyr upone xl dais warnyng and gif thai entyr nocht to remane wythin the burgh as said is the xl dais beand bypast, to tyne thair fredome conforme to the act maid be the conventioun of burrowis at Edinburgh the [...] day of [...].[12]

[6]

Itam that na burges air haif his ayrschip gudis and his bernis pairt of gudis togydder. And gif the air thinkis his airschip gudis nocht sa gude as his bernis pairt of gude, than sall he cast his haill airship gudis wyth the haill[13] bernis pairt of gudis and he to haif his pairt of the haill wyth the laiff of bernis, and alwais landis beand except heirin.

[7]

Item that na man be rassavit nor entrit gildbrodyr in tyme to cum without he serve ane merchand gildbroder in ony burgh within the realme or without the realm for the space of thre yeris and he that beis ressavit to haif nane uther craft and gif he hes ane craft to refuyss his usage of his craft and serve thre yeris as said is. And thaireftyr to present ane testificatioun of thair maister to the dene of gild and consell of the burgh quhar thai desyir to be maid gildbrodyr that thai servit thre yeris as said is.

[8]

Item that na thesaureris of burrowis deburss ony of the commoun gudis intromettit be thame without ane precept subscrivit be the provest baillies and cunsell or maist pairt thairof or ane that maid thairupon of thair

---

11 The word 'be' is inserted above the line.
12 There is no such act in the surviving minutes of the previous convention at Edinburgh (see *RCRBS*, i, 6–9), suggesting that they are incomplete.
13 'pairt' is deleted here.

consenttis of the maist pairt tharof. And gif thai do in the contrar the samyn sall nocht be allowit in thair comptis to thame.

[9][14]

Item it sall nocht be lesum to na burges gildbrodyr freman nor onfreman to by ony staple gudis within the limittis of ony uther burgh sic as woll, skynnis, hydis, fischis reyd and quheit bot allanerlie fra fremen of the burgh quhar thai happin to be.[15] And quha that dois the contrar heirof to be accusit as regrataris and forstallaris.

[10]

Item that na merchand freman nor onfreman be licient to saill in France, Flandris, Danskyn[16] or ony odyr pairtis without the realme in merchandrice except thai be considerit be the provest, deyne of gild, baillyeis and consell or maist [fo. 332r][17] pairt thairof that thai be honnest and qualefeit men in thar abulyement and gudis. And gif the provest, dene of gild, baillies or maist pairt of the cunsell giffis thair ticket to ony unqualefyit persoun by the natur of this act to pay x lib. to the commoun weill of the burgh.

[11]

Item that na skippar within burgh nor utouth[18] burgh rasaiff ony merchand fre or onfre within his schip without ane speciall ticket of the provest, dene of gild, baillyeis or maist pairt of the cunsell under the pane of paiment of v lib. for the first fault and tinsell of his fredome gif ony he hes at the secund tyme. And gif he be onye unfreman to pay x lib. for the secound tyme.

[12]

Item the haill commissionaris of burrowis beand presentlie convenit in Perth hes affixt the xvi day of September nixt to cum to conveyne in Dundye for traitting upone thair commoun weillis of burrowis and confermyng of thar actis and statutis within burrowis conforme to the actis of parliament and lawis of the realme. And quhatsumevir burgh beand warnit be Dundie to send thair commissionaris with sufficient commissionis the said day and compeiris nocht in Dundie the said xvi day of September to pay x lib. to the remanent commissionaris that kepis the said day.

Patrik lord Ruven provest of Perth	Patrik Murraye
Thomas Flemyng	Thomas Menyeiss
David Mar	Hendre Levistoun

---

14   There is another copy of this act in NAS, GD62/6.
15   This is written as 'by' in NAS, GD62/6.
16   Gdansk, or Danzig.
17   The word 'Patrik' appears to the right of centre at the top of the page.
18   A variant of 'outwith'.

Willeam Norvell	Robert Utherspone provest of Linlithquhow
Hendre Fowles commissionar	James Olephant
Johne Forres	George Lowell
Thomas Martyne	Androw Dunlap
Charles Gutthre	Robart Willeamsoun
James Rollok	Willeam Panter
Willyeam Donaldsoun	Thome Flescher

Apud Perth quinto Augusti anno L quinto

Quhilk day comperit Thomas Menyeis provest and David Mar in Abyrdeyne, Hendre Levingstowne provest and William Norvell in Sterling, James Olephant provest and Johne Forres in Hadingtowne, Patrik Murray provest [sic] and Thomas Flemyng in Perth, John Erskyn of Downe provest and William Panter in Montross, as thai ar the maist pairt chosin[19] be the maist [fo. 332v] pairt of the commissionaris of burrowis of Scotland for alteratioun of the text roll of the haill burrowis thairof conforme to the actis of electioun and exceptatioun maid at Edinburgh the xxix day of Maii and the last day of Maii last bypast as the samyn actis mair fullilie preportis, and conforme to the act of porogatioun maid thairupon of the dait, dyittit in Junii anno quo supra. And producit and schew the said text roll of the haill burrowis alterit and chengit be thame eftyr thair conscience subscrivit with [thair][20] handes, eikand the riche burrowis and meneissand the puyr burrowis to stand in effect for the space of thre yeris nixt heireftyr gif na uthir occasioun occuris in the meyne tyme. And ordanis the haill burrowis of Scotland to stand and fulfill this ordinance and deliverance quhen evir the quenis grace chergis the said burrowis of Scotland wyth ony texationes that thai be stentit conforme to the text roll and effeirand to thair particular pairt thairof and na alteratioun to be maid in ony taxationes to cum without ane new conventioun of the haill burrowis or maist pairt thairof.

Item the text roll of iii^m iii^c xxxiii lib. vi s. viii d.

Item in primis Edinburgh wyth Kyngorne and Inchekeyth[21] to supple thame   xi^c xi lib. ii s. 2 d.

---

[19] There is a deletion here but it appears to be the scribal flourish that the copyist used to denote the end of each act, presumably written in error and then scored through.

[20] There is no space but the sense requires this insertion.

[21] Kinghorn, on the south coast of Fife and Inchkeith, an island in the Firth of Forth.

Sterling	iii^{xx}xiiii lib. iiii s. iiii d.
Linlythquhow[22]	xlv lib.
Rosay[23]	xvi lib.
Dumbartane	xxviii lib. vi d. ½ d.
Ramfrow[24]	xxviii lib.
Ruglyng[25]	xviii lib.
Ayr	iii^{xx} xviii lib. xvi s.[26]
Ervyng[27]	xlv lib.
Glasgow	iii^{xx} vii lib. x s.
Kyrkcubre[28]	xxiiii lib.
Wygtoune	xxx lib.[29]
Quhitterne[30]	xxx lib.
Lanryk[31]	xxii lib.
Jedburgh	xxii lib. x s.
Selkyrk	xv lib.
Peblis	xv lib.
Hadingtowne	l lib.
Northberwyk	xi lib
Dunbar	xviii lib.
Laudyr	xii lib. x s.
Dumfreiss	xlvii lib.

The burrowis of the northt Forth

[fo. 333r]

Abyrdene	ii^{c} iiii^{xx} x lib.
Dynde[32]	iii^{c} iii^{xx} x lib. vii s. v d.
Pertht	ii^{c} xxii lib. x s.
Sanctandroiss[33]	iiii^{xx} x lib.
Couper	iii^{xx} x lib.[34]
Carraill[35]	xxxii lib. x s.

22 Linlithgow.
23 Rothesay.
24 Renfrew.
25 Rutherglen.
26 'x' is deleted before 'iii^{xx}'.
27 Irvine.
28 Kirkcudbright.
29 'iiii' is deleted after 'xxx'.
30 Whithorn.
31 Lanark.
32 Dundee.
33 St Andrews.
34 'x' is deleted before 'xxx^{xx}'.
35 Crail.

Dysart	xxxix lib. vii s. vi d. ½ d.
Kyrcade[36]	xxxi lib.
Dumfermelyng	xxxiii lib. xv s.
Banff	xx lib. x s.
Fforfar	xi lib.
Brechyne	lii lib. x s.
Munross[37]	iii^{xx} xv lib.
Elgyne	xxxiii lib. xv s.
Innernis[38]	lvi lib. v s.
Abyrbroith[39]	xl lib.[40]
Cullane	x lib.
Fforres	xxviii lib
Narne[41]	xi lib. v s. vi d. ½ d.
Thane[42]	xvi lib. xvii s. vi d.

Hendre Levingstoune wyth my hand
William Norvell wyth my hand
James Olephant wyth my hand
Johne Forres wyth my hand
Thomas Menyeis wyth my hand
David Mar wyth my hand
Patrik Murray wyth my hand
Thomas Flemyng wyth my hand
William Panter wyth my hand

Apud Perth quinto Augusti anno L quinto
Quhilk day the provestis, commissionaris of burrowis underwreittin hes ratefyit[43] apreiffit this present alteratioun of the text roll of iii^m iii^c xxxiii lib. vi s. viii d. maid and alterit be the personis chosyn thairto be the maist pairt of the commissioners of burrowis to be of effect for the space of thre yeris nixt to cum wythout [fo. 333v] other occasioun occur in the meyne tyme. And in tokin of certificatioun and approbatioun thai haif subscrivit the samyn wyth thair subscriptiounis manuel and hes obleist thame and ilkane of thame as commissionaris of thair townes in name of the saidis burrowis to fermile abyde and defend this present alteratioun and all thingis following

---

36   Kirkcaldy.
37   Montrose.
38   Inverness.
39   Arbroath.
40   This may be 'xl' and not 'xli'.
41   Nairn.
42   Tain.
43   'ass' is deleted.

tharupoun wyth thair substance and gudis ilkane for thair awin pairtis for the commoun weill of burrowis as lawe will.

Subscriptio
Patrik lord Rewen provest of Perth
Robart Widderspone provest of Linlythquhow
Hendre Fowles commissioner of Linlythquhow
George Lowell baillye of Dynde
James Rollok elder wyth my hand
Thomas Martyne baillye of Sanctandroiss
Charles Gutthre wyth my hand
Androw Dunlap baillye of Glasgow wyth my hand
William Donaldson
Thomas Flescher commissioner of Couper
Robert Wilyeamson baillye of Cuper
Henricus Elder scriba manu sua

Off the forsaid stent of iii^m iii^c xxxiii lib. vi s. viii d. the burrowis payit as eftyr followis viz:

Eddinburgh	viii^c xxxiii lib. vii s. vi d.
Abyrdene	iii^c xv lib.
Dundye	iiii^c xxvi lib. xvii s.
Kreill[44]	xxii lib. x s.
Hadingtowne	i^c lib. v s.
Lauder	xxii lib.
Gedburgh[45]	xxxiii lib. xv s.
Salkyrk[46]	xxii lib. x s.
Dunbar	xxii lib. x s.
Sanctandrouss[47]	[...][48]

44 Crail.
45 Jedburgh.
46 Selkirk.
47 St Andrews.
48 The absence of a figure for St Andrews may indicate that the list (and therefore this record) is incomplete.

General Convention at Dysart, July 1631[1]

[fo. 374r]

Actis of the generall conventioun of Burrowes hauldin at Dysert 5 Julii 1631[2]

[fo. 375r]

In the generall conventioun of borrowis haldin at the burght of Dysert the fyft day of Julij the yeir of God ane thowsand sex hundreth threttie ane yeiris be the commissioneris of borrowis underwrittin and produceit the commissiounis as followis

Edinburght	Williame Reid, Williame Carnegye
Perth	Andro Wilsone
Dundie	Thomas Haliburtoun
Aberdene	Patrick Leslie
Stirling	Johnne Cowan
Linlithgow	Andro Bell
Sanct Androis	Symeoun Gregour
Glasgow	James Stewart
Air	Johnne Oisburne
Haddingtoun	Mr James Cockburne
Dysart	David Simpsone, David Chrystisoune
Kirkcaldie	Alexander Law elder
Muntrois	Robert Grahame
Couper	Robert Patersone
Anstruther Eister	Robert Alexander
Dumfreis	Mr Johnne Corsane
Innernes[3]	Be exemptioun produceit be agent
Bruntyland	Williame Mekiljohnne
Innerkeithing[4]	Be exemptioun and ratificatioun produceit be Mark Kinglassie
Kingorne	Patrick Wallace
Breichin	Be exemptioun produceit be Muntrois
Irving	Mr Johnne Peeblis
Jedburgh	Alexander Kirktoun

---

1 ACA, SRO 25/3/2, 'Acts of Convention 4 July 1610 to July 1636', fos. 374r–383r.
2 This is written on what would have been the cover sheet of the minutes as they were brought back to Aberdeen by its commissioner. The verso is blank.
3 Inverness. Placenames with the 'inver' element were often written in this way, which led, for example, to Innerpeffray in Perthshire, and Innerleithen, in Peebleshire.
4 Inverkeithing, another example of the above.

Kirkcudbryght	Johnne Ewart younger
Wigtoun	Thomas McGie
Pittenweame	George Kingyow
Dumfermeling	Petter Love
Anstruther Wester	Williame Dairsie
Selkirk	Williame Mitchellhill
Dumbartane	Be exemptioun and ratificatioun produceit be Glasgow
Renfrew	Williame Sommervell
Lanerk	Jeodeane Jack
Aberbrothock[5]	Be exemptioun and ratificatioun produceit be Dundy

[fo. 375v]

Elgynne	Mr Johnne Hay
Peeblis	James Williamsone
Craill	Patrick Hunter
Tayne	Be exemptioun and ratificatioun produceit be agent
Culros	Mr Adward Blaw
Banff	James Winchester
Quhithorne[6]	Be exemptioun and ratificatioun produceit be Wigtoun
Forfar	Be exemptioun and ratificatioun produceit be agent
Rothesay	Be exemptioun and ratificatioun produceit be agent
Nairne	Be ratificatioun produceit be agent
Forres	Be exemptioun and ratificatioun produceit be agent
Rutherglenn	Be exemptioun produceit be Glasgow
North Berwick	Be exemptioun and ratificatioun produceit be Haddingtoun
Cullane	ratificatioun produceit be Aberdene
Lawder	Alexander Wilkesone
Kilranie[7]	Be exemptioun and ratificatioun produceit be Anstruther Eister
Annand	Be exemptioun and ratificatioun produceit be Dumfreis
Lochmavin[8]	
Sanquhair	
Galloway[9]	Johnne Foullertoun

---

5 Arbroath.
6 Whithorn.
7 Kilrenny.
8 Lochmaben.
9 New Galloway.

1

The same day the commissioner of the burght of Dysert verified the citatioun of the haill borrowis to this present conventioun be George Ramsay
poist

2

{Electio moderatour}

The same day the saidis commissioneris of borrowis electis creatis and
constitutis David Sampsoune first in commissioun for the burght of Dysert
moderatour dureing this present conventioun wha compeirand acceptit the
same in and upoun him and gave his aith *de fideli administratione*.[10]

3

{Houres of meitting}

The same day the saidis commissioneris of borrowis apointit the houres of
meitting to be and beginne daylie at nyne houres in the morning and to last
whill tuelf houres at noone and efter noone at twa houres till sax a clock at
nicht And sic as ar absent at the calling of the rollis to pay ane unlaw of sax
schillingis and they that pas out of the hous without leive to pay ane unlaw
as said is and they that pas fra this present conventioun befoir the disolving
thairof to pay ane unlaw as absentis and that none speik unrequired without
leive askit and gevin nor intermix thair ressouning with thair voiting under
the paine of ane unlaw of sax schillingis *toties quoties*.[11]

[fo. 376r]

4

{Dumbar magistrattis}

The same [day][12] the saidis commissioneris of borrowis ordainis the burgh of
Dumbar to produce the electioun of their majestratis and counsall at Michaelmes nixt to the nixt generall conventioun of burrowis and to proceid
thairintill conforme to the acis of parliament and burrowis under the paine
of twentie pundis. And this to be ane heid of the nixt missive.

5

{Outland burgessis foirstalleris, regraitteris and missive}

The same day the saidis commissioneris of borrowis ordainis as of befoir
ilk burgh to produce in writt mair exact dilligence to the nixt generall

---

10 Literally, 'concerning faithful administration', i.e. he was promising to carry out the duties
    of moderator with diligence.
11 As often as it shall happen, i.e. for each offence.
12 There is no space but the sense requires this insertion.

conventioun of borrowis in restraining thair outland burgesses foirstalleris regraiteris sailleris without ticketis and unfriemen usurping their liberties under the paine of tuentie pundis ilk burght. And this to be ane heid of the nixt missive.

6

{Selkirk Curriour missive}

The same day ordainis the burght of Selkirk to produce in writt mair exact dilligence to the nixt generall conventioun of borrowis in causing George Curryour outland burges to mak his residence within their said burght or elis in depryving him of the liberties thairof. And this to be ane heid of the nixt missive.

7

{Dumfreis unfriemen missive}

The same day annent the saxt act of the last generall conventioun of borrowis haldin at the burgh of Jedburgh the 16 day of Julii last ordaining the burgh of Dumfreis to have usit the dilligence mentioned in the said act against James Andersone, Thomas and Johnne McKilvaillis, Johnne Wylie, James Greir, Johnne Tait and Johnne Schairp compeirit Mr Johnne Corsane present commissioner of the said burgh and declairit that the said Johnne McKilvaill had depairtit this present lyfe, the said James Andersone is past furth of the cuntrie thair to remain, the said Johnne Wylie and the said Thomas McKilvaill and the said James Greir hes suspendit under pretext being burgessis of Sanquhar thair chairge quhilk declaratioun the said commissioneris acceptis for thair dilligence against the saidis personis at this tyme, and ordainis the said burgh to use farder dilligence against the said Johnne Tait in taking and apprehending him till he find cautioun for desisting frome usurping thair liberties and in chairgeing of the said Johnne Schairp to the same effect and to produce the same to the nixt generall conventioun of borrowis under the paine of xx lb. and ordainis the said burgh of Sanquhair to produce thair dilligence to the nixt generall conventioun in writt in causing the saidis Thomas McKillvaill and James Greir thair alledgit, ather mak thair residence with theme or depryve theme off the liberties of their burgh under the paine of xx lb. And this to be ane heid of the nixt missive.

[fo. 376v]

8

{Jedburgh electioun magestratis}

The same day annent the tent act of the last generall conventioun of borrowis haldin at the burght of Jedburgh the 7 of Julii last ordaining the burgh of Jedburgh to produce the forme of the electioun of thair majestratis and

counsall at Michaelmes[13] last and to proceid thairintill in maner prescryvit in
the said act compeirit Alexander Kirktoun present commissioner of the said
burgh and produceit the forme of thair said electioun quhilk being red and
considderit be the saidis commissioneris they accept the same for dilligence
and ordainis the said burgh in all tyme cumming to conforme themeselffis
thairto in thair said electioun.

9
{Perth unfrie tredderis}
The same day, the saidis commissioneris of burrowis annent the elevint act
of the last generall conventioun of borrowis haldin at the burgh of Jedburgh
the 7 of Julii ordaining the burgh of Perth to produce their dilligence in
uplifting frome Johnne Mitchell and Gilchryst McClair the unlawis incurrit
be theme for usurping the liberties of the frie royall burrowis, compeirit
Andro Wilsoun commissioner for the said burgh and declairit that they had
upliftit the saidis unlawis and that sine the persounis hes fled out of their
boundis to remaine in sum uther part of the cuntrie quhilk declaratioun the
saidis borrowis acceptis for dilligence at this time.

Sexto Julii 1631

10
{Aberdaine Fraserburght[14] missive}
The quhilk day the commissioneris of borrowis being conveanit and understanding that the burgh of Fraserburgh being of late erectit in ane burgh of
barronie quhairby they daylie usurpe the libberteis of the frie borrowis to
the great hurt and prejudice of a number of the burghs in the north and
consideering with all that the burgh of Aberden hes intendit summondis
against the inhabitantis of the said burgh quhilk ar by theme suspendit and
lyes over undiscussit, thairfoir they ordaine the said burgh of Aberdeine to
present thair intendit actioun and to produce thair dilligence heirannent to
the nixt generall conventioun of borrowis. And to be ane heid of the nixt
missive.

11
{Factoris in France commissioun missive}
The same day annent the 9 act of the last generall conventioun of burrowis
haldin at the burgh of Jedburght the 7 day of Julii last twiching the remedie

---

[13]   Michaelmas falls on 29 September. Burgh council elections were always held around that
time of year.
[14]   Fraserburgh lies on the coast, 40 miles north of Aberdeen. It had actually been a burgh of
barony since 1546, see Pryde, *The Burghs of Scotland*, no. 227.

of the hurtis sustenit be merchandis traffiqueris in France through occasioun of the factoris thair, quhairby it wes statut and ordainit that no factoris sould be imployit in Normandie bot sick as wer ressavit and admittit be the commissioneris of borrowis and becaus it is not expedient that the said act should tak executioun untill sick tyme as the merchandis and factoris allreddie imployit have maid thair comptis, [fo. 377r] thairfoir they ordaine ilk commissioner present to intimat the said act of new to thair neighbouris to the effect they may end thair comptis betuix and the first day of Julii nixtocum efter which tyme they intend that onlie sick factoris shalbe imployit in these places as salbe ressaveit be the borrowis and to this effect the present commissioneris giffis full power and commissioun to the burghis that salbe apointit to meit and convein at Edinburgh efter the disolving of this present conventioun to mak choyse of sick youthis as sall present theme selffis to theme and sall find cautioun for thair intromissioun and undergoing of the injunctiounis to be set doun to theme, to be factoris thair with power lykewyse to the saidis borrowis to sett doun the saidis conditiounis and to tak cautioun of theme quhairanent the present commissioneris gives thair full power and commissioun and in all uther thingis that may concerne the said mater and the saidis borrowis to repoirt thair diligence heir annent to the nixt generall conventioun of burrowis. And this to be ane heid of the nixt missive.

12
{Commissioun plaidding, yairne, Buchane missive}
The same day the saidis commissioneris of burrowis beand conveanit annent the mater of the plaiding[15] and presenting of the same to the mercat mentioned in the twentie act of the last generall conventioun of burrowis haldin at the burgh of Jedburgh the 7 day of Julii last, the saidis commissioneris considdering that wair to be ane of the pryme commodities of this kingdome quhilk throw occasioun of the falset in wyrking and concealling of the same be presenting the same to the mercant hard roillit up is licklie to decay abroad to the grit hurt of this cuntrie, as lykewyse for considdering that the yairne is becum a greit and necessar commoditie for the merchandis and that thair is ane great falset committit be the selleris in the fals telling thairof to the great prejudice of the merchandis traffiqueris thairwith, for avoyding quhairof, the saidis commissioneris findis thair is no meanis so guid as to obteane the same to be soild be wecht with a pennaltie aganis thoise that sall sell the same utherwyse and ane command to the burghis to sie the same put to executioun. Thairfoir the present commissioneris ordainis the burghis that salbe appoyntit to meit at Edinburgh befoir the

---

15   Twilled woollen cloth, often but not necessarily with a checked pattern, i.e. tartan.

dissolving of this present conventioun to supplicat the lordis of his Majesties counsall anent the premisses and to deall with theme thairannent as they sall find occasioun utherwayis to tak sick course therein as they in thair judgementis sall think most fitt and expedient for the weill of the merchandis. As lykwyse ordainis the said burghis to insist with the lordis for recalling of the patent purchessit be Robert Buchane annent the perrill[16] mentioned in the 12 act of the said last generall conventioun quhairannent and annent all uther thingis that may concerne the premisses the present commissioneris grantis unto theme their full power and commissioun and to doe thairin all and quhatsumever they might doe theme selffis gif they wer personallie [fo. 377v] present firme and stabill haldand and for to hald quhatsumever the said commissioneris sall doe in the premisses And the said burghes to repoirt thair dilligence heir annent to the nixt generall conventioun of borrowis. And this to be ane heid of the nixt missive.

13

{Statute factouris in Flanderis, marriadge, conservatour missive}

The same day the saidis commissioneris of borrowis beand convenit, annent the 21 act of the last generall conventioun of burrowis haldin at the burgh of Jedburgh the 8 day of Julii last for taking ane constant and satled course with the factoris of the staipill poirt of Campheir[17] for prevening of the evillis as in tyme bypast they have suffered through the occasioun of the mariadge of thair factoris as at mair lenth is sett doun in the said act, The present commissioneris considdering the exemple of utheris natiounis in the lyke caise and of the benefeit may redound to this cuntrie through haveing thair awin youth traind up in merchandice abroad. Thairfoir and for eschewing the farder evillis and prejudices they have susteinit through occasioun of mariadge of thair factouris, the said commissioneris be thir presentis statutes and ordainis that all personis to be heirefter admittet factoris at the said stapill poirt salbe unmaried and that at thair mariadge thair office of factorie shall presentlie expyre. As lykewyse for that it sall not be lawfull to theme to maire befoir they repair hame to this cuntrie and mak ane end of thair comptis with all sick merchandis as hes imployit theme and that to this effect they sall find cautioun at thair admissioun quhilk act wes presentlie intimat to the present conservatour And ordainis ilk commissioner present to intimat the same to thair burghis at thair hame cumming.[18]

---

16 For details on the career of this fascinating individual, see S. Murdoch, 'The pearl fisher: Robert Buchan "de Portlethin" in Sweden, 1642–1653', *Northern Scotland*, 40 (2007), 51–70.

17 This is the Scottish staple port of Veere, on what was then the island of Walcheren (now part of the Dutch mainland due to later land reclamation), in the Dutch province of Zeeland.

18 This act is one of those noted in the Abstract of Acts of Convention, reproduced in *RCRBS*, iv, Appendix No. I, 525–44, at 526.

14

{Statute borrowis absent frome particuller conventionis}

The same day the saidis commissioneris of borrowis beand conveinit, annent the saxt act of the particuller conventioun of burrowis haldin at the burght of Edinburgh the third day of Merch last for better keiping of the particuller conventiounis that occurris betuix and thair generall meittingis as at mair lenth is conteinit in the said act, the saidis commissioneris finding that thair is a great necessitie of keiping of the said particuller meitingis inrespect of the wechtie materis that occurris betuix and generall conventiounis so neirlie concerning the estait of burrowis. Thairfoir they have statute and ordainit and be thir presentis statutis and ordainis that all burghis lawfullie wairnit for keipping of the said particullar meittingis and salbe absent ilk ane of theme sall incur ane unlaw of xx lb. but favour; and grantis and gives power to the burrowis meitting for unlawing of the saidis burghis absent in maner foirsaid and decernis and declairis the burghis that depairtis befoir the subscryving of the booke to be accomptit as absentis as gif they had never compeirit; and ordainis this ordour to be kepit in all tyme cumming and ilk burgh to adverteis thair counsall heirof at thair hame cumming and lykewyse ordainis that in the wairning the missives sall conteine the caussis of the meitting.[19]

[fo. 378r]

Septimo Julii I^m vi^c trigesimo primo

15

{Commissioun coyne missive}

The quhilk day the commissioneris of burrowis bean conveinit, annent the nynt act of the last particullar conventioun haldin at the burgh of Edinburght the thrid day of March last[20] ordaining ilk burght to send thair commissioneris sufficientlie instructit with thair best advyses for reforming of the present abuse in the coynis with thair best advyses for inbringing of money within this cuntrey. The present commissioneris haveing considderit the overtour and propositioun maid be the saidis commissioneris then conveinit quhich as yit hes taking no effect and finding as yit the same to be the fittest and savest cour for the weill of the kingdome. Thairfoir they ordaine the commissioneris that salbe appointit to meit at Edinburgh efter the dissolving of this present conventioun to tak the said matter of new to thair consideratiounis and according as they sall find most expedient for reforming of the former abuse and for weill of the kingdome to prosecute

19   This act is noted in the Abstract of Acts of Convention, *RCRBS*, iv, 526.
20   *RCRBS*, iii, 329.

the said matter quhairannent they gif and grantis to the saidis commissioneris and most pairt of theme conveinit their full power and commissioun ratifieing what sumever they sall doe in the premissis and the saidis commissioneris to repoirt thair dilligence heir annent to the nixt generall conventioun of borrowis. And this to be ane heid of the nixt missive.

16
{Commissioun letters to Campheir greivances conservatour missive}
The same day forsamekill as the commissioneris of borrowis considdering that since thair last generall conventioun haldin at the burgh of Edinburght in Julii last they had writtin to the toun of Campheir for sending of commissioneris hither for treating annent the greivances susteanit be the merchandis traffiquand thair and for remeiding thairof which letter wes answerit be the said toun in the moneth of December excusing thair not sending of commissioneris and desiring to be accquant with the saidis grivances promeissing to give all satisfactioun could ly in theme quhairunto thair wes ane answer maid be the commissioneris that convenit at Edinburgh in March last, as lykewyse the saidis commissioneris considdering the letter direct to this present conventioun be the magistratis of the toun desireing as of befoir to be informit of the said alledgit hurtis sustenit be this natioun in the last contract past betuix the borrowis and theme which being knowin they promised all contentment as is conteinit in thair said letter. The present commissioneris considdering that as yit the former greivances ar not takin away and that onlie in default of the saidis magistratis, thairfoir ordanis a letter to be direct to the saidis magistratis of the said toun in thair nameis schewing that the conservatour being heir present had acquaintit thame that his lordship had impairtit to theme the foirsaidis greivances which notwithstanding his nocht bein by them removit and no course takin for removeing of the same to their heavie prejudice quhich they can no longer undergoe and thairfoir to desire theme to communicat thair mindes and intentiounis with the said conservatour; and as they have promeissit to give content so reallie to performe the same, [fo. 378v] utherwyse to hold theme excusit gif they sall tak sum farder resolutioun without ane farder acquainting of theme and ordainis the generall clerk to subscryve the same quhairanent thir presentis salbe his warrand; and ordainis the said greivances to be of new sett doun be the commissioneris that ar apointit to meit at Edinburgh efter the dissolving of this present conventioun and the same to be sett doun with the said letter. As lykewyse ordainis the conservatour being present to travell and commoun with the said majestratis annent the premissis and to sie the saidis grievances removit and the said conservatour thairefter to acquant the burght of Edinburgh in thair names that sum farder cours may be taikin annent the premissis for the weill of the natioun as said, and the saidis burghis and conservatour to repoirt thair dilligence heir annent to

the next generall conventioun of borrowis. And this to be ane heid of the nixt missive.

17

{Conservatouris dewis}

The same day annent the nynt act of the last generall conventioun of borrowis haldin at the burght of Jedburght the 7 day of Julii last for setting doun a tabill to my lord conservatour for his dewis.[21] The present commissioneris haveing sene and considderit the tabill alreddie sett doun at Bruntiland in the moneth of Agust the yeir of God I^m vi^c and sex yeiris[22] and the said conservatour compeirand declairit that he had conforme to the said act caried him selff in uplifting his dewis. Thairfoir ordainis the said tabill to stand, the said conservatour being present to uplift no uther dewes nor hier bot according as he hes ressavit or sall ressave warrand frome the commissioneris of borrowis in thair generall or particular conventiounes.[23]

18

{Commissioun annent the conservatouris dewis missive}

The same day the lord conservatour compeirand declairing how that these sex yeiris bygaine he had servit the burrowis as conservatour of the priviledges of the natioun in the Law Cuntries and had utherwayes servit as they had imployit him and withall declair the great derth of these places and meanis of the dewis allowit be the burrowis for his intertainment and thairfoir desyret that they sould be pleased to tak the same to thair considderatiounis and to grant unto him sum augmentatioun or gratificatioun as they sould pleis. With the quhilk desire the saidis borrowis being advysit and willing sum way to gratifie his bygaine painis and to provyde for his honouris interteinment bot withall considdering that they had not bene fullie acquainted thairwith of befoir they have remitted and be thir presentis remittis the considderatioun thairof to the commissioneris appointit to meit at Edinburght efter the dissolving of this present conventioun, to which borrowis and maist pairt of theme conveanit they grant thair full power and commissioun to doe annent the premissis as they sall think most meit and expedient both for the honour and weill of the natioun promitten *derato*[24]

21   It was actually the 19th act of that convention, see *RCRBS*, iii, 315.

22   *RCRBS*, ii, 227–8.

23   This act is noted in the Abstract of Acts of Convention, *RCRBS*, iv, 526.

24   This literally means 'promising concerning firm/fixed', more commonly and fully expressed in Scots as 'promittand to hauld firme and stabill all and quhatsumevir thingis our said commissionar shall lauchfullie do in the dischairge of this his commissioun' (this example is from NAS, PA7/25/35/2, a parliamentary commission from Aberdeen from 1639). It is therefore an undertaking by a body that delegates its authority to another individual or group to abide by whatever is decided on their behalf by that person or group.

etc. [fo. 379r] And the saidis borrowis to repoirt their dilligence heirannent to the nixt generall conventioun of borrowis. And this to be ane heid of the nixt missive.

19

{Bamph electioun magistratis, commoun guid Aberdeine missive}

The same day annent the aucht act of the last generall conventioun of borrowis[25] haldin at the burgh of Jedburgh the saxt day of Julii last ordaining the burgh of Bamph to have produceit the forme of the electioun of thair magistratis and counsall at Michaelmes last and to have proceidit thair said electioun conforme to the actis of parliament and borrowis with ane perfyte rentall of their commoun guid and commoun landis, compeirit James Winschester present commissioner of the said burght and produceit the forme of thair said electioun at Michaelmes last which being sene and considderit be the commissioneris of burrowis they find the same altogidder informall and against the lawis of this kingdome provydit in that caice and against the actis of borrowis and in speciall in putting of barrounis and knichtis to be upoun the lyttis of their magistratis and theirfoir unlawis theme in the sowme of fourtie pundis and upoun dyvers respectis they continew the uplifting thairof togidder with the uplifting of the unlaw of tuentie pund quhairin they wer adjudgit the said last conventioun for being absent thairfra to the nixt conventioun; and ordainis theme in their nixt electioun to proceid conforme to the actis of parliament and burrowis under the paine of fourtie pundis and to produce the forme thairof to the said nixt generall conventioun and as for their rentall produceit. Ordainis the burgh of Aberdaine to informe themeselffis annent the veritie thairof that nothing is omittit furth of the same and of the validitie of their commoun guid and commoun landis and to produce the same to be sene and considderit be the commissioneris of borrowis their conveinand. And the saidis burghis to repoirt thair diligence heiranent to the nixt generall conventioun of borrowis. And this to be ane heid of the nixt missive.[26]

20

{Commissioun fyre bit May missive}

The same day annent the fyft act of the last particuller conventioun of borrowis haldin at Edinburgh the thrid day of March last annent the expediencie of ane fyre bitt[27] upoun the May and maner of interteinment thairof gif the samene sould have bene fund expedient. The present commissioneris

25 RCRBS, iii, 311.
26 This act is noted in the Abstract of Acts of Convention, RCRBS, iv, 526.
27 RCRBS, iii, 328. This is probably the same word as 'butt', a barrell or bucket, suggesting that the proposal is to erect a brazier.

remitis the consideratioun thairof to the commissioneris of borrowis to be conveinit at Edinburgh efter the dissolving of this present conventioun, and grantis and gifis thair full power and commissioun to the borrowis and maist pairt of theme conveinand to try the expediencie and inexpediencie of the said fyre bitt and according as they sall find to proceid thairintill as they sall think best for the weill of the borrowis. And the saidis borrowis to repoirt thair dilligence heiranent to the nixt generall conventioun of borrowis. And this to be ane heid of the nixt missive.

21

{Edinburght Dundie Muntross Linlithgow Kirkcaldie to present certane thair nighbouris missive}[28]
The same day the commissioneris of borrowis being informit that William Melvill in Kirkcaldie had depairtit furth of the yle of Zeland[29] in January 1627 in Maij 1628 and October 1630 unpayand his dewis to the conservatour or minister, and sicklyke that James Whyte had depairtit with his schip furth of the said yle in October 1630 [fo. 379v] unpaying his dewis, Alexander Blair in Dundie from Campheir in December 1629, Robert Forrester in Dundie in December 1630 unpayand the saidis dewis, Alexander Reid in Monros had transpoirtit stapill waris by the staipill poirt to Rotterdame the 20 of December 1630, David Murray in Edinburgh had lykewyse transportit stapill wairis by the said poirt to Amsterdame in December 1630 and that certane merchandice in Linlithgow had transportit to Rotterdame by the said stapill poirt certaine staipill goodis in ane schip perteining to Robert Mitchell in Borrowstonnes[30] in the moneth of Maii last. Thairfoir the present commissioneris ordainis the burghes of Edinburgh, Dundie, Monros and Kirkcaldie to produce to the nixt generall conventioun of borrowis the saidis persounis ilkane of theme thair awin neighbouris to answer upon the caussis foirsaid under the paine of ane hundreth pundis ilk burgh to be bayit to the borrowis, and the said burght of Linlithgow to try which of thair neighbouris transpoirt anie guidis into the said schip, and haveing tryit to produce theme to the said nixt generall conventioun of borrowis under the paine foirsaid. And this to be ane heid of the nixt missive.

22

{Dischairge selling to certaine in Campheir conservatour missive}
The same day the saidis commissioneris of borrowis being informit that thair is dyvers persounis resident pairtlie at Middilburght[31] and pairtlie at

---

28 This marginal note of the content of the act appears on fo. 379v but has been placed here for the sake of consistency.
29 This is the island of Walcheren in Zeeland, now part of the Dutch mainland.
30 i.e. Bo'ness, on the Firth of Forth.
31 Middelburg, also on Walcheren, had previously been the Scots staple port in the Netherlands.

Campheir who to the heavie prejudice of the haill merchandis trafiking thither with stapill wairis doeth by up the said wairis and impeidis these of Holland and Flanderis to cum to the said poirt to by and being informit that among these thair is Nicollas Clawsone, Jacob Kein, Adriane Isen and Peter Rischellis, Habricht Bone, Barthilmew Bone the widow of Merteine de Roning[32] who dois continuallie by up the commodities of this cuntrie. Thairfoir the present commissioneris dischairges thair neighbouris or anie of the factouris from selling of anie of the commodities of this cuntrie to anie of the saidis persounis under the paine of xx lb. Fleamis to be payit be theme to the conservatour being present to have ane cair to put these actis to executioun, and swa to intimat the same to the saidis factour and ilk burght to intimat this act to thair nighbouris at thair hamecuming that none pretend ignorance. And the said conservatour to repoirt his dilligence heirannent. And this to be ane heid of the nixt missive.[33]

23

{Muntrois Suttie}

The same day it being compleinit be George Suttie merchand in Edinburgh upoun the burgh of Munros that they haveing obteinit ane decreit befoir the commissioneris of borrowis in thair last generall conventioun haldin at the burgh of Jedburght the 8 day of Julii last against the said burght of Munros for payment making to of the soume of I^c xxviij lb. xiiij s.[34] Conforme to the said decreit compeirit Robert Gray ane present commissioner of the said burgh and for obedience of the said decreit band and obleist himselff of his awin consent as commissioner for the said burgh, [fo. 380r] and in thair names to content and pay to the said George Suttie at thair nixt particuller conventioun to be haldin at Edinburgh the 8 of this instant the said sowme of ane hundreth twentie aucht pund fourtene schillingis foirsaid under the paine of fyftie pundis by and attour the said soume in cais of failyie.

24

{Certane unlawis Remittit}

The same day annent the 40 act of the last gennerall conventioun of borrowis haldin at the burgh of Jedburgh the 9 of Julii last unlawing the burghis of Pittinweame and Anstruther Wester ilk ane of theme in xx lb. for being absent frome the said conventioun.[35] Compeirit the commission-

---

32 Clawsone is Claessone, Rischellis is Rischeers, and Roning is Koning. No explanation is offered for a widow called Bartholemew. I am gratefull to Peter Blom of the Zeeland Archives for help with these names.

33 This act is noted in the Abstract of Acts of Convention, *RCRBS*, iv, 526.

34 *RCRBS*, iii, 317.

35 *RCRBS*, iii, 319.

eris of the saidis burghis and humblie intreatit the haill commissioneris for remitting of the saidis unlawis and the saidis commissioneris consideering thair estaitis with sum resonabill excussis schawin, they dispence with the saidis unlawis and dischairges theme thairof. And sicklyke dispenssis with the unlawis incurrit be the burghis of Linlithgow, St Androis, Munrois, Kinghorne, Anstruther Eister and Wester, Craill, Dumbar, Lanerk, Peiblis, Air and St Androis[36] for being absent frome certane particullar conventiounis.

Octavo Julii I^m vi^c tregesimo primo

25

{Ratificatioun of the act annent keiping of the conservatouris hous and dischairging of factouris and utheris to sell beir, wyne etc and the hous to be furnischit with Inglis beir}

The quhilk day the commissioneris of borowis being conveinit, annent the supplicatiounis givin in be Walter Cant merchand in name and behalff of David Peiblis and Elizabeth Cant his spous schawing of the abussis of the consergerie hous quhairby the said David maister thairof is grittumlie prejudgit and in speciall throw the not keiping of sum merchand skipperis merchandis sonnes and utheris their servandis when they ar allone intrustit with their fatheris or maisteris guidis their ordinarrie at the said hous and be the tupping and selling of beir be sundrie of the natioun thair and not authorizit frome the commissioneris of borrowis for doing thairof with the which supplicatioun the saidis commissioneris being advysit and haveing sene the former actis maid thair annent and in speciall the actis maid at Strivilling the 4 of Julii 1616[37] they ratifie and aprove the same in the haill heidis and merchantis sons and servandis when they ar intrustit with thair fatheris or maisteris guidis or hes ane stock of thair awin, that in that caice they salbe subject for the keiping of thair ordinar at the said hous as other merchandis. And sicklyke as of befoir dischairges all factouris or utheris that hes the benefeit of the natioun frome tapping and selling beir and wyne or meit and drink to anie merchandis, marineris or utheris of the natioun under the paine of fyve pund Fleamis to be payit be the said transgressoris to the maister of the saidis consergerie hous and ordainis my lord conservatour to caus intimat this present act to all these at the said stapill poirt that hes intreis heirin and to sie the same put to dew executioun.[fo. 380v] As lykewyse ordainis the said maister of the consergerie to furnisch the said hous with sufficient guid drinking Inglisch beir.[38]

---

36 It is not clear if St Andrews appears a second time merely in error or instead of another burgh.
37 *RCRBS*, iii, 23–4. The convention met at Perth, not Stirling.
38 This act is noted in the Abstract of Acts of Convention, *RCRBS*, iv, 526.

26
{Commissioun fisching, salt, Hay comptis missive}
The same day forsameikill as the commissioneris of burrowis consideding
that in the matter of fisching so long debaittit that it is necessar sum conclusioun be taikin their annent, and finding that befoir Mr Johnne Hay[39] his
returne whoe is apointit commissioner for theme in the said mater and
that his proceiding be hard they can tak no solide course for prosecuting
thairof, and it being schawin to theme lykewyse be the commissioneris of
the burght of Edinburgh that the said Mr Johnne nocht long since hes beine
indewit with commissioun frome theme for theme selffis and in name of the
haill borrowis of this kingdome supplicatting his majestie and concorring
with sum of the gentrie for staying of the course intendit be sum persounis
for rejecting of the salt to be transportit frome this cuntrie to Ingland to ane
certane small quantitie onlie sellabill to sum few persounis and for restraining
of importing of forrane salt within this kingdome; and the saidis commissioneris considdering that the said matter doeth importe verie mutch boith
thair estait in particuller and the haill kingdome in generall, the said restraint
of salt drawing with it ane overthrow of the most profitabill coilheuchis of
this kingdome by which two meanis the shipping of this kingdome sould
mightilie be impairit and trade and negotiatioun mutch diminischit to the
great prejudice of this haill kingdome; and lykewyse considdering that be
restraint of forrane salt the haill fischingis of this kingdomes should prove
unprofitabill. Thairfoir the saidis commissioneris ratiffies and aproves the
saidis burght of Edinburgh their preceidingis thairannent. And to the end
that sum farder conclusioun may be takin for prosecuting of the said matter
of the fisching and for staying of the saidis intendit course of the restraint
of salt gif ane farder neid shalbe they have apointit and ordainit and be thir
presentis appointis and ordainis ane particullar conventioun of borrowis to
be haldin at the burght of Edinburgh the 8 of this instant with continuatioun of dayis and appointis and ordainis to keip the said conventioun the
burghis of Edinburgh, Peirth, Dundie, Aberdeine, Striviling, Linlithgow, St
Androis, Glasgow, Air, Haddingtoun, Munros, Kirkcaldie, Dysart, Bruntyland,
Anstruther Eister and Wester, Couper, Pittinweame, Creall, Kinghorne and
Dumbar to which borrowis and maist pairt of theme convenand the present
commissioneris remitis the considderatioun of the foirsaidis materis, and
grantis and gives unto theme their full power and commissioun for theme
and in thair nameis to heir and ressave the said Mr Johnne Hay his report,
gif he shall returne betuix and the said day or befoir the dissolving of the
said conventioun, of his proceidingis boith in the said matter of the fisching
and in the said matter of the salt conforme to the severall commissiounis

---

[39] Hay was the burghs' representative at court.

givin unto him thairannent and all uther thingis concerning the borrowis, and to heir and ressave the said Mr Johnne Hay his comptis of his debursementis in the borrowis effairis. With power also to theme [fo. 381r] thairefter for taking sum solide course and conclusioun for prosecuting the said matter of the fisching and staying of the said intendit course of the restraint of salt according as they sall think most meit and expedient for the weill of the borrowis and for taking course and ordour for repayment of the soumis the said Mr Johnne salbe fund to have debursit in thair effairis. With power also to theme gif it sallhappin the said Mr Johnne to to returne betuix and the dissolutioun of the said conventioun to appoint ane new day of meitting or to gif commissioun to the burgh of Edinburgh for appointing of ane new day as they sall think it most meit and expedient according to the necessitie of thair effairis. Quhairanent and all and sindrie the premissis the present commissioneris grantis and gifis unto theme full frie plaine power and commissioun to doe as they sall think most requisit for the generall weill of the haill borrowis, and obleissis theme and thair burghis to abyde at and fulfill what sumever the saidis commissioneris sall doe annent the premissis. And grantis lykewyse power and commissioun to the saidis borrowis to unlaw the borrowis absent or that sall depairt befoir the subscryving of the book ilk of theme in ane unlaw of twentie pund and the saidis borrowis to repoirt thair dilligence heiranent to the nixt generall conventioun of borrowis. And this to be ane heid of the nixt missive.[40]

27
{Commissioun Wedderburne grammer Edinburgh}
The same day the saidis commissioneris of borrowis haveing ressavit ane letter direct to theme be the lordis of his majesties most honorabill privie counsall annent ane grammer drawin up be Mr David Wedderburne scoolemaister of Aberdene quhairby disputteris grammer quhich hes formerlie bene taucht is abridgit, facilitat for the profeit of the youth.[41] Compeirit the said Mr David and produceit the said grammer with ane new rudimentis or introductioun thairto quhich being sene and considderit of the univerities and colledgis of this kingdome and uther learnit men, the saidis borrowis considdering that the same being ane mater that requires dew deliberatioun so neirlie concerning the educatioun of the youth whoes progres and profeit in learning dependis mutch upoun their first institutioun and firt groundis, thairfoir they have thocht gude that befoir the saidis rudimentis and grammer salbe farder authorized or imbraiced be the scoolmaisteris that first thair be printed the number of twa hundreth of the said buikis to be distributeit among leirnit men and utheris of this kingdome as salbe thocht

---

[40]   This act is noted in the Abstract of Acts of Convention, *RCRBS*, iv, 527.
[41]   See the Introduction for a discussion of Wedderburn's grammar.

fitt be the saidis lordis of counsall and they desired, betuix and such a day as
the saidis lordis sall apoint to returne their animadversiounis to the burght
of Edinburgh to be thairefter presentit to the said lordis by whois authoritie
their may be maid chois of two or thrie leirnit men with the said Mr David
for reveising of the saidis haill animadversiounis and according as they sall
think necessar the saidis rudimentis and grammer to be correctit [fo. 381v]
and thairefter of new to be imprintit and taught and ressavit in the haill
grammer scooles within this kingdoome and no uther. And becaus the said
Mr David hes taine the paines to be the beginner and layer doun of the
grundis of the saidis rudimentis in grammer, thairfoir they for thair pairt ar
content and consentis that he sall have boith the name thairof, as also the
benefeit of the printing and selling thairof for sick a space as the saidis lordis
sall appoint, the said Mr David alwayis submitting himselff in the pryce
thairof to the commissioneris of borrowis, lyke as he compeir and obleis him
to exact no hier paye for the same nor salbe sett doun be the saidis commissioneris. And to the effect that this thair intentioun for correcting of the
saidis rudimentis and grammer may be maid knowne they find it necessar
that the haill buikis now to be printed sall conteine ane programe befoir
the beginning thairof declairing onlie to the end the same may cum into
the handis of leirnit and juditious men whoe out of thair cair and zeale to
the advancement of learning salbe desired to revise the saidis buikis and to
send thair animadversiounis with the buiks to the burgh of Edinburgh to the
effect that farder course may be tayne thairin as the saidis lordis sall appoint.
And ordainis the burghes that ar appointit to meit at Edinburgh to repoirt
this thair opinioun to the saidis lordis. And farder ordainis the said burght
of Edinburgh to advance for printing of the saidis buikis to the said Mr
David the soume of ane hundreth and twentie pundis mair as they sall find
necessar provyding alwayis that this thair opinioun to the lordis be informit
and that he undertak and assist the printing of the saidis buikis which being
advancit be theme ordainis ilk burght to be requirit for sending thair pairt
of the said soume acording to the taxt roll to the nixt generall conventioun
of borrowis under the paine of ane unlaw of twentie pundis ilk burgh by
and attour the payment of thair pairt of the said soume to the nixt generall
conventioun of borrowis. And thir saidis burghis to repoirt thair dilligence
heirannent to the nixt generall conventioun of borrowis. And this to be ane
heid of the nixt missive.[42]

28
{Commissioun Eilleis, Burnet, ministeris dewis missive}
The same day annent James Eilleis and Johnne Burnet collectouris of the

---

[42]   This act is noted in the Abstract of Acts of Convention, *RCRBS*, iv, 527.

dewis grantit for defraying of the ministeris stipend at Campheir, compeirit Patrick Baxter merchand and produceit the saidis coumptis and the saidis borrowis understanding be these appointit for heiring of the saidis coumptis that the same are a litill intricate.

Thairfoir they ordaine the said Patrick Baxter to present the saidis coumptis moir perfyte to the commissioneris of borrowis appointit to meit at Edinburgh efter the dissolving of this present conventioun, to which borrowis and maist pairt of theme convenand the said borrowis grantis and gifis thair full power and [fo. 382r] commissioun for fitting of the said coumptis and for nominating of ane new collectour and for taking farder ordour for the moir preceis uplifting of the said dewis. As lykewyse for the cons-iddering of the validitie thairof and according as they sall find necessar with power to theme to proceid in augmenting thairof, quhairanent thir presentis salbe ane sufficient warrand to theme and generallie all and sindrie uther thingis to doe annent the premissis as they sall think most meit and expedient and to repoirt thair dilligence heirann-ent to the nixt generall conventioun of borrowis. And this to be ane heid of the nixt missive.

29

{Statutes annent the voitting to remitting of unlawes, missive}

The same day forsamekill as for avoyding of confusioun and better ordour keiping this being formarlie statute and ordainit that when anie burght sall happin to be decernit in ane unlaw for not fulfilling anie heid of the missive or for transgressing anie act or ordinance of the borrowis that the commis-sioner who should happin to voit to the remitting thairof should pay ane unlaw of fyve pundis and not to have place or vote befoir the said soume wer payit, yit nochtwithstanding the same as yit hes not takin full effect [to] the great prejudice of this estait and daylie grouth of the same amongst theme. Thaifoir the present commissioneris ratifies and aproves the former act and of new statutes and ordainis that when ane burght sall happin to be decernit in ane unlaw for nocht keiping of the generall or anie particuller conventioun for not ansewring anie heidis of the missive or for transgressing anie of the actis or ordinance of the borrowis or unlawit be the borrowis for quhatsumever caus that the commissioner voiting to the remitting of the unlaw sall presentlie incur ane penaltie of fyve pundis to be payit pres-entlie, and ordainis him nocht to be hard till the penaltie be produceit, and ordainis ilk burght to intimat this present ordinance to thair counsall at thair hamecuming that none pretend ignorance thairof. And lykewyse to repoirt thair dilligence in intimating the samene to the nixt generall conventioun of borrowis. And this to be ane heid of the nixt missive.[43]

---

43   This act is noted in the Abstract of Acts of Convention, *RCRBS*, iv, 527.

30

{Agent v^c xxi lb. xviij s., missive}

The same day forsamekill as the coumptis of Alexander Aikinheid agent[44] being fittit calculated and alowit be the commissioneris of borrowis of his debursementis in the borrowis effairis since thair last generall conventioun to extend to the soume of fyve hundreth twentie ane pundis auchteine schillingis four pennyis, and theirfoir ordainis ilk burgh to send thair pairt of the said soume with thair commissioneris conforme to the taxt roll to the nixt generall conventioun of burrowis under the paine of xx lb. ilk burgh and that by and attour thair payment of thair said soume. And this to be ane heid of the nixt missive.

[fo. 382v]

31

{Dysart I^m merkis, missive}

The same day annent the supplicatioun giffin in be burght of Dysart schewing the grit and extraordinarie loissis susteinit be the said burgh thir yeiris bygaine togidder with thair harberie which throw thair bygaine loissis they ar altogidder unabill to reedifie and without the same be repairit or buildit of new in ane moir convenient place thair burgh cannot subsist as at mair lenth is conteinit in the said supplicatioun. The said commissioneris of borrowis considdering their great necessities and imminent overthrow gif sum spedie course be not takin for thair supplie, thairfoir they have grantit and giffin and be thir presentis grantis and giffis to the said burghis for their helpis and supplie for building of thair saidis harberie the sowme of ane thowsand merkis guid and usuall money of this realme, with this provisioun that the burrowis be no farder burdenit with anie desire of thair farther supplie heirefter and that they imploy the said soume upoun the saidis harberie and be coumptabill thairof to the borrowis and repoirt to the nixt generall conventioun thair dilligence in repairing and building of their said harberie and that be testimonie of thair nighbour burghis. Lykeas the commissioner of the said burgh obleissis himselff in name of his said burgh for fullfilling of the conditiounis and provisiounis abonewrittin. As also the saidis commissiouneris ordanis ilk burgh to send thair pairt of the said soume to the nixt generall conventioun of borrowis according to the taxt roll under the paine of xx lb. ilk burgh, and that by and attour the payment of thair pairt of the said soume. And this to be ane heid of the nixt missive.

---

[44] Aitkenhead acted as the burghs' legal agent, pursuing and defending cases on their behalf before the courts, and carrying out a range of other duties, including collecting burghs' dues and fines.

32
{Supplicatioun Anstruther Wester, missive}
The same day annent the supplicatioun giffin in be the burgh of Anstruther Wester schawing the grit and extraordinarie charges they have sustenit throw obteining ane decreit annent the asyse of the herring, and thairfoir craveing in respect of thair present povertie lisence and warrand for living[45] of twentie schillingis ilk boit that sall happin to goe this yeir to the Lambes drave[46] as at mair length is conteinit in the said supplicatioun. The saidis commissioneris of borrowis ordainis the saidis burgh to produce the said decreit to the nixt generall conventioun of borrowis and ilk burgh to send thair commissioneris sufficientlie instructit to give answer to the said supplicatioun at the said conventioun. And this to be ane heid of the nixt missive.

[fo. 383r]
33
{Exemptioun Peiblis, Lawder, Renfrew}
The same day the saidis commissioneris grantis and gives to the saidis burghes of Lawder, Peiblis and Renfrew to abyde and remaine fra the generall conventiounis of borrowis for the space of thrie yeiris upoun the conditiounis and provisiounis efterfollowing, provyding alwayis the saimeine be nocht extendit to parliamentis nor quhair the saidis burghis ar citat for anie particullar cuase. And also provyding the said burghis send with thair commissioner of thair nixt adjacent burgh their severall ratificatioun and approbatioun of all thingis to be done yeirlie in the saidis generall conventionis autenticklie subscryvit with all soumis that they sould pay to the borrowis conforme to the missive and that they bestow the expenssis quhilk they sould have bestowit upoun their commissioneris upoun commoun workis and be coumptable thairof to the borrowis at the expyring of the saidis yeiris.

34
Nono Julii I[m] vi[c] trigesimo primo
{Agent, borrowis absent, missive}
The quhilk day the commissioneris beand conveinit, ordainis Alexander Aickinheid agent to adverteis the borrowis absent or exeamit of the strick ordour to be takine heirefter with these that salbe absent or unlawit for anie cause and that they omit not to send to the nixt generall conventioun their speciall ratificatioun as is contenit in thair exemptioun without which thair

---

[45] i.e. levying.
[46] Drave = the annual herring fishing. Lammas is 1 August.

exemptioun will not be steidabill unto theme, togidder with the extract of thair said exemptioun. And the said agent to repoirt his dilligence in doing heirof to the said nixt generall conventioun of borrowis. And this to be ane heid of the nixt missive.

35
{Present conventioune}
The commissioneris dissolvis this present conventioun and affixis thair nixt generall conventioun of borrowis to be and begin at the burgh of Munros the [...] day of Julii nixt with continuatioun of dayis and ordainis thair clerk to direct thair generall missive to the said burgh of Munros for wairning of the haill borrowis for keiping of the said conventioun.

Particular Convention at Edinburgh, July 1631

[fo. 383v]
In the particular conventioun of borrowis haldin at the burgh of Edinburgh the auchtene day of Julij the yeir of God ane thowsand sex hundreth and threttie ane yeiris be the commissioneris of borrowis underwrittin be virtue of ane commissioun givin to theme be the last generall conventioun of borrowis haldin at the burght of Dysart the 8 of this instant.

Edinburght	Williame Reid, Williame Carnegie
Perth	Andro Wilsoun
Dundie	Thomas Haliburtoun
Aberdene	Patrick Leslie
Striviling[1]	Johnne Cowane
Linlithgow	Andro Bell
St Androis	Symoun Gregour
Glasgow	James Stewart
Air	Johnne Oisburne
Hadingtoun	Mr James Cockburne
Munros[2]	Robert Grahame
Kirkcaldie	Johnne Williamsone
Bruntyland	Williame Mekilljohnne
Anstruther Eister	Robert Alexander
Anstruther Wester	John Tollok
Couper	David Andersone
Pettinweame	George Kingyow
Craill	John McKisone
Kingorne	Patrick Wallace
Dumbar	Robert Shorteous

1
The same day electis Williame Reid, merchand, first in comissioun for the burgh of Edinburght, moderatour dureing this present conventioun wha compeir and exceptit the said office in and upoun him and geve his aith *de fideli administratione*.[3]

---

1   Stirling.
2   Montrose.
3   Literally, 'concerning faithful administration', i.e. he was promising to carry out the duties of moderator with diligence.

Vigesimo tertio Julij I^m vi^c trigesimo primo

[2]

The quhilk day anent the coumptis of James Eilleis factour in Campheir and Johnne Burnet factour also their, late collectouris of the impost appointit for defrying of the ministeris stipend at the said toun of Campheir, remittit be the commissioneris of borowis conveinit at the burght of Dysert the [...] day of [fo. 384r] this instant to the comissioneris presentlie conveinit. Compeirit Patrick Baxter merchand in Edinburgh and produceit the said James his comptis from the 10 of Junij 1630 exclusive to the 10 of October exclusive of the same yeir. As also produceit the said Johnne Burnit his coumptis from the first of October 1630 to the 24 of Junii 1631 inclusive. Which being sene and considderit be the saidis commissioneris, they find that the said impost hes not bene preceislie takin up as it schould, nor such attendance givin to the collectouris as wes requisit, and that they have neglectit the uplifting thairof as is cleir be the saidis comptis. Theirfoir they have remittit the fuitting of the saidis coumptis to the burghis of Edinburgh, Stirling, Linlithgow, Hadingtoun, Bruntyland, Kirkcaldie and Dysert, to which borrowis the present commissioneris gifis full power and commissioun for fitting and ending and taking furder ordour as they sall think expedient for uplifting of the said impost and with the saidis factouris. And ordainis the said James and Johnne to be present themselffis. And to this effect hes appointed the saidis commissioneris to meit at the burght of Edinburgh the saxt of March nixt with continuatioun of dayis and the saidis persounis with thair cautiouneris to be wairnit for answering for their dewtie in the gathering of the said impoist and for produceing of more formall coumptis. And the said burghis to repoirt thair dilligence heirannent to the nixt generall conventioun of borrowis. And this to be ane heid of the nixt misive.

[3]

The same day the commissioneris of borrowis apointis and ordainis for ingathering of the impost appointit for the defraying of the minist-eris stipend at Campheir till the first day of September Johnne Burnet present collector and ordanis him till delyver his haill ressaitis and quhat is restand in his handis gif anie be to the nixt enterant collectour, to send his coumptis thairof frome the dait of his last coumptis till the said first day of September nixt, verified be the supperscriptioun of the skipperis and merchandis, or in merchandis absence be his factor to the commissioneris of borrowis appointit to meit att Edinburgh the saxt day of March nixt with continuatioun of dayis. And according to the custom they ordaine and appoint to be collectour of the said impost frome the said first day of September nixt till the first of August thairefter in the yeir of God I^m vi^c xxxii yeiris Robert Ballie present factour in Campheir and ordainis him to give his aith *de fideli administratione*[4] to the conservatour or his deputis to ingather the said impoist and mak payment to the minister, reader and utheris conforme as is allowit be the commissioneris of borrowis and to send hame his coumptis of his intromissioun with the said impost frome the first day of September nixt till the first day of August thairefter till the nixt generall conventioun of borrowis [fo. 384v] verified be the skipper, merchand or factour in absence of the merchand with the said minister and reider thair dischairgis. And sicklyke ordainis the said conservatour or his deputis at his begining to take his aith in opin court to be haldin be theme to that effect that he sall dischairge his leill and trew dewtie in the said collectioun and sall uplift frome the merchandis, factoris and skipperis their trew and just pairt according to the quantie of thair guidis that thei sall happine to have according to his knowledge and sall chairge himselff thairwith and omitt nothing thairof. And that he sall collect it be him selff and no utheris dureing the time of his collectioun except in cais of seiknes or uther necessitie. And ordainis letters to be direct to the saidis persounis in thair names and thair gennerall clerk to subscryve the same, quhairanent thir presentis salbe his warrand. And the saidis persounis with the conservatour to repoirt thair dilligence heiranent to the nixt gennerall conventioun of borrowis. And this to be ane heid of the nixt missive.

Vigesimo septimo Julii I[m] vi[c] trigesimo primo
[4]
The quhilk day anent the supplicatioun giffin in be Johnne Boisweall of Craigsyde to the lordis of his Majesties most honorabill privie counsall desyreing certane skilfull marineris to be nominated for surveying the water of Forth[5] for the impeding of the strangeris and utheris resorteris to the said river of casting furthe of ballest abone the Quenisferrie, with the which supplicatioun the present commissioneris being acquaintit and desyret to answer thairto, the said commissioneris having considderit that thair hes bene in anno 1625 a survey maid and the awneris of the coilheuchis actit that ilk ane of theme sould have clengit the said river foranent thair awin boundis, and lykwyse considdering that thair hes [been][6] ane proclamatioun past for staying boith of natives and strangeris for casting of thair ballest abone the saidis Quenisferrie bot in sick places as sould be designit under the paine of certane pecuniall soumis. And having found that the above nameit supplicant does insist in ane new survey to the effect he might obteane ane gift thairof for surveying of the said river in tyme cuming,

---

4   Literally, 'concerning faithful administration', i.e. he was promising to carry out his duties
    with diligence.
5   The Firth of Forth.
6   There is no space in the MS but the sense requires this insertion.

and that for sum benefeit to himselff, which can no uther wyse be obteinit
bot be impoising of sum dewties to be levied of the natives and strangeris
resortit to the said place, and feiring that through occasioun thairof the
trad thairof might ceis to the great lois of the haill kingdome, and they
haveing desyrit the saidis lordis to rewew the foirsaid proclamatioun and
hier penaltie impoisit upoun the transgressouris conforme to the byrth of
ilk schip, viz tuentie schillingis upoun the tun sua that a schip of fourtie tun
failyeing in casting furth of ane small quantitie of ballest sall pay xl s., and
so proportionallie utheris […]⁷ And to convene of new the saidis heretouris
befoir theme to be actit as they have bene of befoir. [fo. 385r] And haveing
schewin unto theme that through the not executioun thairof of the former
proclamatioun and small regaird the saidis heretouris hes had for seing the
said present executioun, the said river hes not bene kept so cleine as the
necessitie of tred did require. Thairfoir desyred that for the better executing
thairof in tyme cumming, that all schippis at thair making of thair entrie
in Culros salbe astrictit to gif thair aith to the customer anent the casting
out of thair ballest. And gif they have transgressed the said proclamatioun
that thei be punischit accordinglie. And to the end that boith presentlie and
in tyme cuming it may be knowne what and quhair the defectis ar, they
have ordained the burghis of Culros, Bruntyland and Kirkcaldie betuix and
Michelmes nixt to mak ane survey of the saidis water and to repoirt the
same to the burgh of Edinburgh that thairefter they might mak the same
knowne to the saidis lordis. And sicklyke that they mak ane new survey
betuix and the nixt generall conventioun and to repoirt the same be thair
commissioneris to the commissioneris then to be conveinit, that thairefter
they may proceid further as the necessitie of the mater doeth require. And
the saidis lordis of counsell to be acquaintit thairwith. And becaus that the
visiting of the saidis boundis will be chairgeabill to the saidis burghis, thairfoir the present commissioneris [ordainis]⁸ that what chairges salbe debursit
be theme that thei sal be againe repayit at the making of thair repoirt. And
the saidis burghis to repoirt thair dilligence heiranent to the nixt generall
conventioun of borrowis. And this to be ane heid of the nixt missive.⁹

[5]
The same day forsamekill as the commissioneris of borrowis haveing,
conforme to the commissioun givin to theme the last generall conventioun
of borrowis haldin at the burgh of Dysert the [8] day of Julii instant for
giving answer to the lordis of his Majesties most honorabill privie counsall anent the grammer framed be Mr David Wedderburne, scoolmaister of

---

⁷ There is a space of about two words' length here.
⁸ There is no space in the MS but the sense requires this insertion.
⁹ This act is noted in the Abstract of Acts of Convention, *RCRBS*, iv, 527.

Aberdeine, with the rudimentis or introductioun thairto,[10] and the present commissioneris haveing maid repoirt to the saidis lordis as wes injoyned unto theme, the saidis lordis acceptit thairof. And thairfoir they ordaine the burgh of Edinburgh to advance to the said Mr David, conforme to the tennour of the said act, the soumes conteinit thairin. And ilk burgh to be required for sending thair pairt thairof conforme to the taxt roll with thair commissioneris to the nixt generall conventioun of borrowis conforme to the tennour of the said act, the said burgh alwayis ressaveing frome the said Mr David ane noit under his hand for repoirting of the number of bookes conteinit in the said act to the said burgh, and that he salbe roullit be the borrowis in the pryce of the booke when the same sall tak effect.

[fo. 385v]

[6]

The same day, forsamekill as the commissioneris of borrowis in the last generall conventioun of borrowis haldin at the burght of Dysart the 7 of that instant upoun supplicatioun maid to them be my lord conservatour. Haveing considderit the said conservatour his paines and travell takin in certaine important effaires tuiching thair estate, wes pleissit to remit the gratificatioun thair of the commissioneris presentlie conveinit as is at mair lenth contteinit in the auchtene act of the said conventioun. And the present commissioneris haveing takin his bygaine painis to thair firme considderatiounis and being willing in sum measour to gratifie his lordship, thairfoir they for themeselffis and haveing poweris as said is, hes givin, grantit and disponit and be thir presentis givis, grantis and disponis to the said conservatour for his farder manadgement in all thair honorabill imployment, the soume of thrie by and attour 18 stuiris payit of befoir to be levied of ilk seck guidis transportit frome Scotland to the Law Cuntries in maner following, viz: fourteine stuiris be the guidis and four be the schip and this dewtie to indure during the borrowis will allanerlie it is alwayis declairit that in respect of the dewties alreddie impoisit upoun coall that the same salbe frie of the saidis thrie stuiris of new imposed, the same onlie to pay as of befoir. And the saidis commissioneris ordenis the merchandis and skipperis to answer the said conservatour of the dewis abonewrittin. And incais of refuisall or not thankfullie payit, ordanis the said conservatour to distreinyie for the same.[11]

[7]

The same day annent the patent purchessed be Robert Buchen anent the perrill mentioned in the 12 act of the last generall conventioun of borrowis

---

10   See above, 56–7.
11   This act is noted in the Abstract of Acts of Convention, RCRBS, iv, 527.

haldin at the burgh of Dysart the [6] day of this instant[12] remitis to the
present commissioneris, and the said commissioners haveing supplicat the
lordis of his majesties privie counsall thairannent, the saidis lordis ordainis
to be wairnit, quhairfoir the present commissioneris recomendis the same
matter to the burgh of Edinburgh and ordainis theme as they sall find occasioun to prosecute the same and to repoirt thair dilligence heirannent to
the nixt generall conventioun of borrowis. And this to be ane heid of the
nixt missive.[13]

[8]
The same day the saidis commissioneris haveing according to the commissioun giffin to theme be the last generall conventioun of borrowis haldin
at the burgh of Dysart the [6] day of this instant supplicat the lordis of his
Majesties maist honorabill privie counsall for causing of all yairne heirefter
to be sold be wecht onlie.[14] And the saidis lordis considdering the expediencie thairof had ordained the [fo. 386r] same to be done and intimatioun to be maid at the mercat crossis of all burghis necessar. Thairfoir the
present commissioneris ordainis the agent to extract the said proclamatioun
and to send ane doubill thairof to the haill borrowis in print and the[y]
required to intimat the same with all dilligence. As lykewyse ordainis ilk
burgh to be required to send with thair commissioneris thair dilligence be
writt in putting executioun [of] the said ordinance and in seing the samene
observit in time cumming. And ordainis the agent to depurse the expenssis
for printing of twa hundreth thairof. And the same salbe allowit to him in
his accomptis.[15]

[9]
The same day forsamekill as the greivances sustenit be the natioun wer
remittit to be considderit be the commissioneris presentlie conveinit and
they haveing advysit thairwith with the conservatour and haveing condiscendit thairupoun, thairfoir they ordaine thair clerk to send the same with
the conservatour to be delyverit to the magistratis of the said toun[16] and
the said conservatour to repoirt conforme as wes ordainit in the 16 act of
the said last generall conventioun of borrowis the 7 of this instant to the

---

12 See above, 46–7.
13 The first one and a half lines of the next act follow immediately after this sentence, without
    a break, but they are scored through.
14 See above, 46–7.
15 This act is noted in the Abstract of Acts of Convention, *RCRBS*, iv, 527.
16 Clearly, no town has yet been mentioned but this must refer to the Scots staple port of
    Veere, on Walcheren, in Zeeland.

nixt generall conventioun of borrowis. And this to be ane heid of the nixt missive.

[10]

The same day annent the supplicatioun givin in be James Kinninmonth and Johnne Duff skipper in Leith for erecting of lightis upoun the Holie Iland, Fairne Iland and Skair Heidis[17] and places thair about for saiftie of schippis passand to ane frome Scottland that way. The commissioneris of borrowis haveing considderit that these ar places in Ingland and that be the patent produceit purchest be umquhile Mr Johnne Broun and assigned be Hendrie Broun his air to the said Johnne Duff, the Inglish ar exemit from anie dewtie for the saidis lichtis and yit they sall reape allyke benefeit with the schippis of this cuntrie and uther strangeris schippis resoirting to this cuntrie and that be this a preparative might be induceit for causing of the schippis of this cuntrie to contribute and to pay for the lichtis of Yermouth, Wintertoun[18] and uther places of lichtis albeit they never cum into anie poirt of Ingland and so manie unnecessar burdingis be brocht upoun the schippis to thair great prejudice, and withall haveing considderit that for the expediencie or inexpediencie of the saidis lichtis thair being bot ane few number of seaferring men heir present so that thair wer not ane number sufficient for trying thairof nor have they bene acquaintit befoir thair meitting nor instructit frome thair burghis. And the saidis lordis be[ing] acquaintit thairwith wer pleissit not to give anie farder way to the said supplicantis desire. Thairfoir they ordaine [fo. 386v] the agent to extract the saidis lordis declaratioun heiranent and to repoirt the same to the nixt generall conventioun of borrowis.[19]

Vigesimo octavo Julii I^m vi^c trigesimo primo

[11]

The quhilk day the commissioneris of borrowis beand convenit, understanding that the grit constable of Scotland[20] haveing procuired ane commissioun from his Majestie for cognoscing of his right and extent of the office of the constabullarie, which being a mater quhairin the haill borrowis ar greattumlie intrest in thair priviledgis and so neirlie dois concerne theme that without farder advyse frome thair burghis they could not fullie resolve upoun ane perfyte remedie and thairfoir they have ordanit and ordanis that

---

17 The first two, Holy Island and the Farne Islands, lie on the east coast of England, just south of Berwick-upon-Tweed. Skair Head may be the promontory on which Scarborough Castle sits.

18 This refers to Great Yarmouth and, presumably, nearby Winterton-on-Sea in Norfolk.

19 This act is noted in the Abstract of Acts of Convention, RCRBS, iv, 527.

20 An office held heritably by the earls of Erroll.

the burghis that salbe appointit to meit in the mater of the fisching salbe requirit for sending of thair commissioneris sufficientlie instructit for taking ane solid cours for preventing of the incrotching of the said constabill and in the interim they gave commissioun and full power to the burght of Edinburght for taking course for staying of ane patent to be purchassit in favour of the said constabill till farder resolutioun be takin in manner abone writtin. And what chairgis salbe imployit thairupoun the present commissioneris obleissis thame and thair burghes to refound the same. As lykewyse the same commissioneris considdering the infinit hurt they susteine throw the daylie incres of the burghis of barronie and usurping thair liberties and that thairthrough, gif tymous remeid be not takin, thair overthrow is threitned. Thairfoir the saidis commissioneris ordainis the brughis appointit in the matter of the fisching to be requirit for sending of thair commissioneris sufficientlie instructit for taking course for remedie heirof.

[12]
The same day forsamekill as the commissioneris of borrowis haveing according to the commissioun giffin to theme be the last generall conventioun of borrowis haldin at the burght of Dysart the [7] day of Julii instant insistit with the lordis of counsell for the overtour proponit be theme to the saidis lordis in Mairch last annent the coyne.[21] Thairfoir the saidis commissioneris ordainis the agent to extract the proclamatioun and to produce the same to the nixt generall conventioun of borrowis. And this to be ane heid of the nixt missive.

[13]
The same day forsamekill as conforme to the ellevint act of the last generall conventioun of borrowis haldin at the burght of [fo. 387r] Dysert the [6] day of this instant and commissioun thairin conteinit, annent the factouris in France.[22] The present commissioneris considdering that thair hes no personis presentit themeselffis at this time for ressaveing of the office of factorie in these pairtis, thairfoir they continow the matter in the same estait quhairin it is presentlie to the nixt generall conventioun, and ordainis ilk burgh whome the said mater dois concerne to try out among theme such of thair neighbouris sick as will undergoe the said office upoun the conditiounis contenit in the said act maid annent factouris in France, and the said burghis to repoirt thair dilligence heirannent to the nixt generall conventioun of borrow[is]. And this to be ane heid of the nixt missive.

21 See above, 48–9.
22 See above, 45–6.

Vigesimo non Julii I^m vi^c trigesimo primo
[14]
The quhilk day the present commissioneris being conveinit haveing upoun
Tyisday last representit to the lordis of his Majesties counsall thair oppinioun annent the lightis cravit to be erectit be James Kinninmonth and
Johnne Duff upoun the Fairnieland, Holeyland and Skair Heidis, and the
said mater being of new reveillit yisterday befoir the saidis lordis and the
twentie day of September nixt appointit for repoirting thair jugement and
opinioun thairanent of new. Thairfoir the saidis commissioneris ordainis the
burghis that sallbe apointit in the mater of the fisching to be requirit to
send thair commissioneris sufficientlie instructit anent the expediencie and
inexpediencie of the saidis lichtis and to this effect that ilk ane of the said
burghis be requiret for taking advyse thair anent with the most skilfull of
thair neighbouris boith merchandis awneris and skipperis and to repoirt
the same to the commissioneris to be convenit the said 20 of September
nixt. And sicklyke that they be desired to send thair commissioneris sufficientlie instructit anent the lichtis cravit to be erectit upoun the Yle of the
Maii.²³ And lykewyse ordainis thair clerk in thair names to wryte to George
or Alexander Bruces annent thair trying of the opinioun of the strangeris annent the saidis lightis with thair awin particuller advyse thair anent
desiring theme to meit and confer with the said commissioneris appointit to
meit in the said moneth of September nixt. And the saidis commissioneris
to repoirt thair dilligence heirannent to the nixt generall conventioun of
borrowis. And this to be ane heid of the nixt missive.

[15]
The same day, forsamekill as it haveing pleisit the lordis of his Majesties
most honorabill privie counsall to impart unto the present commissioneris his Majesties letter direct to thair lordshippis annent the fisching and
annent the boundis cravit to be reservit in the treattie of the fisching with
the Inglische [fo. 387v] to the natives of this kingdome, as lykewyse efter
heiring it haveing pleissit the saidis lordis to ordaine the burrowis presentlie
to convein amangst themeselffis and to call such other borrowis as they
sall think fitting and to advyse and condiscend upoun sick places as they
crave to be reservit for the fisching of the natives without the which thair
cuntrie cannot subsist and to be present upoun the 20 day of September
nixt to the effect they may repoirt to the saidis lordis of counsall thair
advyse and oppinioun thair annent upoun the 21 of the said moneth. Thairfoir the saidis commissioneris ordainis the burghis of Edinburgh, Perth and
Dundie, Aberdene, Stirling, Linlithgow, St Androis, Glasgow, Air, Hadding-

---

23   The Isle of May, in the Firth of Forth.

toun, Montrois, Kirkcaldie, Dysart, Bruntyland, Anstruther Eister and Wester, Pittinweame, Craill, Kinghorne, and Dumbar to meitt and convein at the saidis burght of Edinburgh the 19 of September nixt with continuatioun of dayis and to send thair commissioneris sufficientlie instruct for discending upoun the saidis places, ilk burght under pain of xx lib. ilk burght, to which borrowis and most pairt of theme conveinand the saidis commissioneris for theme selffis and haveing power frome the last generall conventioun haldin at Dysart in the said mater of the fisching, grantis and giffis full power and commissioun to the commissioneris thene to conveine and most pairt of theme convenand to treate, ressoun, voit and conclude annent the prem-issis in such maner as they sall find best boith for the weill of the cuntrey in generall and guid and weill of this estait in particullar, ratifieing and approveing, lyke as they be thir presentis ratifies and approves quhatsumever the saidis commissioneris or moist pairt of theme convenand sall doe in the premissis, with power lykewyse to theme to unlaw the borrowis absent in maner abonewrittin. And to the effect the commissioneris then to be conveinit may be the better instructit for giffing answer to the saidis boundis and for prepearing and facilitating matteris to the saidis meitting, they have appointit and ordainit and be thir presentis apointis and ordainis the burghis of Edinburgh, Stirling, Linlithgow, Haddingtoun, Glasgow, Air, Bruntyland, Kinghorne, St Androis, Kirkcaldie, Anstruther Eister and Craill to send such of thair nighbouris as ar best qualified in the matter of the fisching for meitting and conveining at the said burght of Edinburgh the fyftein day of the said moneth of September nixt for advysing and treitting annent all such thingis as may be incident in the said matter, and for preparing of such thingis as they sall think meitt to be handlit at the said meitting appointit to be upoun the 19 day of the said moneth thairefter. And the said burghis to repoirt thair dilligence heir annent to the said meitting. As lykewyse the saidis burghis to repoirt thair dilligence to the nixt generall conventioun of borrowis. And this to be ane heid of the nixt missive.[24]

[fo. 388r]
[16]
The same day compeirit Mr Johnne Hay commissioner for the borrowis to his Majestie in the matter of the fisching and desyring that sum course may be takin annent his expenssis debursit in the borrowis effairis. The borrowis ordainis the same to be rememberit to be direct in the matter of the fisching and the burghis then to be conveinit to be requiret for sending thair commissioneris sufficientlie instructit for heiring and ending of the said Master Johnne his coumptis, and for taking ordour for repay-

---

24   This act is noted in the Abstract of Acts of Convention, *RCRBS*, iv, 527.

ment thairof. And the saidis borrowis to repoirt thair dilligence heiranent
to the nixt generall conventioun of borrowis. And this to be ane heid of
the nixt missive.

[17]

The same day forsamekill as it being havilie regraittit that through negligence and raschnes of the inhabitantis of the burghis, manie of theme ar
drawin to put to thair handis to such giftis as oft proves prejudiciall boith
to themeselffis and haill estait. As lykewyse manie of theme becumis sutt-
eris and projectouris of monopolis ather be themeselffis or sum utheris in
thair names. Thairfoir and for preventing thairof in tyme cumming, the
present commissioneris ordainis ilk burght to be required for sending of
their commissioneris sufficientlie instructit for taking sick course and ordour
as the said abuse may be takin away as they in thair judgement sall think
best to the nixt generall conventioun of borrowis. And this to be ane heid
of the nixt missive.

[18]

The same day annent the supplicatioun giffin in be my lord conservatour annent the prejudice susteinit be the tradderis of the staipill wairis to
Campheir and uther tradderis to the Ile of Waker[25] and of the defraud done
to his lordschip and to the minister to the prejudice of theme boith as at
mair length is conteinit in the said supplicatioun. With the which the present
commissioneris being rypelie advysit and for restraining of the lyke abuse
in tyme cuming, they have ordainit and be thir presenttis ordainis the said
conservatour that all such personis as sall pas by the staipill poirt with staipill
guidis that whensoever his lordschip can nather find theme or thair guidis
thairefter at the said poirt to uplift the doubill of all such dewis as they sould
have payit ather to his lordschip or minister at thair passing by the said poirt
and this without prejudice alwayis of the saidis personis furder censuir to be
aflictit upoun theme be the commissioneris of borrowis. And farder, the said
commissioneris understanding that thair is dyvers personis that tradis into
the Law Countries that payis no dewis to the said conservatour. Thairfoir,
and for better cais[26] boith of the merchandis and of the said conservatour,
the present commissioneris ordainis ilk burght upoun adverteisment of the
said conservatour to uplift fra thair neighbouris such dewis allowit to his
lordschip for his honorabill interteinment as salbe dew to have bene payit
be thair neighbouris in the said [fo. 388v] Law Cuntries and to send the
same conforme to the list of thair nameis to be giffin in to theme be the

---

25 Walcheren.
26 This may be a mistranscription of 'ease' by the original copyist.

said conservatour with thair commissioneris the nixt immediat following conventioun to be delyverit to his lordschip or anie haveing power frome him. As lykewyse ordainis the said ordour to be takin annent all such as standis alreaddie addebttit to his lorschip for the caussis foirsaidis and gif neid beis ordainis thair generall clerk to conteine the same in the missive, quhairanent thir presentis salbe his warrand.

[19]

The same day ordainis Alexander Aikinheid agent to pay to James Primrois his sonne thair servand and to the maisseris such soumes of money as is ordainit be the present commissioneris and the same salbe allowit to him in his comptis.

[20]

The same day the saidis commissioneris unlawis the burght of Dumbar in the soume of xx lib. for depairtit frome this present conventioun befoir the dissolveing thairof and ordainis the said burgh to send the said unlaw to the particullar conventioun to be haldin at this burght the 20 of September nixt with thair commissioner. And this to be conteinit in the missive direct to theme thairannent.[27]

---

27 The record of this convention ends here. There are no fos. 389–91 and the next record commences on fo. 392.

Particular Convention at Edinburgh, November 1631

[fo. 392r]

In the particullar conventioun of borrowis haldin at the burgh of Edinburgh the 29 day of November the yeir of God ane thowsand sax hundreth threttie ane yeiris be the commissioneris of borrowis underwrittin be vertew of ane missive letter direct to theme frome the same burght daittit the [...] day of [...] last and produceit thair commissiounis as followis:

Edinburght	William Dick, William Carnaygie
Perth	Andro Wilsone
Dundie	Johnne Ramsay
Aberdene	Mr Robert Forquhair
Stirling	John Cowane
Linlithgow	Androw Bell
St Androis	Robert Tailyeour
Glasgow	Gabriell Cunninghame
Air	Johnne Oisburne
Haddingtoun	Mr James Cockburne
Dumfreis	Johnne Irving
Montrois	Patrick Lightoun
Bruntiland	William Meikilljohnne
Kinghorne	Mr Robert Cunninghame
Kirkcaldie	Johnne Williamsone
Dysert	Alexander Sympsoune
Craill	Johnne Mackisoune
Anstruther Eister	
Couper	Robert Pettersoune
Dumbar	Robert Schortas
Jedburght	Johnne Penman

1

The said day the saidis commissioneris electis William Dick, merchand, first in commissioun for the burght of Edinburgh, to be moderatour dureing this present conventioun who compeirit and annixted[1] the said office in and upoun him and gave his aith *difedilie administratione*.[2]

---

1   This is probably a mistranscription of 'accepted' by the original copyist.
2   An unusual spelling of 'de fideli administratione', it means 'concerning faithful administration', i.e. he was promising to carry out the duties of moderator with diligence.

Quinto Desembris I^m vi^c trigesimo primo
[2]
The quhilk day the commissioneris of borrowis beand conveinit and haveing
tayne to thair considderatiounis how that [fo.

392v] formerlie they have
manie tymes strainit sum unfrie persounis frome unsurping the liberties of
the frie royall borrowis and for making distinctioun betuix the saidis frie
royall burghes and burghis of barronie, yit throw manie interveining occasiounis their saidis travellis hes not tayne the desyrit end. And now considdering that gif it shall pleis God to send his majestie to this his ancient
kingdome their may fall out sum such occasioun the saiddis usurpatiounis
may be remeidit. Thairfoir they have thocht meit that ane signatour may be
drawin up in the best manner that can be devysit conteining ane ratificatioun of their haill priviledges conteinit in actis of parliament and in thair
generall chartour grantit unto theme be umquhile King David of worthie
memorie,³ and the same to be extendit in sa lawfull maner as may be boith
agriabill to the lawis of the cuntrey and may serve for restrayning of unfrie
persounis and burghis of baronie frome usurpeing of thair saidis liberties.
And ordainis the burgh of Edinburgh to advance the soume of four or fyve
hundreth merkis for furthering of the saidis signatour to such persounis as
shalbe desyrit be the generall clerk. And the said borrowis obleissis theme
to pay the same back againe at the nixt generall conventioun. And for this
effect ordainis ilk burgh to send thair pairt thairof with thair saidis commissioneris to the nixt generall conventioun of borrowis conforme to the taxt
roll. And when the said signatour shalbe drawin up ordainis their clark to
retayne the same till the borrowis conveineing in the first occurrent particullar or generall conventioun shall reveise the same and tak farder ordour
as they sall think guid and find cause and occasioun for prosecuting thairof.
And the saidis mater to be rememberit in the missive to be direct to the
said conventioun.

Sexto Decembris I^m vi^c trigesimo primo
[3]
The quhilk day forsamekill as in the matter of the new copper coyne the
new warrandis that should have been procureit be the Maister of Stirling⁴
conforme to the borrowis desyre signified to him thairannent and impairtit
be him to his father, ar nocht as yit comeit to his handis, and the commissioneris of borrowis being willing to sattill that matter in peice and calmenes
to the most advantage of the cuntrie. Thairfor they have conteinued the same

---

³ That is David II, r. 1329–1371, who granted the burghs a general charter of privileges in
   1367.
⁴ Probably William Alexander, younger, eldest son and heir of William Alexander, Viscount
   Stirling. The title was raised to an earldom in 1633.

till the burgh of Edinburgh should be acquintit with the saidis warrandis and gif they sall find the samene agreable in all thingis to [the] saidis articles thairannent to acquiefie as gif nothing had bene done be the saidis borrowis in that mater, and gif the same shall prove disconforme to the saidis articles, ordainis the same burgh with all dilligence to give notize thairof to the haill borrowis presentlie conveinit and to require theme for conveining with such expeditioun as may be that heirefter sik course may be taikin [fo. 402r][5] as may best serve for the commoun weill of the cuntrie. And in the meane tyme they ordaine ane letter to be direct in their names to Mr Johnne Hay thanking him for his travellis and desireing him in thair manes to rander thankis to the said vicount of Stirling for his affectioun, intreitting for continuance thairof as they salbe reddie at all occasiounis to mak knowne thair dewtifull rememberance. And withall to acquaint the said Mr Johnne how far they have proceidit in this matter, and with the articlis proponit and with their minde annent the plackis and the course of the copper coyne mentioned in his letter. And ernestlie to desire him to deill with the saidis vicont that the warrandis to be procurit be in all thingis conforme to the saidis articles and withall to recommend the burrowis effairis to his dilligence. And ordainis the said clerke to subscryve the said letter in thair nameis quhairannent thir presentis shalbe his warrand. And the said burgh of Edinburgh to repoirt thair dilligence hairannent to the nixt generall conventioun of borrowis. And this to be ane heid of the nixt missive.[6]

---

5   It is clear from the text that this folio has been bound out of sequence, as it is in the same hand and completes the act which begins on fo. 392v.

6   This act is noted in the Abstract of Acts of Convention, RCRBS, iv, 529. The rest of the recto and all of the verso of fo. 402 are blank, suggesting that the record of this convention ends here. Fos. 393–4 and 399–401 contain a letter to Aberdeen burgh council from its commissioner and other related papers concerning rates of exchange and coinage. Although relevant to the last act of the preceding particular convention, they are not records of the convention of burghs, and have therefore been omitted from this volume.

Particular Convention at Edinburgh, April 1632[1]

[fo. 396r]
Act Borrowis signatour 26 Aprilis 1632[2]

[fo. 397r]
In the particular conventioun of borrowis haldin at the burgh of Edinburgh the tuentie sext day of Apprile the yeir of God ane thousand sex hundreth threttie tua yeires be the commissioneris of borrowis thair convenit, be vertew of ane missive letter direct to theme frome the said burgh of Edinburgh of the of the dait the sext of Apryle instant. The [same] day the commissioneris of borrowis beand convenit, ffor as the commissioneris of borrowis haiffing this manye yeires bygane endevoured to have maid ane perfyte distinctioun betuixt theme and the burghis of barronye and uther unfrie plaices by whome they have bein so much prejudgit and impoverished, and to have had thair liberties putt to dew executioun whairby the foirsaidis usurpers micht have bein suppressed, and especiallie haveing for this effect upone the first of December last ordaynit ane signature to be drawin up conteining ane ratificatioun of thair haill liberties contenit in the actis of parliament and in thair generall chairtour grauntit to theme be umquhill King David of worthie memorie.[3] Lykas the present commissioneris after mature deliberatioun had anent the said signature has for divers caussis thoght guid that the said chairtour grauntit be the said King David sall not be confirmed, bot rather so much thairof as they have thoght necessar sall be contenit in that pairt of the new signature conteining the haill priveledges of the borrowis and haiffing perused the same they have ordaynit and ordanis the said signature as the samin is conceaved to be writtin over in mundo and docked be the advocat and to be sent to Maister Johnne Hay thair commissioner to be exped be his Majestie. And for that effect ordanis ane letter to be sent thairwith to the said Mr Johnne in thair names earnestlie recommending the prosecutioun thairof to him and withall to intreat his Majestie in thair names for directing ane warrand to the lordis of counsall and exchekquer for passing of the same without questioun since the same is so weill warranted

---

[1]   This consists of a single sheet, folded to create four pages, bound so that the text runs vertically. It is the only record from this convention. It is preceded by fo. 395, which contains a list of acts of parliament in favour of the burghs from the reign of James I onwards. This list may relate to an act of the particular convention of Nov. 1631 but it has not been included as there is no indication that it is an act of the convention of burghs.
[2]   This act is noted in the Abstract of Acts of Convention, *RCRBS*, iv, 529.
[3]   David II, r. 1329–1371.

be actes of parliament. And to desyre him to send the same doun with all the diligence he can to the burgh of Edinburgh which being dune ordanis the said burgh to conveyne with theme the burghis of Perth, Dundye, Aberdein, Stirling, Lynlithgow, Glasgow, Aire and Haddingtoun, with all convenient diligence therefter, to whiche borrowis and most pairt of theme convenand, the present commissioneris for theme selffes and in name of the whole remanent borrowis gives full powar and commissioun for prosecuting of the said signature, and for using of all[4] [fo. 396v] meanes for obteining the same past and debursing of such soumes of money as they sall think necessar for performance thairof, which being so debursed they obleis theme and thair burghis for theme selffes and in name foirsaid to refound the same with the interrest thairof. And farder the saidis commissioneris considdering that they be the actes of parliament hes powar in thair conventiounes to sett doun lawes for the weilfaire of the borrowis and floorisching of the merchand estait and considdering that thair is nothing concernis theme more then the floorisching of schippinge and ane guid governament amangst maisteris and marineris through inlaik quhairof both the merchand estait and schipping is much prejudgit and impairit. Thairfoir thai ordayne thair clerk to eik to the said patent ane commissioun to the saidis commissioneris in thair conventiounes to sett doun lawes and ordoures for the governing of the schipping and for guyding and ordering of maisteris and marineris, unto which lawis and ordours the saidis merchandis, maisteris and marineris of this kingdome whairsoevir thai reside or travaile outwith or within this kingdome salbe subject; with powar to everie burgh within theme selffes to putt the saidis lawis to executioun, and with powar also to the said commissioneris ather be theme selffes or judges foresaid at the instance of the agent or anye uther particular pairtye to execut the same with all uther claussis neidfull, whairanent thir presentis salbe his warrand. And ordanis Maister Johnne Hay to be acquaintit heirwith and to be desyrd to use his best meanes for passing the said signature with this additioun foirsaid, if not to wryte over the said signature leiving out the foirsaid commissioun anent the schipping and with diligence to send the same hither. And ordanis the burgh of Edinburgh to advance the soume of fyve hundreth and threttie merkis for expeding of the said signature. And the saidis commissioneris for theme selffes and in name of the haill remanent borrowis obleissis theme to repay the same at the nixt generall conventioun without any farder wairning or premonitioun to be maid to theme. And incace of not payment at the tyme foresaid to pay the same with interrest dew thairfore. And the saidis borrowis and the said

---

4   A whole line is almost lost in the binding. The text from 'remanent' to 'all' is based on informed guesswork, for only parts of many words can be seen.

Maister Johnne Hay to report thair diligence anent the premissis to the nixt generall conventioun and the said mater to be rememberit at the said nixt conventioun. Extractit furth of the register of the actis of the conventioun of borrowis be me Mr Alexander Guthrie commoun clerk of Edinburgh and clerk also to the saidis borrowis. Witnessing heirto this my signe and subscriptioun manuall.[5]

---

5   There is, however, no signature on this extract, suggesting that it is a copy of an extracted act. Fos. 397v–399r are blank.

General Convention at Montrose, July 1632

[fo. 403r]
At the generall conventioun of borrowes haldin at the burgh of Montrois
the thrid day of Julii, the yeir of God ane thowsand sex hundreth and
threttie twa yeires be the commissioneres of borrowes underwrittin, and
produceit thair commissiounes as followes:

Edinburgh	Cr[1] Johne Macknacht, William Carnegy
Pearth	Androw Willsone
Dundie	Johne Ramsay
Aberdene	Maister Vedast Lowsoun
Striviling[2]	Johne Cowan
Linlithgow	William Bell
Sanctandrois	Williame Geddie
Glasgow	Johne Barnes
Air	Johne Osburne
Haddingtoun	Maister James Cockburne
Dysert	David Crystie
Kirkcaldie	Johne Williamsone
Monttroise	Patrick Lichtoun, Robert Keith
Cowper	David Jamesone
Anstruther Easter	Thomas Mairteine
Drumfreis[3]	Robert Richartsone
Innernnes[4]	Thomas MakWilloche
Burntiland	Gairdin, George Gairdin
Innerkeithing[5]	be exemptioun and ratificatioun producit be Dumfermeling
Kinghorne	Walter Duncane
Breichin	be exemptioun and ratificatioun producit be David Lindsay
Irving	
Jedburgh	Johne Moscrop
Kirkcudbriche	Johne Ewart
Wigtoun	Thomas Mackkie

1   It is not clear what this means, but it could be 'councillor'. It cannot be 'craftsman', since McNaught was a merchant, and Edinburgh's craft commissioner is always named second.
2   Stirling.
3   Dumfries.
4   Inverness.
5   Inverkeithing.

Pettinweime	George Kingyow
Dumfermeling	James Reid
Anstruther Wester	Henry Cunninghame
[fo. 403v]	
Selkirk	Williame Scott
Dumbar	Robert Schorteone
Dumbartane	be exemptioun and ratificatioun producit be Glasgow
Renfrew	
Lannerik[6]	Gedioun Weir
Aberbrothoke[7]	Maister James Peirsone
Elgin	Maister Johne Hay
Peibbles	be exemptioun and ratificatioun producit be the agent
Caraill[8]	Thomas Cunninghame
Taine	David Forrester
Culrose	James Aitkine
Bamfe	James Winchester
Whitehorne	be exemptioun and ratificatioun producit be Wigtoun
Forfar	Maister David Pearsone
Rothesay	be exemptioun and ratificatioun producit be agent
Nairne	Johne Tulloche
Forres	be exemptioun producit be agent
Ruglane[9]	be exemptioun and ratificatioun producit be agent
Northberwick	Johne Mure
Culane	
Kilranie[10]	Thomas Sampsone
Lauder	be exemptioun and ratificatioun producit be agent
Annan	be exemptioun and ratificatioun producit be agent
Galloway[11]	Johne Foullartoun
Lochmabine	
Sanquhar	be exemptioun and ratificatioun producit be agent

1

{Citatioun of the borrowes verefeit}

The same day the commissioneres of the burgh of Montroise verfied the citatioun of the haill borrowis to the present conventioun be George Ramsay post.

---

6   Lanark.
7   Arbroath.
8   Crail.
9   Rutherglen.
10   Kilrenny.
11   New Galloway.

2

{Electio moderator}
The same day the said commissioneres of borrowes electis nominates
and constitutes Patrick Lichtoun, first in commissioun for the burgh of
Montroise, moderator dureing this present conventioun, wha compeirand
accepit and gave his aith *de fideli administratione*.[12]

[fo. 404r]

3

{Houres of meiting}
The same day the saidis commissioneres of borrowes appointed thair houres
of meittinges to be and begin daylie at 9 houres in the morning and to lest
quhill twelff houres at noone and efternoone at twa houres till sex acloack
at nyght. And sik as ar absent at the calling of the rolles to pay ane unlaw[13]
of sex schillinges. And they that passis out of the hous without leive to pay
ane unlaw as saids. And they that passes fra this present conventioun befoir
the dissolveing thairof to pay ane unlaw as absentis. And that nane speak
unrequyrit without leive askitt and gevin nor interimix and thair reassoning
with thair votting under the pane of ane unlaw of sex schillinges *toties
quoties*.[14]

4

{Glasgow}
The same day the saidis commissioneres of borrowis being convenit and
haveing perused and considderit the commissioun gevin be the burgh of
Glasgow to thair commissioner for the present, and finding Johne Andersone
ane craftis man to be convynit in commissioun with thair said commissioner, and that they had bene diverse tymes admonisched for the lyke omis-
sioun, yitt continewed in thair oversight. Thairfoir they dischairged the said
burgh from doing the lyke in tyme coming and that under the pane of ane
hundreth punds. And ordainis the said commissioner to intimatt this ordinance to thair burgh at thair homcoming. As lykwayes to be contenit in the
missive that they pretend no ignorance. And in the meanetyme dischairges
the said Johne Andersone of all vott and place amangs thame.[15]

---

12 Literally, 'concerning faithful administration', i.e. he was promising to carry out the duties
    of moderator with diligence.
13 The phrase 'at the calling of the rollis to pay ane unlaw' is repeated.
14 As often as it shall happen, i.e. for each offence.
15 Although Glasgow's commissioner is John Barnes, it was common for burghs to send an
    'assessor' with their commissioner, to deputise if the commissioner were indisposed. In this
    case, however, because that assessor was a craftsman, he is ineligible as a commissioner.

5

{Dysart}

The same day ordaines the burgh of Dysart to produce thair diligence to the nixt generall conventioun of borrowes in causing Williame Touche, indweller in Leavin,[16] either to mak his reall and actuall resadence within thair burgh or in depryveing him of thair libertie under the pane of twentie punds and to depairt. This to be ane heid of the nixt missive.

6

{Coupare}

The same day ordaines the burgh of Coupare to produce thair diligence to the nixt generall conventioun in causing of Thomas and Williame Andersones, indwelleres in Newburgh[17] in Fyffe, to desist from usurping the liberties of the frie royall burrowes under the paine of twentie punds and to report thair diligence heiranent to the nixt generall conventioun. And this to be ane heid of the nixt missive.

[fo. 404v]

7

{Elgin}

The same day ordaines the burgh of Elgin to produce thair diligence to the nixt generall conventioun of borrowes in restraining of certane inhabitants in Germouthe[18] lyand within thair shereffdome from usurping the libertie of the frie royall borrowes, and ordains the agent to concure and assist with thame and to report thair diligence heiranent to the nixt generall conventioun of borrowes. And this to be ane heid of the nixt missive.

8

{Forfar}

The same day ordaines the burght of Forfar to produce thair diligence to the nixt generall conventioun of borrowes in restraining of the inhabitantes of Killiemure[19] in Anguse from usurping the liberties of the frie royall borrowes, and ordaines the agent to concure and assist thame in the said persute and to report thair diligence heiranent to the nixt generall conventioun of borrowes. And this to be ane heid of the nixt missive.

---

16 Leven lies on the Fife coast to the east of Dysart.

17 Newburgh, on the north coast of Fife, was nominally a royal burgh, having been erected in 1631 (see Pryde, *The Burghs of Scotland*, no. 75). Its failure to be enrolled by the convention or admitted to parliament is testament to the convention's ability effectively to block the erection of royal burghs by the crown.

18 Garmouth, at the mouth of the Spey, in Moray.

19 Kirriemuir, Angus.

9
{Act concerning the restraint of merchandis to sell Scottis wairis at Campheir}
The same day anent the twentie twa act of the last generall conventioun at the burgh of Dysart the sevint day of Julii last anent the restraint of selling of Scotts waires to certane persones indwelleres in Campheir and Middilburgh and suspendit be the commissioneres of borrowes convenit at Edinburgh the fyftene of Marche last.[20] The present commissioneres hes thocht good lykewayes to suspend the said act and ordaines the same to tak na farder executioun till they sall tak farder course thairanent and ordains this act to be intimatt to the conservatour.

10
{Act concerning the yarne}
The same day anent the aucht act of the particular conventioun of borrowes haldin at Edinburgh the twentie sevint of Julii last anent the selling of yairne be weght,[21] the present commissioneres recommendes the executioun thairof to the haill borrowes and ordaines the present commissioneres to recommend the same in thair names to thair borrowes at thair home coming.

[fo. 405r]
11
{Monopolies}
The same day anent the sevintene act of the particular conventioun of borrows haldin at the burghe of Edinburghe the twentie nynt of Julii last for taking course for restraining of thair nichtboures and inhabitantes for putting thair hand to any gift prejudicall to the estate of borrowes and restraining of thame for[22] from suteing or projecting of any monopolies either be thame selves or utherwayes or having hand or pairt with any projectores of monopolies, as at mair lenth is contenit in the said act.[23] The present commissioneres being weill advysit thairanent, and finding suche lyke persones to be very prejudiciall not only to thair estate in particular bot to the haill cuntrey and to be so pernitious memberes as they deserve not to cary the name of ane member of any burghe. For remeid thairof the said commissioneres hes statute and ordanit and be thir presents statutes and ordaines that it be eikit to the burges oath that non procure directlie nor indirectlie any monopolies prejudiciall to thair estate nor to have pairt thairin, and thai thairby to renunce the same. And farder dischairges all thair

20   See above, 51–2.
21   See above, 67.
22   This superfluous word seems to have been written in error but not scored out.
23   See above, 72.

burgesses from puting to thair hands to any gifts or declaration quhairupoun any suchelyke gifts or patentes may be procured without consent of the counsall of thair burgh quhair they dwell or from suteing thairof or haveing hand in any suche lyke patent or gifts under the pane of ane hundreth punds and deprivatioun of their liberties and fridome and punishment of thair persone at the will of the magsitratt. And ordaines ilk commissioner to intimatt the same to thair nichtboures and inact the same amongs thair acts that non pretend ignorance and to report thair diligence heiranent the nixt generall conventioun of borrowes under the pane of xx li. And this to be ane heid of the nixt missive.[24]

12
{Dumbar electioun of thair magistrattis}
The same day anent the fourt act of the last generall conventioun of borrowes haldin at the burgh of Dysart the fyft day of Julii last,[25] compeirit the commissionar for the burgh of Dumbare and produceit the forme of the electioun of thair magistrates and counsall at Michaelmes last. Which being seene and considerat be the present commissioneres, they accept the same for this tyme, and ordaines thame in all tyme coming to proceid in thair electioun conforme to the act of parliament and borrowes.

[fo. 405v]
13
{Selkirk diligence anent thair outland burgessis}
The same day anent the sext [act] of the last genenerall conventioun of borrowes haldin at the burgh of Dysart the fyft day of Julii last,[26] compeirit Williame Scott commissioner of the burgh of Selkirk and produceit ane act quhairin George Curriour in Whitemurehall acted himselff to mak his residence in thair said burgh under the pane of deprivatioun as the said act of the daite the elleventh day of Junii last beares which the present commissioneres [accept][27] for diligence. And ordainis the said burgh to put the said act to executioun.

14
Quarto Julii I[m] vi[c] trigesimo secundo
{Concerning the factouris in France}
The quhilk day the commissioneres of borrowes being convenit anent the threttein act of the particular conventioun of borrowes haldin at the

---

[24] This act is noted in the Abstract of Acts of Convention, *RCRBS*, iv, 531.
[25] See above, 43.
[26] See above, 44.
[27] There is no space in the MS but the sense requires this insertion.

burgh of Edinburgh the twentie aucht of Julii last anent the factores in France and remedies to be taikin for preveining the prejudices sustenit be the merchandis traffiquing in these places mentionat in the said act and in the nynt act of the said generall conventioun of borrowes haldin at the burgh of Jedburgh the sevint day of Julii the yeir of God ane thousand sex hundreth and threttie yeires.[28] The present commissioneres inrespect thair is nane compeirit to offer thameselves to be factores upoun the conditiounes mentionated in the said actes hes continewit and does continew the said matter to be handlitt in the first occurring particular conventioun to which borrowes to be appointed the saids commissioneres grantes and gives full power and commissioun to tak suche course for the farder preveining of these evilles sustenit be the natioun as they sall think expedient. And ordaines the same to be rememberit in the missive to be direct for the said conventioun, and ordaines the said borrowes to report thair diligence heiranent to the nixt generall conventioun of borrowis. And this to be ane heid of the nixt missive.

15

{Dumfreis diligence anent thair forstalleris}

The same day anent the sevint act of the last generall conventioun of borrowes haldin at the burgh of Dysart the fyft day of Julii last ordaining the burgh of Dumfreis to produce thair diligence in writt to this present conventioun in taking and apprehending of Johne Tait till he sould find cautioun for desisting from usurping the liberties of the frie borrowes and in chairging of Johne Scharpe to desist from usurping also of the liberties of the saidis frie royall borrowes.[29] For obedience quhairof compeirit Robert Richartsone present commissioner for the said burgh of Dumfreis and produceit letters of captioun agains the said John Tait and declairit that they had taikin him and that he had fund cautioun to thame to desist and cease from usurpeing of the liberties of the saids frie royall burrowes under the pane of ane hundreth pundis. And siclyke produceit the chairges against the said Johne Scharpe and his denunciatioun [fo. 406r] to the horne which the said borrowes acceptis for diligence, and ordaines the said Robert to produce the said act of cautioun to the nixt generall conventioun of borrowes and to use farder diligence aganis the said Johne Scharpe in taking and apprehending of him till he finde cautioun to desist under the pane of twentie punds. And ordaines the said burghe to report his diligence heiranent to the nixt generall conventioun of borrowes. And this to be ane heid of the nixt missive.

---

[28] See above, 47 and *RCRBS*, iii, 311–12.
[29] See above, 44.

16

{Burrowes agent concerninge the plaiding}

The same day anent the twelft act of the last generall conventioun of borrowes haldin at the burgh of Dysart the sext day of Julii last anent the hurt sustenit be the merchandis and in the commoditie of the plaiding and falsit croppin in of laite and concealled throw the presenting the same to the mercatt hard rolled up in rolles and consideddering that throw the falshood of the said ware the same is becom so suspect abroad that the marcates are fallin so laiche that the merchandis tradderes thairwith maybe forced to leave of that trad and so muche the more that the Inglische hes begun to furnish these places of the seall thairof with seyis,[30] cottones and uther lyke stuff which is occasioned throgh the disloyallty of the said plaiding.[31] For remeid quahirof the present commissioneres of burrowes ordaines the burgh of Edinburgh to supplicat the lords of his Majesties counsall for causing of the workeres of plaiding present the same to the mercatt laide in foldis and trinches and to command the heritores of the faires quhair the same is sold to sie the same ordinance put to executioun. And in caice it sall happin the said lords to caus warne the gentrie of the north, ordains the agent to caus raise letters for warning of thame and to send the same to the burgh of Aberdene whome they ordane to chairge the said gentrie against suche a day as thair sould happin any particular conventioun to be affixt unto. And ordains the burrowes to be conveinit at the said particular conventioun to prosequite the said matter, and to tak suche course thairwith as they sall think expedient for the weill of the burrowes. To which borrowes the present commissioneres gives thair full power and commissioun to do thairin as they micht do themeselvis promitten de rator.[32] And ordaines the said burgh and burghes to report thair diligence heiranent to the nixt generall conventioun of borrowes. And this to be ane heid of the nixt missive.

17

{Concerning coyne}

The same day anent the twelt act of the particular conventioun of borrowes haldin at the burgh of Edinburgh the twentie aucht day of Julii last anent the matter of the coyne and the abuse thairof.[33] The present commissioneres hes thocht good that the lordis of his Majesties secreit counsall be supplicat for renewing and puting to executioun the act of counsall made in Marche 1631. And farder consideddering that thair is no [fo. 406v]

---

[30] A fine woollen cloth.

[31] See above, 46.

[32] This literally means 'promising concerning firm/fixed'. It denotes an undertaking to abide by whatever is decided by the person or persons delegated.

[33] See above, 69.

money passing bot dolloures and that thair is no silver peices for thair
exchange according to the excigenciey of the people for thinges of small
value. Thairfoir they have thocht guid in lykwayes that the said lordis be
supplicat for causing of small peices of silver to be cunyeit differrent from
the ordinare reckoning of England according to the present standart of the
money suche as sexteine penney peices and twentie penney peices, threttie
twa penney peices, and fyve schillinges four penney peices. And for this
effect ordanes the commissioneres that sall conveine in the first particular
conventioun that sall occure, to supplicat the saidis lordis in thair names,
to which borrowes the present commissioners gives thair full power and
commissioun thairanent and ordaines thame to report thair diligence heiranent to the nixt generall conventioun of borrowes. And this to be ane heid
of the nixt missive.[34]

18
{Sanchar[35] contra thair outland burgessis}
The same day anent the sevint act of the last generall conventioun of
borrowes haldin at the burgh of Dysart the fyft day of Julii last, ordaining the
burgh of Sanquhar to have produced thair diligence to this present conventioun in writt in causing of Thomas Maxwell and James Greir thair allegit
burges ather mak thair residence within thair burgh or els in depryveing of
thame of the liberties of the same.[36] Compeirit Alexander Aikinheid agent
and produceit ane act of thair court depryveing the said Thomas Maxwell
and James Greir of the liberties of the said burghe of Sanquhar which the
said burrowes attestes for diligence. And ordaines the burgh Drumfreis to
use diligence against thame in discusing of the suspensioun raisit at thair
instance and in prosequiteing of thair chairges against thame and to report
thair diligence heiranent to the nixt generall conventioun of borrowes. And
this to be ane heid of the nixt missive.

19
{Aberdeines diligence contra Fraserburghe}
The same day anent the tent act of the last generall conventioune of borrowes
haldin at the burghe of Dysart the sext day of Julii last ordaining the burghe
of Aberdeine to prosecute thair actioun intentit be thame against the burgh
of Fraserburghe laitly created in ane burgh of barronie and usurping the
liberties of the frie borrowes, and that the samyne is suspendit and lyes over
undiscust.[37] Thairfoir they ordane the said burgh of Aberdeine to prosecute

---

34 This act is noted in the Abstract of Acts of Convention, *RCRBS*, iv, 531.
35 Sanquhar.
36 See above, 44, although the act primarily concerned Dumfries.
37 See above, 45.

thair said intendit actioun and to produce thair diligence heiranent to the nixt generall conventioun of borrowes. And this to be ane heid of the nixt missive.

20

{Ratificatioun of the act maid agains these that passis by the steppill port}[38] The same day anent the auchtene act of the particulare conventioun of borrowes haldin at the burgh of Edinburgh the twentie nynt day of Julii last ordaining the lord conservator that all suche persones as sall pas by the [fo. 407r] stapill port with staipill goodes that whensoever his lordship can finde thame or thair goodes thairefter at the said port, to uplift the doubill of all suche dewes as thai sould have payed ather to his lordship or his ministeres at thair passingby the said port, and this without prejudice allwayes of the saidis persones farder censure to be inflicted upoun thame be the commissioneres of borrowes. And siclyke ordaining ilk burgh upoun adverteisment of the said conservator to uplifte fra thair nichtboures suche dewes allowed to his lordship for his honorabill interteanement as salbe dew to have bene payed be thair nichtboures in the Low Cuntreyes.[39] The present commissioners of borrowes ratifies[40] and approves the said act in the haill heidis and claussis, articles thairof, and ordaines the same to be keeped in all tyme coming.[41]

Quinto Julii I[m] vi[c] trigesimo secundo

21

{Bamff}
The quhilk day the commissioneres of borrowes being conveinit anent the nyntene act of the last generall conventioun of borrowes haldin at the burghe of Dysart the sevint day of Julii last ordaining the burghe of Bamff to produce the form of the electioun of thair magistrates at Michaelmes last till this present conventioun and the burghe of Aberdene to try the estate of that toun and the validitie of thair commoun landis.[42] Compeirit the present commissioner of the said burgh of Bamff and produced the forme of the electioun of thair magistrates at Michaelmes last, which being seine and considderit be the saidis commissioneres of borrowes, they accept the same for diligence at this tyme, and ordaines thame to conforme thame selvis in thair electioun in all tyme coming conforme to the actis of parlia-

---

38 This marginal title appears on the recto of the next folio but is placed here for the sake of consistency.
39 See above, 72–3.
40 The phrase 'the present commissioneres of borrowes ratifies' is repeated.
41 This act is noted in the Abstract of Acts of Convention, *RCRBS*, iv, 531.
42 See above, 51.

ment and borrowes. And siclyke compeirit the commissioner of the burght
of Aberdene and declairit that he was imployed be his burgh conform to
the ordinance of the borrowes and had tryed the estate of the said toun and
fand the same to be verie poore and that thair haill commoun landis war in
the possessione of gentillmen about thame and that thair evidentis war all
abstracted so that no certane thing could be reportit thairanent. With the
quhilk report the present commissioneres being advysed and being willing if
possibillie they could to mak sum helpe for the preveining of the utter decay
of the said burgh, they have remitted and remites the said matter to the first
occurring particular conventioun, and ordaines the commissioneres than to
be convenit to take the same to thair [fo. 407v] serious consideratioun and
to tak suche course for finding out of thair evidentis and for thair farder
help as they sall think expedient. Quhairanent the present commissioneres
grantis and gives to the burghes thair to be convenit thair full power and
commissioun, siclyke in all thinges to do as they micht do themselves and
to use all the meanes they can finde out for the standing of the said toun.
And ordaines the said burgh of Bamff to be present at the said conventioun
and to give thair best advyse and concurence in all thinges as they sall be
requyrit under the pane of xx li. And the said burghes to report thair diligence heiranent to the nixt generall conventioun of borrowes. And this to
be ane heid of the nixt missive.

22

{Burrowes agent}

The same day ordains Alexander Aikinheid agent to advance to the burgh of
Elgyne the sowme off thrie hundreth pundis, grauntit unto them for helpe
to build ane brigge upon the Walter of Rossie[43] be the commissioneris of
borrowis haldin at the last generall conventioun of borrowis haldin att the
burgh of Dysart in the moneth of Julii last, and omitted furth of the register
and missive. And the said sowme, togidder with the anuellrent thairoff sall be
allowit to him in his comptis. And ordainis ilk burgh to be requirit to send
thair pairt thairoff conforme to the taxt roll to the nixt generall conventioune of borrowis, under the payne of tuentie pundis ilk burgh, and that
by and attour the payment of thair pairt of the said sowme. And this to be
ane heid of the nixt missive.

23

{Collectour of the minister at Camphearis dewis and Sanctandrois}

The same day forsameikle as the burgh of St Androis haveing bein ordainit
to produce Walter Mitchell or els to pay the sowme of threttine schillingis

---

43   This is probably the Water of Lossie, which flows through Elgin.

sax grit Flemes money for his dewes dew to the minister att Campheir, haveing past frome thair unpayeing the same. Compeirit William Geddie commissioner of the burgh of St Androes and producet Johnne Burnett collectour that yeire of the said dewes his dischairge thairoff. And the saidis commissioneris finding the same omitted furth of his comptis thairfor they ordaine him to pay the samen to Robert Batyche, present collectour of the saidis dewes, and he to be chairged thairwith in his comptis. And iff neid beis ordanis the conservator being present to interpone his authoritie and the said conservator to report his diligence heiranent to the nixt generall conventioune of borrowis. And this to be ane heid off the nixt missive.

24
{Anent the chairge of the steppill at Campheir}[44]
The same day anent the saxtein act of the last generall conventioune of borrowis haldin att the burgh of Dysart the sevint day of Julii last anent the [fo. 408r] grivances sustenit be the natioun att Campheir in defalt of the magistrattis and ordaining the conservatour to report the saidis magistrattis thair answer theranent conforme to the said act and nynt act of the particular conventioune haldin at Edinburgh in Julii last.[45] Compeared the said conservatour and reporit that he had delivered the saidis borrowis letter to the magistrattis of the said toun with the grivances sett doun be the borrowis and had oft tymes required ane particular answer to the said letter and grivances and had nather obtined the same be himselff nor be his depute, notwithstanding he had travellit with them thairanent. And the saidis commissioneris finding themselffis neglected be the said toun and nether thair letter answered nor thair grivances taikin away, thairfoir thei ordaine as befor ane letter to be direct to the said magistrattis requyreing them reallie to tak away the saidis grivances betuixt and Mertymes nixt or utherwayes to expect no forder fromthem. And in that caice lyckwayis the present commissioneris ordaines the said conservatour to trye the myndis of the magistrattis of Midleburgh[46] or such uther tounes in the Low Cuntryeis as he thinkis meitt anent such conditiones as may be obtenit of them if the borrowis sall heirefter be plised to establish thair staiple with them and to adverteis the toun of Edinburgh thairanent betuixt and Januarii nixt that thairefter it bein knowen that nether the magistrattis of Campheir or any of them does not remove thair just grivances and that the said toun off Middilburgh ar willing to give honorabill and sufficient conditiones, ilk burgh may be required for sending thair commissioneris sufficientlie instructed for changeing of the

---

[44] This marginal title appears on the recto of the next folio but is placed here for the sake of consistency.
[45] See above, 49–50.
[46] Middelburg, also on the island of Walcheren, Zeeland.

said staiple. And the said conservatour to report his diligence heiranent to
the nixt generall conventioune of borrowis. And this to be ane heid of the
nixt missive.[47]

25
{Anent Mr Johne Hayes comptis}
The same day enent the twentie sext act of the last generall conventioun
of borrowes haldin at the burgh of Dysart the viii day of Julii last and
the sextene act of the particular conventioun of borrowes haldin at the
burgh of Edinburgh the xxix day of Julii last and fyfte act of the particular conventioun haldin at the burgh of Pearth the twentie twa day of
September last concerning the severall sowmes of money advanced be the
toun of Edinburgh be[48] Mr Johne Hay commissioner for the borrowes to
his Majestie in his severall imploymentis, and anent the report to have bene
maid this tyme be the said Mr Johne Hay in his severall imploymentis
conforme to the aucht act maid at the particular conventioun of borrowes
haldin at the burgh of Pearth the xxiii of September last.[49] Compeirit Johne
McNaght and William Carnegy commissioneres of the burgh of Edinburgh
and produced ane compt of the haill sowmes of money advanced be the
burgh of Edinburghe to the said Mr Johne since the [fo. 408v] moneth of
Junii 1629 yeires till this present tyme and desyred the said sowmes with
the enterest dew for the same to be repayed [or] at least ane ordour and
course taikin for repayment for the same. And the present commissioners
considepring the greatnes of the sowmes quhairunto by the necessitie of
thair effaires they have bene drawin to thir yeires bygane, and being willing
that the said burgh of Edinburgh sould be no losseres at thair handis of
what hes bene dewlie and trewlie depursit by thame, and in respect of the
absence of the said Mr Johne Hay thair commissioner foirsaid, thairfoir
they have appointed and ordanit and be thir presents appointis and ordaines
ane particulare conventioun to be haldin at the burgh of Edinburgh be the
most pairt of the borrowes of this kingdome, viz the burghes of Edinburgh,
Pearth, Dundie, Aberdene, Striviling, Linlithgow, Sanctandrewes, Glasgow,
Air, Haddingtoun, Dysart, Kirkcaldie, Montrose, Cowpar, Anstruther Easter
and Wester, Drumfreis, Bruntilland, Kinghorne, Innerkeithing, Jedburgh,
Pettinweime, Dumfermeling, Selkirk, Dumbar, Lannerk, Aberbrothok, Elgin,
Peibles, Carraill, Culrose, Bamff, upoun ane missive letter to be direct be
the said burgh of Edinburgh to the remanent borrowis to that effect as

---

47 This act is noted in the Abstract of Acts of Convention, *RCRBS*, iv, 531.
48 This should be 'to'.
49 See above, 55–6, 71–2. No record of the convention at Perth is preserved in the volume
    held in Aberdeen.

they salbe adverteised be the said Mr Johne Hay of his returne. To which borrowis and maiste pairte of them convenand, the present commissioneris for themselffis and in name and behalffe of thair borrowis and haill borrowis of this kingdome, grantis and gives full power and commissioune for heareing, ressaveing and allowing of the comptis of the sowmes of money advancit be the said toune of Edinburgh in maner forsaid and for taking course for repayment thairoff, with the interest dew for the same, since the severall debursementis thairoff till the payment, which course to be takin in maner forsaid. The present commissioneris for themselffis and in name of the whole borrowis obleissis thame to obey and fullfill the samen but gaine calling or contradictioune quhatsumever. And becaus throw the long lying over of the saidis comptes, the saidis sowmes of money advancit be the said burgh of Ediburgh hes growin to ane grit height, and the present commissioneris being willing thairfor that sum present and spedye course soulde be takin for repayment of the saidis sowmes and interest of the same, thairfor they ordaine the commissioneris to be conveined in maner forsaid to appoint the firste termes payment to be and begin at the nixt generall conventioun of borrowis. As also thei ordaine ilk commissioner present seriouslie to recommend to thair burghis att thair home cuming the taking ordour with the saidis sowmes of money and for directing of thair commissioneris to the said burgh of Edinburgh to that effect being requirit in maner forsaid. And grantis and gives full powar and commissioune to the burghis conveanand to unlaw the burghis absent ilk ane of them in any unlaw off [fo. 409r] fourtie pundis and to heir and ressave the said Mr Johnne Hay his report of his proceidingis in thair severall imploymentis conforme to the severall commissiouns givin unto thame theranent and thairefter with powar to them to take such course in all thingis as they sall think most expedient for the weill of thair estaite.

26

The same day anent the supplicatione gevin in be the presbeterie of the Mearnis for helpe to the reparatioun of the bridge off [...]50 the commissioneris recommendis the same to the charitie of the burghis whose inhabitantis passes that way earnestlie intreatting them to considder the necessitie and expediencie thairoff to all travelleris in winter.

---

50 There is a blank space sufficient for the name of the river. The supplication probably came from the presbytery because the Mearns (Kincardineshire) contained no royal burghs. Inverbervie, although a medieval creation, was not enrolled until 1670, so could not seek financial aid from the convention (see Pryde, *The Burghs of Scotland*, no. 44). While this could be a bridge over any of a number of rivers, the most likely are the Bervie Water at Inverbervie, the Carron Water or the Cowie Water, both at Stonehaven.

27

{Anent the factouris in Campheir}

The same day the commissioneris of borrowis being informet that the
factouris at thair staiple port of Campheir does sell thair merchand commodities to ane day, and beare the hasart and for that caus they have tua and ane
halffe for the hundreth yit without warrand or commissioun they rebaitt the
breiffes whiche is without hazard and takis thair full factour fie, and makis
thair merchandis pay the rebait. As lyckwayes thei compell the merchandis to
abyd the day of thair breiffes, and mak thair rebaittis notwithstanding. And
also the factouris drinking with thair merchandis is growen to ane grit abuse
as they make feastis therupoun. And lyckwayes when anye merchand cumes
over with his awine guidis and makkis seall of any pairt thairoff, they refuise
to accepte of the rest. Item the saidis factouris when upoun warrand they
mak any rebait, they tak ten per cent be the yeir whair they sould tak bot
aucht. Whairwith the borrowis being advysit and finding the same against
all law, reassoune and commoun equitie, thairfor thei ordaine the conservatour being present to trye the giltines of the saidis factouris theranent and
to acquant them that the borrowis are informet thairoff and to report thair
answere. As lyckwayes ordaines him upoun complaint of anye nichtbouris
to caus the saidis factouris repair the losse sustenit be thair merchandis
thairthrugh and utherwayes to punishe them. And the said conservatour to
report his diligence heiranent to the nixt generall conventioun of borrowis.
And this to be ane heid of the nixte missive.[51]

28

{Anent Wedderburnes grammer and price thairof}

The same day anent the supplicatioun gevin in be Mr David Wedderburne
scoole maister att Aberdein desyreing the grammer with the rudimentis
and introductioun thairto newlie maid be him and reveised, corrected and
amendit to be ressavit into the haill scooles of the frie borrowis of this kingdome and ane pryce to be sette thairupoun as att mair lenth is contenit in
his said supplicatioun. The present commissioneris of borrowis considdering
that conforme to the 27 act of the last generall [fo. 409v] conventioune of
borrowis haldin at the burcht of Dysart the aucht day of Julii last,[52] thair had
bein the nomber of twa hundreth of the saidis bookis imprinted and distrib-
uted amongs the universities, colledges, scoolemaisters, principall borrowis
and uther learned men of this kingdome and they required to haiff sent
thair animadversiounes to the burgh of Edinburgh to have bene presentit
to the lordis of his Majesties most honorabill secreit counsall betuixt and

---

51 This act is noted in the Abstract of Acts of Convention, RCRBS, iv, 532.
52 See above, 56–7.

the first of Februar last that be thair advyse farder ordour micht have bein
taikin for ane newe impressioune of the saidis bookis to have bein ressavit
and taught within the wholle scoolles of this kingdome. Lyckas they had
some animadversiounes bein directit and presentit to the saidis lordis, who
had appointit ane committe of certan learned men for reveising of the
saidis animadversiounes togidder with the saidis bookis quho had lyckwayes
reveised the same and condiscendit and agreit upoun ane new impressioune
of the saidis bookis, allowing and approving the samen being amendit in
maner forsaid to be ressavit and taught within the scoolles of this kingdome.
Lyckas the saidis lordis had allowit thairof and gevin and grantit sole benefeit
and printing and selling thairof to the said Mr David Wedderburne for the
space of twentie ane yeires following as the said act of borrowes and act of
his Majesties most honorabill privie counsall daitit at Halierudhous the 26 of
Junii last at mair lenth beires. Thairfoir they ordane the haill scholemaisteris
of the borrowes of this kingdome to teache the said new correctit grammer
and rudimentis and to begin the samyne with all these that salbe enterit to
the scholes efter Mertemes nixt. And appoynt, appoyntis and ordanes the
pryce of the saidis rudimentis newlie corrected and amendit in maner foirsaid to be twa schillingis Scottes and the pryce of the said grammer newlie
lykwayes correctit and amendit conteining thairin the etimologie, syntax,
orthographie and prosodie, to be four schilling Scottis money. And ordaines
the said Mr David to sell the samyne at the prices foirsaid and not to exact
or tak any heigher pryces for the samyne. Lykas the said Mr David compeirand aggreit and consentit thairto and obleist him his aires and assignayes
to sell the samyne at the pryces foirsaid and to exact no heicher pryces
for the same and to imprint the samyne with all diligence in better paeper
and greatter letter. And farder the said commissioneres ordanes ilk burgh to
report thair diligence in ressaveing and teaching of the said rudimentis and
grammer in thair scholes with thair advyce and oppinion anent the profeit
that sall redound thairby to the youth of this kingdome to the nixt generall
conventioun of borrowes. And this to be ane heid of the nixt missive.[53]

[fo. 410r]
Sexto Julii I^m vi^c trigesimo secundo

29
{Act concerning Robert Batie his intromissioun with the ministeris dewis}
The quhilk day the commissioneris of borrowis being convenit anent the
comptis of Robert Bawtye factor collector of the ministeres dewties att
Campheir from the auchtein of November last inclusive till the tuentie

---

[53] This act is noted in the Abstract of Acts of Convention, *RCRBS*, iv, 532.

nynt of Junii last, *stilo novo*,[54] being hard they finde the same altogither informall and confused and the dewes not preceislie as they sould have bein uplifted and many uther thinges omitted. Thairfor the present commissioneris ordaines the said Robert Bawtye to make over of new his comptis, from the fyftein of September last inclusive, till the firste of September nixt conteining the just quantities of the leadiningis of everie ship, and of the impost upliftit, accordinglie togidder with the merchand, skipper and factouris dewes following togidder, and to verifie the same to be the hande writt of the factouris or skipperis at the tyme off his resaittes and to send the samen to the burght of Edinburgh to be presentit to the first occurring conventioune to which borrowis conveined, the present commissioneris given full power and commissioun for heiring, allowing or dissalowing according as thei sall find the saidis comptis to deserve and to take suche course with the said collectour as they sall think good. And ordaines ane letter to be direct in thair names schewing him heiroff, and certifieing him if his said comptes salbe found defective ather in maiter or forme he sall be accordinglie punisched, and als the sowme of ane hundreth pundis Scottis money addebted be Johne Burnett and to pay him the rest of his debt. As lyckwayes ordaines the conservatour to have ane caire to sie the present ordinance fullfilled and obeyeit be the said Robert Bawtye. And siclyck the said commissioneris according to the custome they ordaine and appoint to be collectour of the saide impost, from the said firste day of September nixt, till the first of September thairefter in the yeire of God ane thousand, sex hundreth threttie thrie yeires, James Weir factour, and ordaines him to give his aith *de fideli administratione*[55] to the conservatour, or his deputtis to ingather the saide impost and to mak payment to the minister, reidder and utheris conforme as is allowit to thame be the saidis commissioneris of borrowis and to sende home his comptes of his intromissioune with the said impost frome the said first day of September nixt till the nixt generall conventioun of borrowis, verified be the skipper and merchand or factour in absence of the merchand with [fo. 410v] the said minister and reidder thair dischairges. And siclyck ordaines the conservatour or his deputtes att his beginning to take his aith in oppin court to be haldin be them to that effect that he sall dischairge his leill and true duetye in the said collectioune, and sall uplift frome the merchandis, factouris and skipper, thair true and just pairt according to the quantitie of thair guides that thei sall happin to have according to his knowledge, and sall chairge himselffe thairwith and omitt

---

54 This is the only reference to the fact that, while Scotland continued to adhere to the Julian calendar (albeit that it adopted 1 January as the first day of the calendar year from 1600), most continental countries had switched to the Gregorian calendar by this time.

55 Literally, 'concerning faithful administration', i.e. he was promising to carry out his duties with diligence.

nothing therof, and that he sall collecte it be himselffe, and na uther during the tyme of his collectioun except of seiknes or necessitie. And ordaines letters to be direct to the saidis persounes in thair names and thair generall clerk to subscryve the same. Quhairanent thir presentis salbe his warrand and the saidis persounes with the conservatour to report thair diligence heiranent to the nixt generall conventioun of borrowis. And this to be ane heid off the nixt missive.

30
{Conservatour, skipperis anent the ministeris dewis}
The same day forsameikle as the commissioneris of borrowis finding that thair is ane grit fraude committit be the skipperis in upgiving of thair lead-iningis to the collectouris of the minister dewes quhair the sowmes allotted for the ministeris stipend can schairlie be maid out of the small collectioun nor the validitie of that impost tryed. For remeid quhairoff, the present commissioneris ordaines the skippers att the upgiving of thair leadiningis to the said collectour to make faith that he hes conceallet na pairt thairoff, bot hes gevin the same trewlie uppe. And incaice he sall refuis, ordaines the conservatour and his deputtes to interpone thair authoritie for compelling of thaime thairto. And ordaines ilke burgh to intimat this statut to thair nichtboures att thair home cuming, that nane pretent ignorance and the extract theroff to be sent over to the present collectour and the saidis burghis to report thair diligence [in] intimatting heirof to the nixt generall conven-tioune of borrowis. And this to be ane heid off the nixt missive.

31
{Invernes diligence against thair outland burgessis}
{Aberdeine diligence agains Alexander Murray}[56]
The same day the saidis commissioneris of borrowis ordaines the burgh of Innernes to produce Donald Fullour and Donald Talyeour thair burgessis for transporting staiple waires by the staiple port, and the burgh of Aberdein [fo. 411r] to produce Alexander Murray and to putt them under cautioune for compeirance the nixt generall conventioune. And the same to be remem-berit in the nixt missive.

32
{Anent the visitatioun of the Watter of Forth[57]}
The same day anent the elevint act of the particular conventioune of borrowis haldin att the burgh of Perth the 23 of September last,[58] ordaining

---

[56] The second marginal title appears on the recto of the next folio but is placed here for the sake of consistency.

[57] The Firth of Forth.

[58] No record of the convention at Perth is preserved in the volume held in Aberdeen.

the burgessis of Bruntyland, Kirkcaldie, and Culros to produce thair diligence in writt of the visitatioun of the walter of Forth to this present
conventioune, as also ordaineing the burgessis of Culroeis, Kinghorne and
Dysart to make ane visitatioun thairoff betuixt and this present generall
conventioune. For obedience quhairoff compeirit the commissioneris of the
saidis burghes and producit thair reportis of thair visitatione of the Walter of
Forth, both for this laste yeire and yeire preceiding. Which being considederit
be the saidis borrowis, they ordaine the burgh of Edinburgh att thair home
cuming to report this laste yeires visitatioun to the lordis of secreit counsell
and to desyre the saidis lordis to recommend to the gentrie of new the
proclamatione maid thairanent the twentie aucht of Junii ane thousand sax
hundreth ane yeiris and did respect that the lordis of counsell hes appointed
report to be maid yeirlie of the estaite of the said watter abone Queines
Ferrie. Thairfor they appoint for this yeire the burghis of Anstruther Easter,
Pettinweyme and Culroies to visite the said watter abone the said Queines
Ferrie upoun both the sydis thairoff and produce the same in writt to the
nixte generall conventioun to be reportit be thaime to the saidis lordis of
counsell under the payne off tuentie poundis ilk burgh. And ordaines the
burghe off Culroise to conveine the uther twa and the agent to pay the
sowme of threttie sax poundis, fyftein schillingis debursit be the last visi-
touris and the sowme sall be allowed to him in his comptis. And this to be
ane heid off the nixte missive.

33
{Anent the passing of ane signature in favouris of the burrowes}
The same day forsameikle as the commissioneris of borrowis conveinet att
Edinburgh the tuentie saxt of April last hadde, conforme to the commissioun given them, drawen upp ane signatour of the borrowis liberties and
sent the samen to Mr Johne Hay to pas his Majesties handis. Considdering
the said Mr Johne hes not as yett returnit, thairfoir they give full powar and
commissioun to the burghis appointit to meitt att Edinburgh efter the
[fo. 411v] saide Mr Johne his returne to prosecute the passing of the saide
signatur and to use all meanes for doeing of the same and perfyting thairoff.
And ordaines the saidis borrowis to report thair diligence heiranent to the
nixt generall conventioune of borrowis. And this to be ane heid of the nixt
missive.

34
{A tabill to be drawin up of the actis of burrowis}
The same day forsameikle as the commissioneris off borrowis, finding that
through the inlacke off the knawledge of the actes statutis and proceidingis
of the commissioneris of borrowis in former tymes money omissiounes
are committit and the good ordour that sould be keapet is neglected. For

remeid quhairoff the present commissioneris ordaines thair generall clerk to drawe upp ane index of the holle actes, statutis and ordinances and maitteris contenit in the registeris of the acts of borrowis, haveing the number of the booke and leives thairoff. And the same to be presentit with the registeris ilk conventioune to the end the borrowis may informe themselffes anent all thinges hes formerlie past amongest thame. And the said clerke to report his diligence heiranent to the nixt generall conventioune off borrowis. And this to be ane heid of the nixt missive.[59]

35
{Anent particular conventiounes}
The same day the commissioneris sufficientlie instructed for taking ane course anent the keaping of particular conventiounis and to this effect ordaines the same to be rememberit in the missive.

36
{Unfrie skipperis useing tred}
The same day anent the supplicatioun givin in complening of the trade and negotiatioun used be many skipperis unfriemen under collour of portage, the commissioneris ordaines the same to be rememberit in the missive and ilk burgh to be requirit for sending thair commissioneres sufficientlie instructed for sum remeid thairoff.

37
{Aberdeine contra Dik anent thair birne[60]}
The same day anent the complent givin be the burgh of Aberdein against Frances Dick for selling in France of salmound efter Michaelmes last under the byrne of Abirdein which hes bein counterfute be some persounes heir. Thairfor the present commissioneris ordaines the burgh of Edinburgh to take such tryell anent the persounes to whome the said wair did appertein, and iff it be possibill to find them out that sum solide course may be taikin theranent and the said burgh to report thair diligence heiranent to the nixt generall conventioun of borrowis. And this to be ane heid of the nixte missive.

[fo. 412r]
38
{Northberwick craving support to thair herberie}
The same day anent the supplicatioun gevin in be the commissioner of the

---

59 This act is noted in the Abstract of Acts of Convention, *RCRBS*, iv, 532.
60 i.e. 'burn', a burned brand mark on a barrel in this case.

burgh of Northberwick in name of the said burghe craveing ane voluntar support for helpe to the reprairatioun of ane harberie by whiche thair burghe doeth stand. The present commissioneres does recommend the povertie of the said burghe and necessetie thariof to the haill borrowes and grantis them licence to seik the said contributioun of the majestrates and counsall of the burghes provyding allwayes they imploy the same to the repairatioun of the said harberie and be comptabill to the said borrowes when they salbe requyreit.

39
{Montrose craveing help to thair herberie}
The same day anent the supplicatioun gevin in be the burghe of Montroise craveing help to the building of ane harberie, inrespect of the meannes of thair comoun good. The commissioneres ordaines the sam to be rememberit in the missive and ilk burghe to be requyrit to send thair commissioneres sufficientlie instructed to give anser thairto to the nixt generall conventioun of borrowes.

40
{Jedburghe craveing help to thair bridge of Twed[61]}
The same day anent the supplicatioun gewin in be the burgh of Jedburgh craveing help to the uphalding of ane bridge over the[62] water of Tuiet being the cheiff and ordinarie passage to thair burghe without the whiche the same cannot subsist, the standing thairof consisting be the resort of cuntrey people hither. The commissioneres ordaines the burghes of Haddingtoun and Selkirk to visite the said bridge and report the necessity thairof to the generall conventioun of borrowes and ilk burghe to be requyrit to send thair commissioneres sufficientlie instructed to give answer thairto. And this to be ane heid of the nixt missive.

41
{Baetie admittit factour at Campheir}
The same day the commissioneres of borrowes being convenit, anent the supplicatioune gevin in be Alexander Baety present resident within the toun of Campheir craveing thair consent, ratificatioun and aprobatioun for his admissioun to the office of factorie at the staple port of Campheir as at mair lenth is contenit in his said supplicatioun. Quhairwith the said commis-

---

61   This probably refers to the Tweed rather than the Teviot. The river flowing through Jedburgh is the Jed Water, a tributary of the Teviot, which is a tributary of the Tweed. The Tweed, which lies to the north of the burgh, would have been the principal barrier to communication between Jedburgh and Edinburgh.

62   'over the' is repeated here in error.

sioneres of borrowes being rypelie advysit and understanding of the said
Alexander Baety his qualificatioun and habilitie for the dischairgeing of ane
sufficient dewty in the said office of factorie. Thairfoir they grant and gives
him consent, [fo. 412v] ratificatioun and approbatioun to the admissioun
of the said Alexander Baety to the said office of factorie for the natioun at
thair said staipill port of Campheir, provyding allwayes the same sall onlie
indure indureing his non mariage and efter the same *hoc ipso facto*[63] the said
office to expyre. As lykewayes indureing the saidis borrowes will allanerlie
and with provisioun and conditioun that he will behave himselff honestlie
and dewtifullie in the said office and mak just thankfull compt reckoning
and payment of his intromissioun with whatsumever goodis or geir, sowmes
of money intrometted with be him perteining to whatsumever persones that
sall happin to imploy him in the said office or utherwayes salbe intrometted
with be him at command and directioun of the commissioneres of borrowes
and that he sall obey all actis and statutes maid or to be maid be the saidis
commissioneres of borrowes anent factores and sall undergo suche offices
and services as it sall please thame to burdene him withall. And for his better
performance heirof, compeirit Patrick Guthrie merchand burges of Dundie,
Alexander Mure merchand burges of Edinburgh and Robert Learmonth
burges of Haddingtoun and band and obleist thameselvis conjunctlie and
severally thair aires executouris and assignayes as cautiouneris souerties and
full debitoures for the said Alexander Baety, that he sall faithfully and trewlie
dischairge his dewty in the said office of factorie and all utheres his imploymentis and sall mak just compt reckoning and payment to all merchandis
of the natioun that sall happin to imploy him of quhatsumever soumes of
money, merchandice goodis and geir it sall happin him to intromett with
or utherwayes sall ressave be any uther imployment. As lykewayes they band
and obleist thame and thair foirsaid as said that the said Alexander Baety sall
fullfill and obey all actes and statutes maid or to be maid be the commissioneres of borrowes in thair generall or particular conventiones conforme
to the tenores thairof, and under the paines thairin contenit. And espectiallie
befoir his mariage (if he sall happin to marie) that he sall make just compt
reckoning and payment to the merchandis of all his [fo. 413r] imploymentis.
As lykewayes that he sall befoir his admissione compeir judiciallie befoir
the conservatour or his deputes and mak faith for the dischairge of his
dewty and the said office and for obeying and fullfilling of the said actes of
borrowes maid or to be maid. Quhairunto the said Alexander Baety being
personallie present band and obleist himselff under suche paines as it sould
please the commissioneres of borrowes to inflict upoun him. As lykewayes
band and obleist him his aires and executouris to releve and skaithles keepe

---

[63] By that very fact/action, i.e. automatically.

the said cautiouneris and thair foirsaidis of all cost, skaith, damnage and entrest which sould happin thame or uther foirsaid to incur or sustene throw thair becuming souertie for him in maner foirsaid. In witnes quhairof the said Alexander Baety and his cautiouneris hes subscrivit this present act with thair handes, day, yeir and moneth foirsaid.

42
{Selkirk}
The same day anent the supplicatioun gevin in be the burghe of Selkirk craving helpe for thair defence in the persutes intendit and depending against thame be certane of thair nichtboures quhairby thair haill commoun landes and customes are intendit to be evicted from them to thair utter ruine. The present commissioneres findes they deserve and aucht to be helpit and thairfoir remittes the samyne to be gevine and appointed be the commissioneres to be convenit at Edinburgh unto quhom the present commissioneres gives thair full power and commissioun to do thairin as they sall think expedient for the standing and weill of the said burghe. And the said burghes to report diligence heiranent to the nixt generall conventioun of borrowes. And this to be ane heid of the nixt missive.

43
{Exemptioun to certane burrowes}
The same day the said commissioneres of borrowes gives and grantis licence to the burghes of Galloway, Tayne and Nairne, Kilranie to abyd and remaine fra all generall conventiounes of borrowes for the space efterspecefeit: viz the said burgh of Galloway for the space of fyve yeires and the burghes of Tayne, Kilranie, Nairne for the space of three yeiris, upoun the conditiones and provisiounes efter following: provyding allwayes the samyne be not extendit to parliament nor quhair the said burghes ar cited for any particulare caus. And also provyding the saidis [fo. 413v] burghis send with the commissioner of the nixt adjacent burgh thair severall ratificatoune and approbatioune of all thingis to be done yeirlie in the said generall conventiounes authenticklie subscryvit, with all soumes that they sould pay to the borrowis conforme to the missive and that they bestow the expences that they sould have bestowed upon thair commissioneris upoun comon workis and be comptable thairoff to the borrowes, att the expyring of the saidis yeires.

44
{Dumbartan Renfrew}
The same day anent the complent givin in name of the burgh of Dumbartan against the burgh of Ranfrew for suffering of unfriemen within thair boundis to usurpe the libertie of the frie borrowis. The commissioneris ordaines the said burgh of Ranfrew to come sufficientlie instructed to the nixt generall

conventioune of borrowis to give answer thairto under the paine of xx li. And this to be ane heid of the nixt missive.

45
{Impost grantit to Kirkcaldie}
The same day the saidis commissioneris off borrowis grantis and gives licence to the burgh of Kirkcaldie to impetrat of our soveraine lorde a gifte of the impost following for the spaice off sevin yeiris nixt and immediatlie following for reparatioune of thair heaven and shoore. That is to say of ilk toun guidis losset[64] in the herberie tua schillingis at thair incuming and att thair outpassing tua schillingis and of the veschell 12 d. for ilk tunn att the incuming and 12 d. att the out pasing and this of all sort of geir except lyme, coall, sklaitt and friestane quhilk is ordainit to be frie of the said impost. Item ilk chalder of victuallis dischairged and lost in the said harberie twa schillingis at thair entrie and ilk chalder vittual transportit furth thairof twa schillinges and of the veschell twelff penneyes of ilk chalder lost or schipped. Item ane trie of ilk hundreth lost or laidned in the said harberie, and ilk chalder salt of unfrie men sex schilling aucht peneyes and of frie men three schilling four peneyes and of the veschell of unfriemen twa schillinges and of frie men 12 d. provyding the said burghe imploy the said impost to the [fo. 414r] effect foirsaid and mak yeirlie compt to the borrowes thairof under the paine of twentie pundes to be payed to the borrowes.

Septimo Julii I^m vi^c trigesimo secundo

[46]
{Agentis comptis}
The quhilk day the commissioneres of borrowes beand convenit, haveing hard, seine, fited, calcullat and allowed the comptis of Alexander Aikinheid agent from the last generall conventioun to this present conventioun, they finde thame selvis restand awand to him the sowme of fyve hundreth twentie aucht punds ten schillinges ten penneyes, which with the annuelrent duew since his debursementis to the nixt conventioun will extend to the sowme of sex hundreth threttie twa pounds. Which sowme of sex hundreth threttie twa pounds ten schillinges ten penneyes togidder with the sowme of three hundreth pounds presentlie advanced be him to the burgh of Elgin with the annuelrent thairof extending to the sowm of threttie punds, togidder with the sowme of fourty poundis debursit for surveying of the watter of Forth extending in the haill to the sowme of nyne hundreth threescoir sevin poundis, they ordane ilk burgh to send thair pairt thairof conforme to the

---

[64] i.e. loosed, unpacked.

taxt roll with thair commissioner with[65] the nixt generall conventioun under the pane of twentie poundis ilk burgh by and attour ther pairt of the said principall sowme. And this to be ane heid of the nixt missive.

47
{Act againis merchandis treding with unfrie skipperis}
The same day forsameikill as the commissioneris of borrowes understanding that the greattest caus of the encreas of unfrie tradderes is in default of the burgesses wha takes pairt and becomes pairtners with skipperes dwelling at unfrie portis. For remeid quhairof, they ordane ilk burgh to send thair commissioneres sufficientlie instructed with thair best advyse for remeiding the samyne under the payne of twentie pound. And this to be ane heid of the nixt missive.

[fo. 414v]
48
{Anent the conserjarie hous}
The same day anent the complaint gevin in be certane burghes anent the consergerie hous, the commissioneres recommendes to the conservatour to have ane cair to sie the same provydit with Inglis beir and to have the brode contening the lawis of the said hous sett up thair.

49
The same day ordaines the burghes of Brechin, Dumbartane and Rossay[66] to send thair pairt conforme to the taxt roll with thair commissioneres to the nixt conventioun of the sowme of fyve hundreth threttie merkes payit presentlie be the borrowes for the drawing up of thair signatur. And this to be ane head of the nixt missive.

50
{Certane burrowes unlawit}
The same day unlawes the burghes of Ranfrew and Lochmabine ilk ane of thame of the sowme of xx li. for being absent from this present conventioun being lauchfullie wairnit thairto be George Ramsay, post, as was presentlie verefied and for not sending thair pairt of the dewes of the missive. The said burgh of Ranfrew thair pairt extending to the sowme of fourtie aucht schillinges, the burgh of Lochmabane for thair dewes this yeir and the last yeir to fyve poundis thre schillinges sex penneyes. And they ordane the said burghes to send with thair commissioneres the samyne to the nixt generall

---

65   This should be 'to'.
66   Rothesay.

conventioun, togidder with the unlawes incurrit be thame and thair pairt of the fyve hundreth and threttie merkes presentlie advanced be the borrowes in thair proper efferes with all uther dewties contenit in the missive. And this to be ane heid of the missive.

[fo. 415r]

51

Compeirit Alexander Aikinheid agent and grantit him to have ressavit the haill dewes of the missive from the present commissioneres together with thair pairtis of fyve hundreth and threttie merkis not contenit in the missive. And thairfoir dischairges the saidis haill commissioneres and thair burghe[s] thairof for ever.

52

The same day the present commissioneres of borrowes dissolves this present conventioun and affixis thair nixt generall conventioun to be begun and haldin at the burght of Sanctandrewes [...][67] the day of Julii nixt with continewatioun of dayes. And ordanes thair clarke to direct thair generall missive to the said burgh of Sanctandrewes for wairning of the haill borrowes for keepeing of the said conventioun.[68]

[fo. 416v]

Actis of the generall conventioun of Burrowes hauldin at Montrois in Julii 1632[69]

---

67   This should say 'the [...] day of Julii'. The convention, originally planned for July, did not meet until 6 August 1633 because of the visit of Charles I to Scotland. The change of date was decided at a particular convention at Edinburgh in June 1633 (see below, 126).

68   The rest of fo. 415 is blank, as is fo. 416r.

69   This is the title on the exterior of the minutes as they would have been given to Aberdeen's commissioner to take back to Aberdeen at the end of the convention.

Particular Convention at Edinburgh, October 1632

[fo. 418r]

In the particular conventioun of borrowis haldin at the burghe of Edinburghe the tuelft day of October the yeir of God I^m vi^c threttie two yeiris be the commissioneris of borrowis underwreittin be vertew of ane missive letter direct to thame from the said burght of Edinburght conforme to ane commissioune gevin to thame from the last generall conventioune haldin at the burght of Munrose[1] the fyft day of Julii last and tuentie fyft act of the said conventioune, and produceit thair commissiounis as followis:

Edinburgh	Williame Dick, James Danielstoune
Perth	Andro Wilsoune
Dundye	Johne Ramsay
Abirdein	Maister Vedast Lowsoune
Stirling	Johne Cowane
Lynlighow[2]	Williame Bell
St Androis	James Watsoune
Glasgow	Gabriell Cunyinghame
Aire	Johne Osburne
Haddingtoun	Mr James Cockburne
Montrose	Robert Keyth
Dysert	Johne Gay
Kirkcaldie	Johne Williamesoune
Cowpar	George Jamesoune
Anstruther Eister	David Alexander
Anstruther Wester	Robert Pullow
Drumfreis[3]	Robert Richardsoune
Bruntyland	Williame Meikiljohne
Kinghorne	Patrik Wallace
Innerkeithing[4]	Williame Blaikburne
Carraill[5]	Johne Mackiesoune
Jedburght	Johne Penman
Pittinweme	George Kingyow
Dumfermling	James Reid
Selkirk	Williame Scott

---

1   Montrose.
2   Linlithgow.
3   Dumfries.
4   Inverkeithing.
5   Crail.

Dunbar   Robert Schortas
Lanerick[6]   Gediane Weir
[fo. 418v]
Abirbrothock[7]
Elgyne
Peiblis   Patrick Weitche
Culrose   Adame Prymrois
Bamff

1
{Moderator}
The same day the saidis commisioneris of borrowis electis, creatis and constitutis Williame Dick, mercheand, first in commissioun for the burght of Edinburght, moderator during this present conventioune wha comperand acceptit the said office in and upoun him and *de fidelie administratione*[8] gave his aithe.

2
{Discharge of Sir Johne Hay his commission}[9]
The same day anent the severall heidis of the missive concerning the severall commissiounes gevin to Sir Johne Hay for dealling with his Majestie in the materis efterspecefeitt. Compeirit the said Sir Johne and declairit that:
{1. Equalitie of custome in England, Scotland and Irland}
First, conforme to ane of the instructiounes gevin to him be the commissioneres convenit at Perth the [23] of September 1631[10] ordaining him to deall with his Majestie for ane ratificatioune of the patent grantit to the borrowes of the kingdome of thair schipis and gudis in payment of craftsmen in Ingland and Irland as the natives thair, and especiallie for making the same effectuall in Irland, he had procurit ane new gift of the equalitie of customes in all his Majesties kingdomes under his Majesties gryt seill of England datit at Westminster the nynteine[11] of Aprill last, which the said Sir John producit, conforme whairunto thair was the lyke grantit in Scotland under the gryt seill thairof to his Majesties subjectis in England and Ireland, and declairit

---

6   Lanark.
7   Arbroath.
8   Literally, 'concerning faithful administration', i.e. he was promising to carry out the duties of moderator with diligence.
9   This act is recorded in full in the Abstract of Acts of Convention, *RCRBS*, iv, 532–3, with only minor differences, largely involving slight abbreviation in the Abstract, except where noted.
10 There is no surviving record of this convention, but the date has been obtained from the printed Abstract.
11 The abstract has '10th April'.

that the same was lauchfullie intimat throuche the poirtis and borrowis of England. As lykwayis produced ane coppye of the same patent signed be his Majestie direct to the deputye of Ireland with ane letter from his Majestie for publischeing thairof thair.

{2. Burghis of baronie}

And anent the aucht act of the particular conventioune haldin at the said burgh of Peirthe the 23 September last 1631 anent the burghis of barronie and commissioune gevin unto him for suppressing of thair incroachementis upoune the frie borrowis, declaired that he had procured ane letter frome his Majestie to the lordis of sessioune conforme to thair commissioune which was delivered to thame. And lykwayis producit ane letter direct to the lordis of counsell willing thame that in no erectioune of burghis of [fo. 419r] baronye heirefter, thair be no farder libertie grantit to thame in any patent then by the lawis of this kingdome is competent to ony burghe of baronye, and that none of thame heirefter be erected with ony priviledgis which be the lawis and statutis of this kingdome ar onlye popper to the burghis royall as the letter produced daittit the last of Julii last beiris.

{3. Pearle patent Robert Buchan}

And anent the patent procurit be Robert Buchane of the fischeing of the perll in Scotland, which by the commissioun contenit in the said act at Peirthe he was ordained to procure the recalling thairof. The said Sir Johne producit ane lettir frome his Majestie to the lordis of counsell with ane copy thairof willing thame to conveine befoir thame the said Robert and to dischairge the said patent and to publische the said dischairge and to exped no uther thairefter as the letter daittit at Oatlandis the last of Julii last beiris.

{4. Maltmen}

And anent the fyft act[12] of the last conventioune haldin at Edinburght the 25 of Aprill last ordaining the said Sir Johne to deall with his Majestie anent the act of parliament maid anent maltmen, the said Sir Johne producit ane letter from his Majestie to the lordis of counsell willing thame to sett ane new pryce according to the tyme betuix the boll of barley and boll of malt, and in the meantyme dischairgeing the executioun of the former act daittit at Oatlandis the last of Julii last.

{5. Heigh constabill}

And anent the commissioune gevin to him anent the heiche constable[13] mentioned in the said act of the said particular conventioune haldin at Peirthe the 23 of September last 1631, the said Sir Johne producit ane letter direct be his Majestie to the lordis of counsell willing thame that no new

---

12 This act does not survive as the record of that convention is incomplete, but it is mentioned in the Abstract, see *RCRBS*, iv, 531.

13 William Hay, 10th earl of Erroll, had inherited the title in July 1631 on the death of his father Francis, the 9th earl.

gift be exped tuitching the office of constabularie iff any sould be presentit to[14] the commissioneris of the frie borrowis be lauchfullie cited and hard to object,[15] and giff any questioune arryis anent thair liberties to remitt the same to the judge ordiner, daittit at Oatlandis the last of Julii last.

{6. Manufactories}

And siclyk the said Sir Johne repoirtit that he being informit that thair was sum persounes busied in procuring of certaine patentis for manufactories of cloathe and stuffis within this kingdome and leist the burghis sould suffer prejudice thairin, that he had procured ane letter from his Majestie to the counsell willing thame to call befoir thame the counsell of Edinburgh or such uther burghis as they sall find willing to undertak the inbringing of headis men[16] and to grant to thame suche priviledgis as may encourage thame, restrayning all utheris during thair tyme, datit at Oatlandis the last of Julii last.

{6[17]. Fishing} And siclyk producit ane lettir from his Majestie direct to the present commissioneris of burrowis willing thame to contribute thair indevouris for bringing the work of [fo. 419v] fischeing to perfectioune, for the which his Majestie promeises to menteine and defend thair liberties, dattit at Beaulyre[18] the 15 of August last.

3

Vigesimo Octobris I[m] vi[c] trigesimo secundo

{Ratification Pettinweime}

The quhilk day the commissioneris of borrowis being convenit, compeirit George Kingyow commissioner for the burght of Pittinweme and for himselff and in name and behalff of his said burght ratifiet and approvit all actis, statutis and ordinances and conclusiounes takin and to be takin be the present commissioneris of borrowis at this present conventioun and oblissed and his said burght to abyd and remaine thairat but contraditoune or againe calling quhatsumever.

4

Vigesimo quinto Octobris I[m]vi[c] trigesimo secundo

{Sir Johne Hay payment of his charges}

The quhilk day the commissioneris of borrowis being convenit, anent that pairt of the missive concerning Sir Johne Hay thair commissioner to his

14 In the Abstract this is 'till', making it less ambiguous, see *RCRBS*, iv, 533.
15 Although this is garbled, it is a true transcription of the text.
16 In the Abstrct this is 'tradesmen', see *RCRBS*, iv, 533.
17 This should clearly be 7.
18 In the Abstract this is, more correctly, 'Beaulie', i.e. Beaulieu Palace in Essex, see *RCRBS*, iv, 533.

Majestie his chairges anent thair severall imploymentis since the moneth of Junii ane thowsand sex hundrethe tuentie nyne yeiris debursit be the burgh of Edinburght conforme to the severall actis maid thairanent, they have agriet and condiscendit and be thir presentis agries and condiscendis and for thame selffis and in name of thair burghis and having power and commisioun from the generall conventioun of borrowis haldin at the burght of Muntrose in July last, bindis and obleissis thame to content and pay to the said burght of Edinburgh and ony haiffing power from thame, the sowme of tuentie four thowsand pund usuall money of this realme at thrie severall termes efterfollowing, viz The sowme of aucht thowsand pundis at the nixt generall conventioune[19] to be haldin at the burght of St Androis in July nixt 1633 yeiris, and the sowme of uther aucht thowsand pundis at the nixt generall conventioun thairefter following in Julii I^m vi^c threttie four, and the last aucht thowsand pundis at the generall conventioune to cum in Julii 1635. And for this effect ordaines the same to be rememberit in ilk missive during the non payment of the saidis sowmes and ilk burgh conforme to the termes abonewrittin, requirit to send thair pairt of the said sowme to the saidis conventiounes conforme to the taxt roll under the paine of tuentie burght[20] ilk burght, and that by and attour the payment of thair pairt of the said principall sowme, the said burght of Edinburgh bearing alwayis thair proportionall pairt of the saidis sowmes conforme to the taxt roll. Which sowmes [fo. 420r] aggriet and condiscendit upoune as said is ar declairit to be in full contentatioune and satisfactioune of all sowmes of money or annuelrentis thairof debursit be the said burgh of Edinburgh and thair said commissioner conforme to the severall actis maid thairanent befoir the day and dait heirof.[21]

5

Vigesimo sexto Octobris I^m vi^c trigesimo secundo

The quhilk day the commissioneris of borrowis being convenit, forsamekill as Sir Johne Hay, commissioner to his Majestie did procure ane patent under the gryt seall of England of the equalitie of customes in all his Majestie dominions which hes not bein publisched in his Majesties kingdome of Irland, and for this caus the said Sir John producit ane letter and lykwayis the dowble of the saidis letters patentis under his Majesties handis with the missive letter direct to the deputye of Ireland for publischeing of the saidis letters patentis in the said kingdome. Thairfoir the saidis commissioneris ordaines the saidis letter patentis with the said lettir to be deliverit to Gabriel Cunynghame commissioner for the burght of Glasgow, to whome

---

19   This word is repeated.
20   This should be 'pundis'.
21   This act is noted in the Abstract of Acts of Convention, RCRBS, iv, 533.

they recommend the deliverie of the said letter and letters patentis to the said deputye and repoirting of his answer, and in the publischeing thairof and effectuating of his Majesties desyre thairanent and of his said answer to be deliverit to the burght of Edinburgh to whome the present commissioneris gevis full power and commissioune for prosequuting of the said mater according as they sall think best and the said answer sall requyre. As lykwayis the said Sir Johne having procured ane warrand anent the burghtis of barrony togidder with ane uther letter anent Buchanes patent of the perle as is contenit in the secund act of this conventioun, which the present commissioneris deliverit to the lordis of his Majesties most honorabill privie counsell and quhairof the said lordis ordanit to be insert and registrat in the buikis of excheker, and the uther they have inactit in the saidis buikis of counsell, and ordaines the said Robert Buchane to be cited for heiring of the said patent dischairgit in all tyme cuming. Thairfoir they ordainit thair agent to extract the said warrand out of the buikis of excheker and to intimat the same to all whome it effeiris. As lykwayis to caus raise letteris for citing of the said Robert Buchane with all diligence, and ordaines the burght of Edinburgh to concure and assist in dischairgeing of the said patent befoir the lordis of counsell, to whome they give thair full power and commissioune to compeir befoir the saidis lords of counsell for insisting in the said actioune. And lykwayis the said commissioneris grantis full power and commissioune to the said burght of Edinburgh for prosequuting of that letter procured be the said Sir Johne anent the modefeing of ane competent [fo. 420v]
pryce betuix the boll of beir and boll of malt which letter was lykwayis producit [befoir][22] the saidis lordis of counsell and which they continowit to the [...] day of [...] nixtocum, and seriouslie recommendis to thair cair that suche competent pryce be sett doun betuix the saidis bollis that the said maltmen may have competent gaine and the lieges not too far prejudgit. And lykwayis the said Sir Johne haiffing procurit ane letter anent the gryt constable and ane uther concerning manufactories as is contained in the said secund act of this present conventioune, thairfoir the present commissioneris gevis full power and commissioune to the burght of Edinburght for prosequuting of the said mater concerning the constable to the saidis lordis of counsell and in thair names for prosequuting of the said mater as they sall think maist neidfull and expedient. And anent the uther concerning the manufactories, the saidis borrowis continows the prosequuting thairof till they sall find ane fitt occasioune for the same. And the said burghis of Edinburgh and Glasgow togidder with the agent to repoirt thair diligence

---

22   There is no space in the MS but the sense requires this insertion.

heiranent in ane generall conventioune of borrowis. And this to be in head
of the nixt missive.

6

{Small coyne}

The same day anent the point of the missive concerning the prejudice this
cuntrie sustaines throw laik of small spaces of money for exchange mentionit
in the sevinteine act of the last generall conventioune haldin in the burght of
Muntrose, the present commissioneris findis expedient that his majest[ie] be
his[23] supplicat for causing ane yeirlie builyeoun be printit in spaces different
from the Inglische reckining, as also since that this cuntrie and especiallie
the mercheandis estaitt is infinitlie prejudgit be sindrie occasiounes and
burdingis muche impoverischeit and nothing done for the advancement of
traid, and withall considdering that the victuall throuch all Europe is becum
the pryme and chief commoditie quhairby all traid is mantained, which
commodityes is heir suppressit evin in tymes not fitting, and ane unnecessar
restraint of importing establischeit. Thairfoir the saidis commissioneris findis
expedient that his Majestie be supplicat for causing ane satlit ordour to be
takin quhairby it may be licentiat that at all tymes it be lauchfull to the
mercheandis without ony impositiounes or customes to import victuall from
forrane cuntries to girnell and keip the same, and to transpoirt the samyne
againe als frielie provyding always at the incuming of the said victuall the
importar sall find cautioun not to sell the samyne againe within the cuntrie
the boll being of quhytt bot xiiii merkis[24] and the boll beir at xi merkis the
boll, and the boll of aitmeall at aucht [fo. 421r] merkis which licence micht
tend to the gryt inricheing of the cuntrie and prove ane gryt meanes for
holding of money within the same the tyme of necessitie. And for this effect,
they ordaine Sir Johne Hay to deall with his Majestie heiranent and to lay
oppin to his Majestie quhat commoditie may redound to this cuntrie thairby
and quhat incommoditie they susteine be the restraint foirsaid. As lykwayis
the[y][25] supplicat his Majestie in the said mater of the money in maner foirsaid and the said Sir Johne to repoirt his diligence heiranent in ane generall
conventioune of borrowis. And this to be in head of the nixt missive.[26]

7

{Crying in of douloures}

The same day anent the mater of crying in of doulouris and coyning of ane

---

23 This word seems to have been inserted in error.
24 The Abstract has '40 merks' and makes no mention of malt, see *RCRBS*, iv, 533.
25 The word is written as 'the', presumably in error for 'they', although it could be in error
    for 'he', referring to Sir John Hay.
26 This act is given almost in full in the Abstract of Acts of Convention, *RCRBS*, iv, 533–4,
    although there it is described as an act concerning imported victuals, rather than coin.

new money of ten pennie fyne mentionat in the missive and in the overtouris send doun be his Majestie to his counsell, the present commissioneris
gives power and commissioune to the burght of Edinburght in thair names
to compeir befoir the saidis lordis of counsell and to oppose againes the
same, and giff neid beis to convene sua many of the burghis as they sall think
neidfull, recommending the said mater seriouslie to thair cair and to repoirt
thair diligence heiranent to the nixt generall conventioune of borrowis. And
this to be in head of the nixt missive.

8

{Plaiding trinched referred}
The same day anent the supplicatioune to have bein presentit to the lordis of
counsell be the commissioneris for obtaining the pleading heirefter to have
bein presentit to the mercatt in foldis conforme to the xvi act of the last
generall conventioun haldin at Muntrose, the saidis commissioneris ordainis
the same to be rememberit in the first missive to be direct for convening of
the burrowis and they requirit for cuming instructit for supplicating of the
saidis lordis thairanent.

9

{His Majestie to be supplicat for helping of some indempnities may aryse
by the fishing patent}[27]
The same day the said commissioneris understanding that the mater of
the treattie of the fischeing betuix this kingdome and the kingdome of
England is now endit and that in the patent [fo. 421v] thairof, thair is sum
thingis which ar necessar to be farder cleirit and without his Majesties farder
declaratioune micht prejudge the whole cuntrie, and especiallie anent the
buscheing in the ylis and within the samyne and in the fischeing upon that
coast of this kingdome lyand betuix Buchaneness and Reidheid[28] which be
the incroacheing of busches neirer then fourteine myles to the coast thairof
wald prejudge the salmound fischeing. Also anent the farder cleiring of all
indemnitie or prejudice, the said borrowis micht mainteine in the whole
rest of thair priviledgis, they geving way to the said patent of associatioun.
And thairfoir ordaines the missive letter in all humane maner to be drawin
up to be direct to his Majestie for cleiring of the pointis abonewrittin,
and with all to mak humle offer to his Majestie of thair willingnes to
contribute to the advancement of the said intendit wark of fischeing, which

---

[27] This marginal title appears on the verso of the folio but is placed here for the sake of
consistency.

[28] Buchan Ness is the promontory immediately south of Peterhead, Aberdeenshire; Red Head
is a sea cliff in Angus, to the south of Lunan Bay, in the parish of Inverkielor.

letter they ordaine Sir Johne Hay to present to his Majestie and during his abod thair to seriouslie advert to all thingis which may fall out thair ather generall or particular and to use his best indevour for opposing and staying of what micht tend to thair prejudice, to whome thairanent they give full power and commissioune and to contribute thair best meanes for procuiring thair saidis desyris conteanit in the said letter obtanit in thair favouris. As lykwayis to prease in the dounsetting of the lawis to obtaine that the said busche fischeing in the ilis conforme to the said letter be dischairgit and that the beginning of the busche fischeing upoune the eist coast of this kingdome begin the 24 of Julii yeirlie and the fischeing in the fischeing[29] of the ilis begin the first of September, and to condiscend upoun the maner of administrating of the justice and ressaving of suche as desyris to be in the said associatioun, quhair thair is not of bothe natiounes resyling. And generallie to advert that thairin so far as he can that nothing be done to the prejudice of the natioune and as materis sall occur bothe in generall as also anent the said letter and lawis to be establischeitt, to acquaint the burght of Edinburght, that they thairefter according to the expediencie of the effairis may communicat the same to the rest of the borrowis. And for the said Sir Johne Hay his paines to be takin be him in the said effairis, the present commissioneris in name of thair burghis promittis to tak the same to thair consideratioune and accordinglie to remember the same thankfullie.[30]

[fo. 422r]

[10]

{Factors in France}

The same day anent the course to have bein takin for preveining the huirt sustanit be the natioune throw the factouris in France conforme to the 14 act in the last generall conventioun haldin in the burght of Muntrose,[31] and the saidis commissioneris finding no uther meanes for preveining thairof bot ather be restrayning of the mercheandis trafficking in these places from imploying of any bot such as hes approbatioune from the burrowis or be restricting the present factouris with thair awin consent to certaine condi-tiounes suche as that thair waires be not sauld bot at ane destinct pryce for exchange money, that no rebaitt should be ressavit nor allowit efter the deliverie of the mercheandis gudis that sum course sould be takin for the extraordinar exactioune be governouris, that the saidis factouris give the compt of chairges to thair mercheandis be particularis, that they sett doune in thair comptis the particular reasounes of the devalling off the pryce quhen any happin that they chairge the mercheand with no bankerroppis, that the

---

[29] The phrase 'in the fischeing' is repeated.
[30] This act is noted in the Abstract of Acts of Convention, *RCRBS*, iv, 534.
[31] See above, 84–5.

factouris with the first occasioun send home the mercheand thair comptis immediatlie efter the seall of thair waires. Quhairanent the present commissioneris ordaines ilk burgh to be requirit for sending thair commissioneris sufficientlie instructit with thair best advyse thairanent or quhat ellis they think may occure [to] the nixt generall conventioune. And this to be in head of the nixt missive.

[11]
{Help to Selkirk}
The same day anent that heid of the missive concerning the supplicatioune gevin in be the burght of Selkirk to the last generall conventioune for thair helpe in the defence of thair commoun land and remittit to the present conventioun.[32] The saidis commissioneris finding the necessitie of the said burgh, hes agreit and consentit to give to thame the sowme of fyve hundrethe pundis usuall money of this realme to be imployet be thame upoune defence of the actiounes intendit againes thame and no utherwayis and ordained ilk burgh to be requirit for sending of thair pairt of the said sowme with thair commissioner to the nixt generall conventioune of borrowis under the paine of tuentie pundis. And that by and attour the payment of thair pairt of the said principall sowme. And this to be in head of the nixt missive.

[fo. 422v]
[12]
{Bamff}
The same day anent that heid of the missive concerning the toun of Bamff mentioned in the 21 act in the last generall conventioune.[33] The saidis commissioneris being informit that they war in agriement with some persounes for thair evidentis, thairfoir they ordaine the said burgh to repoirt thair diligence anent thair proceidingis in the said mater to the nixt generall conventioun of borrowis. And this to be in the head of the nixt missive.

[13]
{Montrois conservatour}
The same day anent the complaint gevin in be the burght of Montrose alledging certaine of thair nichtbouris to have sufferit wrong be the conservatour in the arreisting of thair schip and guidis and deteining the same to thair prejudice as at mair lenthe is contenit in the said complaint gevin in thairanent. The said commissioneris finding that they could determein nothing thairanent befoir the conservatour war first hard thairanent

---

32 See above, 102.
33 See above, 89–90.

or lauchfullie cited to that effect, thairfoir they ordaine ane missive letter
to be direct to the said conservatour with ane copye of the said complaint,
desyring him giff he hes no just caus for deteaning of the saidis gudis and
schip to louse the saidis arreistmentis or utherwayis to answer thairanent to
the commissioneris of borrowis the nixt generall conventioune to be haldin
in the burght of St Androis the […] day of Julii nixt with continuatioun of
dayis. And the same to be rememberit in the nixt missive.

[14]
{Johne Burnet his unlaw remittit}
The same day anent the supplicatioun gevin in be Johne Burnet factour
creaving the sowme of ane hundreth pundis quhairin he was adjudgit for
certaine negligence committit be him in uplifting of the ministeris dewis
at Campheir the year he was appointit collectour, and which Robert Batie
last collectour was be ane act of the last conventioun ordanit to deteine
in the payment which was dew unto him in his comptis as at mair lenthe
is contenit in the said supplicatioune. The said commissioneris for caussis
moving theme dispensis with the said unlaw and ordaines ane letter to be
direct to the said Robert Batie for payment making to him of the said
sowme notwithstanding of any forme of warrand in the contrair giff he sall
have any sowmes in his hand or utherwayis ordaines the present collectour
to pay the same, and the said sowme salbe allowit to him in his comptis.

[fo. 423r]
[15]
The same day the commissioneris ordaynes Alexander Aikinheid, agent, to
pay to James Prymrois and to his servand and to Mr James Durhame and
the measseris of the counsell for thair paines takin in thair effairis sic sowmes
as he sall think expedient and quhat he sall deburse to thame salbe allowit
to him in his comptis.

[16]
The same day quhairas the commissioneris hes apppointit Sir John Hay to
present to his Majestie thair letter conforme to the nynt act of this present
conventioune, finding it necessar that ane moir ample lettir of thankisgeving
be drawin up, they ordainit the sam to be pennit in moist submissive maner,
which they likwayis ordanit the said Sir Johne to deliver to his Majestie, and
withall to represent thair humle obedience and to desyre the continuance
of his Majesties royall favour toward thame. And to repoirt his Majesties
acceptance of boith.

[17]
Followis the instructiounes gevin in to Mr Johne Hay thair commissioner

in the particular conventioune of borrowis haldin at the burght of Peirthe the 23 of September 1631.[34]

Imprimis, thair said commissioner sall informe his Majestie of the necessitie of reservatioun of the loches in the maine land and yles and utheris convenient[35] in the declaratioun gevin be thame to the lordis of his Majesties most honorabill counsell, and to humlie supplicat his Majestie to ratefie the same.

Nixt, iff his Majestie sall insist for the farder inlargement of the saidis places to declair to his Majestie thair willingnes to contribute thair best helpes to secund all his Majesties royall intentiounes especiallie in this his Majesties gryt work of the fischeingis, and that they to this effect haiffing takin to thair consideratioune how the samyne work may be moist proffitablie and upoun suire groundis begun and continowit, have thocht fitt in all humilitie to represent to his Majestie the gryt oppressioune and wrongis done to his Majesties subjectis be the subjectis of the estaittis of the Low Cuntries and the Hamburgeris and Brymeris[36] and be incroatcheing upoun the seas and coistis of Scotland and upoun the ilis of Schetland and Orknay, and now laitlie [fo. 423v] upoun the iles of the Lewis to the gryt detriment of his Majesties subjectis, and how giff the samyne be continowit as is liklie, that boith riche fischeingis which formerlie hes bein the meanes for thair traid salbe maid unproffitable to his Majesties subjectis. And thairfoir to shew thair willingnes to advance all his Majesties royall designes that they wald humlie intreate his Majestie to frie the seas of his Majesties native kingdome of Scotland and iles of the samyne of the inundatioune of the busches of the saidis Nather Landis and utheris straingeris Hamburgeris and Brymeris resorting to the iles of Yetland[37] and Orknay at leist to frie the coistis of the said kingdome of the saidis busches or uther fischer boattis of the Nether Landis be the space of 28 or 14 myles, and to dischairge thame any fischeing neir the coastis of the said Maneland or iles, and the Hamburgeris and Brymeris of thair traid within Yetland or Orknay utherwayis nor according to the lawis of the realme of Scotland, for the which they as his Majesties moist humle and obedient subjectis will offer his Majestie to advance his royall wark of fischeing to the uttermoist of thair power be setting furth of suche ane competent number of busches as sall proportionallie fall to thair pairt, and use all uther meanes for improving of these fischeingis of the iles and loches of the samyne and of the mane land of the kingdome. Bot also

---

34   This act is in the Abstract of Acts of Convention, *RCRBS*, iv, 534–6, although in slightly
     abbreviated form.
35   This is 'contained' in the Abstract, see *RCRBS*, iv, 534.
36   People from Bremen, a Hanseatic port on the river Weser in north-western Germany.
37   Shetland, sometimes still written as 'Zetland' due to confusion with the original initial
     'yogh' which, with aspiration, gave rise to the modern initial 'Sh'.

will consent that his Majestie grant libertie to the subjectis of his Majesties kingdome of Ingland and Ireland who salbe frie of the associatioun of the fischeingis intendit, frielie to fische in all the seas of the said kingdom and iles thairof and loches of the maine land and iles of the samyne in the same maner as they doe (exceptand alwayis the particular firthes of Lowtheane, Murray and Dumbartane,[38] and the boundis reservit for the salmound fischeing and indemnitie thairof contenit in the declaratioune gevin in to the lordis of his Majesties privie counsell be the nobilitie, gentrie and the saidis commissioneris of borrowis[39]), in the which caise and no uther wayis they declair they ar able to grant the said inlargement without thair awin utter undoing. Thairfoir humlie to supplicat his Majestie that since the fischeing within the iles and loches of the samyne and maine landis of this kingdome wilbe improffitable giff any busche fischeing be permittit betuix the Fairayheid in Stranaver[40] and the northeistmaist pairt of the Lewis and xiiii mylis from the eistmaist poynt of the said ile of the Lewis, and thairfoir his Majestie wald be pleasit to dischairge any busche fischeing thair, with libertie alwayis to the [fo. 424r] associatioun to fische within thair said boundis in maner as is presentlie accustomet be the natives quhilk is moist usefull in these pairtis. As also that his Majestie wald remove the straingeris furth of the Lewis and the iles adjacent to the samyn. As also that his Majestie wald appoint the particular tymes boith of busche fischeing and iles fischeing as salbe moist commodious for the samyne, which is fittest to be done in maner following, to witt the busche fischeing upoun the eist coast not to begin befoir the 24 day of Junii yeirlie and the iles fischeing upoune the first of September yeirlie.

Farder, since the libertie of traid and of packing and peilling of fisches does apperteine be grantis from his Majesties predicessouris to the frie royall borrowis of this realme, and that they at his Majesties desyre ar content and consentis that all dependaris of the said associatioune, Englische and Ires, salbe frie to pack and peill fisches and expoirt the samyne, that thairfoir his Majestie micht dischairge thame frome any uther traid within the said kingdome and iles thairof, and from all importatioune or exportatioune of any uther commodities ather forrane or native, utherwayis nor is aggriable to the lawis of the kingdome. And that they hyre none of the fischeris of the said kingdome to the prejudice of the natives. And that they expoirt no fisches bot these fisches which salbe takin be thame selffis. And that they buy none frome the native bot for thair present consumptioune. And that they

---

38 i.e. the Firth of Forth, the Moray Firth and the Firth of Clyde.

39 This seems a more true rendering than the Abstract, which has 'given in be the lords of his Majesties privie counsell, both nobilitie and gentry, and the said commissioners of burrows', see *RCRBS*, iv, 534–5.

40 Probably Farr Point, Caithness.

associat no strainger to thame selffis nor cullour straingeouris gudis under cullour of thair awin. And that nather Englische nor Ires fische any salmond fischeing within the said kingdome or iles thairof.

As also it may please his Majestie to grant to the subjectis of Scotland of the said associatioun libertie to fische frielie in all the coistis and seas of England and Ireland and iles of the samyne, and that alsweill heiringis and quhyt fische as pilschairtis, and that upoun the same conditoune, liberties and payment of customes as the natives doe and with the lyk libertie to pak and peill upoun the maineland and expoirt the samyne furthe thairof.

They ar also to supplicat his Majestie that this inlargement of traid in the matter of the fischeing may be no prejudice to the liberties of the saidis frie royall borrowis in no uther [fo. 424v] point of the same, and it wald pleis his Majestie to ratefie and approve the liberties alsweill in packing and peilling of fisches and exportatioune of the samyne as in all uther pointis grantit to thame ather be grantis frome his Majestie [or his][41] predecessouris.

They ar also to will thair commissioner in all the treattie of the fischeingis to advert the samyne be done to the utmoist advantage and leist prejudice of the borrowis that can be to his utmoist.

Item, to procure of his Majestie ane ratificatioun of the patent grantit to the borrowis of his Majesties kingdome of thair schipis and gudis in payment of customes in England and Irland as the natives thair. And since in Ireland notwithstanding of the said patent thair is ten schillingis of custome or impoist exactit of the tun of wines impoirtit within Ireland in Scottis bottomes, that his Majestie wald dischairge the samyne and ordaine the said patent to be obeyit in all pointis conforme to the tennour thairof.

Lastlie to informe his Majestie anent the prejudice sustainit be the frie royall borrowis in erectioune of the burghis of baronye with liberties of frie royall borrowis and in the usurpatioune maid be the saidis burghis of baronye upoun thair liberties. And thairfoir to supplicat his Majestie for remeid of the same conforme to his commissioun and act maid thairanent.

And finallie quhatsumever salbe incident and which may concerne the borrowis to obviat the same and to adverteis the toun of Edinburgh et sic subscribitur Andro Gray moderatour, Andro Ayinslie, Alexander Rid, Andro Wilsoune for Perth, Thomas Collingstoune for Aberdeine, Johne Cowane for Stirling, Andro Bell for Lynlythgow, Johne Leaper for St Androis, James Stewart, Mr James Cockburne, Johne Cunyinghame for Aire, Johne Mackiesoune, Johne Williamsoune Kirkcaldie, William Meikiljohne Bruntyland, David Alexander, George Kingyow, Patrick Wallace, Robert Grahame Montrose

---

[41] There is no space in the MS but the sense requires this insertion.

Vigesimo septimo Octobris I^m vi^c trigesimo secundo

[18]

The quhilk day thet commissioneris of borrowis being convenit, unlawis the borrowis of St Androis and Montrose ilkane of thame in ane unlaw of xx li. of money for depairting from this present conventioune befoir the subscryving of the buik and the saidis burghis to send the same with thair commissioner [to] [fo. 425r] the nixt generall conventioune of borrowis. And this to be in head off thair missive.[42]

---

42 The rest of fo. 425 is blank. There are no fos. 426–31, which suggests the loss of the minutes of a particular convention (see below, 123).

Particular Convention at Edinburgh, January 1633

[fo. 432r]

In the particular conventioun of borrowis haldin at the burgh of Edinburgh the aucht day of Januar the yeir of God 1633 yeiris be the commissioneris of borrowis underwrittin be vertew of ane missive letter direct to theme frome the said burgh of Edinburgh daittit the 14 of December last and produceit thair commissiounis as followis:

Edinburgh	Johnne Sinclair, James Danielstoune
Perth	Andro Gray
Dundye	James Boyter
Abirdein	Patrick Leslie
Stirling	Johnne Cowan
Lynlythgow	Williame Hamiltoun
Sanctandroes[1]	Robert Taelyeour
Glasgow	Gabriell Cuninghame
Aire	
Haddingtoun	Maister James Cokburne
Kirkcaldie	Johnne Williamesoun
Montrose	
Bruntyland	Williame Miklejohne

1

The same day the saidis commissioneris of borrowis electis, creattis and constituttis Johnne Sinclare, merchand, first in commissioun for the burght of Edinburgh, moderator during this present conventioun, wha compeirand accepted the said office in and upone him and gaive his aith *de fideli adminstratione*.[2]

2

Penultimo Januarii I^m vi^c trigesimo tertio

The quhilk day forsameikle as it haiveing pleased his Majestie upone ane remonstrance maid to him of the present abuse of the coyne within this kingdome, to direct ane letter to the lordis of his Majesties most honorabill privie counsall requyring thair advyse anent certan overtoures proponit be

---

1   St Andrews.
2   Literally, 'concerning faithful administration', i.e. he was promising to carry out the duties of moderator with diligence.

Monseur Briott[3] for [fo. 432v] reforming of the said abuse, which being impairtit to the commissioneris of borrowis togither with ane declaratioun made be him in certificatioun of the said propositouns, the saids commissioneris find the samin to conteyne in effect the cryeing doun of the haill dollouris and levelling of the same with his Majesties awin coyne, togither with ane overture for coyning of sum small speces of silver ten dynneir fynes, which both was fund be theme to be verie prejudiciall and hurtfull to the cuntrey for the reassounes more at lenth givin in to the saidis lordis theranent. Which propositioun and declaratioune of the said Maister Briott was lyikwayis communicat to the generall and maister of the coynyiehous, which was lyikwayis refutit be theme. As also the said maister coynyier proponit certan overtoures for reforming of the said abuse which in effect wer nathing bot heichting of the moneyis to fyve merks the unce, the enlairging of the bulyeoun, and the making of ane stock to him of the said bulyeoun and of ane gritt pairt of the pryce of the commoditie transportit into England and uther native commodities transportit be straingers be returning of ane grit pairt of the price thairof to him ather in the kingis owne money or in foraine money of ellevin dynneir fyne. Which overtoures being impairtit lyikwayis to the saids commissioneris they fand the same to be verie hurtfull and prejudiciall to the cuntrey and to be no sufficient remedie for reforming of the present abuse, for the ressounes more at lenth contenit in the answeris givin in be theme to the saidis overtoures. And thairfore desyrit the saidis lordis inrespect the whole mass of the money of this kingdome did consist in dollouris, and of the grit losse to ensew to the liedges of the sam sould at one tyme be levelled with his Majesties awin coyne, to crye doun the same by littill and littill, viz 12 d. at one tyme, 12 d. at one uther tyme, and according as the cuntrey sould be fund to abound with his Majesties awin coyne to dischairge the farder course thairof. As lyikwayis desyrit that such ordour micht be taiken with the bulyeoun that all compositioun or transporting thirfore sould be dischairged and everie merchand ordanit to bring in his owne bulyeoun in forrane coyne, and to ressave bak againe his Majesties awin coyne. As lyikwayis that sum small speces of coyne, different frome the Inglish reckning sould be struckin for the present supplie of the inlaik of small money within this kingdome. Whairwith the saids lordis of his Majesties secreit counsall being advysit they haif continewit the taking ordour with the dollouris till they be farder advysit theranent and hes promised to take ane satled course for the bulyeoun [fo. 433r] quhairby the money proceiding therof may disperse through the whole kingdome. As lyikwayis hes ordainit that sum small speces of silver, different frome

3   M. Nicolas Briot was engaged by Charles I to strike medals to commemorate the king's Scottish coronation and to rectify problems with the copper content of Scottish coin: see *RPC*, 2nd series, v, 107–8, 550.

the english reckning be coyned. And becaus the present commissioneris haiffing so long attendit can no longer abyid to disput the said mater of the dollouris and quhat may be maid out thairanent. And thairfore they ordaine the burgh of Edinburgh to attend such dyettes as salbe appointit be the saids lordis for the said mater to whome they for theme selffis and in name of the haill remanent borrowis give full powar and commissioun for ressaiving ane answer fra the saidis lordis and for agrieing and concluding anent the saids dollours conforme and in maner as is contenit in the propositiounis givin in be the saids borrowis and if they find the samin in anywayis to be disagrieable to protest against the same till the saids borrowis be furder hard and in thair names to disassent therfra, in which cair and as the said mater sall require farder advyse the present commissioners ordanis the said burgh of Edinburgh to conveyne with theme suche ane competent nomber of the borrowis as thai sall think neidfull for taking farder course in the said mater as salbe fund most expedient both for the weill of the kingdome and for thair owne estait. And the said burgh of Edinburgh to repoirt thair diligence heiranent till the nixt generall conventioun of borrowis. And this to be ane heid of the nixt missive. And the commissioner of Abirdein disassentit heirfra and protestit in the contrare.[4]

3

The same day forsamikle as the present commissioners of the borrowis understanding that his Majestie hes resolvit to visit his ancient kingdome this sommer and considdering that it is necessar for thair estait that some solid course be taiken for advancing of thair effaires in all tyme heirefter, thairfore they ordayne the burgh of Edinburgh to conveyne the haill remanent borrowis in dew tyme for advysing and concluding anent all such thingis as may concerne the weill of thair estait and to require ilk burgh to sand thair commissioneris sufficientlie instructit theranent under the payne of tuentie pundis ilk burgh. As lyikwayis concerning the dyet of the meitting of the burrowis at Sanctandroes the beginning of Julii nixt and the said burgh to report thair diligence heiranent to the nixt generall conventioun of borrowis. And this to be ane heid of the nixt missive.

[fo. 433v]
Particular conventioun of borrowis haldin at Edinburgh 14 December 1632 and upon the penult of Januarii 1633.[5]

---

4   This act is noted in the Abstract of Acts of Convention, *RCRBS*, iv, 536.
5   This seems to be the cover sheet for the preceding minutes, although there are no minutes of the December 1632 session, which may originally have been on fos. 426–31, which must have been lost at some point after the records were first foliated. Fo. 434 is blank and there appears to be no fo. 435.

Particular Convention at Edinburgh, June 1633

[fo. 436r]
In the particular conventioun of borrowes haldin at the burgh of Edinburgh the threttene day of Junii, the yeir of God ane thousand, sex hundreth and threttie three yeires be the commissioneres of borrowes underwrittin, be vertew of severall commissiounes or missives direct to thame from the said burgh of Edinburgh daitit the thrid and twentie twa dayes of Maii lastbypast, and produced thair commissiounes as followes:

Edinburgh	Johne Sinclare, Gilbert Kirkwood
Perth	Andro Gray
Dundye	Maister Alexander Wedderburne
Aberdeine	Paull Meinyeis
Striviling[1]	Thomas Bruce
Linlithgow	Andro Bell
Sanctandroes[2]	Johne Lepar
Glasgow	Gabriell Cuninghame
Aire	James Blaire
Haddingtoun	Maister James Cockburne
Dysert	Alexander Simpsoun
Kirkcaldie	Johne Williamesone
Montrose	Robert Keath
Cowpar	Robert Pitersone
Anstruther Easter	Robert Alexander
Drumfreis[3]	Maister Johne Corsine
Innernes[4]	Duncan Forbes
Bruntyland	Williame Mekiljohne
Innerkeithing[5]	Williame Blaikburne
Breichin	Johne Skynner
Irrwyne[6]	Robert Broun
Jedburgh	Alexander Kirktoun
Kirkcudbricht	Williame Glendinning
Caraill[7]	Johne Mackesone

1 Stirling.
2 St Andrews.
3 Dumfries.
4 Inverness.
5 Inverkeithing.
6 Irvine.
7 Crail.

Wigtoun	Thomas Mackie
Pettinweyme	James Stevinsone
Dumfermeling[8]	Patrick Cowpar
Anstruther Wester	Robert Richardsone
Selkirk	Williame Scott
Dumbar	George Purves
Dumbartane	Johne Sempill
[fo. 436v]	
Ranffrew[9]	Robert Hall
Lanerick[10]	Gedioun Jacke
Aberbrothok[11]	
Elgyne	Maister Johne Hay
Peibles	James Williamesone
Tayne	David Forrester
Culros	Adame Prymrois
Bamffe	Andro Baird
Quhitehorne[12]	Robert Creichtoun
Forfar	Maister David Pearsone
Rothesay	Mathow Spence
Nairne	
Forres	James Dumbare
Rutherglen	Johne Scott
Northberuick	Johne Mure
Culane	James Lawty
Kilranie[13]	Thomas Simpsone
Lawder	Alexander Wilkiesone
Annand	Edward Johnestoun
Lochmaeben	
Sanquhaire	Johne Creichtoun
Galloway[14]	Robert Gordoun

[1]
The same day the said commissioneres of borrowes electis, creates and
constitutes Johne Sincelare, merchand, first in commissioun for the burgh
of Edinburgh, moderator dureing the tyme of this present conventioun, wha

---

8   Dunfermline.
9   Renfrew.
10 Lanark.
11 Arbroath.
12 Whithorn.
13 Kilrenny.
14 New Galloway.

compeirand acceptit the said office in and upoun him and gave his aith *de fidelie adminstratione.*[15]

[fo. 437r]
Vigesimo nono Junii I^m vi^c trigesimo tertio
[2]
The quhilk day the commissioneres of borrowes being convenit, finding the course of thair affaires so to presse thame that thairby the dyet appointit of the generall meiting at Sanctandroes the beginning of Julii nixt cannot possibillie be keeped thairfore. Thairfoir they have continewed and continewes that dyet to the sext of August nixt, and ordanes the present commissioneres to acquaint thair borrowes herewith at thair home cuming and to send thair commissioneres sufficientlie instructed for anwereing the haill heades of the missive direct last to them be the burgh of Sanctandroes with full commissioun to them to conclud in al materes that may be incident at the said conventioun, and in speciall in the mater of the fischeing and inequalitie of the liberties betuix this[16] kingdome and the kingdome of England, and in the mater[17] of the impositiounes in France, oppressiounes of his Majestie of Spayne his subjectis, twa extraordinarie taxatiounes in the materes referrit be parliament to the lordis of his Majesties privie counsall. For the which caus they dissolve this present conventioun and continewes the said dyet in maner forsaid. And ordanes ane missive letter to this effect to be direct to the haill borrowes be thair agent upoun the borrowes chairges requyreing thame for keepeing of the said new dyet[18] under the pane of twentie punds, and for the takeing ordour with disordoures in this present conventioun and parliament. And thair generall clarke to subscryve the same in thair names, quhairanent thir presents salbe thair warrand.

[3]
The same day the said commissioneres considering the necessitie of thair effaires in the mater of the fischeing and the prejudice which this kingdome susteanes in the inequalitie of the libertie betuixt this kingdome and the kingdome of England and the necessitie in the taking cours in the materes of the twa extraordinare taxatiounes, customes of France and oppressiounes of the Dunkirkeres and utheres subjectis of his Majestie of Spaine, and

---

15 Literally, 'concerning faithful administration', i.e. he was promising to carry out the duties of moderator with diligence.
16 This word is preceded by 'thes'. The copyist presumably started to write 'these', realised his mistake but did not cross it out.
17 The phrase 'in the mater' is repeated.
18 This is preceded by 'said dyet the', presumably because of the omission of the word 'new' the first time the phrase was written.

how expedient it is that sum conclusioun be maid thairanent before his Majestie pas in to England. Thairfoir they give full power and commissioun to the burghes of Edinburgh, Aberdein, Glasgow, Aire, Haddingtoun, Dumfreis, Dumbartane, Anstruther Easter, Bruntyland, Krikcudbricht, to tak sum course anent the premissis in sua far as they may think may tend to the weill of the borrowes. And to report to the nixt generall conventioun of borrowis thair proceidinges thairanent.

Particular Convention at Edinburgh, July 1633

[fo. 437v]
In the particulare conventioun of borrowes haldin at the burght of Edinburgh the first day of Julij the yeir of God ane thousand sex hundreth and threttie three yeeres be vertew of the commissioun gevin to thame be the last preceiding conventioun be the commissioneres of borrowes underwrittin, viz

Edinburgh	Johne Sinclare
Aberdeine	Patrick Leslie
Glasgow	Gabriell Cuninghame
Haddingtoun	Maister James Cockburne
Dumfreis	Maister Johne Corsine
Dumbartane	Johne Sempill
Bamffe	Andro Bairde
Aire	James Blaire

[1]
The quhilk day the said commissioneres being con[venit ... con]siddered[1] the particulares remited unto them be the last preceiding conventioun, and finding no opportunitie for speakeing with his Majestie thairanent, thairfoir they ordane Johne Sinclare, Mr James Cockburne, Maister Alexander Guthrie or any two of thame with suche utheres of the borrowes as they can finde for the tyme to attend his Majestie at his cuming backe to this toun the tend of this instant, and to acquaint his Majestie with the said particulares remitted unto this present conventioun and to obtene his Majesties answer thairanent giff possibillie they can befoir his passing into England, and to report thair diligence thairanent to the nixt generall conventioun of borrowes that sum farder course may be takin thairanent.

---

1   This is a copying error, as the first line ends with 'con' which must have been the beginning of 'convenit'. Presumably because the second or a subsequent line also ended with 'con' and another began with 'siddered', the copyist's eye jumped from the end of the first line to the beginning of that one, and thus one or more whole lines were omitted. It is likely that the missing text was something like 'venit anent the third act of the last particular convention at Edinburgh on the 29th of June and having con'.

General Convention at St Andrews, August 1633

[fo. 438r]

In the generall conventioun of borrowes haldin at the burgh of[1] Sanctandroes the sext day of August the yeir of God I^m vi^c and threttie three yeires:

Edinburgh	Johne Sincelare, Gilbert Kirkwood
Perth	Andro Gray
Dundye	James Simpsone
Aberdeine	Patrick Leslie
Stirling	Johne Johnestoun
Linlithgow	Williame Hammiltoun
Sanctandroes[2]	Robert Taelyeour, Johne Lepar
Glasgow	Gabriell Cuninghame
Aire	George Maessoun
Haddingtoun	Patrick Broun
Dysart	Alexander Simpsone
Kirkcaldie	Johne Williamesone
Montrose	James Williamesone
Cowpar	Robert Pitersone
Anstruther Eister	George Hammiltoun
Dumfreis	
Innernes[3]	be ratificatioun
Bruntyland	Capitane Andro Watsone
Innerkeithing[4]	be exemptioun and ratificatioun produced be
Dumfermeling	
Kinghorne	Maister Robert Cunninghame
Breichin	produced thair exemptioun produced be agent
Irrwyne[5]	Maister Johne Peibles
Jedburgh	Johne Moscrope
Kirkcudbricht	Johne Ewart younger
Wigtoun	
Pettinweyme	George Kingyew
Dumfermeling[6]	Peter Law

---

1 There is a scribal error here, with 'Ed' written presumably because the copyist began to write 'Edinburgh' but realised his mistake.
2 St Andrews.
3 Inverness.
4 Inverkeithing.
5 Irvine.
6 Dunfermline.

Anstruther Wester	Robert Richardsone
Selkirk	Williame Scott
Dumbar	George Purves
Dumbartane	Johne Sempill
Ranffrew[7]	David Monte[gomerie][8]
[fo. 438v]	
Lanerick[9]	Gedioun Jacke
Aberbrothok[10]	Maister James Pearsoune
Elgyne	
Peibles	be exemptioun and ratificatioun produced be agent
Carraill[11]	David Maxwell
Tayne	be exemptioun and ratificatioun produced be agent
Culros	Maister Edward Blaw[12]
Bamffe	be Andro Bairde
Quhitehorne[13]	be exemptioun and ratificatioun produced be agent
Forfar	Maister David Pearsone
Rothesay	
Nairne	
Forres	be exemptioun and ratificatioun produced be agent
Rutherglen	Johne Pinkartoun
Northberwick	Johne Mure
Culane	
Kilranie[14]	be exemptioun and ratificatioun produced be agent
Lochmaben	
Sanquhair	
Galloway[15]	

[1]
{Electioun of the moderator}
The same day the said commissioneres of borrow[es] electes, creates

---

7 Renfrew.
8 The name is written as 'Monte' but see act no '[20]', below, which identifies this
   commissioner.
9 Lanark.
10 Arbroath.
11 Crail.
12 This is probably the same person as Mr Edward Blair, commissioner to a convention of
    estates in 1630 (RPS, A1630/7/1) but here, and at the general convention in 1634, his name
    is clearly 'Blaw'. G.F. Black, The Surnames of Scotland (Edinburgh, 1993), 82, contains other
    instances of the name in Culross and the surrounding district, so it could be that his name
    is incorrectly recorded in the parliamentary record.
13 Whithorn.
14 Kilrenny.
15 New Galloway.

and constitutes Robert Taileyour, first in commissioun for the burch of
Sanctandroes, to be moderator dureing this present conventioun, wha
compeirand, acceptit the said office in and upoun him and gave his aith *de
fideli adminstratione*.[16]

[fo. 439r]

2

The same day the said commissioneres of borrowes appointis thair houres
of meitting to be and begun at nyne houres in the morning and to lest
quhill twelff houres at noon, and efter noone at twa houres till sex acloake
at nicht and sic as ar absent at the calling of the rolles to pay ane unlaw of
sex schillinges, and they that passis out of the hous without leave askit, to
pay ane unlaw as said is, and they that passis fra this present conventioun[17]
befoir the dissolveing thairof, to pay ane unlaw as absentis, and that nane
speake unrequyrat without leave askit and gevin nor yit to interrup[18] thair
reassoning with thair voiting under the pane of ane unlaw of sex schillinges
toties quoties.[19]

3

The same day the said commissioneres for better ordour keepeing in all
conventiounes heirefter statute and ordanit, lykeas they be thir presents statutes and ordanes that in all tyme coming, the burgh quhair any meiting of
the borrowis salbe indicted either generall or particular sall caus warne the
borrowes who are to direct thair commissioneris to the said conventioun
and sall report the delyverie of the missive quhair they sall requyre the
said borrowes for sending of thair commissioneres be ane certificat under
the hand of sum of the magistrates of the burgh who are wairnit of thair
ressaveing of the said missive, which being reportit, it is declairit and aggreit
upoun be the commissioneres present that the same salbe ane sufficient
warrand for unlawing these that sallhappin to be absent as also for proceiding
against them or any persone wairnit to compeir. And lykewayes ordaines ilk
burgh that salbe requyrit to give thair certificatt of the ressaveing of the said
missive under the pane of xx li., and ordanes ilk commissioner to report this
act and statute to thair borrowes at thair home cuming that non pretend
ignorance. And ordaines the same to be contenit in the nixt missive.[20]

---

16 Literally, 'concerning faithful administration', i.e. he was promising to carry out the duties
    of moderator with diligence.
17 This phrase is preceded by 'fra this conventioun'.
18 This is usually written as 'intermix', i.e. once it comes to voting, which was oral, further
    argument was not permitted.
19 As often as it shall happen, i.e. for each offence.
20 This act is noted in the Abstract of Acts of Convention, *RCRBS*, iv, 536.

[fo. 439v]

[4]

The same day ordanes the burgh of Irrvyn to produce thair diligence in writt to the nixt generall conventioun of burrowes in restraining of the inhabitantes of the Larges, Fairlie, Kelburne and Saltscoates[21] from the usurping the liberties of the said royall borrowes under[22] the pane of twentie pundis. And this to be ane heid of the nixt missive.

[5]

The same day the commissioneres ordanes the burght of Caraill to produce thair diligence in writt to the nixt generall conventioun of borrowes in restraining of the inhabitantis of Levin and Sanct Minnence[23] from usurpeing the liberties of the frie royall borrowes under the pane of twentie punds. And this to be ane heid of the nixt misive.

[6]

The same day anent the eleventh act of the last generall conventioun of borrowes haldin at the burgh of Montrose the thrid day of Julii last 1632 yeires, anent the restraining of burgessis from projecting of monopolies or being partineres in monopolies directlie nor indirectlie,[24] and for this caus ordanes that it salbe aded to the burghes aithe[25] that nane sould project the same or be partineres thairin. The present commissioneres ordanes ilk commissioner of new to intimat the said act to thair burghes at thair homecuming. And ilk burgh to report thair diligence in writt in keepeing and fulfilling of the said act to the nixt generall conventioun of borrowes under the pane of xx li. And this to be ane head of the nixt missive.

[fo. 440r]

[7]

The same day the said commissioneres anent the threttie fyfte act of the last generall conventioun of borrowes haldin at the burgh of Monterose the sext day of Julii last 1632 yeires concerning the particular conventiounes.[26] The present commissioneres haiffing considered the thrid act of the particular conventiounes haldin at Edinburgh the 22 of Appryll 1626[27] and the fourtene act of the last generall conventioun of borrowes haldin at Dysart the

---

21 Largs, Fairlie, Kilbirnie, Saltcoats, in Ayrshire.
22 'under' is repeated.
23 St Monans, Fife.
24 See above, 84–5.
25 This should probably be 'burges aithe', i.e. the oath a new burgess took upon entry.
26 See above, 99.
27 RCRBS, iii, 219.

6 of Julii 1632,[28] they ratifie and approve the same and ordanes the ordour prescryved be the said actis to be keeped in all tyme coming.

Septimo Augusti I^m vi^c trigesimo tertio

[8]

The same day the said commissioneres of borrowes being convenit, anent the threttye sext and fourtie sevin actis of the last generall conventioun of borrowes haldin at the burghe of Monterose in the moneth of Julii 1632 yeires concerning the treding of unfrie skipperes and the restraineing of the nychtboures of the burghes from being partineres with them.[29] The present commissioneres findes it expedient and thairfor statutes and ordaines that thair be no pairt nor portage be allowed to maisteres or marineres bot that suche ane competent allowance be gevin to thame in thair hyres quhairby they may leave in ane honest maner. And quhairas in the mater of the fisching it micht seeme the allowance of portage to be necessar, in that caice it is thocht fitt and ordanit that the merchand that imployes thame sould aggrie with them for thair portage befoir hand. And so all evill that that way does incure may be takin away. And farder for restraining of unfrie skipperes dwelling at unfrie ports, it is statute and ordainit that in na tyme coming any merchand be partneres either in schippes or goods with the said unfrie skipperes under the paine of ane hundreth punds, and deprivatioun of thair libertie. And becaus for the present thair is many burgessis that are partineres with them, thairfoir the said commissioneres ordaines that all suche burgessiss will betuixt this and the nixt [fo. 440v] generall conventioun of borrowes frie themselffes of the schipes belongin unto them or uther wayes drawe them to thair awin pairtis under the same pane to be exacted without favour of the transgressoures of this present ordinance be the burghe quhair they dwell. And ordanes ilk commissioner to intimat the same[30] to thair burghes and nixt nichtboures, and to put the same to dew executioun against them under the paine of fourtie pundis, and to report thair diligence heirin to the nixt generall conventioun of borrowes in intimating and executing of this present act under the said pane. And this to be ane head of the nixt missive.[31]

[9]

The samen day the said commissioneris being convenit, anent the tuentie aucht act of the last generall conventioune of borrowis haldin at the burght

---

28 This should be 1631 and is therefore the last general convention but one. See above, 148.
29 See above, 99, 104.
30 This phrase (from 'And') is repeated in the MS.
31 Another version of this act is contained in the Abstract of Acts of Convention, RCRBS, iv, 536.

of Montrose the fyft day of Julii 1632 yeires concerneing Mr David Wedderburne his grammer.[32] The commissioneris of borrowis ratifies and approves
the samen and ordainis the samen to be taucht within the whole grammer
scholes of the frie borrowes of this realme and to begin at Michaelmes nixt
and ordaines ilk burght to caus thair schole maisteris imbrace and teache the
samen and to report thair diligence thairanent to the nixt generall conventioune of borrowis under the paine of tuentie pundis. And this to be ane
heid of the nixt missive.

[10]
The same day anent that heid of the missive concerning the factouris in
France mentionat in the tent act of the particular conventioun of borrowis
haldin at the burght of Edinburgh the teuntie saxt of October last.[33] The
said commissioneris finding the evillis mentionat in the said act to continew
and that nane is presentlie themselffis to undergoe that burding, thairfoir
it is thought guid that ilk commissioner present sall requyre thair burghes
for advysing upon sum solid course to be takin thairin, and for restraneing
of thair nightbouris for imployment of him bot sic salbe authorised be
the borrowes and sall subject themselffis to the lawis to be sett doune be
them. And ordaines the burght of Edinburgh to requyre the borrowis to be
wairnit to the said meting for setting doune ane solide and constant course
thairin to which borrowis the present commissioneris gives thair full pwer
and commissioun to doe thairin all and quhatsumevir thai might doe themselffis. [fo. 441r] And to report thair diligence heiranent to the nixt generall
conventioune of borrowis. And this to be ane heid of the nixt missive.

[11]
The same day the said commissioneris of borrowis being convenit, anent the
fourt act of the last generall conventioun of borrowis haldin at the burght
of Montrose the thrid day of Julii 1632 yeiris concerneing the burght of
Glasgow in sending thair commissioneris to the last generall conventioune
of borrowis.[34] The saidis commissioneris findis the said act satisfied be thame
and ordaines them so to continew in all tyme cumeing under the paine of
all hiest sensuir.

[12]
The same day anent the saxt act of the last generall conventioune of
borrowis haldin at the burght of Montrose the thrid day of Julii 1632 yeiris,
ordaineing the burght of Cowper to have producet thair diligence to this

32 See above, 94–5.
33 See above, 114–15.
34 See above, 82.

present conventioun in causing of Thomas and William Andersones indwelleris in Newburghe in Fyff to desist frome usurping the liberties of the
frie royall borrowes under the paine of tuentie pundis. Compeirit Robert
Peittersone commissioner for the said burghe of Cowper and reportit his
diligence thairanent with the which report the said commissioneris being
advysit they find the said burght to have done no diligence and thairoir to
have incurrit the unlaw contenit in the said act. And thairfoir ordaines the
said burght to produce sufficient diligence againes the said persones to the
nixt generall conventioun of borrowis in causing them ayther find cautioun
to desist or in making thame selffis frie in sum frie burghe under the paine
of fourtie pundis and continewis the uplifting of the said former unlaw to
the said nixt generall conventioune of borrowis. And to be ane heid of the
nixt missive.

[13]
The same day anent the aucht act of the last generall conventioun of
borrowis haldin at Montrose the thrid day of Julii 1632 yeiris, ordaineing the
burght of Forfar to have producet thair diligence to this present conventioun
in the restraineing the inhabitantis of Killemuire[35] in Angus frome usurping
the liberties of the frie royall borrowis.[36] Compeirit Mr David Pearsone
commissioner for the said burght of Forfar and producet letteres raissit at
thair instance againes the said inhabitantis quhilk the present commissioneris
acceptis for diligence at this tyme, and ordaines them to produce thair farder
diligence in executing and discussing of the said letteris to the nixt generall
conventioun of borrowis under the paine of fourtie pundis. And this to be
ane heid of the nixt missive.

[fo. 441v]
[14]
The same day anent the fyft act of the last generall conventioune haldin at
the burght of Montrose the fourt day of Julii last 1632 yeiris and auchtein
act of the said conventioune anent the burghe of Dumfreis to have producet
thair diligence to this present conventioun againes certane unfrie persones
mentionat in the said actis.[37] The said burghe of Dumfreis not compeiring
be thair commissioner, the said commissioneris ordaines them to produce
the lyk diligence as they sould have producet to this present conventioun to
the nixt generall conventioune of borrowis againes the said unfrie persones
mentionat in the said actis under the paine of fourtie pundis. And this to be
ane heid of the nixt missive.

---

35 Kirriemuir, Angus.
36 See above, 83.
37 That should be 15th rather than 5th. See above, 86.

[15]

The same day anent the tuentie aucht act of the last generall conventioun of borrowis haldin at the burghe of Montrose the fourt day of Julii 1632 yeiries and the twelft act of the particular conventioun of borrowis haldin at Edinburgh in October last, ordaineing the burgh of Bamff to produce thair diligence to this present conventioun in searching and finding out of the auld evidentitis.[38] For obedience quhairof compeirit Androw Baird commissioner for the said burght of Bamff and reportit his diligence in seiking of the auld evidentis of the said burght and lykwayes producet ane chairtour of the said burghe with the ratificatioun thairof in this last parliament which the borrowis acceptis for diligence.

[16]

The same day compeirit Mr Alexander Guthrie and producet ane table of the actis of borrowis maid and sett doun be him whiche the saidis borrowis acceptis and ordaines to be keipit amonges thair registeris and yeirlie actis that pass to be addit thairto.[39]

[17]

The same day anent the threttie twa act of the last generall conventioune of borrowis haldin at the burght of Montrose the saxt day of Julii 1632 yeiris concerneing the visitatioun of the Walter of Forthe.[40] Compeirit the commissioneris of Cullros, Pettinweyme, Anstruther Eister and excuisit thair broughes thairanent, quhairwith the present commissioneris being advysit they find and declair that burghes of Pettinweyme and Anstruther Eister to have done no diligence and thairfoir to have incurrit the unlaw contenit in the said act. Yet for caussis moveing them, they dispens with the uplifting thairof till the nixt generall conventioun and as of befoir ordaine the saidis thrie frie broughes to vissit the said walter [fo. 442r] and for this effect they ordaine the brughes of Anstruther Eister and Pettinweyme to send commissioneris for theme to the burghe of Culross the secund of September nixt without any farder advertisment to be maid to them. And the said burght of Culross to have thair commissioneris reddy againes the said day and all thrie with all convenient diligence to visit and try the said walter and deipis thairof one both the sydis and to sett doune the samen in writt with thair oppinions anent the estait thairof since the last yeir. Whiche being doun, ordaines them betuixt the aucht of the samen monethe to direct the samen to the burghe of Edinburgh under the paine of fourty pundis ilk burghe,

---

38 That should be 21st rather than 28th. See above, 89–90, 115.
39 No such table appears to be extant among the records of the convention. Presumably it formed part of the lost volume covering the years 1631–1649.
40 The Firth of Forth, see above, 97–8.

whiche being ressaveit be them they ordaine the burghe of Edinburgh to aquant the lordis of his Majesties counsall thairwith, that gif neid beis sum convenient course may be takin for redres of any hurt doune to the said walter and the said burghe and burghes to report ane diligence heireanent to the nixt generall conventioun of borrowis. And this to be ane heid of the nixt missive.

Octavo Augusti I^m vi^c trigesimo tertio
[18]
The quhilk day the commissioneris of borrowis being conveinet, anent the fyft act of the last generall conventioun of borrowis haldin at the burghe of Montrose the thrid day of Julii 1632 yeiris ordaineing the burghe of Dysart to have producet thair diligence to this present conventioun in causing Williame Touche indueller in Levin ather mak his residence within thair broughe or in depryving him of thair liberties under the paine of tuentie pundis.[41] Compeirit Alexander Simpsoun commissioner for the said burght of Dysart and producet ane act of thair court of thair said burght under the subscriptioune of thair clerk of the dait the 17 Aprile last, depryving the said Williame Touche of thair liberties and friedomes of thair said burghe, whiche the borrowis acceptis for diligence.

[19]
The same day ordaines the burghe of Elgin to produce thair diligence to the nixt generall conventioune of borrowis in restrayneing of certane inhabitantis in Garmouthe[42] lyand within thair shereffdome from usurping of the liberties of the frie royall borrowis and ordaines the agent to concure and assist with thame in thair persuit and to report thair diligence heiranent to the nixt generall conventioun of borrowis. And this to be ane heid of the nixt missive.

[fo. 442v]
[20]
The same day anent the fourtie fourt act of the last generall conventioune of borrowis haldin at the burght of Montrose the saxt day of Julii 1632 yeiris ordaining the burght of Ranfrew to use diligence againes certaine of thair unfriemen.[43] Compeirit David Montgomerie commissioner for the said burght of Renfrew and producet letteres raissit and execuit at thair instance againes certaine persones whiche being consideered be the said borrowis they ordainet the burght of Dumbartane to give in the names of suche

---

41 See above, 83.
42 Garmouth, at the mouth of the Spey, in Moray.
43 See above, 102–3.

unfrie persones dwelling within the liberties of the said frie burght as they sall find out to the agent. Whiche being delyverit ordaines the said agent to send the same under his hand to the burght of Ranfrew and the said burght to produce thair diligence heiranent to the nixt generall conventioune of borrowis in causing the said persones to be givin upe to them be the agent to desist frome usurping the liberties of the frie borrowis conforme to the act maid in this last conventioune of estaittis[44] under the paine of tuentie pundis. And this to be ane heid of the nixt missive.

[21]

The same day ordaines the burghe of Glasgow to produce thair diligence to the nixt generall conventioun of borrowes in causeing Williame Hill in Grinocke thair alledged burges mak his actuall residence with them or in depryveing him of thair liberties. As also if he sall reside with them to caus him desist from selling of any merchandice in unfrie places conforme to the ordour observit amangst the borrowes. And this to be ane heade of the nixt missive.

[22]

The same day anent that head of the missive concerning the supplicatioun gevin in be the burgh of Jedburghe craveing helpe to that bridge leading to thair toun over Tyet.[45] The commissioneres considering how necessar that brige is for the standing of that burgh hes grantit and gevin for helpe and building and reparatioun of that brige[46] the sowme of twa hundreth punds usuall money of this realme, and ordaines ilk burghe to send thair pairt thairof conforme to the taxt roll to the nixt generall conventioun of the borrowes under the pane of twentie punds and that by and attour the payment of thair pairt of the said sowme. And this to be ane head of the nixt missive.

[23]

The same day anent the twentie fourt act of the last generall conventioun of borrowes haldin at the burgh of Montrose the fyft day of Julii the yeir of God 1632 yeires anent the greivances sustanit be the natioun at thair staippill port of Campheir in default of the [fo. 443r] magistrates of the said toun and the conservatores dealling with them thairanent.[47] Compeirit

---

44 This may refer to the general ratification of burgh privileges by parliament in 1633 (*RPS*, 1633/6/39), rather than the last convention of estates which met in 1630 but passed no such ratification (see *RPS*, A1630/7).

45 The river Tweed, or possibly the Teviot. See above, 100.

46 The MS also includes the phrase 'of the the said brige' here.

47 See above, 91–2.

Maister Patrick Drummond conservatour and declairit his deallings in the said mater and of the obstacle he had throw the not cumming of the borrowes letter. With the which the present commissioneres being advysed, ordaines ane letter to be direct to the magistrates of the said toun in thair names requyring thame reallie to tak away the said grievances betuixt and Mertemes nixt or utherwayes to expect no farder from them. And in that caice lykewayes ordained the said conservatour to try the myndes of the magistrates of Middelburgh or suche uther tounes in the Low Cuntreyes as he thinkes meit anent suche conditiounes as may be obtenit be thame of them if the borrowes sall herefter be pleassed to establish thair staippill with them, and to adverties the toun of Edinburgh thairanent betuixt and Januarii nixt that thairefter it being knawin that the magistrattis of Campheir does not remove thair just greivances and that the said toun of Middelburgh are willing to give honourabill and sufficient conditiounes, ilk burgh may be requyrit for sending thair commissioneres sufficientlie instructed for tham chainging of the said staippill. And the said conservatour to report his diligence heiranent to the nixt generall conventioun of borrowes. And this to be ane heade of the nixt missive.

[24]

The same day quhairas the commissioneres of borrowes being informit that thair factoures at thair staippill port of Campheir does by all equitie and reassoun mak rebaites upoun thair merchand billes at thair awin hand without any warrand from thair merchand, notwithstanding of the former act maid thairanent at thair last generall conventioun haldin at the burghe of Montrose whiche is lickelie to grow to ane great abuse to the heavie prejudice of the merchandis of this kingdome. For remeid quhairof it is statute and ordanit lykeas the present commissioneres statutes and ordaines that no factor sall heirefter attempt to mak rebaites of the merchand billes at thair awin handes without any warrand as said is under the paine of deprivatioun of thair said office. And ordaines the said conservatour being present when any complaintes salbe maid to him thairanent to caus the said factores to refound the hurt susteanit be the saidis merchandis, and to intimat this present act to the said factores in ane court to be haldin be him to that effect. And to report his diligence heiranent to that effect and to report his diligence heiranent in the nixt generall conventioun of borrowes. And this to ane head of the nixt missive.

[fo. 443v]

[25]

The same day anent the twentie nynte act of the last generall conventioun of borrowes haldin at the burghe of Montrose the sext day of Julii 1632 yeires anent the compts of Robert Baetie factor, collector for the ministeres dewties at Campheir.[48] Compeirit Patrick Suittie, indweller in Campheir and produced the said Robert Bawties his comptis subscryvit with his hand of his intromissioun with the impost from the sextene of September 1631 inclusive till the sextene of August thairefter 1632 allso inclusive. Whiche being examined they finde the same to extend to the sowme of ane hundreth threttie twa punds four schillinges Fleymes money and his depursementis to the sowme of twa hundreth threttie nyne pundis aucht schillinges ane great Fleymes money.[49] And sua they finde thair is addebtit to the compter the sowme of ane hundreth and sevin pundes ane great Fleymes money whiche they ordane James Weir, present collector, to pay to him of the readiest of the said collectioun and the said sowme salbe allowed to him in his comptes of his intromissioun with the said impost.

[26]
The same day quhairas the said commissioneres of borrowes be thair twentie nynt act of thair last generall conventioun of borrowes haldin at the burgh of Montrose the sext day of Julii 1632 yeires did appoint James Weir to be collector of the ministeres dewties at Campheir from the first of September last 1632 yeires till the first of September thairefter in this instant yeir of God 1633 yeires,[50] and ordaines him to give his aithe *de fideli administratione officii*[51] to the conservator or his deputes and to ingadder the said impost and to mak payment to the minister, reader and utheres conforme as is allowed to them be the said commissioneres and to send home his comptis of his intromissioun with the said impost from the first of September last till this present conventioun verified be the skipper and merchand as factor in absence of the merchant as at mair lenth is contenit in the said act. Thairfoir the said commissioneres ordaines the said James Weir with Charles Hammiltoun and Thomas Weir his souerties to be wairnit to compeir to the nixt generall conventioun for produceing of the said comptis with his intromissioun with the said impost and for answearing [fo. 444r] for not fullfilling the heades of the said act under the paine of deprivatioun. And this to be ane head of the nixt missive. And ordains thair clerke be ane letter in thair names to requyre the said James Weir for his effect, quhairanent thir presentis salbe his warrand.

---

48 See above, 95–6.
49 The word 'which' appears here, probably a copying error resulting from its appearance immediately after the phrase 'ane great Fleymes money' a few lines below – presumably the copyist's eye missed a couple of lines, the error was noticed but the superfluous word was retained.
50 See above, 95–6.
51 A longer version of the normal phrase, this literally means, 'concerning faithful administration of [his] office', i.e. he was promising to carry out his duties with diligence.

[27]

The same day the said commissioneres of borrowes electes, creates and constitutes Thomas Cunninghame, factor at Campheir, according to the custome to be collector of the impost grantit for defraying of the minister, readeris thair chairges at thair staippill port of Campheir from the first of September nixt till the first of September nixt thairefter in the yeir of God 1634 yeires. And ordaines him to give his aithe *de fideli administratione* to the conservator or his deputes, to ingadder the said impost and to mak payment to the said minister, reader and otheres as is allowed to them be the said commissioneres of borrowes, and to send hom his accompt of his intromissioun with the said impost from the said first day of September nixt till the nixt generall conventioun of borrowes verified be the skipper and merchand or factor in absence of the merchandis with the said minister and reader thair dischairges. And sicklyke ordaines the conservator or his deputis at the beginning to tak his aithe in oppin court to be haldin be thame to that effect and that he sall dischairge his lealle[52] and trew dewtie at the said collectioun and sall uplifte from the merchandis fa[c]tores and skipperes thair trew and just pairt according to the quantitie of thair goodis that thai sall happin to have according to his knawledge and that he sall chairge him selff thairwith and omit no thing thairof and that he sall collect it be himselff and no uther wayes dureing the tyme of his collectioun except in caice of seiknes or necessitie. And ordaines letteres to be direct to the said Thomas Cunninghame factor in thair names for that effect. And thair generall clerk to subscryve the samyne, quhairanent thir presents salbe his warrand. And the said Thomas with the said conservator to report thair diligence heiranent to the nixt generall conventioun of borrowes. And this to be ane heade of the nixt missive.

[28]

The same day compeirit Mr Alexander Guthrie and produced the act of parliament maid in favoures of the borrowes at this last parliament, whiche they ordaine to be insert in thair borrow court bookes and quhairof the tennour followes. In the parliament haldin at Edinburgh upoun the [fo. 444v] twentie aucht day of Junii 1633 yeires our soverane lord and[53] estates of this present parliament hes ratified and approved, and be the tennor heirof ratifies and approves of new all actis and statutes of parliament maid be his Majesties predicessoures in favoures of the frie borrowes of this realme and burgesses and inhabitantis of the samyne with all priviledges, fridomes, liberties and immunities grantit and gevin to the haill borrowes in the gennerall in any

---

52 This word is repeated in the MS.
53 The MS contains the additional phrase 'estates of parliament' here.

tyme bypast be any of our soverane lord his Majesties most nobill progeni-
tores, with all that hes followit or may follow thairupoun,[54] and decernes
and declaires the samyne to haiff full strenth, force and effect in all tymes
heirefter, sua that the samyne may be put to full and dew executioun in
all pointis and specaillie without prejudice of the generallie abonewrittin,
his Majestie and estates ratifies the act of parliament maid be his hienes
grandfather umquhill King James the thrid,[55] 16, 1466, 2, P, C, 11,[56] ordeaning
that nane saile nor pas in merchandice out of the realme bot frie men or
burgesses dwelling within burghe or thair familiares, factores, servandes being
with thame in houshold at meit and drink, except and reserveand to the
prelattes, lordis, barrounes clerkis as in the said act is contenit and all uther
exceptiounes contenit in any uther act of parliament in force preceiding
the day and daite heirof. And siclyke the act of parliament maid be King
James the fourt of worthie memorie in the parliament haldin at Edinburgh
the elluenth day of Marche 1503 yeires, Ca, 84,[57] ordering that na persone
dwelling out of borrowes use any merchandice nor topsell wyne, walx nor
silk, spycerie, wade, nor yit sicklyke stuffe nor staippill goodis, and that nane
packe nor peall in Leith nor uther places without the kinges borrowes under
the pane of escheat of the goodis thatt beis peilit or topped sauld packit
contrair that statute. And sickelyke the 152 act of umquhill King James the
sext his twelff parliament,[58] ordaining that na persone exerce the traffique
of [fo. 445r] mairchandice bot burgesses of frie borrowes under the paine of
escheatt of thair haill goodis and geir, the ane halff to his Majestie and the
uther halff to the burgh apprehender and geveing power to everie burgh
be thame selves or ane collector commissioner deput be thame, to searche
the said unfrie menis goods intromet thairwith as escheatt either within the
cuntrey or in any uther pairt, to arreist, call, follow or persew befoir unsus-
pect baillies to be creat be thame. As also the sext act of King James the
sext his nynt parliament[59] ordaining letteres of horning to be direct against
unfrie men not being burgesses of frie royall borrowes to finde cautioun
for desisiting fra usurpeing thair liberties in all the heades, clausses and
circumstances and articles thairof. Lykeas his Majestie and estates declaires
that the said liberties and priviledges mentionat in the said acts are onlie

---

54 The MS contains the additional phrase 'and decernes and ordaines the samyne' here.
55 James III was actually Charles I's great-great-great-grandfather.
56 This appears to refer to the second parliament of 1466 which met in January 1466/7, the
    first (not the eleventh) act of which is the one referred to here: see RPS, 1467/1/1.
57 See RPS, 1504/3/55. This parliament sat in 1504 by modern reckoning and the statute in
    question was passed on 15 March 1503/4.
58 See RPS, 1592/4/96.
59 If 1592 was James VI's twelfth parliament, then 1584 was the ninth but no act relating to
    unfree traders was passed in 1584. It may refer to one of two acts from 1579: see RPS,
    1579/10/51–2.

proper and competent to the frie royall borrowes that hes voatt in parliament and beares burthen with the rest of the frie royall borrowes and na utheres, prohibeiting and dischairgeing all persones wha are not burgesses of the said frie royall borrowes and beares no burthen with the rest off all useing and exerceing of the liberties and priviledges forsaid in all tyme cuming. And ordaines letteres of horning may be direct to the lords of counsall at the instance of all borrowes upoun the foirsaidis priviledges and former actes of parliament maid thairupoun and this present act in all tymes to cum for puting the samyne to dew executioun with all rigour against them that does in the contrare or cumes in the contrair of the said actes and priviledges forsaid without calling of any pairtie. Extractit furthe of the bookis of parliament be me Sir John Hay of Land[60] knicht, clerke of our soverane lordis register, counsall and rollis, under my signe and subscriptioun manuall. Sic subscribitur JHay, Clericus Registri.[61]

Nono Augusti I^m vi^c trigesimo tertio
[29]
The quhilk day the commissioneres of borrowes being convenit, anent that heade of the missive concerning the disordoures amangst the borrowes in parliament and utheres conventiounes, the present commissioneres considering the many evillis redounding to thair estate throw dew advyse in materes of estate proponit throw the inlaike of lauchfull and uniforme concurrence as is requisit and expedient in the membres of ane body, and finding that in the conventioun haldin at Cowpare the nynt of Maii 1586 for eschewing of all disordoures and avoyding of differences in voates, it hes bene statute that all thair conventiounes sould be keeped be the commissioneres of [fo. 445v] borrowes befoir the said publict meittinges and that thair commissioneres sould be men favouring and practised in thinges concerning thair estate and of thair degrie and rankes,[62] as also the conventioun haldin at Aberdene the 14 of Junii 1590 ordanit that all matteres to be proponit in suche lyke meittinges sould be first reassounit[63] and concluded amang themselves and quhat sould be concluded they sould remaine constant in that and at that conclusioun to abyde but variance,[64] and sickelyke in that conventioun haldin at Glasgow in Julii 1508[65] the commissioneres thene convenit statute and ordanit that

---

60 This is either 'Lane' or 'Land', the latter being most likely judging by the size of the terminal letter. He was normally known as Sir John Hay of Barro, then Lord Barro after his appointment in 1634 as an ordinary lord of session, see J.A. Inglis, 'Sir John Hay, the "Incendiary"', *Scottish Historical Review*, 15 (1918), 124–45.

61 This act is given in full in the Abstract of Acts of Convention, *RCRBS*, iv, 536–7.

62 *RCRBS*, i, 209–10.

63 The MS also contains the phrase 'and reassounit' here.

64 *RCRBS*, i, 339.

65 This should be 1598, see *RCRBS*, ii, 31–2.

na burghe sould send to parliamentis, conventiounes of estates or borrowes ane commissioner above the degre of ane merchand traffiquare indweller within thair burghe and bearing burdene with the same within the same and for whom the burghe sould be answeirable, and in that conventioun haldin at Haddingtoun in Julii 1603 ordaining them to be suche as may tyne and wyne in the commoun causes of the borrowes[66] or in the particular of thair awin burghe, and farder in the conventioun haldin at Selkirk the sext of Julii 1608 it was ordanit that all burghes sould send thair commissioneres twa dayes befoir the parliament without the citatioun to convyne at the burghe quhair the same sould be indicted with sufficient commissiounes not onlie in the materes in the parliament bot also in the materes in the borrowes to concure and with another[67] and last in the conventioun haldin at the burghe of Glasgowe the fyft day of Julii 1625 for avoyding of confusioun it was statute and ordanit that na burghe sould conteine in thair commissiounes direct to any parliament or conventioun of estates mae commissioneres then one exceptand the burghe of Edinburghe[68] as at mair lenth is contenit in the said actes whithe the whiche the said commissioneres being advysed and finding these actes and constitutiounes to be most necesssare for the weall of thair estate and for keepeing ane mutuall estate and mutuall harmonie in all thinges and impeding the renting of the body whiche so long by thair mutuall concurrence and correspondence hes bene preserved inteir. Thairfoir they ratifie and approve the haill actes abovewrittin in all the heades, clausses and articles thairof, and declaires the samyne to have full force strenth and effect in all tyme cuming to be put to executioun against the transgressouris of any of thame conforme to the tennor thairof, and in caice of necessare absence declaires that it salbe lauchfull to the borrowes as may send assessores [fo. 446r] with thair commissioneres that thair assessour sall have voat[69] in the commissioneres absence, the commissioner being of the qualitie abonewrittin and for whom the burghe salbe answerabill. And least the samyne sould fall in oblivioun, ordaines the burgh quhair any publict meitting of parliament or conventioun of estates is appointed, to requyre the remanent borrowes for sending commissioneres sufficientlie instructed in maner foirsaid. And that nane pretend ignorance, ordaines ilk commissioner present to intimat the samyne to thair nichtboures at thair home cuming and ilk burghe to report in writt to the nixt generall conventioun of borrowes the intimatioun thairof under the pane of twentie punds. And this to be ane heade of the nixt missive.[70]

---

66 *RCRBS*, ii, 156–7.
67 *RCRBS*, ii, 262.
68 *RCRBS*, ii, 193.
69 The phrase 'with thair commissioner sall have voat' also occurs here.
70 This act is noted in the Abstract of Acts of Convention, *RCRBS*, iv, 537.

[30]

The same day forsamekill as the commissioneres of borrowes considering the heades of the last missive and materes referrit be the parliament to the lordis of privie counsall, viz the inlairgeing of the places reservit in the mater of the fisching, the enequalitie of trade betuix this kingdome and the kingdome of England, new impositiounes in France, oppressiounes of the Dunkirkers, the twa extraordinare taxatiounes, anent the tanneres, maltmen, correctoun housses, forbidden goodis out of England, manufactories, presenting to the mercattes the plaidinges in foldes, Robert Buchannis patent of the pearle, bleiching with lyme, importing of victuall, and the mater of the coyne and course of dollouris, and the penall statute anent transporting of money, and finding the said materes of so great ane weight, and that it is necessare that sume course be taikin for preventing of all hurt that may occure to this estate thairin. Theirfoir they have appointit and appointis ane particulare conventioun of borrowes to be haldin at[71] the burghes following, viz, the burgh of Edinburghe, Perthe, Dundy, Aberdene, Stirling, Linlithgow, Aire, Haddingtoun, Sanctandroes, Glasgow,[72] Montorose, Kirkcaldie, Cowpar, Bruntyland, Kinghorne, Dumbar, Caraill, Dumbartane, Dumfreis, to meit at the burgh of Edinburgh the aucht of October nixt with continuatioun of dayes, and ordanes the said burghes to send thair commissioneres for keepeing of the said conventioun sufficientlie instructed anent the foirsaid particularis and in any uther thinges concerning thair estate under the paine of twentie punds, and ordaines the burghe of Edinburgh be thair missive to requyre them to that effect in dew tyme, to whiche borrowes and maist pairt [fo. 446v] of them convenand, the present commissioneres give full powar and commissioune to tak all sufficient and lauchfull course for establisching of all suche thinges as may tend to the good of the borrowes and for prevening thair hurt in any of the particulares abovewrittin, with poware to deall with his Majesite, lords of counsall and all utheres whom the samyne sall concerne, in sua far as they sall think expedient for the weall of this estate, recommending seriouslie the prosecutioun of thairof to thair diligence, quhairanent and quhatsumever they sall do thairin the present commissioneres for themselves and thair borrowes and in name of the haill remanent borrowes grantis and gives to them and maist pairt of thame convenand full power and commissioun ratifieing and approveing quhatsumever they sall do in the premissis. And the said borrowes to report thair diligence heiranent to the nixt generall conventioun of borrowes. And this to be ane heade of the nixt missive.[73]

---

71 This should be 'by'.
72 'Sanctandroes' is repeated here.
73 This act is noted in the Abstract of Acts of Convention, RCRBS, iv, 537–8.

[31]

The same day anent the supplicatioun gevin in be Patrick Suttie indweller in the toun of Campheir craving the commissioneres of borrowes thair approbatioun to his office of factorie at the said staippill port of Campheir the said commissioneres being advysit thairwith and understanding of the sufficiencie abilitie and qualificatioun of the said Patrick for the dischairge of his dewtie in the said office of factorie, at the earniest desyre and requeist of my lord conservator notwithstanding of many former actis in the contraire whairanent the present commissioneres hes dispensit and dispenssis for this tyme, grantes and gives thair allowances ratificatioun and approbatioun for his admissioun to the said office, to indure for the space of threttene yeir heirefter, upoun the provisiounes and conditiounes efter following: viz, that he behave himselff honestlie and dewtifullie in the said office and that he sall mak just compt and reckoning and thankfull payment of his intromissioun with quhatsumever goodis and geir or sowmes of money that he sall happin to intromet with perteaning to quhatsumever persone salbe pleassed to imploy him in the said office or that he sall intromet with at command and directioun of the said borrowes and that he sall obey and fulfill all actis and statutes maid or to be maid be the commissioneres of the said borrowes in the generall or particulare conventiounes and sall undergo [fo. 447r] all suche offices and services as they salbe pleassed to burdene him withall, and sall dischairge ane honest dewtie to all merchandis and sall not refuis to accept of thair imployment howsoever meane the same salbe whensoever he salbe requyrit thairto be thame or any ane of thame. And that he sall caus his wyfe compeir judiciallie befoir the conservator or his deputes and renunce all benefeitt sche may acclame in caise hir husband sall deceas befoir hir or utherwayes that schee may have or pretend be the lawes of that cuntrey, and sall submit hir selff to the lawes of this kingdome in all thinges and jurisdictioun of the said conservator. And with provisioun allwayes that not withstanding of the tyme gevin yit the samyne sall no longer indure nor the borrowes good will allanerlie. For better performance of whiche provisioun and conditiounes, George Sutty younger, merchand burges of Edinburgh, and David Duff, merchand burges of Perthe obleissis thame selves conjunctlie and severallie thair aires [and] executoures, as cautiouneres sourertes and full debtoures for the said Patrick that he sall dischairge faithfullie and trewlie dischairge his dewtie in the said office. And for obedience of the said actes of borrowes maid and to be maid and that he sall mak just compt and reckoning and payment of all goodis, geir and sowmes of money or quhatsumever he sall happin to intromet with be vertew of his office or utherwayes in maner forsaid. And that befoir his admissioun he sall compeir judiciallie befoir the conservatour and mak faith *de fideli administratione officii*[74] and obedience of the provisiounes above writtin in all thinges. For doing quhairof and fulfilling of the haill provisitiounes and conditiounes abovewrittin, the said Patrick Suttie compeirand, band and obleist himselff his airis executouris and be thir presenis bindes and obleissis him and his forsaid to freith, releiff and skaithles keepe his said cautioneres and thair forsaid of all skaith and damnage that they or ony of thame may incure thairthrow, throw thair becoming cautioneres in maner abonewrittin. In witnes quhairof the said Patrick Suttie and his cautioneres hes subscrivit thir presentis with thair handis, at Sanctandroes the tent day of August, and at Edinburgh the [...] day of [...] the yeir of God 1633 yeires. Patrick Suttie.

[32]

The same day forsamekill as the commissioneres of borrowes resenting[75] the favour and kyndnes done be thair freindes at last parliament, thairfoir gives and grantis for passing of the act of parliament maid in favoures of the borrowes the sowme of ane thowsand merkes and ordaines the agent to borrow the same upoun ordinare profeit and to have it in readines against the nixt particulare meitting of the borrowes whom they ordane to delyver with the borrowes good will. And ordaines ilk burgh to be requyrit for sending of thair pairt of the said sowme with the said interrest to the nixt generall conventioun of borrowes conforme to the taxt roll under the paine of tuenty pundis ilk burgh and that by and attour thair payment of thair pairt of the said principall sowme and enterrest. And this to be ane head of the nixt missive.[76]

[fo. 447v]

[33]

The same day grantis and gives thair generall clerke for his travellis takin be him for making of ane taibill be him of the generall actes of borrowes the sowme of fyve hundreth merks and to Alexander Mackcartnay his servand the soume of fourtie pundis. And ordanes ilk burgh to be requyrit for sending thair pairt[77] of the said soumes conforme to the taxt roll to the nixt generall conventioun of borrowes. And that under the paine of twentie

---

74 A longer version of the normal phrase, this literally means 'concerning faithful administration of [his] office', i.e. he was promising to carry out his duties with diligence.

75 The sense of this word has changed considerably since the seventeenth century. Here it means 'being aware of'.

76 This act is given in full in the Abstract of Acts of Convention, *RCRBS*, iv, 537.

77 The phrase 'for sending thair pairt' is repeated.

pundis ilk burgh and that by and attour the payment of thair pairt of the forsaid sowmes. And this to be ane head of the nixt missive.[78]

[34]

The same day forsameikill as the commissioneres of borrowes findeing that it is necessar that thair be ane constant soume set doun upoun everie ordinare in all burghes quhair the conventioun of borrowes is appointed. Thairfoir appointis ane ordinare[79] that no greatter ordinare be taikin heirefter in any burgh at thair meittinges and conventiounes then the sowme of twelff schillings and ordanes ilk commissioner present to intimat the same to thair nichtboures at thair homecumming and that nane pretend ignorance and to see the same dewlie put to dew executioun under pane of being censured be the rest of the borrowes. And ilk burghe to report thair diligence in intimating thairof to the nixt generall conventioun under the pane of twentie pundis ilk burgh. And this to be ane head of the nixt missive.[80]

[35]

The same day ordaines the burgh of Dumfermeling, Cowpare and Rothesay to produce the formes of the electioun of thair magistrates and counsall at Michaelmes nixt to the nixt generall conventioun of borrowes and to conforme thame selves in thair electioun conforme to the actes of parliament and borrowes under the pane of twentie pundis ilk burgh. And this to be ane head of the nixt missive.

[36]

The same day anent the supplicatioun gewin in be Marjerie Davidsone relict of umquhill George Corstor sumtyme factor at Campheir now spous to George Riddell indweller in Campheir craiveing to be excyse frie for hir familie of certane beir and wyne as is contenit in the said supplicatioun. The said commissioneres seriouslie intreates my Lord Conservator to deall with the magistrates of the toun of Campheir for obtaining the quantitie of twelff barrellis of beir and twa punscheounes of wyne or thairby excyse frie to be spent into thair awin hous and familie and not to be topped out. Which matter they be thir presents recomendes to the said conservatores cair and diligence.

[fo. 448r]
[37]

The same day ordaines ilk burgh to be requyrit for sending thair commissioneres sufficientlie instructed to the nixt generall conventioun of borrowes

78 This act is noted in the Abstract of Acts of Convention, *RCRBS*, iv, 538.
79 Either this should read 'ordinance' or the words 'ane ordinare' should be omitted.
80 This act is noted in the Abstract of Acts of Convention, *RCRBS*, iv, 538.

whither it salbe expedient to alter the taxt roll or not. And this to be ane head of the nixt missive.

[38]

The same day the said commissioneres of borrowes gives and grantis licence to the burghes of Bamff, Forfar, Aberbrothoke and Anstruther Wester to abyde and remaine fra all generall conventioun[es] of borrowes for the space of thrie yeires upone the conditiounes and provisiounes efter following, provyding the samyne be not extended to parliamentis nor quhen the burghes[81] are citatte for any particulare caus, and also provyding the said burghes send with the commissioneres of the nixt adjacent burghes thair severall ratificatiounes and thair probatiounes of all thinges to be done yeirlie in the said generall conventiounes autenticklie subscryvit, with all sowmes that they sould pay to the borrowes conforme to the missive. And that they bestow the expenssis that they sould have bestowed upoun thair commissioneres upoun commoun workis and be compttabill thairfoir to the borrowes at the expyreing of the said yeires.

[39]

The same day anent the supplicatioun gevin in for helpe to the clenging of and making ane harberie to the braidheaven within Speyhoupe.[82] Ordaines ilk burgh to be requyrit for sending thair commissioneres sufficientlie instructed to the nixt generall conventioun of borrowes to have answeare thairto. And ordaines the burghes of Aberdene, Bamff and Elgyne to visit the same and to report the necessitie and the expediencie thairof to the said nixt generall conventioun of borrowes. And this to be ane head of the nixt missive.

[40]

The same day the said commissioneres understanding that the persones after following had passed by the staippill port [with] staippill waires, viz Williame Ferrie burges and inhabitant of the burgh of Edinburgh, Johne Burges, James Nobill, Robert Ormistoun, Alexander Smyth, George Stirling, James Fowller, Harie Robertsone, Johne Boig, Thomas Gray, Williame Alexander, Johne Coblae burgesses indwelleres in Edinburgh, Williame Andersone burges in Stirling, William Govane, John Stirling, Johne Andersone younger, Johne Burges, Johne Wilsone, [fo. 448v] Johne Moresone, Williame Andersone and James Tod, burgesses indwelleres in Glasgow, Robert Doik, John Mackmillane burgesses indwelleres in the burgh of Aire, Alexander

81 The phrase 'are not citatt' occurs here apparently in error.
82 Hope = a small bay or haven. This probably refers to Findochtie, Banffshire: see the 34th act of the general convention of 1634 (below, 183).

[...] of Culros, Thomas Gray, Thomas Annand,[83] Thomas Watsone, Alexander Blaire, Thomas Gray, Alexander Forrester, George Dunning and Andro [...] burgesses indwelleres in Dundye, Andro Bennet and Williame Diskie burgesses indwelleres in Bruntylland, Johne Simpsone, Alexander Lindesay and James Whytt, James Smyth of Montrose, Johne Howiesone, Alexander Schandie, Peter Mure and James Robertsone burgesses indwelleres in Aberdene, James Fergussone in Haddingtoun and Andro Geddie in Sanctandroes had passed by the staippill port and not maid payment of the dewes to the lord conservator and minister, contrair the act of borrowes and to the violatioun of thair contract betuixt thame and the toun of Campheir. As lykewayes understanding that the persones underwrittin viz George Stirling in Edinburgh, James Sowter thair, Patrick Andersone in Perth, Johne Uddert in Dundy, Andro Bennet in Bruntyland, James [...] in Aire, James Nicolsone in Dysart, James Law alias Bischop thair, and Johne Simpsone in Kirkaldie, had not maid payment of thair said dewtyes at the said port conforme to the act of borrowes maid at Dumbare in anno 1626.[84] Thaifore the said commissioneres of borrowes ordaines the said burghes ilk ane of thame for thair awin pairtis to put thair said nichtbouris under cautioun for thair compeirance befoir the said commissioneres at the nixt generall conventioun of borrowes ilkane of thame under the pane of ane hundreth pundis for answering for passing by the staippill port and for not payment of thair dettes. And the said burghes to report thair diligence heiranent to the nixt generall conventioun of borrowes. And this to be ane heade of the nixt missive.[85]

[41]
The same day the said commissioneres understanding that they haif grantit to the burgh of Monteberwick[86] at thair last generall conventioun of borrowes licence to seik thair charitabill support of the whole remanent borrowes for the reparatioun of thair harberie, which hes not bene performit universallie be thame. Thairfoir the said commissioneres recommendes the necessitie of thair said harberie of new to thair charitabill support, earnestlie intreating thame that they would not mak no delay thairin.

Decimo Augustie I^m vi^c Trigesimo tertio
[42]
The quhilk day the commissioneres of borrowes being conveinit, compeirit Alexander Aikinheid agent and produced his comptis of his depursementis in the borrowes affaires sine the last generall conventioun which being seine,

---

83 This name is repeated.
84 RCRBS, iii, 227.
85 This act is noted in the Abstract of Acts of Convention, RCRBS, iv, 538.
86 This must be a mistranscription of North Berwick.

[fo. 449r] concluded and allowed, they fand the borrowes to be restand awand to him the sowme of three hundreth fourescore sevineteine punds ten schillinges, which with the interrest bygane and till the nixt generall conventioun they finde it to extend to the sowme of foure hundreth fyftie ane punds vi s. viii d., and thairfoir ordaines ilk burgh to send thair pairt thairof to the nixt generall conventioun of borrowes with thair commissioner conforme to the taxt roll and that by and attour thair pairt of the said principall sowme. And this to be ane heade of the nixt missive.

[43]
The same day the commissioneres of borrowes understanding the paines of thair minister at Campheir, thairfore they ordaine ilk burgh to send thair commissioner sufficientlie instructed anent augmentatioun of his stipend craived and for consideratioun and considering the impost grantit for defraying thairof if the same sall be funde sufficient for doeing thairof and to tak suche course thairin as they sall think expedient to the nixt generall conventioun of borrowes. And the same to be contenit in the nixt missive.

[44]
The same day the said commissioneres of borrowes being conveinit haveing seine and considered the excuse sent fra the burgh of Dumfreis excuseing thair absence of thair commissioner be his seiknes, and finding be the sameing excuse that they micht both have elected and send ane uther in his place in dew tym. Thairfoir they unlaw the said burgh in the sowme of twentie punds for thair absence fra this present conventioun and ordaines the agent to uplift the samyne, and he to be chairged thairwith in his accomptis.

[45]
The same day unlawes the burghes of Dumfreis, Lochemaben, Sanquhair, ilk ane of thame for being absent fra this present conventioun and for not sending of the dewtie of the missive and alse to produce the sowme of twentie punds ilk ane of thame quhairin they ware unlawit at the last generall conventioun for being lykewayes absent fra the same and ordaines to chairge thame for payment making of the samen unlawes and to report his diligence heiranent to the nixt generall conventioun. And this to be ane heade of the nixt missive.

[46]
The same day the said commissioneres dissolves this present conventioun and affixes thair nixt generall conventioun to be and begin at the burghe of Edinburgh the [...] day of Julii nixt and ordaines ilk burghe to send thair commissioneres sufficientlie instructit for keepeing of the said conventioun conforme to the ordour under the paine of twentie punds ilk burgh.

[fo. 449v]

[47]

The same day the said commissioneres for causses moveing thame ordaines thair agent to give to Andro Forret the sowme of ane hundreth punds, and ordaines ilk burgh to send thair pairt thairof to the nixt generall conventioune of borrowes with the annuelrent thairof conforme to the taxt roll under the pane of twentie pundis ilk burgh by and attour thair pairt of the payment of the said sowme. And this to be ane heid of the nixt missive.

Finis[87]

---

[87] There is no fo. 450.

Particular Convention at Edinburgh, October 1633

[fo. 451r]

In the particular conventioun of borrowis haldin at the burgh of Edinburgh the 8 day of October the yeir of God 1633 yeires be the commissioneris of borrowis thair convenit be vertew of ane commissioun givin to theme be the last generall conventioun of borrowis haldin in the burgh of Sanctrandrois the nynt day of August last be the commissioneris of borrowis underwrittin and produceit thair commissiounes as followis

Edinburgh	William Dick, Robert Miklejohnn
Perth	
Dundye	James Simpsoun
Abirdein	Mr Alexander Japhray
Stirling	Johnne Johnnestoun
Lynlithgow	James Gibbesoun
Sanctandroes[1]	Johnne Lepar
Glasgow	James Stewart
Aire	George Maissoun
Haddingtoun	Mr James Cockburne
Kirkcaldye	Johnne Williamsoun
Montrose	Thomas Reanye
Coupar	Robert Pitersoun
Dumfreis	Johnne Williamsoun
Bruntyland	
Kinghorne	Walter Duncan
Caraill[2]	Johnne Mackesoun
Dumbar	George Purves
Dumbartan	Johnne Sempill

1

The same day the saids commissioneris electes William Dick, deyne of gild, first in commissioun for the burgh of Edinburgh, to be moderator during this present conventioun, quha compeirand and accepted the said office in and upon him and gaive his aith *de fideli administratione*.[3]

---

1   St Andrews.
2   Crail.
3   Literally, 'concerning faithful administration', i.e. he was promising to carry out the duties of moderator with diligence.

Decimo Octobris 1633

[2]

The quhilk day the commissioneris of borrowis being convenit, forsamikle as after dew and mature deliberatioun taiken be thame anent the severall heids contenit in the last missive direct to theme be the burgh of Edinburgh and especiallie haiveing considderit the mater of the fischings and associatioun with England [fo. 451v] with England quhairin notwithstanding that the petitioun anent the plaices craived be the kingdome to be reservit to the natives for thair use and maintenance and goode of thair uther fischingis hes not yit ressavit ane answer and that thair is now with mutuall consent conforme to the paitent of the said fisching as yit ressavit into that companie, nor any lawes nor any lawes sett doun for governing thairof, nor no libertie grauntit for doeing of anye farder then for to fische, yit the Inglish as thai ar informit hes not onlie outraid to the said fisching, fisched whair thai aucht to haif bein prohibited, bot also hes incroached upon the whole tred upon the mayne and by thair factors whome thai haive establischit in these remote plaices of this kingdome bocht up the whole commodities this cuntrey does affoord to the no small prejudice of all the rest of the kingdome and absolute takin away of these merchandices, whairupone the cheiff and mayne trade thairof does depend and does committ sindrie uther thinges which in ane small space of tyme will tend to our absolute undoeing of this natioun quhairof thai have not ressavit yit full informatioun. Thairfoir they have continewit[4] the further handling of the said mater to ane uther tyme and hes appointit and apointes and particular meitting and conventioun of the borrowes deputt be the last generall conventioun togither with the burghis of Anstruther Eister and Wester and Irrwyne to be at this burgh of Edinburgh the 7 of Januarij nixt with continuatioun of dayis, to quhome and maist pairt of theme convenand the present commissioneris for theme selffes and in name and behalff of the haill remanent borrowis and haiving commissioun frome theme, for treatting resolving and concluding anent the said mater and all that may be made thairin as thai sall think maist meit and expedient for the weill of the kingdome and thair estait and that ather at home with the lordis of his Majesties most honorabill privie counsall or abroad with his Majestie, in such mater as thai sall think best, firme and stable haldand and for to hald quhatsumevir the said commissioneres then convenand sall doe or lauchfullie leids to be done anent the premisses. And to the effect the saidis commissioneris may be sufficientlie informit of the procedor of the Inglish in these pairts, thairfore thai ordaine the burghis of Aire, Glasgow and Dumbartan with the burghis of Caraill, Sanctandroes, Montrose and Kirkcaldye to tak speciall notice and tryell of thair nych-

---

4   The phrase 'they have continewit' is repeated.

tbouris upone the west coast and eist coast of this kingdome of the said Inglish thair doeings be sea or land and to notifie the same to the commissioneris to be convenit under the hand writt of thair saidis nichtbouris and magistrattis. And for better doeing heirof ordains the burgh of Edinburgh to require in dew tyme the saidis borrowis for sending thair commissioneres sufficientlie instructit in maner foresaid under the payne of xx lib. ilk burgh and the missive to be direct to the saidis borrowis ordainit to tak tryell as said is [fo. 452r] As said is to require theme lyikwayes to that effect. And lyikwayes inrespect that the remanent heids in the present missive may be more commodiouslie handlit and followed at the said tyme nor now in tyme of vacance, thairfore thai have lyikwayes continewit the saidis haill remanent heids to be treatted and concludit upone be the saids commissioneris of borrowis apointed to be conveinit in Januarij nixt, to whome thai give thair full powar in commissioun in maner abonewrittin and which particulares they ordayne to be insert in the said missive to be direct to theme and the saidis burghis to report thair proceidings anent the premissis to the nixt generall conventioun of borrowis and this to be ane heid of the nixt missive.[5]

[3]

The same day the present commissioneris haiffing considderit and perused the extent roll of the borrowis sett doun be the burgh of Edinburgh in 1633 conforme to the extent roll of the hundreth pundis sett doun be the borrowis whairwith thai collationat and calculat the said roll sett doun be the burght of Edinburgh, the present commissioneris conforme quhairunto ordaines thair generall clerke to give out ane roll of the soumes grantit be the estaittes last convenit to the lordis of his Majesties colledge of justice, and also of the last ordiner taxatioun grantit to his Majestie quhairanent thir presentis salbe his warrand.

[4]

The same day foresamikle as the commissioneris of borrowis being informit that tua of thair schippes hes bein of late takin and seasit upone be ane capitan Queist of Enensen[6] in Holland goeing in to Ostent and making mercat of thair guidis thair, haiveing caryed no guids which could cum under the name of bastiamento and the saids ships declaired lauchfull pryse be ane sentance of the admiraltie of horne which being suffered micht induce ane exampill to move those of West Flanders to doo the lyik to all such of thair shippis as goes or cumes from eany pairts subject to the estaittis generall, quhairby the haill traid of this kingdome is licklie to suffer prejudice. With

---

5   This act is noted in the Abstract of Acts of Convention, *RCRBS*, iv, 538.
6   This is Captain Quast, of Enkhuizen, Vice-Admiral of North Holland. See National Archives, SP84/150, fos. 139–42. I am very grateful to Martine Van Ittersum for this reference.

the which the lordis of his Majesties privie counsall being informit thai
have writtin to his Majestie theranent and to certain of the counsall of this
kingdome presentlie resident thair. Which letters thai ordayne the burgh of
Edinburgh to direct to Patrick Wood, merchand presentlie thair with ane
letter to him desyring him to deliver the same to the conservator desyring
him to sollicite his Majestie in thair behalff and to delyver the saidis letteris
and to tak such ourse as may be most stedabill for recalling of the sentence
givin and to report his diligence heiranent to the nixt generall conventioun
of borrowis. And this to be ane heid of the nixt missive.

[fo. 452v]
[5]
The same day forsamikle as the commissioneris of the borrowis being
informit that the toun of Lynlitgow does not proceid formallie conforme
to the actes of parliament and borrowis in the electioun of thair magistrattis
and counsell. Thairfore ordains the said burgh to be required for sending
with thair commissioner the forme of the electioun of thair counsell and
magistratis at Michaelmes last autenticklie subscrivit under the payne of
xx lb. and to report thair diligence heiranent to the nixt generall conventioun of borrowis. And this to be ane heid of the nixt missive.

[6]
The same day the saids commissioners of borrowis unlawes the burghis of
Perth and Bruntyland ilk ane of theme in ane unlaw of xx lb. for being
absent frome this present conventioun being lauchfullie wairnit to have
compeirit as was verifiet be the agent be productioun of thair deyne of gild
of Perth and thair baillie of Bruntyland of thair ressait of the missive direct
to theme for keiping of this present conventioun and ordanis the [a]gent to
uplift the same with diligence and to be chairgit thairwith in his comptis.[7]

---

7   There are no fos. 453–4.

Particular Convention at Edinburgh, January 1634

[fo. 455r]

In the particular convention of borrowis halden at the brughe of Edinburgh the sevint day of Januari 1634 yeires be the commissioneris of borrowes underwrittin be vertew of ane missive letter direct them from the said brughe of Edinburgh the dait the fourth day of December last and produced ther commissiones as followis:

Edinburgh	William Dick, Robert Micklejohne
Pearth	Andro Wilsoun
Dundye	James Fletcher
Abirdein	Mr Robert Farquhair
Stirling	Johne Johnstoune
Lynlithgow	James Gibbersoun
Santandrois[1]	Johne Lepar
Glasgow	Gabriell Cunningham
Aire	George Massoun
Haddingtoun	Mr James Cokburne
Kirkcadie	Johne Willamsoune
Montrose	Johne Erskein
Couper	Robert Patersoune
Brountyland[2]	Andro Watson
Kinghorne	Mr Robert Cunninghame
Dumbar	George Purves
Caraile[3]	Patrick Hunter
Dumbertoune[4]	Johne Semple
Dumfreis	Johne Ireving
Anstruther Eister	Johne Alexander
Anstruther Wester	Johne Pullo

1

The same day electis William Dick merchand, first in commissioun for the brugh of Edinbrughe, to be moderator during this present convention, who compeirand excepted the said office in and upon him and gave his aithe *de fideli administratione*.[5]

---

1 St Andrews.
2 Burntisland.
3 Crail.
4 Dumbarton.
5 Literally, 'concerning faithful administration', i.e. he was promising to carry out the duties of moderator with diligence.

2

Vigesimo quarto Januari 1634

The quhilk day the commissioneres of borrowes being conveined appoyntis to follow the supplicationes alredy presented to the lordes of his Majesties privie counsel anent the matter of the fisching and patent of the generall association and anent the matter of the mutuall traide betuix this kingdome and the kingdome of Ingland and establisching of manufactories as also anent the oppression of the Dunkirkeres [fo. 455v] and last the supplicationes given upon the reference in aid be the estaites last convenit to the saides lordis anent the price betuix the bolle of beir and bolle of mate,[6] the presenting of plaiding in foldes to the market, establisching of correction houses and forbidding of bleitching with lime, the present commissioneres of Edinburgh, Aberdein, Glasgo, Dumbartan and Irrvynge and ordeines them and most pairt of them to procure sua far as in them lyes the borrowes desires thairin mentionat and what they sall finde derogative to ther estat to live the same. As lykwayes ordaines them to supplicat the lordes for crying doune the dolleres 12 d. for sex monethes and so proportionallie whill they be ballanced and brought equall with the course they have in Ingland, and for causing the bulyeoune to be coyned in small peices and to be received from everie persone and thairin in particular be the mynte masteres and not in coumon be the customeris. And the said burghes to report ther diligence heir anent to the nixt generall convention of borrowes. And this to be in heid of the nixt missive.

3

The same day compeired James Barnes merchand burgis of Edinburgh and declaired that he having becum souerty for Robert Bautie factor at Campheir at his admission to the said office and desires to be fred therof, the saides commissioneris ordaines the said Robert Bautye to be cited be ane messive for compeiring the nixt generall convention to find caution of new, reforme[7] to the ordour with certification if he failye they will discharge him of his said office and in the meintyme ordeines the said cautioner to stand.

4

Vigesimo quinto Januarii 1634

The quhilke day the commissioneres of borrowes being conveinet and being informit that the toune of Ramfrew hade to the prejudice of the borrowes nix adjacent to them and to ther aune ruine entred in paxion with the lard of Grinocke and disponit ther liberties contrair to the actes of parliament

---

6   i.e. malt.
7   This should be 'conforme'.

and borrowis. Thairfoir ordeines the said burghe to be cited to answer theranent to the nixt generall convention of borrowes under the paine of xx lib.
And this to be in the heid of the nixt missive.

5

The same day forsameikill as the commissioneres of borrowes resentes[8] the
great intrest of this kingdome hes in the matter of traide with Ingland and
Irland which not being ballanced in due tyme the manufactores and tred
in all thinges within his Majesties wholle dominiones, which may tend to
the great prejudice of the kingdome. As lykwayes considering that some
thinges in the matter of the generall association of fisching ar required to
be ratified for the gud and liberties of the borrowes. Whairanent and anent
sundrie other matteres proponit to the estatis last conveined in parliament
and remited be them to the lordis of his majesties most honorable privie
counsell, and hes appoyn[t]it certaine of thair number for attending and
resaving ther answer. And they considering that the most pairt of the saides
maitteres cannot receive ane determinat and full conclusion without his
Majesties speciall favour be declaired thairanent, thairfoir the said commissioneres and as nominated and elec[t]ed and be the present nominates and
electes Williame Gray merchand of Edinburgh and Mr Alexander Guthrie
ther generalle clerke commissioneres for them for passing and deiling with
his Majestie in the particular underwritten, videlicet in the matter of the
fischeing, [fo. 456r] in the matter of traide with Ingland and Ireland and
establisching of companyes for inbringing of manufactory and procuring
of certaine liberties to them for incuraging of them, anent the oppres-
siones of the Dunkirkeris and all uther particulares mentioned in the last
missive to which persones the saides borrowis grauntis and gives ther full
power and commissioun [for] deilling with his Majestie theranent conforme
to the instructiones to be set doune be the said commissioneres of the
brughe of Edinburgh, Pearthe, Dundie, Aberdein, Glasgow, Dumbartein,
Dumfreis, Irwinge and Bruntyland or any four of them to whome the
presentis commissioneres gifes ther fulle power and commission theranent[9]
and ordaines the said commissioneres to deil with his Majestie in the said
particulares conforme therto and doe quhat in them shall lye for procuring
the borrowes satsifaction theranent and generall grauntis and giftis them full
power and commissioun in all matteres that sall occure that sall cume to
ther knowledge that may concerne ther estat and to deill with his Majestie
for procuring what they sall finde may tend to the borrowes weill, ratifeing

---

8   i.e. appreciates.
9   The phrase 'to be set doune ... theranent' is repeated, the only differences being variant
     spellings of some of the placenames.

and approving what ther comissioneres [do] anent [the][10] premises lykas the said commissioneres for themselves and in name of ther brughes as also in name of the haile remanent borrowes ratifies and approves the same and obleissis themselves in name forsaid to abyde thairat but contradiction or againe calling whatsomever. And for ther said commissioneres charges they ordaine the brughe of Edinburgh to advanse for them and eich of them suche soumes of money as they sall stand in neid for defraying of ther charges, which soumes so advanced and payed the present commissioneres for themselves and in name and behalfe of the saides borrowes and hail remanent borrowes obleissis them to refound this same with all intrest therfoir. And ordaines the said commissioneres to report ther procedinges in the said hail particulares to the nixt generall conventioun of borrowes. And this to be ane heid of the nixt missive.

[6]
The same day wheras the commissioneres considering the necestie of ther affaires wherby they ar drawen oft to repaire to his Majestie to thair great charges, thairfoir ordaines ilk brughe to be required for sending ther commissioneres sufficientlie instructed for condiscending anent the necessitie of ane agent at courte and ordaines the same to be remembered in the nixt missive.

[7]
The same day forsameikill as the borrowes understanding that ther liberties in France ar likly to be impaired be ane new exaction imposed thair upon al gudis. For remeid quhairof the present commissioneres ordaines the bruge of Edinburgh to deall with some of ther nightboures best expert in thes affaires of France for passing to France and dealing with the Frenche kinge for discharge of the said new exaction and to graunt unto him such ane soume of money as they sall thinke may effectuat that busines to be repayed to him againe be ane impost to be laid upon the guides cuming from Normandie, quhairanent the said commissioneres obleisses them and there burghes and ordaines ther commissioneres that sall goe in Ingland to procure ane letter from his Majestie to the [fo. 456v] said French king heiranent. And the said burghe to report ther diligence heiranent to the nixt generall conventiones of borrowes. And this to be ane heid of the nixt missive.

[8]
The same day forsomeikill as the commissioneres of borrowes being informed be the agent of certaine enormities within the burghe of Linlithgow conforme to ane remonstrance given in be him theranent, the

---

10   These two omissions appear to be the result of copying errors.

present commissioneres ordaines the burghe of Edinburgh with the present commissioneres of Pearthe, Stirling and Hadingtoun to cognose the veritie of the said remonstrance givin in be him theranent. And to that effect to pas to the said burghe and gife anie apearance be therof, to advertise ther clerke that the burgh may be required for answering anent the said particulares. And the same to be ane heid of the nixt missive.

[9]
The same day the saide commissioneres unlawes the burghs of Sanctandrois and Munrose ilke ane of them in the soume of twentie pundis for depairting from this present conventioun befoir the desolving thairof and ordaines the said burghes to be required for sending ther saides unlawes to the nixt generall conventioun of borrowis with ther said commissioneres. And this to be ane heid of the nixt missive.

Actis off the conventioun of burrowis at Edinburgh January 1634.[11]

---

11   This title appears at the bottom of the folio. It would have been on the outside of the record as it was folded. There is no fo. 457 and fo. 458 is blank.

General Convention at Edinburgh, July 1634

[fo. 459r]
In the generall conventioun of borrowes haldine at the burgh of Edinburgh the first of Julii the yeire of God ane thousand sex hundreth threttie four yeires be the comissioneres of borrowes undirwrittin and producit thair comissiones as followes:

Edinburgh	Williame Gray, Williame Carnagye
Pearth	Andro Gray
Dundie	Thomas Halyburtoun younger
Aberdeine	Mr Alexander Jophray
Stirling	Johne Johnstoun
Linlithgow	Andro Bell
Sanctandrois[1]	Robert Tailyeour
Glasgow	Patrick Bell
Aire	Johne Osburne
Haddingtoun	Mr James Cokburne
Dysert	Alexander Sympsoun
Kirkadie	Williame Tenent
Montrose	Patrick Lichtoun
Couper	Robert Pittersoun
Anstruther Eister	Robert Alexander
Dumfries	Johne Williamsone
Invernes	Johne Forbis
Brunteilland[2]	Andro Watsoun
Inverkeithing	Williame Blaickburne
Kinghorne	Maister Robert Cunninghame
Breichine[3]	be exemptioun producit be Thomas Carnegye
Irrvyne	James Blair
Jedburgh	Mr Johne Rutherfuird
Kirkcudbright	Robert Glenduning
Wigtoun	Thomas Makgie
Pettinwym	George Kingyow
Dumfermling[4]	

---

1 St Andrews.
2 Burntisland.
3 This appears originally to have been written as 'Buchane'. It was then overwritten as 'Brehine' and then 'Breichine' was added in the margin just to be sure.
4 Dunfermline.

Anstruther Wester	be exemtioun and ratificatioun producit be Pittinwyme
Selkirk	Williame Ellott
Dumbare	George Purves
Dumbartoun	Johne Semple
Ramfrew[5]	Johne Spreull
Lanerick[6]	Gedioun Jack
Abirbrothok[7]	be exemptioun and ratificatioun producit be Mr James Peirsoun
Elgine	Mr Johne Hay
Peibles	Be exemptioun and ratificatioun producit be agent
Carell[8]	John Mackesoun
Thayne[9]	be exemptioun and ratificatioun producit be agent
Culrois	Mr Edward Blaw[10]
[fo. 459v]	
Bamff	be exemptioun and ratificatioun producit be agent
Quhythorne[11]	
Forfar	
Rothesay	
Nairne	be exemptioun and ratificatioun producit be the agent
Forris	Airthour Foirbis
Rutherglen	Johne Pinkartoun
Northe Berwick	Johne Muire
Cullane	
Kilrainie[12]	be exemptioun and ratificatioun producit be Anstruther Eister
Lauder	
Annand	
Lochmaben	
Sanchquhair	Hew Dick
Galloway[13]	

5   Renfrew.
6   Lanark.
7   Arbroath.
8   Crail.
9   Tain.
10 This is probably the same person as Mr Edward 'Blair', commissioner to a convention of estates in 1630 (*RPS*, A1630/7/1), but here, and at the general convention in 1633, his name is clearly 'Blaw'.
11 Whithorn.
12 Kilrenny.
13 New Galloway.

[1]
{Electioun Moderator}
The same day the said comissioneres of borrowes ellectes creattes and constitutes Williame Gray, merchand, first in commissioun foir the burgh of Edinburgh, to be moderator during this present conventioun, quha compeirand
acceptand the said place in and upoun him and gave his aith *de fideli administratione*.[14]

[2]
{Houres of meiting}
The same day the comissioneres of borrowes appoyntes thair houres of
meiting to be and begine daylie at nyne houres in the morning and till
least till tuellff houres at none and efter non at tua houres till sex of clok at
night, and sick as are absent at the calling of the rollis to pey ane unlay of
sex schillingis, and they that passes out of the house without leive pey ane
unlay as said is and they that passis fra this present conventioun befoir the
dissolving thairof pey ane unlay as absentes. And that nane speak unrequyrit
without leive askit and gevine nor intermix thair reassouning with thair
voting under the paine of ane unlay of sex schillingis *toties quoties*.[15]

3
{Citatioun borrowes verifiet}
The same day Williame Gray comissioner foir the burgh of Edinburgh
verifiet the citatioun of the haill borrowes to this present conventioun be
George Ramsay post quho producit his book of the subscriptiones of all
suche as receavit the generall missive.

[fo. 460r]
4
{Unfrie skipperes factoures in France missive}
The same day the saidis comissioneres ordaines the aucht act of the last
generall conventioun of borrowes haldine at Sanctandrois the sevint of
August last maid anent the dischairge of portage and prohibiting frie men
to be perteneres with unfrie skipperes dwelling at unfrie portes[16] to be
remembrit in the missive and ilk burgh to be requyrid concerning thair
dilligence to the nixt generall conventioun in observing and execuiting of
the said act under the paine of tuentie pundis. And siclyk ordaines ilk burgh
to be requyrit foir sending thair commissioneres suficientlie instructit to the

---

14 Literally, 'concerning faithful administration', i.e. he was promising to carry out the duties
    of moderator with diligence.
15 As often as it shall happen, i.e. for each offence.
16 See above, 133.

nixt generall conventioun of borrowes foir taking ane solid course anent the
factoures in France conforme to the tent act of the last generall conventioun
under the paine foirsaid.

5

{Couper unfrie persones}

The same day anent the tuellfft act of the last generall conventioun haldine at
the burgh of Sanctandrois the sevint day of [August] last ordaining the burgh
of Couper to have producit thair dilligence to this present conventioun and
causing of Thomas and William Andersones indwelleres in Newburgh in Fyff
to desist from usurping the liberties of the frie royall borrowes.[17] Compeirit
Robert Pattersone, present comissioner of the said burgh and producit our
soverane lordis letters raisit and execuit againes the saidis persones. As also
producit ane act of thair owne court quhair the saidis persones compeirand
befoir them and actit themsellffis with thair owine consent to desist from
usurping the libertie of the said borrowes wiche the saidis commissioneres
acceptes foir ane dilligence at this tyme.

Secundo Julii I[m] vi[c] trigesimo quarto

[6]

The quhilk day the commissioneres of borrowes being conveined understanding that diverse burgesses does resort to the Chanarie of Ros,[18] Rosemarkie, Dingwall and Crumartie[19] and makis markit losses and leadis contrair
to the actes of parliament and borrowes in prejudice of the borrowes, and in
speciall David Murray merchand burges of Edinburgh with sundrie utheres
in Dundie and Aberdeine. Quhairanent the said David being conveined
and compeirand, confessit the samyn. And thairfoir the saidis comissioneres
dischairges him of the lyk doeing in tyme cuming, and also the inhabitantes
of Dundie and Abirdeine and ordaines the present comissioneres of the said
twa burghes to prohibit thear nightboures from attempting the lyk in tyme
cuming under the paines conteined in the actes of old borrowes maid of old
thairanent. [fo. 460v] As also ordaines the burgh of Invernes to produce thair
dilligence in restraining the inhabitantes of the saidis places from holding of
buithes and usurping the liberteis of the saidis borrowis to the nixt generall
conventioun of borrowis under the paine of fourtie pundis. And allwayes
ordaines the burgh of Elgine to try suche persones as dwellis in the saidis
places and keipes buithes or attempttis upoun the liberteis of the saidis
borrowis contrair to the lawis of the kingdome, and to report thair names

---

17   See above, 134–5.
18   Fortrose.
19   Cromarty.

to the nixt generall conventioun of borrowes. And this to be ane heid of the nixt missive.[20]

7

The same day anent the fourt act of the last generall conventioun of borrowes haldine at the burgh of Sanctandrois the sext day of August last, ordaining the burgh of Irrving to have producit to this present conventioun thair dilligence in writt in restrayning the inhabitantes of the Largis, Fairlie, Kelburne and Salcoattes[21] from usurping the libertie of the frie royall borrowes under the paine of twentie pundis.[22] The said comissioneres considdering that the inhabitantes of thes places does not onlie prejudice and hurt the said burgh of Irrving but also the haill borrowes of the wast and that thair number daylie does grow to the ruine and decay of the saidis borrowes. Thairfoir ordaines the said burgh of Irrving to report thair dilligence in causing the haill inhabitantes in the said places to desist under the paine of fourtie pundis. And ordaines them to tak tryell of all thair outland burgessis dwelling outwith thair liberteis and to report thair dilligence in causing them ather mak thair residence within thair burgh or in depryving them of the liberteis thairof under the paine of twentie pundis to be payit be them foir ilk ane of thair burgesses salbe fund to dwell outwith thair burgh but favoure. And ordaines the agent to concure with them anent the premissis. As lykwayes becaus of the greatnes of the persones with whome they have to doe, ordaines ilk burgh to be requyrit foir sending thair comissioneres sufficientlie instructed to the nixt generall conventioun with thair best advyse foir taking course foir surppressing the inhabitantes of the said places foir attempting againest the liberteis of the borrowis. And this to be ane heid of the nixt missive.

8

The same day anent the fyft act of the last generall conventioun of borrowis haldine at the burgh of Sanctandrois the sext day of August last ordaineing the burgh of Caraill to have producit thair dilligence in wreitt to this present conventioun in restraineing the inhabitantes of Levin and Sanctmeinan[23] frome usurpeing the liberteis of the frie royall borrowes under the paine of xx pundis.[24] The comissioneres foir caussis moving them hes thought guid to continow the said maitter [fo. 461r] to the nixt generall conventioun and in the mean tyme ordaines ilk burgh to send thair comissioneres suficientlie

20   This act is noted in the Abstract of Acts of Convention, *RCRBS*, iv, 538.
21   Largs, Fairlie, Kilbirnie and Saltcoats, in Ayrshire.
22   See above, 132.
23   St Monans, Fife.
24   See above, 132.

instructid with thair best advyse and consent thairanent to the nixt generall conventioun and the same to be remembrit in the missive.

[9]

The same day anent the auchteine act of the last generall conventioun of borrowis haldin at the burgh of Montrose the fourt of Julii 1632[25] yeires ordaines the burgh of Dumfreis to use dilligence against Thomas Makillwaill and James Greir in discussing the suspentioun raised againest them and prosecuting thair chairges againest them and to have reportid thair dilligence thairanent to the last generall conventioun haldine at St Androis. Compeirit Johne Williamsone present commissioner foir the said burgh of Dumfreis and producit tua actes of thair court whairin the saidis persones compeirand actid themselffis to desist from usurping the liberteis of the said burgh under the paine of ane hundreth pundis, wiche the borrowes acceptes foir dilligence and recomendis to the said burgh to be cairfull that nane usurpe upoun thair liberteis heirefter.

[10]

The same day anent the threteine act of the last generall conventioun of borrowis haldine at the burgh of Sanctandrois the sevint day of August last ordaining the burgh of Forfar to have produced thair dilligence to this conventioun in restrayning the inhabitantes of Killiemure[26] in Angus from usurping the liberteis of the frie royall borrowes.[27] Compeirid Alexander Aikinheid agent and declarid that they had beine willing to prosecuit thair former letters raised againest the inhabitantes of Killiemure but be advyse of law had raised new letters which he produced raisit and execuit againes the saidis inhabitantes which they ordaine the said burgh to prosecuit and to produce thair dilligence thairanent to the nixt generall conventioun undir the paine of tuentie pundis. And this to be ane heid of the nixt missive.

11

The same day anent the tuentie ane act of the last generall conventioun of borrowis haldine at the burgh of St Androis the aucht day of Julii last ordaining the burgh of Glasgow to have produced thair dilligence to this present conventioun in causing William Hill in Grienock thair addledgit burges mak his actuall residence with them or in depryving him of thair liberties.[28] Compeirand the comissioner of Glasgow and producit ane act

---

25 That was actually the last but one, the last having been in July 1633 at St Andrews. For this act, see above, 88.

26 Kirriemuir, Angus.

27 See above, 135.

28 See above, 137–8.

of thair court depryving him of thair liberteis as the samyn daitit the 7 of Junii last beires whiche the saidis borrowes accepted foir dilligence and ordaines the said burgh in respect he continowes in using merchandrice to report thair dilligence in searching of his guidis and escheiting of the same conforme to the actes of parliament and in causing him desist from using the liberteis of the borrowes conforme to the law of this kingdome under the paine of tuentie pundis. And this to be ane heid of the nixt missive.

[fo. 461v]

12

The same day the saidis comissioneres of borrowis being conveined and heaving takine to thair consideratioun the augmentatioun creaved be Mr William Spang thair present minister for the natioun at the port of Campheir his stipend and the impost appoyntid for defraying thairof mentionat in the 34 act haldine at the burgh of St Androis the tent day of August last[29] and finding the great and exhorbitant derth in thes places in respect of the present warres hed thought guid to augment the said stipend and in respect of the former impostis not able for defrying fo the ordinarie chairges of the churche lykwayes to alter the said impost. And thairfoir grantes and gives unto the said Mr William during his thankfull service at the said place and induring thair will the soume of thrie hundreth guidlingis foirmerlie grantit unto him for his stipend making upe in the haill the soume of elevine hundreth guidlinges to be payid unto him in the name of stipend during his thankfull service at the said kirk and thair will. And ordaines the collectour of the impost following to be appoyntid foir defraying of the chairges of the church to mak guid and thankfull payment to him thairof at the four ordinarie termes in the yeire, beginning the first termes payment at the Lambes nixt, quhairanent thir presentis sall be unto them ane warrand. And becaus and in respect the said impostes [are] not suficient foir defraying of the chairges of the churches as said is, thairfoir they have appoyntit and appoyntes the impost following to be takine upe yeirlie and ingadderit be the collectores of the samyn, viz the soume of tuelff stoures and doittes Flymes mony to be payid be the merchand of ilk seck of guidis perteining to him or his factour in his name and four stuires and odis Flymes mony to be payid be the skipper and awneres of the schipe of ilk seck arryving at the said stable; Item of ilk merchand that sall happine to arryve thair not heaving of ane seck of stable guidis threttie steveres ilk voyag; Item of ilk hundreth collis arryving thair nyne stiveres; Item of ilk schip leadonit with corne nyne guidlinges quhairof sex to be payit be the merchand and thrie be the skipper; Item of ilk schipe arryving within Ile albeit frachtit be ane stranger and

---

29   It was actually the 43rd act, not the 34th. See above, 151.

coming from for any[30] pairtes ten schillingis gritt; Item of ilk seck of guidis that any factour sall happine to ressave aucht striveres tua doittes Flymes mony; Item of ilk seck of guidis arryving at the said port, quhairunto thair is na factour imployid aucht stiveres tua doittes to be payit be the merchand by and attour his uther dewes. And incaice any persones dew in payment of the said impost sall refuis to mak dew and thankfull [fo. 462r] peyment thairof ordaines the said collectour to arreist poynd and distrenyie thairfoir, and the conservator and his deputes to concure and assist with him nocht-withstanding without payment declares the saidis persones to be subject in the double quhair they sould have peyit at the said port of Campheir or Ill of Waker.[31] And ordaines the burgh quhairunto the said persone sall perteine ather to produce him befoir the comissioneres of borrowis being laufullie requirid or to mak payment thairof. As also ordaines the conservatour and his deputtes to arreist poynd and distrenyie foir the double of the said impost if they or thair guidis can be apprehendit at the said port of Campheir or within the said Ile. And farder the saidis comissioneres declares that if the said Mr Williame shall procuire the factores to augment thair saidis dewes to the soume of ten stures tua doittes Flymes mony to be payit of ilk seck of guidis to be intrometit with be them appoyntid foir thair pairt of his said stipend and sall report the samyn under thair handis laufullie subscrivit to the nixt generall conventioun of borrowes, than and in that caice the said augmentatioun to be extendit to the soume of foure hundreth guidlinges to be payid to him in maner foirsaid.[32]

13

The same day the saidis commissioneres of borrowes considdering that the tymes appoyntid to the factores of befoir foir collecting of the impost appoyntid foir defraying of the ministeres stipend yeirlie hes beine fra September till September yeirlie quhairby the saidis collectores comptes hes bein ather takine upe atture tymes or the borrowes forcid to let the samyn ly over a lang tyme. Thairfoir they have thought guid to alter the saidis tymes and to ordaine and ordaines in all tyme cuming everie collectour that salbe chosine heirefter to collect from the first of Maii the ensueing yeere and send home thair comptes to the generall conventioun following the said moneth of Maii and this ordour to be keiped in all tyme cuming. And becaus Thomas Cunninghame, present collector, hes not at this tyme sent home his comptes of his intromissioun with the said impost since the first of Se[p]tember last. Thairfoir ordaines thair generall clerk to writte to him in thair names and to requyre him to send home his comptes from the said

---

30 This should probably read 'forane' but was transcribed as 'for any' in error.
31 The Scots staple port of Veere, on the island of Walcheren, Zeeland.
32 This act is noted in the Abstract of Acts of Convention, *RCRBS*, iv, 538.

first of September last to the first of September nixt to the burgh of Edinburgh betuix and the first of November thairefter, togidder with the verifi-
cationes of the said comptes under the merchand, factor or skipperes hand
to the effect the said burgh of Edinburgh may present the samyn to the nixt
particular conventioun that sall occure, which comissioneres then conveined
the present commissioneres ordaines to fit the said [fo. 462v] Thomas his
comptes and to report the samyn to the nixt general conventioun following,
wheranent they grant unto them full power and commissioun. And also the
present commissioneres ellectis, nominates and appoyntes Alexander Boutye
to be collector of the said impost from the first of September nixt to the
first of Maii I^m vi^c threttie fyve yeires and ordaines him to give his aith *de
fideli administratione*[33] to the conservatour or his deputtis to ingadder the
said impost and to mak payment to the minister reidder and utheres as is
allowit to them be the saidis comissioneres of borrowis and to send home
his comptes of his intromissioun with the said impost frome the first of
September nixt till the first of Maii thairefter till the nixt generall conventioun of borrowis, verifiet be the skipper, merchand or factor in absence of
the merchand, with the said minister and reidder thair dischairges. And siclyk
ordaines the said conservatour or his deputtes at the begining to tak his
aith in oppene court to be haldine be them to that effect and that he shall
dischairge his leall and trew dewetie in the said collectioun and sall uplift
fra the merchandis factores and skipperes thair true and just pairt according
to the quantitie of thair guidis they sall happine to have according to his
knowledge and that he sall chairge himselff thairwith and omitt nothing
thairof and that he sall collect it be himselff and not utherwayes during the
tyme of his collectioun except in sicknes or necessitie. And also ordaines
the said Alexander Bautye to tak speciall notice and tryell of suche as sall
not mak thankfull payment of thair saidis dewes and of all suche as sall pas
by the staiple port during the tyme of his collectioun and to send home
thair names with sic notice and attestatioun as he can find of them passing
by the said staiple port with the places of thair abode, quantitie of guidis,
the maisteres of the schippis thair names, and tymes and places quhen and
quhither the saidis guidis ware transported. As also the saidis comissioneres
hes nominatid ellectid and appoyntid, lykas they be thir presenttis nominates,
ellectes and appoyntes Robert Greirsoun at Campheir to be collectour of
the said impost from the said first of Maii I^m vi^c threttie five yeires till the
first of Maii thairefter, ane thousand sex hundreth threttie sex yeires, and
ordaines him to send his comptes thairof to the comissioneres of borrowes
to the generall conventioun to be haldine in Julii thairefter to be seine and

---

33 Literally, 'concerning faithful administration', i.e. he was promising to carry out his duties
    with diligence.

considderit and fitit be them. And also to give his aith *de fideli administra-tioni*[34] and performe al uther thingis in maner abovwrettin and for this effect ordaines the generall clerk to wreat to the haill persones in maner [fo. 463r] abonwrettin foir fullfilling and obeying quhat is requyrit of them in maner foirsaid. As also to acquaint the conservatour with thair preceidinges anent the premessis and to requyre each of them for produceing thair dilligence heiranent to this generall conventioun of borrowes. And this to be ane heid of the nixt missive.

Tertio Julii I[m] vi[c] trigesimo quarto

14

The quhilk day the comissioneres of the borrowes being conveined anent the threttie sevint act of the last generall conventioun of borrowes haldine at the burgh of St Androis the nynt day of August last, ordaining thair burgh to be requyrid for sending of thair comissioneres suficientlie instructed to this present conventioun quhither it be expedient to alter the taxt rooll or not.[35] The saidis comissioneres in respect the said taxt rooll hes not bein this long tyme alterit and manifest decay of sum borrowes and increase of utheres, thairfoir hes thought fit that the same be alterit and that ilk burgh sall be requyrid foir sending thair comissioneres suficientlie instructid to the nixt generall conventioun of borrowes anent the alteratioun of the taxt rooll, forme and maner thairof under the paine of tuentie pundis. And this to be ane heid of the nixt missive.

15

The same day anent the tuentie act of the last generall conventioun of borrowes haldine at the burgh of St Androis the sevint day of August last, ordaining the burgh of Ramfrew to have producit thair dilligence to this conventioun for the restraining the inhabitantes of Grienok, Gorrock, Kartis burne, Killmcculme and Intherkip[36] from usurping the liberteis of the frie borrowes.[37] Compeirit the comissioner of the said burg and producit our soverane lordis letters raisit and execuit at thair instance and the agentes againes them and declarit that the maist pairt of thos that wer chairgit had suspendit, wiche the saidis commissioneres acceptes foir dilligence. And considdering that the saidis unfrie persones are increasit within thir few yeires to ane greit multitud and are lyk to grow in suche maner that not

---

34 Literally, 'concerning faithful administration', i.e. he was promising to carry out his duties with diligence.
35 See above, 148–9.
36 Greenock, Gourock, Cartsburn, Kilmacolm and Inverkip, Renfrewshire.
37 See above, 137–8.

onlie the said toun of Ramfrew but the wholl borrowes of the west are
licklie to decay, to the grit hurt and prejudice and lose of the wholl estait
of the borrowes of this kingdome, thairfoir the present commissioneres hes
thought guid and ordainet ane particular conventioun to be haldine at the
burgh of Edinburgh the fourt day of November nixt with continowatioun
of dayes be the burges of Edinburgh, Pearth, Dundie, Abirdeine, Stirling,
Linlithgow, Glasgow, St Androis, Air, Haddingtoun, Dumbarton, Irrving,
Ramfrew and Kinghorne, and ordaines the said burghes to be requyrit for
sending thair comissioneres suficientlie [fo. 463v] instructed for conveining
the said tyme, not onlie with thair best advyse foir preveining the said
evill and restraining of the saidis persones, but also for taking ane present
course for prosecuiting under the paine of tuentie pundis ilk burgh. To
whiche borrowes and most pairt of them conveanand the present comissioneres grantis and gives thair full power and comissioun foir taking ane
solid course anent the premisses and prosecuiting thairof, and gif neid sall
be to borrow moneyes upoun interest foir performing of thair does, and
obleisses them and thair burghes to abyd thairat and to pey suche soumes
as the[y] sall borrow to the effect foirsaid, and generallie all and sundrie
uther thingis to doe use and exerce anent the premessis quhilk the present
comissioneres might have done themselffis. As also ordaines the burgh of
Ramfrew to produce thair saidis comissioneres thair evidentes to the effect
they being considderit such course may be followit as the saidis comissioneres sall think expedient. As also ordaines the burgh of Irrving wit[h]
all dilligence to chairge the inhabitantes of the Lagis, Fairlie, Saltcottes and
Kellburnei[38] from usurping thair liberteis and to produce thair dilligence to
the said particular conventioun under the paine of fourtie pundis togidder
with thair evidentes that the lyk course may be takine with the saidis inhabitantes of the saidis places as thes that remaines within the boundis of the
said burgh of Ramfrew. Quhairanent the present comissioneres gives thair
full power and comissioun in maner abonwrettin and ordaines the same to
be ane heid of the nixt missive.

16
The same day anent the threttie fyft act of the last generall conventioun
of borrowis haldine at the burgh of St Androis the nynt day of August last,
ordaines the burgh of Dumfermling to have producit the forme of the
ellectioun of thair magistrates and counsell at Michaelmes last to this present
conventioun and to conforme themselffis in the said ellectioun conforme to
the actes of parliament and borrowes.[39] The said burgh not compeirand be

38   Largs, Fairlie, Saltcoats, Kilbirnie, Ayrshire.
39   See above, 148.

nan of thair names to have satisfiet the desyre of the missive thairanent direct
to them and being lauchfullie wairnit, the saidis comissioneres unlayes the
said burgh in the soume of tuentie pundis and ordaines the agent to uplift
the same and to report his dilligence heiranent. As also of new ordaines them
to produce the forme of the ellectioun of thair majestrates and counsell at
Michaelmis last and Michaelmes nixt and to proceid at Michaelmes nixt in
the ellectioun of thair majestrates and counsell conforme to the saidis actes
of parliament and borrowis under the paine of fourtie pundis. And this to
be ane heid of the nixt missive.

17

The same day ordaines the burgh of Rothesay foir not productioun of the
forme of the electioun of thair majestrates and counsell at Michaelmes last
being lauchfullie wairnit [fo. 464r] to that effect in the soume of tuentie
pundis and ordaines them to be requyrid foir sending of the said unlaw and
producing of thair said electioun at Michaelmes last and Michaelmes nixt
to the said nixt conventioun and foir proceiding thairin at Michaelmes nixt
conforme to the actes of parliament and borrowes undir the paine of fourtie
pundis. And this to be ane heid of the nixt missive.

18

The same day anent the sevinteine act of the last generall conventioun of
borrowis haldine at the burgh of St Androis the sevint day of August last
concerning the visitt of the Watter of Forth,[40] compeirand the comissioneres
of Anstruther Eister and Pittinwyme and gave in thair visitatioun in writt
whiche they ordaine to be delyverit to the lordis of counsell. Whiche being
done and the comissioneres finding the watter to be muche damnifiet yeirlie
notwithstanding of thair report, thairfoir gives power and comissioun to
the burghis that salbe appoyntid to remaine heirat at Edinburgh efter the
disolving of this present conventioun anent certaine uther particulares to
supplicat at the saidis lordis foir puting thair former proclamatioune maid
anent the said river againes the heretores to executioun and in causing the
custumeres in Culrois to mak thair report of thair dilligence, at the making
of thair enterie, of thair tryell of the transgressores, or utherwayes to releive
the borrowis of thair yeirlie visitatioun; to whiche borrowis the present
comissioneres giffis full power and comissioun thairanent and for doeing
quhatsumever they sall think expedient anent the premessis and to report
thair dilligence and appoyntes to visit the said watter the burghes of Kirkcaldie, Dysert and Brunteilland. And Brunteilland to conveine the uther two
and ilk burgh to report thair dilligence to the nixt generall conventioun

---

40 See above, 136–7.

anent the true estait of the said watter and deipes thairof on both sydes
under the paine of tuentie pundis ilk burgh. And this to be ane heid of the
nixt missive.

Quarto Julii I^m vi^c trigesimo quarto
[19]
The quhilk day the comissioneres of borrowis being conveinet anent the
nynteine act of the last generall conventioun of borrowis haldine at the
burgh of St Androis the aucht day of August last ordaining the burgh of
Elgine to have producit to this present conventioun thair dilligence in
restraining of certaine inhabitantes in Gairmoch[41] lyand within thair shereffdome usurping the liberteis of the frie royall borrowis.[42] Compeirid Mr
Johne Hay comissioner foir the said burgh and declarit that they haid raisit
letters foir chairging of the saidis inhabitantes and upone the desyre of the
laird of Innies of giving thair burgh satisfactioun had contenued any farder
procedour againes them. The saidis comissioneres ordaines them to proceid
with all dilligence ay and quhill they find cautioun to desist conforme to
the lawis of the kingdome [fo. 464v] and to report thair dilligence theiranent
under the paine of fourtie pundis. And this to be ane heid of the nixt missive.

20
The same day the present comissioneres being informit be ane letter of
missive direct to them from the lord conservatour schewing conforme to the
warrand givine him the last generall conventioun foir causing James Weir
collector of the ministeres stipend compeir befoir them foir geving his aith
as is prescryvid in the said act maid thairanent his deputt had requyrid the
said James who refuised to doe the same and also schewing that Thomas
Cuninghame, present collectour, had also refuised. The present comissioneres ordaines the saidis persones to be requyred foir compeiring befoir the
comissioneres to be conveinet at Edinburgh the fourt of November nixt
the said day foir answering foir thair contempt in refuising to give thair aith
under the paine of diprivatioun, as also to cite thair souerteis. And ordaines
thair clerk to direct ane missive to eich of them in thair names to the effect
foirsaid. And also ordaines the conservatour or his deputt to intimatt the
same to them in ane fencid court and to report his dilligence to the said
particular conventioun. At last the present comissioneres gives full power and
comissioun to the comissioneres then conveinand to cognose the pairteis
thair contempt and to punische them as they shall think guid thairfoir, and
generallie all and sundrie uther thinges to doe and exerce thairanent, quhilk

---

41   Garmouth, at the mouth of the Spey, in Moray.
42   See above, 137.

the present commissioneres micht doe themsellffis, and to report thair dilligence heiranent to the nixt generall conventioun of borrowes. And this to
be ane heid of the nixt missive.

21

The same day anent the tentie fourt act of the last generall conventioun
of borrowis haldine at the burgh of St Androis the aucht day of August
last dischairging the factores of Campheir from making rebaittes of thair
merchand billis at thair owine hand, ordaining the conservatour to intimat
the same to the saidis factores,[43] wheranent the said conservatour in his
missive direct to the present comissioneres declarid he had intimat the samyn
to them. As also the borrowes understanding they doe not desist, thairfoir
ordaines the conservatour to give justice to all sall compleine conforme to
the tenor of the said act. As also ordaines the said conservatour to intimat the
same of new to them and to requyre them to act themselffis foir obedience
of the same certifeing also that suche as salbe fund to have transgresid, the
comissioneres will not onlie to punische them in certaine pecuniall sowmes
but also depryve them of thair office and all priviledges of the natioune in
tyme heirefter. And the said conservatour to report his dilligence heiranent
to the nixt generall conventioun of borrowis. And this to be ane heid of
the nixt missive.

[fo. 465r]

22

The same day anent the tentie thrid act of the last generall conventioun
of borrowis haldine at the burgh of St Androis the sevint day of August last
anent the conservatour his dealling with the majestrates of Campheir for
removing of the greivancis the merchandis traffiquing thither does susteine.[44]
The present comissioneres finding manie dificulties to arryse theiranent and
thair grievances just to grow in default of the said toun, as lykwayes finding
manie thingis to be defective in thair former contract, thairfoir they give
full power and comissioun to the burghis appoyntid to conveine at Edinburgh the fourt of November nixt not onlie to try the saidis grivances and
defectes of the said contract but also to cognosce of all thingis concerning
the weill of the said staiple and to tak all course lauchfull foir suppleing
the foirsaid defectes, remeiding of the said grievancis and taiking suche
course in all thinges concerning the said staiple as they sall think neidfull,
and for heiring all supplicatiounes to be gevine in to them be the factour
and taking course thairanent, and generallie all and sundrie uther thinges to

43 See above, 139.
44 See above, 138–9.

doe, use and exerce anent the premessis whiche the present comissioneres might doe themsellffis obleissing them and thair saidis burghis to abyd and remaine at quhatsumever thinges they sall doe anent the premessis. As also ordaines the conservatour to be acquaintid with this conclussioun and thair clerk to wreitt in thair names to desyre his lordship ather be himsellff or be his letter to acquaint the borrowes with his advyse theranent and the saidis borrowes to report thair dilligence heiranent to the nixt generall conventioun of borrowes. And this to be ane heid of the nixt missive.

23
The same day anent the fourtie fourt and fourtie fyft actis of the last generall conventioun of borrowis haldin at the burgh of St Androis the nynt day of August last, ordaining the agent to uplift from the burgh of Dumfreis the soume of tuentie pundis of unlaw for being absent fra the said conventioun, as also from the burghis of Lochmaben and Sanquhair ilk ane of them the soume of tuentie pundis of unlaw foir being absent from the said conventioun and foir not sending the dewes of the missive to the samyn and foir chairging them foir payment making of the said unlawes and to haif reportid his dilligence heiranent to the present conventioun.[45] The saidis comissioneres ordaines the agent to produce the lyk dilligence he sould haiff used againes the said burghis betuix and the fourt of November nixt to the comissioneres thair to be conveinet at Edinburgh under the paine of tuentie pundis and to report his dilligence heir anent to the nixt generall conventioun. And this to be ane heid of the nixt missive.

[fo. 465v]
24
The same day the saidis comissioneres understanding be the missive direct to them be the conservatour of his paines takine anent the schipes perteining to Johne Arnit and Andro Reanie confiscat be the admirallitie of Horne for traffiquing in West Flanderes in procuiring thair satisfactioun foir the said wrong. As also considdering that in the same missive he desyres sum retributioun in his yeirlie dewetie foir his paines. Thairfoir the saidis comissioneres ordaines ane missive letter to be direct to him be thair clerk in thair names accknowledging them his debtour for his paines and returning him thankis foir his paines and desyring the continowance thairof and to eschew him that. Thairfoir they have ordainet ilk burgh to be requyrid foir sending thair comissioneres sufficientlie instructid with thair advyse foir ane retributioun foir his saidis paines and foir taking course foir finding out sum better meines for his honorable intertynement wheranent thir presentis sall be his

---

45 See above, 151.

warrand. As also ordaines ilk burgh to be requyrid to the said effect and foir augmentatioun of his saidis dewes and this to be ane heid of the nixt missive.

25

The same day the saidis comissioneres efter perussall of the letter direct to them from the factores of Campheir finding that sundrie propositiones thairine maid does not deserve ane answer and that foir utheres whiche seimes more reassonable it had beine necessare to have followit be sum of thair owne presences. Thairfoir they ordaine thair clerk to wrytt to them in thair names schewing how refractorie they fund them in all thair actiones be thair constitutiounes notwithstanding of thair severall obleismentes and thairefter to desyre them to give full obedience and satisfactioun to what hes bein and is injoynit to them, and therefter they may expect ane reassonable answer of thair reassonable demandis. And becaus they have ordainet sum of thair noumber to compeir befoir theme upoun the fourt of November nixt, thairfoir to desyre them if they have anything to sute to acquaint the saidis persones with thair desyre, quhairanent according to thair obedience they may exspect ane favourable answer as said is, quhairanent thir presentis sall be unto him ane warrand.

26

The same day the comptes of James Weir, leat collectour of the impost grantit foir difraying of the ministeres stipend at Campheir, of his intromissioun thairwith frome the first of September I^m vi^c threttie tua yeires to the tuentie fyft of August I^m vi^c threttie thrie yeires inclusive being hard, seine, fitted and callcullat be the saidis comissioneres, they fand the same to extend to the soume of ane hundreth thriescoir fourteine pundis tua grit Fleymes mony. As also findis him to have ressavit, whiche was omittit furth of Robert Bawtyes comptes, the soume of foure pundis fyve schillinges greit mony foirsaid, which being adit to his said intromissioun makis his chairge in the haill to amount to the soume of ane hundreth [fo. 466r] thriescoir auchteine pundis fyve schillinges tua grit mony foirsaid and findis his dischairge of the soumes payid be him to the minister and reider to extend to the soume of ane hundreth thriescoir tua pund mony foirsaid. Sua they find the compter to be addebtid to the borrowes in the soume of sexteine pundis tua schillinges tua gritt mony foirsaid whiche they ordaine the said James to delyver to Thomas Cunninghame, present collectour, whereanent thir presenttis sallbe his warrand and the said Thomas to be chairgid thairwith in his comptes. As also the saidis borrowes considdering that Robert Bawtye, preceiding collectour to the said James, was superexpendit the yeir of his accomptes in the soume of ane hundreth sevine pundis ane grit Fleymes whiche hes not beine payid to him be the said James, thairfoir they ordaine the said Thomas to pey to him the said soume out of the readiest of his intromissioun and the samyn sall be unto him ane warrand foir allowing thairof in his comptes. And ordaines lykwayes ane letter to be wrettine to the said Thomas for this effect be thair clerk, quhairanent thir presenttis salbe unto him ane warrand. And last the saidis comissioneres understanding be the said James his comptes that sundrie persones hes past both out of the yle as also from Campheir not paying thair dewes, thairfore ordaines the burghis to whome the saidis persones does belong to exact the double of suche soumes of mony as they sould have payid thair conforme to the inventar following: viz in September 1632 Thomas Gray, Johne Stirling, Williame Johnestoun, Archibald Pattone, David Grahame, George Laurie, Alexander Lockart in Edinburgh, in October thairefter Johne Glen, Johne Somervaill, Robert Pringill, Johne Gibsone, Williame Bicked, in Appryll 1633 Walter Borthwik, Robert Black, Robert Stirling, Hendrie Robertsone, Johne Bisset, Alexander Lockart, George Reid, George Campbell, Thomas Gray, in September thairefter Thomas Gray, Johne Merteine, Johne Dehnholme, George Jarden merchandis in Edinburgh, in October 1632 Adam Gordoun in Aberdeine, in Appryll 1633 Robert Alexander, Walter Willsone, Williame Lawsone, Johne Williamsone, Patrick Park, Johne Moreisone, Johne Stirling, Williame Andersone, Johne Andersone merchandis in Glasgow, which persones did come out of the yle of Walker[46] not peying thair dewes and wes dew ilk ane of them in the soume of fyve schillinges Fleymes in respect nan of them had ane seck of guidis thair. Item the persones underwrittin past out of the said yle unpaying thair dewes the yeire of the said James Weir his comptes, viz Williame Sympsone in Dysert with Inglis crallis from Flussen,[47] David Spens in Kirkcadie with ane hundreth collis from Middillburgh, Thomas Law and George Hackid in Kirkcadie from Flussen, David Robertsone in Leith from Flussen, James Dowar in Leith from Middilburgh cam from France and ordaines the saidis burghis to send with thair comissioneres the double of the saidis dewes to the nixt generall conventioun or utherwayes to present the saidis persones under the paine of tuentie pundis ilk burgh, provyding allwayes that suche burghis as makis payment of the singill foir thair nichtboures at the conventioun of November nixt sall be frie of the said double.

[fo. 466v]

27

The same day anent that heid of the missive ordaining William Gray and Mr Alexander Guthrie thair laitt comissioneres to mak thair reportes of thair proceidinges with his Majestie of the matteres concredit unto them

---

46 Walcheren, in Zeeland.
47 Vlissingen, or Flushing, on the island of Walcheren, in Zeeland.

conforme to the instructiones givine to them and severall actes of borrowes maid thairanent and contenit in diverse heidis of the present missive. Compeirid the saidis Williame Gray and Mr Alexander Guthrie and maid report of thair haill preceidinges with his Majestie of the haill particulares following and producit the coppie of his Majesties letter direct to the lordis of the sessioun dischairging them to proceid in the matter of the tythis of the Iles. As lykwayes the coppie of the letter foir the same effect direct to the bischope of the Illes, the principallis quhairof wer delyverit to the saidis lordis of sessioun and bishope of the Iles. As lykwayes producit tua severall letters direct to the comissioneres of borrowes quhilkes ware instantlie red, the ane thairof foir devyding thair inhabitantes in severall companies foir better managing of trade, the other foir erecting of companies of maniefactoreis amongist them foir advanceing the native comiditeis of the kingdome conteining his Majesties promeis foir contributing to both the saidis workes and protecting of them thairin. As also producit ane signatour anent the erectioun of correctioun houssis within the saidis frie borrowes. As also ane letter direct to the lordis of counsell foir dischairging the monopollie of perll with ane letter to them restraining the frequent granting of protectiones with ane uther foir dischairging the renewing of the patent anent tanning. As also producid the coppie of ane letter direct be his Majestie to his thesaurers principall and deputt dischairging the farder execuitioun of that penale statutt maid anent transporting of mony, the principall quhairof they have delyverit to the saidis thesaureres since thair home cuming. As lykwayes declarit thair proceidinges anent the Lord Spynnie his pattent referrit be the parliament to the counsell againes whiche the comissioneres of borrowes with certaine thair nobillitie and gentrie had gevine in sume informatiounes to the saidis lordis of counsell, quhairupoun the saidis lordis remettit the samyn to his Majestie and declarit that they heaving petitiounid his Majestie thairanent, who was graciouslie pleisid to remeitt the same back to the saidis lordis willing them to proceid thairin as sould best tend to his service and weill of the countrie, as the coppie thairof whiche they produced beires, the principall quhairof was delyverit to the saidis lordis. And last declarid thair proceidinges in the matter of the associatioun of the fischinges with thair proceidinges anent the leatt restraint in Irland and mutuall participatioun of all native comodities betuixt his Majesties thrie kingdomes, quhairin they declarid they did find his Majestie werie willing and that they onlie laickit tyme foir prosecuiting the same to the finall perfectioun thairof. With thair whiche haill proceidinges the present comissioneres ware weall pleisid and be thir presentis allowes thairof and foir delyvere of the said letters and foir farder prosecutioun [fo. 467r] of the haill letteres and materes thairin contenit and in the report abovwrittin the present comissioneres ordaines the comissioneres of the borrowes of Edinburgh, Perth, Dundie, Abirdeine, Stirling, Linlithgow, St Androis, Glasgow, Air, Haddingtoun, Dunbartoun,

Suther Eister,[48] Kirkcadie, Dumfreis, Monrois, Irrving, Kinghorne, Couper, Carrell, Brunteilland, Krikcudbright and Jedburgh to meit and conveine at this burgh the aucht of this instant with continowatioun of dayes and prosecuit the saidis purpossis recomending the same to thair caire seriouslie and earnest dilligence, granting, giving and commiting unto them thair full power and comissioun foir doeing thairof and all and quhatsumever thinges they think neidfull may tend to the weill of the borrowes and performing of the saidis effaires ather be imployment at home or abrod and bestowing thairupoun as they in thair judgment sall think best. All which thair procei- dinges the present comissioneres ratifies and approves and obleissis them and thair burghis to abyd thairat but contradictioun or againe calling. And lastlie the saidis comissioneres understanding that the burgh of Edinburgh had advancit to thair saidis comissioneres the soume of sex thousand merkes, quhairof they ordaine ilk burgh to be requyrid to send thair pairt of the soume of thrie thousand merkes conforme to the taxt roll with thair comis- sioneres to the nixt generall conventioun of borrowes with thair pairt of the soume of sex hundreth merkes as foir the anuelrent thairof fra the feist of Witsonday last to the feist of Witsonday nixt. As also ordaines the rest of the said soume extending to the soume of thrie thousand merkes to be payid at the nixt generall conventioun to be haldine in Julii I^m vi^c threttie sex yeires and the same to be rememberit in the missive to be direct the said yeire. And the said borrowes to report thair dilligence heiranent to the nixt generall conventioun of borrowes. And this to be ane heid of the nixt missive.[49]

28

The same day anent the sext act of the particular conventioun of borrowes haldine at the burgh of Edinburgh the tuentie fourt day of Januarii last ordaining ilk burghe sending thair comissioneres sufficientlie instructid to the present conventioun foir condiscending anent the necessitie of ane agent at court.[50] The saidis comissioneres findis it expedient and necessare that thair be ane agent establisched at court foir attending thair affaires and anent the persoun and exersione of the place hes thought guid to continow the samyn to the nixt generall conventioun and thairfoir ordaines ilk burgh to be requyrid foir sending thair comissioneres suficientlie instructid. And the samyn to be ane heid of the nixt missive.

---

48 Anstruther Easter.
49 This act is given in slightly abbreviated form in the Abstract of Acts of Convention, *RCRBS*, iv, 538–9.
50 See above, 160.

29

The same day anent the nynt act of the last generall conventioun of borrowis haldine at the burgh of St Androis the sevint day of August last concerning Maister David Weddirburnes grammer and ordaining the samyn to be taucht within the wholl grammer scollis of the frie borrowis of this realme and to begine at Michaelmes last.[51] The present comissioneres recomendis the samyn of new and ordaines ilk burgh to report thair dilligence in causing thair scoll maisteris to receave and teiche the samyn under the paine of xx lib. And this to be remembrit in the missive.

[fo. 467v]
30

The same day anent the sevint act of the last particular conventioun of borrowes haldin at the burgh of Edinburgh in Januarii last anent the new and heavie impositiones in France,[52] the present comissioneres considdering the wecht and importance of the said matter hes thoucht guid that presentlie sum course salbe taikine foir remeiding thairof and restoring the natioun to thair ancient liberties. And thairfoir ordaines the comissioneres appointit to meitt at this burgh the aucht of this instant to tak the same to thair serious considderationes and to use all meines possible foir remeiding of the said evill and if neid salbe to condischend upoun suche persones as they sall think most fitt foir prosecuiting thairof abroad and to aggrie anent thair chairges and quhat may be incident in that purpos and quhatsumever the saidis comissioneres sall doe anent the premessis the present comissioneres ratifies and approves the samyn and obleissis them and thair burghis to abyd thairat but contradictioun or againe calling. And ordaines them to report thair proceidinges in the said matter to the nixt generall conventioun of borrowis. And this to be ane heid of the nixt missive.

Quinto Julii I[m] vi[c] trigesimo quarto

31

The quhilk day anent the fyft act of the particular conventioun of borrowis haldine at Edinburgh the fyft day of October last ordaining the burgh of Linlithgow to be requyrit foir sending with thair commissioner to this present conventioun the forme of the ellectioun of thair counsell and magistrates at Michaelmes last autenticklie subscryvit under the paine of tuentie pund,[53] compeired Andro Bell comissioner of the said burgh and confest that thair ellectioun was informall, and thairfoir in name of the said burgh

---

51 See above, 133–4.
52 See above, 160.
53 See above, 156.

submittid himselff in the borrowes will to abyd thair will and determinatioun thairanent in all thinges. The present comissioneres being advysit
thairwith thought good to dispense withall thair bygaine escaipes upoun
houpe of thair more formall proceidinges in all tyme cumming and ordaines
the said burgh with consent of thair present commissioneres in tyme cuming
in the ellectioun of thair majestrates, proveist, baillies, deane of gild, thesaurer
and wholl counsell, to conforme themsellffes to the actes of parliament and
borrowes and especiallie in the persones ellectores and quallitie of persones
to be ellectid under the paine of ane hundreth pund *toties quoties*.[54] And to
the effect the samyne may be knowine, to produce the forme of thair said
ellectioun at Michaelmes nixt to the nixt generall conventioun of borrowes
under the paine of tuentie pundis. Lykas thair said comissioner in name of
the said burgh [o]bleised himsellff to the effect foirsaid. And siclyk understanding that thair is ane greit inorminitie in the matter of thair gildrie
whiche although they have ane deine of gild yeirlie chosine, yit his office
hes never beine knowine within the said burgh to the greit confussioun
and hurt of the merchand tredderes thair. And thairfoir the saidis comissioneres ordaines the said burgh to sett doun ane gildrie in suche sort as
they sall find to be most agreiable to the estait of thair burgh and conforme
to the actes of parliament [fo. 468r] and to present the samyn to the nixt
generall conventioun to be seine and consdderit be the comissioneres then
conveinand to the effect that quhat salbe defective may be supplied be the
said commissioneres and ane course takine foir better establisching thairof
in amongist them in tyme cuming under the paine of tuentie pundis. And
this to be ane heid of the nixt missive.

32

The same day anent the thrid act of the last particular conventioun haldine
at Edinburgh the tuentie fourt day of Januarii last ordaining Robert Bawtye
factour to be cited be the missive foir compeiring [before][55] this present
conventioun to find cautioun of new conforme to the ordour, with certificatioun if he failyeid they wald dischairge him of his said office, and in the
meantyme James Barnes merchand in Edinburgh his cautioner to stand.[56]
Compeired the said James Barnes merchand and past from his former
complent and declared that he was content to stand cautioun conforme to
his act of cautionrie maid of befoir.

---

54 As often as it shall happen, i.e. for each offence.
55 There is no space in the MS but the sense requires this insertion.
56 See above, 158.

33

The same day anent the letter procuired be the burgh of Dundye anent the alteratioun of thair taxt from his Majestie direct to the lordis of counsell, the comissioner of the said burgh compeirand, produced the said principall letter whiche the saidis borrowes remitted to be considderit be the comissioneres conveinand the aucht of this instant whom they ordaine to tak suche course thairin as they sall think may most tend to the weill of the borrowes. Quhairanent they grant them thair full power and comissioun and the said burgh to report thair dilligence heiranent to the nixt generall conventioun of borrowis. And this to be ane heid of the nixt missive.

34

The same day anent the threttie nynt act of the last generall conventioun of borrowes haldine at the burgh of St Androis the nynt day of August last anent the heaven of Braidheaven of Fyndochtie[57] and expedience thairof, the saidis comissioneres understanding the expedience thairof foir all schippis, barkes and creares passing and goeing to and from the north hes thought guid that the burgh of Elgyne sall deall with the heretores of the land thairanent and try the chairges thairof and the said burgh to report thair dilligence heiranent to the nixt generall conventioun of borrowes. And this to be ane heid of the nixt missive.

35

The same day ordaines the burgh of Invernes to produce the forme of the ellectioun of thair majestrates at[58] counsell at Michaelmes nixt to the nixt generall conventioun of borrowis and to conforme themsellffis in thair said ellectioun conforme to the actes of parliament and borrowes under the paine of tuentie pundis. And this to be ane heid of the nixt missive.

[fo. 468v]
36

The same day anent the supplicatioun gevine tuitching the laite patent procuired be Sir James Leslie and Thomas Dallmahoy anent the selling of tubaco, quhairwith the comissioneres being advysitt finding the prejudice thair nichtbouris shall susteine and dangerous preparative foir ane exemple to otheres and the impairing of thair liberteis hes thairfoir remeittid and remittis the samyn to the comissioneres of borrowis to be conveined at this burgh the aucht of this instant with continowatioun of dayes, to whiche borrowes they grant thair full power and comissioun to doe thairin as they

---

57   Findochty lies east of Buckie on the Banffshire coast. It is called 'the braidheavin within Speyhoupe' in the 39th act of the general convention of 1633 (see above, 149.
58   This should be 'and'.

shall think most meit and expedient foir the weill of the borrowes in suche frie and ample maner as the present comissioneres might doe themsellffis presentlie. And the said borrowes to report thair dilligence heiranent to the nixt generall conventioun of borrowes. And this to be ane heid of the nixt missive.

37

The same day wheras the comissioneres of borrowes upoun the necessitie of ane herbarie of Northberwick wer formerlie pleged to recomend the same to the charitable and vollunter support of the haill borrowes, and finding that sum hes not as yit rememberit the said work in defect of ane collectour which wold eat upe the support of the remote borrowis. Thairfoir does of new recomend the same to thair chiratable consideratioun desyring suche as hes not contribute as they salbe moved to pittie ane old burgh and to send thair chiritable support to the agent to the effect the samyn may cum to the said burgh frie of chairges.

38

The same day the saidis comissioneres understanding be ane supplicatioun gevine in be Katherine Muire relict of umquhill James Cowane in Dysert of ane great insolencie comittid be ane Pitter Jacobsone, Capitane of ane friebutter in Ostend [against][59] the said James Cowane as he was reddie to goe in to Ostend in killing of the said skipper and taking of the said scheipe and confiscutting the same with hir wholl guidis being ane frie schipe leadonit with wynes frome France to certaine persones dwelling in Ostend. Thairfoir ordaines thair clerk to writt to the conservatour recomending the said purpose to his cair and prosecuitioun four the whiche his paynis and all his uther travell they salbe readie to requytt the samyn when occasioun sall offer and sall not be unmyndfull thairof.

39

The same day anent the supplicatioun gevine in name of Alexander Speir, younger, merchand presentlie resident in Campheir, craveing the said comissioneres thair ratificatioun and approbatioun to his admissioun to be ane factour at the said staiple port. The saidis commissioneres being weill advysit thairwith and understanding perfytlie of the said Alexander his suficiencie, qualificatioun and abillitie of the dischairge of ane honest and perfyt dewetie in the office of factorie, hes grantit and gevine lykeas they be thir presentis grantes and geves [fo. 469r] thair allowance, ratificatioun and approbatioun foir his admissioun to the said office provyding allwayes that the samyn sall

---

[59]   There is no space in the MS but the sense requires this insertion.

indure during the comissioneres of borrowes thair will allanerlie and his non
mariage and efter he be mariet his said office *hoc ipso facto*[60] to expyre and
that he behave himsellff honestlie and dewtifullie in the said office, and sall
mak just and thankfull compt reckoning and payment of his intromissioun
with quhatsumever guidis or geire or soumes of mony that he sall happine
to intromett or to be intrustid with perteining to quhatsumever persone or
persones salbe pleisid to imploy him in the said office or that he sall intromet
with at comand and directioun of the borrowes. And that he sall obey and
fullfill all and quhatsumever actes and statutes maid or to be maid be the
comissioneres of borrowes in thair generall or particular conventiones. And
sall undergoe all suche offices as they sall pleis to burdeine him withall and
sall dischairge ane honest dewtye to all merchandis and sall not refuis to
accept of thair imploymentes, howsoever meine the samyn sall happine to
be, quhensoever he salbe requireid be them or ony of them. And that he
salbe obedient to the discipline of churches thair, and sall mak no rebaittes
of merchandis billis at his owine hand conforme to the act of borrowes
dischairgeing the samyn, and last that he find cautioun for fullfilling and
obeying of the haill premessis. For the whiche caus compeirid Alexander
Speir elder, merchand, James Inglis portioner of Craumound, Johne Rynd,
David Jonkying, Patrick Woode and Williame Mitchell merchand burgesses
of the said burgh of Edinburgh, became actit and obleist themsellffes lykas
they be thir presentis actes and obleissis themsellffes conjunctlie and severallie thair aires, executouris and assignayes, that the said Alexander sall behave
himsellff honestlie and dewtifullie in the said office, and that he sall make just
and thankfull compt, reckoning and payment off all soumes of mony guidis
and geire quhatsumever that he sall happin to intromett or be intrustid with
be vertew of his said office to all suche persones as sall happine to imploy
himsellff and of all soumes of mony he sall intromett with at comand of
the saidis borrowes. And generallie foir his fullfilling and obeying of the
haill premessis abonwrittin and especiallie if he sall happine to marye that
he sall mak just compt, reckoning and payment befoir his marieige of all
his imploymentes. As also befoir his admissioun he sall compeir judiciallie
befoir the conservatour or his deputes and mak faith *de fideli administratione*[61]
and foir obeying of the saidis actes maid or to be maid and fullfilling of the
haill premessis. As also the saidis persones obleissis them that he sall compeir
befoir the comissioneres of borrowes the nixt particular conventioun of
borrowes to be haldin within this burgh in the moneth of November nixt
for fullfilling and obeying the haill premessis. And last the saidis persones
actit and obleist themselffes each on to relieve utheres and thair foirsaidis *pro*

---

60 By that very fact/action, i.e. automatically.
61 Literally, 'concerning faithful administration', i.e. he was promising to carry out his duties
    with diligence.

rato[62] foir all coist, skaith, damnage and interest that they or ony of them or thair foirsaidis sall susteine in maner abonwrittin and in taikine thairof hes subscryvit thir presentis with thair handis in presence of the saidis comissioneres. Sic subscribitur Alexander Speire, James Inglis, Johne Rynd, David Jonkine, Williame Mitchellsone, Patrick Wood.

[fo. 469v]

40

The same day anent the supplicatioun gevine in be Richard Weir, laufull sone to Thomas Weir pewderer burges of Edinburght creaving the saidis comissioneres thair ratificatioun and approbatioun to his admissioun to be ane factour at thair lordshipis staiple port at Campheir, the saidis comissioneres being advysit and understanding perfytlie of the said Richard his sufficiencie abillitie and qualificatioun of the dischairge of ane honest and perfyt dewtye in the said office of factorie, hes grantit and gevine lykas they be thir presentis grantes and geves thair allowance ratificatioun and approbatioun foir his admissioun to the said office provyding allwayes that the same sall indure during the comissioneres of borrowes thair will allanerlie and his non mariage and efter he be maryet his said office *hoc ipso facto*[63] to expyre. And that he behave himsellff honestlie and dewtifullie in the said office and sall mak just and thankfull compt, reckoning and payment of his intromitioun with quhatsumever guidis and geir or soumes of mony that he sall happine to intromet or be intrusted with pertening to quhatsumever persone or persones salbe pleised to imploy him in the said office or that he sall intromett with at comand and directioun of the borrowes. And that he sall obey and fullfill all and quhatsumever actes and satutes maid or to be made be the comissioneres of borrowes in thair generall or particular conventiounes, and sall undergoe all suche offices and service as they salbe pleised to burdeine him withall, and sall dischairge ane honest dewtye to all merchandis, and sall nocht refuis to accept of thair imploymentes, howsoever meine it sall happine the samyn to be, quhensoever he salbe requyrit be them or ony of them. And that he shall be obedient to the discipline of the churche thair, and sall mak no rebaittes of merchandis billis at his owine hand conforme to the act of borrowes dischairgeing the same. And last that he find cautioun foir fullfilling and obeying of the haill premessis. For the which caus compeired Robert Sandilandis, merchand, the said Thomas Weir and Adame Levingstoun merchand and becane actit lykas they be thir presentis actes and obleissis themsellffes conjunctlie and severallie thair aires, executouris and assignayes that the said Richard Weir sall behave himselff

62 This seems to mean that they will pay equal shares of compensation as the act does not indicate that the individuals undertook different shares of the caution (surety).

63 By that very fact/action, i.e. automatically.

honestlie and dewtifullie in the said office and that he sall mak just and thankfull compt, reckoning and payment of all soumes of mony he sall intromet with at comand of the saidis borrowes. And also that he sall mak just compt, reckoning and payment of all soumes of mony guidis and geir quhatsumever that he sallhappin to intromet or be intrustid with be vertew of his said office to all suche persones as sall happine to imploy him, and generallie foir his fullfilling and obeying of the haill premissis abonwrittin. And especiallie that iff he sall happen to marye that he sall mak just compt reckoning and payment befoir his mariage of all his imploymentes, as also befoir his admissioun he sall compeir judiciallie befoir the conservatour or his deputes and mak faith *de fideli administatione*[64] and foir obeying the said actes maid or to be maid, [fo. 470r] and foir fullfilling of the haill premessis. And last the saidis persones actit and obleist themsellfes each on to relieve utheres and thair foirsaidis *pro rato*[65] off all coist, skaith, damnage and interest that they or ony of them or thair foirsaidis sall susteine in maner abonwrittin. And in taikine subscryvit thir presentis with thair handis. Sic subscribitur Richard Weir, Thomas Weir, Robert Sandilandis, Adame Levingstoun.

41

The same day anent the supplicatioun gevine in be David Drumond creaving the saidis comissioneres thair ratificatioun and approbatioun to his admissioun to be ane factour foir the natioun at the staiple port of Campheir, the saidis comissioneres being weill advysit and understanding perfytle of the said David his suficiencie, abillitie and qualificatioun of the dischairge of ane honest and perfyt dewtye in the office of factorie hes grantit and gevine, lykas they be thir presentis grantes and geves allowance, ratificatioun and approbatioun foir his admissioun to the said office provyding allwayes that the same sall indure during the comissioneres thair will allanerlie and his non marieige and efter he be maryet his said office *hoc ipso facto*[66] to expyre. And that he sall mak just and thankfull compt, reckoning and payment of his intromissioun with quhatsumever guidis or geire or soumes of mony that he sall happine to intromet or be intrustid with perteining to quhatsumever persone or persones sall be pleised to imploy him in the said office or that he sall intromet with at comand or directioun of the borrowes. And that he sall obey and fullfill all and quhatsumever actes and statutes maid or to be maid be the comissioneres of borrowes in thair generall or particular conventiones, and sall undergoe all suche offices and service as they salbe

---

[64] Literally, 'concerning faithful administration', i.e. he was promising to carry out his duties with diligence.

[65] This seems to mean that they will pay equal shares of compensation as the act does not indicate that the individuals undertook different shares of the caution (surety).

[66] Literally, 'by that very fact', i.e. automatically.

pleised to burdeine him withall, and sall dischairge ane honest dewtye to all merchandis and sall nocht refuis to accept of thair imploymentes, howsoever meine the samyn sall happine to be, quhensoever he salbe requyrit be them or ony of them. And that he salbe obedient to the disipline of the churche thair and sall mak no rebaittes of merchandis billis at his owine hand, conforme to the act of borrowes, dischairging the samyn. And last that he find cautioun foir fullfilling and obeying of the haill premessis. Foir the whiche caus compeired William Butter of Newtounleyes and Walter Cant merchand bourges of Edinburgh and became actit, lykas they be thir presentis actes and obleissis themsellffes conjunctlie and severallie thair aires, executouris and assignayes that the said David Drummond sall behave himselff honestlie and dewtifullie in the said office and that he sall mak just and thankfull compt, reckoning and payment of all soumes of mony, guidis and geire quhatsumever that he sall happine to intromet or be intrustid with, be vertew of his said office, to all suche persones as sall happine to imploy him and of all soumes of mony he sall intromett with at comand of the said borrowes [fo. 470v] and generallie foir his fullfilling and obeying of the haill premessis abovwrettin, and especiallie if he sall happine to mary that he sall mak just compt, reckoning and payment befoir his mariage of all his imploymentes. As also, befoir his admissioun he sall compeir judiciallie befoir the conservatour or his deputes and mak faith *de fideli administratione*[67] and foir obeying the saidis actes maid or to be maid, and foir fullfilling of the haill premessis. And last the saidis persones actit and obleist themsellffes each on to relieve utheres and thair foirsaid *pro rato*[68] off all coist, skaith, damnage and interest that they or ony of them or thair foirsaidis sall susteine in maner abovwrettin. And the said David Drummond obleissis him to warrand friely releive and skaithles keipe his said cautioneris of all damnage, interrest and expenssis that they or thair foirsaidis sall happine to incure in tyme cuming. In witnes quhairof they have subscrivit thir presentis with thair handis in presens of the saidis commissioneres. Sic subscribitur David Drummond, Walter Cant, W Butter.

42

The same day anent the supplicatioun gevine in be the baillies of Anstruther Eister creaving the borrowes thair concurance and helpe foir building thair ane churche within thair toun, being necessitie[69] to seik that benefite ane myll from thair burgh, with all uther benefites of the churche to thair greit

---

67 Literally, 'concerning faithful administration', i.e. he was promising to carry out his duties with diligence.

68 This seems to mean that they will pay equal shares of compensation as the act does not indicate that the individuals undertook different shares of the caution (surety).

69 This should probably be 'necessitat', i.e. compelled.

discomfort. The borrowes ordaines ilk burgh to be requyrit foir sending thair comissioneres suficientlie instructid to the nixt generall conventioun to give answer thairto under the paine of tuentie pundis. And this to be ane heid of the nixt missive.

43

The same day upoun the supplicatioun gevine in be the comissioneres of Dumfreis foir the unlaw incurid be thair absence at the last generall conventioun and evident remonstrance being maid and thair absence was in default of thair comissioner his seiknes. The present comissioneres dispenssis with the said unlaw and dischairges the agent from uplifting thairof, quhairanent thir presentis salbe unto him ane warrand.

44

The same day the said comissioneres grantes and geves licences to the burghes of Sanquhair, Forres, and Rutherglen to abyd and remaine severall[70] generall conventioun of borrowes for the space of thrie yeires upoun the conditiones and provisiones efter following: provyding the samyn be not extendit to parliamentes nor quhen the said burghis are citat foir ony particular caus, and also provyding the saidis burghes send with the comissioneres of thair nixt adjacent burghes the severall ratificatiounes autenticklie subscryvit of all thinges to be done yeirlie at the saidis generall or particular conventiones, with all somever that they sould pey to the borrowes conforme to the missive and that they bestow thair expenssis that they sould have bestowed upoun thair comissioneres upoun comoun workis and be comptable thairof to the borrowes at the expyring of the said yeires.

[fo. 471r]
45

The same day ordaines the burgh of Linlithgow to produce thair dilligence to the nixt generall conventioun of borrowes in restrayning the inhabitantes of the South Ferrie[71] frome usurping the liberteis of the frie royall borrowes, viz Robert Hill, James Dawling elder and younger, Edward Litill, David Willsone, George Logie, Samuell Willsone, James Jamiesone, George Hill, Johne Allane, Williame Allane, Robert Allane, Pitter Logie, George Patoun, Johne Ewing, James Finlay, Robert Dawling and Archibald Logie under the paine of tuentie pundis. And this to be ane heid of the nixt missive.

---

[70] It is assumed that this is a copyist's error for something like 'fra the' since the text makes no sense as it stands.
[71] South Queensferry.

46

The same day ordaines ane letter to be direct to the conservatour foir seing the Saboth day at Campheir keiped and ordaines thair generall clerk to subscryve the same, quhairanent thir presentis salbe his warrand.[72]

47

The same day ordaines thair clerk to ressave fra the conseravatour or ony in his name suche persones names as hes depairted fra the Law Countrye not paying thair dewes to the conservatour at suche tymes as they salbe gevine in to him and to requyre the burgh or[73] to whom they doe belong to uplift the said dewes from the saidis persones and to send the samyn to the nixt generall conventioun with thair comissioneres, or to produce the saidis persones before them with certificatioun contenit in the former actes maid thairanent.

48

The same day the comptes of the agent being heard and seing him supper expendit in the borrowes effaires in the soume of fyve hundreth fyfteine pundis auchteine schillinges four penyes. And thairfoir ordaines ilk burgh to be requyrit foir sending thair pairt thairof conforme to the taxt roll with thair comissioneres to the nixt generall conventioun togidder with the bygaine annuelrent and annuelrent foir the yeire to cum extending in the haill to the soume of sex hundreth fyfteine pundis auchteine schillinges four penyes under the paine of tuentie pundis by and attour thair pairt of the said soume, togidder also with the soume of tuellff pundis sevine schillinges sex penyes to the burgh of Culrois, to the burgh of Anstruther Eister tuentie pundis, to the burgh of Pittinwyme tuentie pundis foir thair paines taikine in surveying of the Watter [of] Forth. And the samyn to be ane heid of the nixt missive.

[fo. 471v]

49

The same day wheras the commissioneres understanding the burghes to be inclyned to policie upoun the comoune expenssis of the burgh or nichtboures does intend to build sum comoune workes, and yit suche is the presumptioun of sum to perpetuat thair names and vindicat the credit of the saidis workes to themsellffes does intend to fix thair names thairupoun to the discouragment of the rest of thair nichtbouris, quhairby they prove slak in promoving thairof or attempting of the lyk in tyme cumming, for

---

72 This act is noted in the Abstract of Acts of Convention, *RCRBS*, iv, 539.
73 Either something has been omitted here or the word 'or' is superfluous.

the whiche caus the present comissioneres statutes and ordaines that no particular inhabitant or burges of quhatsumever qualitie or degrie presume to doe the lyk upoun ony suche wallis in tyme cuming under the paine of depryving of them of the liberteis of thair burgh and ordaines ilk burgh to be cairfull in execuiting heirof under the paine of ane hundreth pundis to be peyid to the bearer and ilk comissioner present to intimat the same to thair burgh at thair home cuming and the saidis burghes thair dilligence in intimating the samyn to thair nichtboures and keiping thairof under the paine of tuentie pundis. And this to be ane heid of the nixt missive.[74]

50

The same day ordaines the agent to pey to George Ramsay, post, the soume of fyftie pundis and the said soume salbe allowed to him in his comptes.

51

The same day unlawes the burgh of Dumfermling from being absent from this present conventioun being lawfullie wairnit thairto in the soume of tuentie pundis by and attour the former unlaw incurrit be them and ordaines the agent to uplift the same and to produce his dilligence in uplifting thairof to the nixt generall conventioun. And this to be ane heid of the nixt missive.

52

The samyn day unlawes the burgh of Lochmaben foir being absent and foir not sending the dewes of the missive in tuentie pund, and ordaines the agent to uplift the samyn and to produce his dilligence in doeing thairof to the nixt generall conventioun of borrowes. And this to be ane heid of the nixt missive.

[fo. 472r]

53

The same day the present comissioneres desolves this present conventioun and affixis thair generall conventioun of borrowes to be haldine at the burgh of Pearth the [...] day of Julii nixt.[75]

---

[74] This act is noted in the Abstract of Acts of Convention, RCRBS, iv, 539.

[75] The rest of the folio is blank and the record of the next convention begins on the verso of this folio, presumably because it followed immediately afterwards and the same Aberdonian commissioner attended both, bringing back a copy of their acts in a single, continuous record.

Particular Convention at Edinburgh, 8 July 1634

[fo. 472v]
In the particular conventioun of borrowes haldine at the burgh of Edinburgh
the aucht day of Julii the yeir of God ane thousand sex hundreth threttie
four yeires be the comissioneres of borrowes underwrittin be vertew of ane
comissioun gevine to them be the last generall conventioun of borrowes
haldine at the said burgh the fourt of this instant.

Edinburgh	Williame Gray, Williame Carnegye
Pearth	Andro Gray
Dundie	Thomas Halyburtoun younger
Abirdeine	Mr Alexander Jaffray
Stirling	Johne Johnestoun
Lynlithgow	Andro Bell
St Androis	Robert Tailyeour
Glasgow	Patrick Bell
Air	Johne Osburne
Dumbarton	Johne Sempill
Anstruther Eister	
Kirkcaldie	Williame Tennent
Dumfreis	Johne Williamsone
Montrose	Patrik Lichtoun
Cowper	Robert Pittersone
Kinghorne	Mr Robert Cuninghame
Caraill[1]	Johne Mckesone
Brunteilland[2]	Andro Watsone
Kirkcudbright	
Jedburgh	Mr Johne Rutherfuird

1
The same day the saidis comissioneres ellectes Williame Gray, first in comissioun foir the burgh of Edinburgh, to be moderatour during this present
conventioun quha compeirand acceptid the said office in and upoun him
and gave his aith *de fideli administratione*.[3]

Nono Julii I[m] vi[c] trigesimo quarto

---

1   Crail.
2   Burntisland.
3   Literally, 'concerning faithful administration', i.e. he was promising to carry out the duties
    of moderator with diligence.

2

The quhilk day the comissioneres of borrowes being conveined anent the report of thair late comissioneres concerning the errecting of companies for the weill managing of tred and advanceing of the native comoditeis, the present comissioneres considering the good redoundis to these citteis where traid is ordourlie rewlit and confussioun takine away, [fo. 473r] hes thairfoir thought good and ordainet the burgh of Edinburgh to sett doun suche articles, patentes, lawes and suche uther thinges thairanent as they sall think meitt and to present the samyn to the nixt occurring particular conventioun, and failyeing thairof to the nixt generall conventioun, and that ilk burgh be requyrid foir sending thair comissioneres suficientlie instructid with thair best advyse and oppinioun thairanent. And the samyn to be ane heid of the nixt missive.[4]

3

The same day the said comissioneres of borrowes presentlie conveinet, heaving takine to thair consideratioun the matter of the restraint of tobacco togither with the late restraint maid in Irland dischairgeing the transporting from thence unto this kingdome suche comodities as they have bein in use of befoir, to the grit hurt and prejudice of the haill borrowes of the west. As also considdering that the kingdome of England does participat indefferentlie of quhat this kingdome does yeild, alsweill in forbidden guidis restraynit in the treattye of the unioun and be the lawes of the kingdome as utherwayes. As also this kingdome is ane great meanes to the ventt of the wholl manufactoreis thairof to the hinderance of manfactoreis within itselff quhairby vertew micht be advancit and all peiple putt to work. Thairfoir the saidis commissioneres hes thoucht guid conforme to the 36 act of this last generall conventioun and power gevine to them thairin, that his Majestie be pet[it]ioned in the saidis purpossis foir the calling of the said patent of tobacco, inlairging of the tred of Irland and mutuall participatioun of all comodities betuix the thrie kingdomes indifferentlie. And becaus the prosecutioun of thir matteres with what may ocoure betuix and the nixt generall conventioun will requyre dilligent and continuall attendance of sum persone at court, thairfoir they have ellectid and chosine, lykas they be thir presentis ellectes and cheises Harye Alexander, sone to the erle of Stirling[5] foir prosecuiting of the said purpossis and quhatsumever salbe farder inci-

---

[4] This act is noted in the Abstract of Acts of Convention, *RCRBS*, iv, 539.

[5] Henry Alexander was the third son of William Alexander, first earl of Stirling (1577–1640), succeeding to the title in 1640 on the death of his infant nephew (the son of the first earl's first son, also William). See David Reid, 'Alexander, William, first earl of Stirling (1577–1640)', *Oxford Dictionary of National Biography* (Oxford, 2004/online edition, Oct. 2006) [http://oxforddnb.com/view/article/335, accessed 22 April 2010].

dent to the nixt generall conventioun. And foir his paines and travell they obleis themsellffes and thair burghes to thankfullie recompens the same. And foir this cause ordaines ilk burgh to be requyrit foir sending thair comissioneres suficientlie instructid thairanent to the nixt conventioun. And ordaines this course to indure to the nixt conventioun allanerlie and foir the said Harie his better informatioun in the saidis particulares, [fo. 473v] ordaines thair generall clerk be advyse of the burghes of Edinburgh, Pearth, Dundye, Abirdeine, Glasgow, Haddingtoun, Burnteilland, Kinghorne and Kirkcaldie, and most pairt of them conveinand, to sett doun his particular instructiones and to send the samyn to him. As also to wryt to him anent the premessis in thair names. And incaice the wecht and importance of the saidis effaires sall requyre ane farder treatie, ordaines the burgh of Edinburgh, upoun advertisment or intelligence from Ingland, to accquaint the cheiff borrowes and suche utheres as they sall think meit thairwith and to conveine them to the effect that according to the exigence of the effaires, course may be takine. And ordaines the saidis burghes to attend my Lord Stirling[6] his returne and to thank him foir his bygaine favoure and to intreat the concurance thairof. As also ordaines the saidis burghes to supplict the lordis of counsell foir thair concurrance with his Majestie anent the said restraint in Yreland and mutuall participatioun, and thir particulares to be rememberit in the missive.[7]

[4]
The same day anent the matter of new impositiones in France mentionat in the 39 act of the last generall conventioun haldine at this burgh the fourt of Julii instant,[8] the present commissioneres resenting the greit prejudice they susteine thairthrow be the heavie burdeine thairof, as also in the breaking of thair ancient libertyes in the said kingdome of France and that it is hie tyme that some course sould be takine thairwith foir remeid thairof. And considdering that thair is no meines foir effectuating of thair desyres heirin but be the French king himsellff allanerlie and his declaratioun thairanent, thairfoir they have thoucht good that his Majestie be petitionid heirin foir wrytting to the said Frenche king. As lykwayes that paines be taikine foir dealling with the said Frenche king himsellff heiranent, and foir that effect they have ellectit and nominat and be thir presentis ellectes and nominates Johne Trotter, younger, merchand burges of Edinburgh foir passing to his Majestie and procuiring of his letter to the said Frenche king foir reduceing of the present customes to the old dewetyes conforme to the saidis liberteis, as also for passing to the said Frenche king and useing all convenient meines

6   Presumably William, the first earl.
7   This act is noted in the Abstract of Acts of Convention, RCRBS, iv, 539.
8   It was actually the 30th act. See above, 181.

foir dealling with him to the same effect, and also foir procuiring ane sentance in thair favoures. And quhatsumever chairges the said Johne sall bestow
in the said materes, the present commissioneres foir themsellffis and thair
borrowes and in name of the remanent borrowes and heaving comissioun
from them bindis and obleissis them sellfes to repey the samyn to him upoun
the compt to be maid be him thairof. [fo. 474r] And declares that in respect
thair is na uther meines foir his repayment but be imposing upoun the
guidis transportid into Normandie and out of the same, that thairfoir iff he
sall procuire ane immunitie from the present new customes imposed upoun
the inward and outward guidis that then and in that caice the impost to be
appoyntid foir difraying of his chairges to be lykwayes lyand upoun both
outward and inward guidis. And in cais the fruittes of his travelles sall onlie
be extendit to guidis transportid out of Normandie, than the said impost to
be layid upoun thos guidis allanerlie. And howsoever matteres sall succeid
with him obleissis them to tak ane course foir payment thairof. And ordaines
the burgh of Edinburgh to sett doun his instructiones anent the premessis
to whome the present comissioneres gives thair full power and comissioun
thairanent and wrytting in thair names to suche freindis as they sall think
expedient. And the said burgh with the said Johne Trotter to produce thair
dilligence in the premessis to the nixt generall conventioun. And this to be
ane heid of the nixt missive.[9]

[5]
The same day anent the tuentie tua act of the last generall conventioun of
borrowes haldine within this burgh the four of this instant concerning the
staiple and grievances sustenit in default of the magistrates of the toun of
Campheir,[10] the present comissioneres ordaines ane letter to be direct to the
said toun intreating them to tak thair just greivancis in thair considdera-
tiounes and to tak suche course foir amending thairof that all occassioun of
complent may be taikine away and to assure them that as they have long
expectid sum amendement, so now requyring them seriouslie to considder
thairof in sa muche that according to thair pr[ec]edinges they will tak suche
farder course foir thair owine weill without ony farder accquytting of them
as they will think meit and to schaw them that they have wrettine to the
conservatour to deall with them quhom they may be pleised to trust in thair
behalff and to ressave frome him the double of the said greivancis whiche
they have directed unto him. As also ordaines ane letter to be directid to
the said conservatour foir dealling with them and for procuireing the saidis
grievanceis to be takine away togither with ane nott of the same and foir

9   This act is noted in the Abstract of Acts of Convention, *RCRBS*, iv, 539.
10   See above, 175–6.

setting doun thairof ordaines the comissioneres remayning to sett doun the samyn and to have ane cair of directing of the said letters. And the said borrowes with the said conservatour to report thair dilligence heiranent to the nixt generall conventioun of borrowes. And this to be ane heid of the nixt missive.

[fo. 474v]
[6]
The same day the saidis comissioneres heaving presentid to the lordis of counsell, conforme to the comissioun gevine them be the 27 act of the last generall conventioun haldine at this burgh the fourt of this instant,[11] his Majesties letter dischairging the frequent granting of protectiones, with ane letter dischairging the monopollie of the perrle, with ane uther ordaining the plaiding to be presentid to the mercat in foldes, and requyring them foir answering the particular materes presentit to the borrowes to the late parliament and referrit be them to the saidis lordis of counsell amongist whiche particulares thair wes ane petitioun foir dischairging all persones frome blitching with lyme, anent the pryce betuix the booll of beire and booll of malt, and anent correctioun houssis within the saidis borrowes. With the whiche the saidis lordis being advysit, they have inactid the said letter anent protectiones whiche the present comissioneres ordaines the agent to extract, and anent the plaiding and pryce betuix boollis the saidis lordis hes ordainet the comissioneres appoyntid to remayne to attend the saidis lordis and in thair names to deall with them thairanent. Anent the blitching with lyme ordaines the saidis comissioneres to deall with the lordis that the samyn may be inactid and the executioun thairof comittid to the shereffis or justicis of peace to landwart and the proveist and bailyeis within burgh. And last anent correctioun houssis, ordaines the saidis comissioneres to deall with the lordis foir expeding of the said patent. And the saidis borrowes with the agent to report thair dilligence heiranent to the nixt generall conventioun of borrowes. And this to be ane heid of the nixt missive.

[7]
The same day the saidis comissioneres of borrowes being conveinet anent the threttie thrid act of the last generall conventioun of borrowes haldine at this burgh the fyft of this instant concerning the letter procuired be the burgh of Dundye direct to the lordis of counsell foir alteratioun of the taxt roll,[12] [fo. 475r] the saidis comissioneres efter dew considderatioun ordaines ane letter to be direct to Harie Alexander be thair clerk in thair names foir

---

11 See above, 177–8.
12 See above, 183.

procuiring ane letter unto the borrowes foir altering the taxt roll quhen they shall think expedient and that be themsellffes efter thair accustomed maner notwithstanding of quhatsumever former warrand in the contrair. And the said letter to be direct to the comissioneres to be conveined in Julii nixt at Pearth. And the burgh of Edinburgh to have ane cair heirof and to report thair dilligence heiranent to the nixt generall conventioun. And this to be ane heid of the nixt missive.

[8]
The same day compeirid Alexander Aikinheid and producit ane dischairge be the burght of Edinburgh of the last yeires dewes and ordaines him to procuire ane uther of this yeires dewes. As also grantit him to have ressavit the haill dewes of the last missive except the burgh of Dumfermling and becaus in this dischairge he hes acceptid into his owine hand sum small borrowes whiche he hes not ressavid, thairfoir ordaines the said Alexander notwithstanding of this dischairge to chairge foir the same suche as hes not peyid. As lykwayes foir the unlaw quhairanent thir presentis salbe unto him ane warrand. And becaus thair occures yeirlie dischairges, thairfoir ordaines him to mak ane box of tymber lockid upoun the borrowes chairges to be delyverit to thair clerk and the expenssis deburssit be him thairupoun salbe allowit to him in his comptes.

[9]
The same day the saidis comissioneres of borrowes ordaines the burghes that remaines efter this day to intreat the lordis of counsell in thair names ather to put to executioun thair actes maid anent the casting of ballast at the Queinesferrie or to frie the borrowes of thair yeirlie visitatioun. Quhairanent they give them full power and comissioun and to report thair dilligence heiranent to the nixt generall conventioun of borrowes. And this to be ane heid of the nixt missive.

Particular Convention at Edinburgh, 16 July 1634

[fo. 475v]

In the particular conventioun of borrowis haldin at the burgh of Edinburgh the 16 day of Julij the yeir of God 1634 yeiris be the commissioneris of borrowis underwrittin be vertew of the commissioun givin to theme upoun the [9] day of this instant.

Edinburgh	William Gray
Perth	
Dundye	
Abirdein	Mr Alexander Japhray
Lynlithgow	Andro Bell
Glasgow	Patrick Bell
Haddingtoun	Mr James Cokburne
Bruntyland	Andro Watsoun
Kinghorne	Maister Robert Cuninghame
Kirkcaldye	Williame Tennent

1

The same day electis William Gray commissioner for the burgh of Edinburgh to be moderator during this present conventioun, wha compeirand accepted the samin in and upon him and gaive his aith *de fideli administratione*.[1]

2

The same day the saidis commissioneris ordanis the burgh of Edinburgh to wryte to Harye Alexander anent the mater of tobacco for supplicatting of his Majestie for recalling the patent purchest for restrayning therof and to send him the informatioun drawin up be them theranent. As also ordanis theme to wryte to him concerning the late restraint in Yreland togither with the mutuall participatioun desyred of the kingdome of England of the native commodities thairof. As also the toun of Edinburgh to sett doun the greivances anent the staiple port and to send the samin to the conservatour and to the toun of Campheir, anent which particulars the present comissioneris grauntis and givis unto thame thair full powar and commissioun and the said burgh to report thair diligence heiranent to the nixt generall conventioun of borrowis. And this to be ane heid of the nixt missive.

---

1   Literally, 'concerning faithful administration', i.e. he was promising to carry out the duties of moderator with diligence.

3

The same day forsamikle as the lordis of his Majesties privie counsall hes apointed thrie of the gentrie and thrie of the borrowis for attending the faires of Lambes, Sanct Laurence and Sanct Bartill for trying the enormities and abuses committit in the mater of the plaiding and the mettage therof and to report to thame the first counsall day of November nixt. Thairfoir the present commissioneris ordanis the burgh of Aberdein to mak choice of thrie of the best qualifiet [fo. 483r][2] and sufficient persounis of thair nichtbouris for attending the saidis mercattis with thrie of the gentrie and reporting in maner abonewrittin to quhome they recommend the preceis tryall of the abuses committed in working of the said plaiding and covered be presenting of the same to the mercatt in hard rollis. And the said burgh to report thair tryall anent the premissis to the commissioneris of borrowis to be convenit the fourt day of November nixt. To quhich commissioneris then convennand they commit the prosecutioune of the reformatioune of the said abuse befor the saidis lordis of counsell conforme to his Majesteis will signified to the saidis lordis alreddie. And this mater to be remembrit in the nixt missive.

4

The same day ordainis Alexander Aikinheid, agent, till caus summound Robert Buchan for heiring his Majesteis will anent his patent of the perll. As also to insist with the lordis of counsell and his Majesteis advocat anent the expeding of the patent for erectioune of correctioune houssis. And last ordainis him to extract the act dischairgeing the bleitching with lyme and to caus the same be lauchfullie publischit and the expenssis debursit be him upone the premissis salbe allowit to him in his comptis he reporting his diligence to the nixt generall conventioune of borrowis. And this to be ane heid of the nixt missive.[3]

---

2   There seems to have been a mistake in the binding of these folios, that which is labelled as fo. 483 having been separated from fo. 475 before folio numbers were added.

3   The verso of this folio is blank.

Particular Convention at Edinburgh, November 1634

[fo. 476r]
Act's off the particular conventioune off borrow's haldine att Edinbrught in November 1634[1]

[fo. 477r]
In the particular conventioune of borrowis haldin at the burght of Edinburgh the 4 of November 1634 yeires be commissioneris of borrowis underwrittin be vertew of ane missive letter direct to theme frome the said burght of Edinburgh of the daite the 3 of October last 1634, and produced thair commissiounis as followis viz:

Edinburgh	Johnne Sinclair, deane of gild, Rychard Maxwell
Peirth	Andro Wilsone
Dundie	Thomas Haliburtoun younger
Aberdene	Mr Mathow Lumbisdaine baillie
Stirling	Johnne Johnestoun
Linlithgow	William Hamiltoun
St Androis	Robert Tailyeour
Glasgow	Johnne Barnis
Air	Johnne Kennadie
Hadingtoun	Mr James Cockburne
Dumbartane	Johnne Sempill
Irwing	James Scott
Remfrew	Johnne Sprewle
Kinghorne	Mr Robert Cunninghame

[1]
The same day electis Johnne Sinclair, first in commissioun for the burgh of Edinburgh, to be moderatour dureing this present conventioun, wha compeirand acceptit the said office in and upon him and gave his aith *de fideli administrationi*.[2]

Quinto Novembris I^m vi^c xxxiiii

[2]
The quhilk day the commissioneris of borrowis being convenit apoyntis to

---

1   Unusually, there are apostrophes in 'Act's' and 'borrow's'. The verso of this folio is blank.
2   Literally, 'concerning faithful administration', i.e. he was promising to carry out the duties of moderator with diligence.

heir Thomas Cunningham factour his coumptis, George Sutie merchand and burges of Edinburgh and the burghes of Aberdene, St Androis, Air and Glasgow.

Sexto Novembris I^m vi^c trigesimo quarto

[3]
The quhilk day the coumptis of Thomas Cuninghame, collectour of the impost appoyntit for defraying of the ministeris stipend at Campheir frome the 17 of September 1633 yeiris inclusive till the 20 of September 1634 yeiris also inclusive, being hard fuitit, calculat and allowit, they fund his chairge to extend to the soume of twa hundreth twentie nyne pund thre schilling four pennyes great Flemis money and his discharige to be the soume of [fo. 477v] twa hundreth fourscoir fyve pund threttene schillingis fyve pennyes great. Swa the borrowis is fund resting addebtit to the said collectour in the soume of fyftie sax pund ten schilling 1 penny great, which soume they ordaine Alexander Bawtie, present collectour of the said impost, to pay to him of the reddiest of the same which salbe allowit to him in his coumptis. And becaus the personis underwrittin hes pest away not paying thair dewes, viz Robert Black, Robert Stirling, Thomas Gray, Johnne Gibsone, Robert Hadden, Johnne Coupland, Andro Sandis merchandis in Edinburgh, Patrick Park, Johnne Young, Johne Morisone, Johne Andersone, Johne Stirling, merchandis in Glasgow, which wer addettit ilk ane of theme in the soume of fyve schillingis Fleamis in respect they had not ane seck of goodes. And sicklyke the persounis under writtin past away not paying thair dewis, viz Johne Cowane of Dysart with ane laidnyng of wyne at Middilburght, David Spence in Dysart with ane laidnyng of goodes at Middilburght in Januarii last, Thomas Richardsone in Dysart at Flussing³ with coillis in Apryle last, George Dawling in Leith at Middilburght with strangeris goodis the 24 of the said moneth, Johne Hutchesone of Kirkcaldie at Flussing with coalis the 22 of Agust last, Samuell Wilsone in the Quienisferrie for ane voyadge at Campheir with coallis, Johne Distoun in Leivin in Apryle last with coallis at Flussing. And thairfoir ordanis the burghis to whome the saidis personis doe belong ather to uplift frome [them]⁴ the doubill of such soumes as they should have payit thair or to present theme to the nixt generall conventioun of borrowis under the paine of xx lib. As also ordanis the burght of Edinburgh to search for the said Samuell Wilsone and Johne Distoun and George Dawling gif they can find theme in Leith and cause theme to pay the double quhat they should have payit their or to find cautioun for thair

---

³   Vlissingen, or Flushing, on the island of Walcheren, in Zeeland.
⁴   There is no space in the MS but the sense requires this insertion.

compeirance befoir the commissioneris of borrowis in thair nixt generall conventioun under the paine of xx lib. each of theme.

[4]
The same day compeired Alexander Aickinheid agent and produced the burgh of Edinburgh thair dischairge of the soumes of money payit to the said burgh be theme the last generall conventioun.

Septimo Novembris I^m vi^c tregesimo quarto

[5]
The quhilk day the commissioneris of borrowis being conveinit compeirit Mr Johnne Corsane, late provest of Dumfreis, and George Rig, ane of the bailleis thairof, commissioneris for the said burght, and gave in ane missive letter direct to the present commissioneris for the said burgh authorizing theme in commissioun and desyring the borrowis approbatioun to the prorogatioun grantit be the lordis of counsell to theme of ane impost grantit for help to the uphalding of thair bridge for the caussis conteinit in the said missive, quhairwith the present commissioneris being advysit grantis and giffis thair consent and approbatioun to the impetratioun of the said impost frome his Majestie and the saidis lordis of counsall, provyding alwayis, lykas with consent of the saidis commissioneris, they ordaine the said burgh to imploy the same allanerlie towardis the upholding of the said bridge. As also to be countable to the borrowis thairfoir at the expyring [fo. 478r] of the said last grant which they ordaine to be insert and registrat in thair bookes quhairof the tennor followis: At Edinburgh the 17 day of September the yeir of God I^m vi^c threttie four yeires, annent the supplicatioun presentit to the lordis of secreit counsall be the provest, baillies and counsall of the burght of Dumfreis makand mentioun that quhair the saidis lordis haveing taine to thair consideratioun the great charges and expenssis quhilk the bodie of the said toun did sustein of late yeiris by the bigging and reedifieing of thair bridge quhilk by the violence of water and storme of wether wes for the most pairt throwne doun to the grund, and how that the supplicantis interprysit and held fordward that work by theme selffis without anie help or supplie frome utheris, altho if it had fallin out in anie uther pairtis or burght in the kingdome supplies had bene cravit frome the whole estaitis of the kingdome, and the saidis lordis knowing thairwithall that the intertenying and upholding of the said bridge wold require yeirlie great chairges. Thairfoir and for pairt of the supplie and help thairof, the saidis lordis, be ane act and ordinance of counsall of the dait the 17 day of Julii 1627 yeiris, gave and grantit to the supplicantis and to thair successouris provost, bailleis and counsall of the burght of Dumfreis the impost and dewtie following, quhilk by former warrandis they bruikit thir manie yeiris bygane, of all the

commodities and goodes cuming or going allongis their bridge for the space of 7 yeiris nixt efter the daitt of the saidis lordis warrand, to witt, of ilk pack twa schillingis, of ilk hors saxteine pennyis, of ilk kow saxtene pennyis, of ilk scheip twa pennys, of ilk lambe a penny, of ilk pak of skins 2 schillingis, of ilk daiker of hydes twelf pennyes. And sicklyke of everie bark cuming up the river towardis thair toun threttene schilling four pennyes, and of ilk ladnit boate thrie schillingis four pennyes, as the said act maid and grantit be the lordis to that effect schawin beiris. Quhilk tyme and space of 7 yeiris being now expyrit the necessitie of the intertenying and upholding of the bridge is als urgent as it wes at anie tyme heirtofoir and thair passis few weikis in the yeir bot one thing or other fallis out towardis the said bridge quhilk requires ane present help and supplie. Humblie desyring thairfoir the saidis lordis to prorogat and contenew thair said former act of the dait the 17 day of Julii 1627 for such space as they shall think fitt, lyke as at moir length is conteinit in the said supplicatioun. Quhilk being red, hard, considderit be the saidis lordis and thei consideddering the charges and expenssis susteinit be the said burgh in the reedifieing of thair bridge and the necessitie of the interte-anyng and upholding of the same in tyme cuming, thairfoir the saidis lordis of secreit counsall hes prorogatit and continewit be the tennor heirof proro-gatis and continewis the said former act [of the dait][5] the 17 day of Julii 1627 dureing the space of 7 yeiris nixt efter the dait heirof, indureing that space the saidis lordis gives and grantis to the provest and baillies of the said burght of Dumfreis now present and being for the tyme, the impost and dewtie foirsaid of the commodities and guidis cuming and going allongst the said bridge and the barkis and boatis aryving towardis the said toun, [fo. 478v] with power to theme and to the collectouris to be nominat be theme, for quhome thei salbe answerable, to ask, crave, ressave, intromett with, uplift the impost and dewtie abonewrittin dureing the yeiris and space abonespecefeit and gif neid beis to pynde and distreinyie thairfoir and to convert and aply the same to the intertenying and upholding of the said bridge and all thingis necessar for the uplifting of this impost to doe and use which in such cassis ar usuall and necessar, firme and stabill hauld[ing] and for to hald all and quhatsumever thingis shalbe lawfullie done heirin. *Extractum delibere actorum secreti consilii S.D.N. regis per me Magistrum Gilbertum Prymrois Clericum eiusdem sub meis signo et subscriptione manualibus et sic subscribitur.*[6]

[6]
The same day quhairas the commissioneris of the borrowis conforme to the 15 act of the last generall conventioun haldin at this burgh in Julii last,

---

5   There is no space in the MS but the sense requires this insertion.
6   Extracted from the acts of the king's privy council by me Mr Gilbert Primrose, clerk to the same, under my signature.

finding that of longtyme the commissioneris hes dyvers and manie tymis intendit to have had the solide and commoun differences betuix theme and the burghes of barronie decydit and such ane distinktioun maid that the said burghes of barronie should no longer incroatch upon theme,[7] for the furtherance quhairof it pleissit his Majestie of his gracious favour and guid will to his awin ancient borrowis to grant, with advyse of the estaitis then conveinit, ane act of parliament at his last parliament haldin at this burgh in Julii 1633,[8] quhairupon no dissitioun nor sentence hes as yit followit, and yit understanding that the incres of unfrie peiple is such that the borrowis ar licklie to fall into decay and inspeciall in the west. Which consideratiounis movit theme to grant to the present commissioneris full power and commissioun for prosecuting of the actiounis intendit be the burches of Irving and Remfrew aganis the unfrie people within thair severall boundis, as also for borrowing of soumes of money for effectuating thair desyre annent the premissis. Thairfoir the present commissioneris taking the same notice to thair consideratiounis, efter dew and long advyse hes thocht guid to mak choyce of sum qualified persoun to whome the prosecuteing of these actiounis shalbe committit upon the generall chairges alwayes of the borrowis. And to this effect hes maid [choice of][9] Mr James Cockburne, provest of the burght of Hadingtoun, and be thir presentis grantis and giffis him thair full power and commissioun for prosequting of these actiounis according as he in his judgement shall find fitt occasiounis and to bestow such soumis of money thairin as he shall think expedient, which with his awin charges salbe thankfullie repayit and allowit unto him for his better furtherance. They have apoyntit Johne Sinclair, deane of gild of Edinburgh, and Mr Alexander Guthrie, their generall clerk, or anie ane of theme, to concurr and assist with him at all occasiounis as he sall require. As lykewyse ordanis the present commissioneris of Remfrew and Irving to attend as parties in the foirsaidis actiounis, the said commissioneris[10] of Remfrew being payit for his chairges at the discretioun and sight of the borrowis. And becaus thair will be requisit that soumes of money may be advansit for prosecuteing the said actioun be the said commissioner, thairfoir ordanis the agent presentlie [fo. 479r] to borrow the soume of twa thousand merkis upon interest and to delyver the same to the said commissioner with what farder he sall think expedient, be advyse of the said deane of gild and thair said clerk, to be imployit be him to the effect foirsaid. Quhilk soumis the saidis commissioneris for theme selffis and in name of thair burghes and haill

---

7 See above, 171–2.
8 See RPS, 1633/6/39.
9 There is no space in the MS but the sense requires this insertion.
10 This should be 'commissioner' (singular) as there is only one commissioner from Renfrew at this convention.

remanent borrowis and haveing commissioun frome theme as said is obleissis theme to refound the same bak againe with the interest thairof swa lang as the samene shall happin to be unpayit and tak course for payment thairof at the nixt generall conventioun.[11]

Octavo Novembris I^m vi^c trigesimo quarto

[7]

The quhilk day the commissioneris of borrowis being conveinit, quhairas Thomas Cuninghame and James Weir being conveinit for thair alledgit contempt in refoosing at thair acceptatioun of the collectioun of the dewis appoyntit for defreying the ministeris stipend at Campheir to gif thair aithes for collecting the same conforme as wes injoynit to theme be the borrowis, and the saidis personis compeirand, declairit the same wes nowayes refusit upon ane contempt bot upoun ane simpill scrupill that they had in thair conscience that they did foirsie ane absolute impossibilitie to keip the said aith in the strick termes this same wes creavit which wes to collect the same be theme selffis and no uther wyse, quhich being cleirit they wer content to giff obedience lyke as they wer reddie to declair upon thair aithes that the coumptis giffin up be theme wer trew and nothing omitted to thair knowledge. Quhairwith the borrowis being advysit and haveing hard theme at length annent the said porte, they dispence with thair refusall at this tyme and for ane aith to be givin in all tyme cuming ordanis this tennour to be keipit, viz: That the said collectour shall leillilie and trewlie dischairge his dewtie in the said collectioun in uplifting frome ilk persone dew in the said impost thair just pairt thairof and that he shall omit nothing furth of his coumptis quhairwith he sould be chairged and sall doe his uttermost dilligence according to his knowledge for the ingathering thairof, boith frome these that aryves at the stapill poirt as also frome theme that aryves at anie port of the said yland[12] conforme to the tabill of the said impost, and sall gif trew notiz to the borrowis of all that escaipis unpaying of thair dewis or gois by the stapill poirt and tymes and quantities of thair escaipis sua far as he cane leirne, sua help me God, be God him selff. As also he sall at the giving of the aith abonewrittin declair whither he is to imploy ane servant or not, quhilk gif he sall doe he sall lykewyse bring the same servand with him wha sall mak the lyke aith and for whom he salbe answerabill, and gif anie commissioun sallbe, and sall nocht imploy him in anie thing which he cannot convenientlie overtak be him selff. And to the effect better ordour may be keipit and more assured payment and of ilk persone dew to pay

---

11   This act is noted in the Abstract of Acts of Convention, *RCRBS*, iv, 539.
12   The island of Walcheren, in Zeeland.

ony dewtie, the commissioneris understanding that the bygane escaipis hes fallin out be ressoun [fo. 479v] of the delaying of the ressaveing of payment till the wagoing of the personis dew thairin, whairfoir the commissioneris hes statute and ordanit and be thir presentis statutis and ordanis that the skipper at his first aryvell at the said poirt and making of his entrie shall asigne ane sufficient pand[13] in the collectouris hand for payment of the haill dewis quhairinto his schip or goodes ar subject. And becaus divers subject in payment of the said impost dois nocht cum to the said stapill port bot aryves at Flussing or Middillburgh or sum uther poirt of the yland, thairfoir ordanis the saidis collectouris when they sall first apprehend theme to require the said pand for thair dewis, and gif they sall apprehend theme at the said stapill port to cause theme gif the same. For the which cause they ordaine the conservatour and his deputis to concurr and assist with thair said collectour heirin as he or they shalbe required at all tymis. As also ordainis the coppie of this aith to be sent over to the said conservatour, and according thairto the said collectouris to be required to mak faith at thair first entrie under paine of deprivatioun and this ordour to be keipit in all tyme cuming.

Decimo Novembris I[m] vi[c] trigesimo quarto

[8]
The quhilk day the commissioneris of borrowis being conveinit conforme to the 22 act of the last generall conventioun of borrowis haldin at this burght in Julii last and commissioun thairin conteinit,[14] enterit in ane particuller considderatioun of these thingis concerning the stapill, and in speciall annent the late contract past betuix the commissioneris of the borrowis and the magistratis of the said toun of Campheir in anno 1622 and the faillis committit be the said toun and thair divers neglectis, and calling to minde that they had in anno 1631 writtin thairanent to the said toun, and at that tyme and dyvers tymes since had acquaintit the conservatour thairwith whome they had authorized to deill with theme thairannent, and finding these auld greivances to stand and that at this tyme they have not hard frome the said conservatour thairannent as they expectit, thairfoir ordanis ane missive letter to be direct to the said conservatour for ressaveing nocht onlie thair finall answer annent the former greivances sent to him bot also to crave quhat farder assurance they will give for amending quhat shalbe fund defective in the said contract and quhat may be expectit frome theme be the commissioneris, and last to desyre his lordship to try quhat conditiounis may be had at Middilburght or anie poirt ellis whair he may

---

13   i.e. monetary pledge.
14   See above, 175–6.

think the saidis stapill may conveneint[lie] be sattellit and to acquaintt the commissioneris to be convenit in Pearth the begining of Julii nixt with the said toun thair answer with his awin particullar advyse annent the premissis. And ordanis thair generall clerk to subscryve the said letter in thair names, quhairanent thir presentis shalbe unto him ane warran, and to send ane coppie of the auld grevances. As also ilk burght to be required for sending thair commissioneris sufficientlie instructit annent all and quhatsumever may [fo. 480r] concerne the said staple to the nixt generall conventioun. And this to be ane heid of the nixt missive.

[9]
The same day annent the secund act of the particullar conventioun of borrowis haldin at Edinburgh the 9 of Julii last ordaining the said burght of Edinburgh to sett doun such articles, patent lawis and such uther thingis as they sall think meit concerning the erecting of companies for the weill mannadgeing of the trade and for advanceing of the native commodities, concerning the guid redoundis to the cities quhair trade is ordourlie rewlit and confusioun takin away,[15] the present commissioneris consiidering the weghtines and importance of the said matter hes thocht goode againe of new to recommend the same to the said toun of Edinburgh and ordanis theme to repoirt thair dilligence thairanent to the nixt generall conventioun of borrowis. And this to be ane heid of the nixt missive.

Undecimo Novembris I[m] vi[c] trigesimo quarto

[10]
The quhilk day the commissioneris of borrowis being conveined, quhairas it being regraited be Thomas Cunninghame and James Wear factouris for themeselffis and in name of the remanent factouris at the port of Campheir that sindrie personis dois resoirt to the said poirt nocht onlie with thair awin goodes bot also ar imployit frome thair nighbouris for selling of thair goodes and nocht content heirwith dois receed thairfoir allong tyme and ressaves new schipis to theme, quhilk in effect is nothing bot the usurping of the office of factorie without being lawfullie authorized thairin which is far contrair to the estaites[16] of the borrowis forbidding anie to exerse the said office without they be first approvin be the borrowis and admitted thairto. Quhairwith the present commissioneris being advysit thairwith and willing that iveill should be remedied, they ordaneing ilk burgh to be required for sending thair commissioneris sufficientlie instructed for setting doun

---

15 See above, 193.
16 This should probably be 'statutes'.

sum constant law and course thairanent in tyme cuming, as also for preveining the incrotching of sum wha tak occasioun for thair privat gayne of
fraughting of schippis be the grip[17] and will nocht let the same furth againe
bot upon disadvantagious conditiounis to the prejudice boith of thair neighbouris and trade. And the same to be ane heid of the nixt missive.

[11]
The same day quhairas Thomas Cuninghame and James Weir factouris in
Campheir compeirand and being demandit anent thair obedience to the 21
act of the last generall conventioun haldin at this burght in Julii last anent
the rebaitting of breiffis,[18] they wer content to gif obedience thairunto, and
presentlie to act themselffis for fulfilling thairof, and the present commissioneris finding it expedient that they be actit with the rest conforme as
wes ordainit in the said act. Thairfoir they ordane ane missive letter to be
direct in thair names to the conservatour and his deputis willing theme to
conveine the said Thomas and James with the haill remanent factouris and
to act theme selffis in ane course to be haldin be theme to that effect under
the paines conteinit in the said act and to report the same to the nixt general
conventioun. And this to be ane heid of the nixt missive.

[fo. 480v]
[12]
The same day the saidis commissioneris being conveinit annent the 3 act of
the particullar conventioun of borrowis haldin at this burght the 16 of Julii
last, ordaining the burgh of Aberdene to apoint sum of the neighbouris for
attending certane faires in the north with sum of the gentrie apoyntit be
the lordis of counsall for trying of the abooses of plaiding conforme to ane
commissioun giffin to theme be the saidis lordis.[19] Compeirit Mr Mathow
Lumbsdail commissioner for the said burght of Aberdene and declarit that
the personis apoyntit be theme for attending the said fairis with these of the
gentrie had done thair dilligence and had fund such enormities committit
in the working thairof and coverit and sufferit to be presentit to the mercat
in hard roll and gif tymous remeid wer not had that commoditie schould
becum altogidder unsufficient and unsellabill abrod, and produceit lykewyse
thair saidis neighbouris attestatioun heirupon under thair handis which
the saidis commissioneris acceptit for dilligence and ordanis the burghes

---

17 This may mean 'by taking possession of them', that is, seizing a ship and extorting
    unreasonable terms of carriage in return for its release: see 'grip, v.1', OED Online, Oxford
    University Press, November 2010: http://www.oed.com/view/Entry/81557?rskey=96pdO
    4&result=3&isAdvanced=false (accessed 11 March 2011).
18 See above, 175.
19 See above, 199.

of Edinburgh, Aberdene, St Androis and Haddingtoun to present the said attestatioun upon Foorsday[20] nixt and consist[21] with the saidis lordis for procuiring the said plaiding to be presentit to the mercat in foldis so far as in theme lyeth, to whome they give thair full power and commissioun for prosecuting the said actioun and ordane theme to report thair dilligence heirannent to the nixt generall conventioun of borrowis. And this to be ane heid of the nixt missive.

[13]

The same day the saidis commissioneris understanding the mater of tobacco now restraynit to be sauld onlie by licence of Sir James Leslie and Thomas Dalmahoy is not lyke to tak the desyred end as hes bene signified unto theme from Harie Alexander, presentlie thair agent at court, quhairwith they being advysit hes thocht goode that the said Harie shall yit againe petitioun his Majestie in thair names desyring that ather for the ressounis alreddie sent unto him, his Majestie wold be pleisit to recall the said patent utherwyse that his Majestie wald grant unto the borrowis the benefeit of the commoun law and to this effect wold wryte unto the lordis of sessioun that upon remonstrance to be maid to theme be the borrowis, gif they should find the same consonent to law and ressoun, that they sould suspend the said gift and quhat hes followit thairupoun till thair ressounis wer lawfullie discussit. And last gif he could nocht in these prevaill to mak offer in thair names, gif his Majestie sould be pleisit to recall the said patent, of the doubill of the custome the same dois presentlie yeild which will farr surmount anie present benefeit his Majestie ressaves of the said patent, and to desyre the said Harie to performe this with all dilligence, and to returne his answer thairannent to the burgh of Edinburgh to the end farder course may be takin as sall effair and the same to be rememberit lykewyse in the nixt missive. As lykewyse ordanis the said Harie to be desyred to acquaint the burght of Edinburgh with his proceidingis anent the matteris of Ingland and Ireland conforme as was of befoir writtin unto him.

[fo. 481r]
[14]

The same day the said commissioneris conforme to the dyet assignd unto theme in that actioun depending betuix theme and Robert Buchane annent the mater of the perle, haveing incistit thairin, it hes pleisit the lordis of counsall till continew the same till the first counsall day of March. Theirfoir the present commissioneris apoyntis the burght of Edinburgh and Aberdene to attend the said dyet and to insist befoir the saidis lordis untill thair finall desisioun thairof. Quhairannent the present commissioneris grantis unto theme thair full power and commissioun and ordainis theme to repoirt thair dilligence heirannent to the nixt generall conventioun of borrowis. And this to be ane heid of the nixt missive.

[15]
The same day the saidis commissioneris ordanis the burght of Wigtoun for productioun of the electioun of thair magistratis and counsall at Michaelmes last to the nixt generall conventioun of borrowis to be seine and considderit be theme under the paine of xx li. And this to be ane heid of the nixt missive.

18 November[22]
The lordis of counsell have assingd the aucht day of January nixt to the barronns appoynted to visit the faris of the northe to produce thair diligence and mak thair report thairanent peremptorie.[23]

---

22 This entry which relates to the matter mentioned in the 12th act, above, is in a different hand and is preceded by a blank space of about half a page.
23 fo. 481v plus two fos. '482' are blank.

General Convention at Perth, July 1635

[fo. 484r]

Actis of the generall convention of Burrowes hauldin at Perth in Julii 1635[1]

[fo. 485r]

In the generall conventioun of burrowis haldin at the burghe of Perth the sevint day of Julii the yeir of God I^m vi^c and threttie fyve yeiris be the commissioneris of burrowes underwrittin, and produced thair commissiounes as followis:

Edinburghe	Johnne Sinclair, James Leslie
Perth	Andro Gray
Dundie	James Fletcher
Abirdeine	Mr Mathow Lumisdeane
Striveling[2]	Johnne Johnestoun
Linlythgow	Robert Stewart
Sanctandrois[3]	Johnne Lepar
Glasgow	Gabriell Cunynghame
Air	George Maissoun
Hadingtoun	Mr George Gray
Dysert	Alexander Sympsoun
Kirkcaldy	Johnne Williamesoun
Montrois	Johnne Gairdyne
Couper	Robert Petersoun
Anstruther Eister	Robert Alexander
Dumfreis	Mr Johnne Carsane
Innernes[4]	Johnne Cuthbert
Bruntyland	Captaine Androw Watsoun
Innerkeithing[5]	Mr Williame Blaikburne
Kinghorne	James Lochore
Brechin	Johnne Auchterlony
Irving	Robert Broun
Jedburghe	Alexander Kirktoun
Kirkcudbricht	Robert Glendinning
Wigtoun	Thomas Mackie

[1]   The verso of this folio is blank.
[2]   Stirling.
[3]   St Andrews.
[4]   Inverness.
[5]   Inverkeithing.

Pettinnweyme	James Airth
Dumfermeling[6]	Peter Law
Anstruther Wester	be exemptioun and ratificatioun produceit be Pettinweyme
Selkirk	Williame Scott
Dumbar	George Purves
Dumbartane	Johnne Sempill
Ramfrew[7]	Johnne Spreull
Lanerk	Gedione Weir
Abirbrothok[8]	[be] exemptioun and ratificatioun produceit be agent
Elgyne	Robert Hardy
Peiblis	James Williamesoun
Carraill	Patrik Hunter
[fo. 485v]	
Tayne	be exemptioun and ratificatioun produced be agent
Culros	Patrik[9]
Bamff	
Quhithorne	
Forfar	be exemptioun and ratificatioun produced be agent
Rothesay	Mathow Spence
Nairne	be exemptioun and ratificatioun produced be agent
Forres	be exemptioun and ratificatioun produced be agent
Rutherglen	be exemptioun and ratificatioun produced be agent
Northberwik	Johnne Muire
Culane	
Lauder	
Kilrinny	be exemptioun and ratificatioun produced be Anstruther Eister
Annand	be exemptioun and ratificatioun produced be Dumfreis
Lochmaben	
Sanquhair	be ratificatioun produced be agent
Galloway[10]	

---

6   Dunfermline.
7   Renfrew.
8   Arbroath.
9   The name is incomplete. It could be Patrick Keir, who represented Culross at the general convention at Glasgow in 1625 (see *RCRBS*, iii, 185). There is a gap in Culross council minutes from 1600 to 1652.
10 New Galloway.

1
{Ellectioun moderatour}
The same day the saidis commissioneris of burrowes ellectis, creatis and
constitutes Andro Gray, first in commissioun for the burght of Perth, to be
moderatour dureing this present conventioun, quha compeirand, accepted
the said place in and upoun him and gave his aith *de fideli administratione*.[11]

2
{Houres of meitting}
The same day the saidis commissioneris of burrowes appointes thair houres
of meitting to be and beginne daylie at [nine][12] houres in the morning
and till last till tuelff houres at noone and efternoone at tua houris till sex
a cloak at nicht and sick as ar absent at the calling of the rollis to pay ane
unlaw of sex schillingis and they that passes out of the house without leave
to pay ane unlaw as said is; and they that passis fra this present conventioun
untill the dissolveing thairof to pay ane unlaw as absentis; and that nane
speik unrequyred without leave askitt and gevin nor intermixe thair reassoning with thair voitting under the paine of ane unlaw of sex schillingis
toties quoties.[13]

3
The same day Andro Gray commissioner for the burght of Perth verified
the citatioun of the haill burrowis to this conventioun be George Ramsay
post, quho produced the buik of the subscriptiounes of all suche burrowes
as haid ressaved the generall missive.

[fo. 486r]
4
The same day ordaines the burghe of Kirkcudbricht to produce thair diligence to the nixt generall conventioun in restraineing the inhabitantis of
Monygoiff[14] from the usurpeing the liberties of the frie royall burrowes and
in causeing them find cautioun to that effect under the paine of tuentie
pundis and to report thair diligence thairanent to the nixt generall conventioun of borrowes. And this to be ane heid of the nixt missive.

5
The same day ordaines the burghe of Dumfermeling to produce thair

---

11 Literally, 'concerning faithful administration', i.e. he was promising to carry out the duties
    of moderator with diligence.
12 Sessions normally began at 9 am.
13 As often as it shall happen, i.e. for each offence.
14 Minnigaff, near Newton Stewart, Wigtownshire.

diligence to the nixt generall conventioun in causeing of James Dawling, indweller in the Quenisferrie, aither to mak his residence with them or in depryveing him of the liberties of the burrowes under the paine of tuentie pundis. And this to be ane heid of the nixt missive.

6

The same day ordaines the burght of Edinburgh to restraine James Vauss thair alledged burges from useing tread within the Quenisferrie and keiping of ane buith and selling merchandice thair. And ordaines the burght of Linlythgow betuixt and the first day of August nixt to qualifie the said James his tredding within the said toun. And the saidis burghes to report thair diligence heiranent to the nixt generall conventioun of burrowes under the paine of tuentie pundis. And this to be ane heid of the nixt missive.

7

The same day ordaines the burght of Linlythgow to produce further diligence against David Wilsoun, Samuell Wilsoun, Edward Littill, James Hill, Robert Hill, Peter Logy in presenting the suspensiounes raisit be thame against the said burght and obteining the same discussed ay and quhill they find cautioun to desist from usurpeing the liberties of the frie royall burrowes under the paine of tuentie pundis and to report thair diligence heiranent to the nixt generall conventioun of burrowes. And this to be ane heid of the nixt missive.

8

{Anent the admissioun of burgesses not dwelling within burgh}

The same day quhairas it being universallie complained that quhen diverse burghes for vindicating thair liberties hes falling and enterit in proces against sindrie unfriemen dwelling within thair boundis, yitt such is [fo. 486v] the craft of these people and negligence of the burrowes that they find meanes to eluid the saidis chairges by making themselffis frie in some burghes, and yitt notwithstanding does not resort with thair house and familie thairto but abydes in thair former unfrie places. Quhairwith the present commissioneris being weill advysed, thairfoir they have statute and ordainit and be thir presentis statutes and ordaines that quhansoever any burghe sall heirefter admitt any outland persoun dwelling without thair burghe to thair freddome that the said persoun sall first mak faith solemnlie that he is not persewit be any other burght or burghes in generall for usurpeing against the libertie of any burght or burghes in generall, whiche declaratioun being takin and the said persoun fand to be persewed in manner foirsaid, it sall not be leisum to any burght to admitt him to thair freddome befor first he satisfie the desyre of the said persuite and become ane actuall resident and indweller with them and fand cautioun not to remove under the paine of ane hundreth pundis and deprivatioun of thair liberties *ipso facto*.[15] And ordaines the burght that efter tryall sall be fund to have done in contraire this act, to incurre ane unlaw of ane hundreth pundis to be payit to the burrowes *toties quoties*.[16] And ordaines ilk commissioner present to intimatt this ordinance to thair burrowes at thair home comeing, and ilk burght to report thair diligence anent the intimatioun heirof to the nixt generall conventioun of burrowes under the paine of tuentie pundis ilk burght. And this to be ane heid of the nixt missive.[17]

9

The same day the saidis commissioneris of burrowes ordaines the burght of Ramfrew to produce thair diligence to the nixt generall conventioun of burrowis in causeing of Hendrie Kelso, indweller in the Largis,[18] aither mak his residence with them or uplifting from him the unlaw of ane hundreth pundis quhairin he is inacted incaice of his not residence, as is affirmit be the commissioner of the burghe of Ramfrew, as also in depryveing him of thair liberties under the paine of tuentie pundis. And this to be ane heid of the nixt missive.

10

The same day anent the aucht act of the last generall conventioun of burrowes upoun the sevint day of August 1633 yeiris dischargeing portage and inhibiteing friemen from being partineris with unfrie skipperis dwelling at unfrie portis as at mair lenth is contenit in the said act.[19] The present commissioneris ordaines ilk burght to intimat the same of new to thair neighbouris [fo. 487r] and to tak suche course with those that sall be fund amongst them to be pairtineris with the saidis unfrie persounes betuixt and suche competent tyme as they sall assigne to them for frieing of themselffis of thair said pairtinership. And quho sall be fund to be remiss thairefter, the said act to be put to executioun against them but favour. And the burght also quha sall be fund remiss heirin to be punisched lykwayes conforme to the said act. And ilk burght whom thir presentis does concerne to produce thair diligence heiranent to the nixt generall conventioun of burrowes under the paine of tuentie pundis. And this to be ane heid of the nixt missive.

---

15 By that action, i.e. automatically.
16 As often as it shall happen, i.e. for each offence.
17 This act is noted in the Abstract of Acts of Convention, *RCRBS*, iv, 539.
18 Largs, Ayrshire.
19 It was actually the 4th act of the last general convention, which was in 1634, and the 8th act of the general convention of 1633. See above, 133, 164–5.

11

Octavo Julii I^m vi^c trigesimo quinto

The quhilk day the commissioneris of burrowes being conveinit anent the 29 act of the last generall conventioun of burrowes haldin att Edinburght the fourt day of Julii last concerning Mr David Wedderburnes grammer[20] and ordaining the same to be taucht within the whole grammer schooles of the frie burrowes of this realme and to be begun at Michaelmes lastbypast. The present commissioneris, finding as of before the said grammer necessar to be taucht, they ordaine ilk burght to have ane caire to sie the samyne taucht within thair schooles and to report thair diligence thairanent to the nixt generall conventioun of burrowes under the paine of tuentie pundis ilk burght. And this to be ane heid of the nixt missive.

12

The same day anent the sext act of the last generall conventioun of burrowes haldin at the burght of Edinburght the secound day of Julii last, ordaining the burghes of Dundie and Aberdeine to restraine thair neighbouris from traiding, lossing or laidning in the Channorie of Ross,[21] Crommartie or Rosemarkie, and ordaining the burght of Innernes to use thair diligence in restraining the unfrie persounes thair from usurpeing the liberties of the frie royall burrowes, and last ordaining the burght of Elgyne to give in all suche the names of those unfrie persounes as at mair lenth is contenit in the said act.[22] Compeired the commissioneris of Dundy and Aberdeine and declared that they hade inhibite thair neighboures and that none of them did the contrair. As also the commissioner of Elgyne gave in the names following viz, Alexander Hardie, Alexander Robsoun, Gavine McCullo, Johnne McKraw and Donald McKillen in the Channorie, Duncane Baine and Angus McMurchie in Dingwell, Johnne McKillen and James Tailyeour within the toun of Annas[23] in Ross, whome they hade tryed to have usurped within the saidis boundis upoun the liberties of the saidis burrowes, quhiche the present commissioneris [fo. 487v] acceptis for diligence. And findis that the said burght of Innernes hes produced no diligence and thairfoir to have incurred the unlaw conteinit in the said act whairwith the burrowes for the present dispenssis upoun the promeis of thair commissioneris farder diligence. And ordaines the said burght to use diligence in restraining the persounes abonewrittin and all otheris thair usurpeing upoun thair liberties

---

[20] See above, 181. For details of Wedderburn and his grammar, see Introduction 28–30.
[21] Fortrose, Ross.
[22] See above, 165–6.
[23] Probably Alness, on the north shore of the Cromarty Firth.

under the paine of fourtie pundis and to produce the same to the said nixt
generall conventioun under the said paine. And this to be ane heid of the
nixt missive.

13

The same day anent the tent act of the said last generall conventioun of
burrowis haldin at Edinburght the secound day of Julii last ordaineing the
burght of Forfare to have produced thair diligence to this present conventioun in restraineing the inhabitantis of Killiemuire[24] in Angus from usurpeing the liberties of the frie royall burrowes.[25] The present commissioneris
understanding that now thair is ane preparative past in thair favour in
the lyk caice, thairfoir ordaines the saidis burghe to prosecute the former
letters raisit and execuite at thair instance againes the saidis inhabitantis of
Killiemuire under the paine of fourtie pundis and to produce the same to
the nixt generall conventioun of burrowes. And this to be ane heid of the
nixt missive.

14

The same day ordaines the burght of Dumfermeling to produce the forme
of the electioun of thair magistrattis and counsell at Michalmes nixt and to
proceid thairin conforme to the actis of parliament and burrowes under the
paine of ane hundreth pundis and to produce the same to the nixt generall
conventioun of burrowes under the said paine. And this to be ane heid of
the nixt missive.

15

The same day anent the sevinteine act of the last generall conventioune
of burrowes haldin att Edinburght the thrid day of Julii last, ordaining the
burght of Rothesay to produce the forme of the electioune of thair magis-
traitis and counsall at Michaelmes last to this present conventioun and for
sending the soume of tuentie pundis of unlaw for not productioun of the
forme of the electioun of thair magistrattis and counsell to the last generall
conventioun haldin at the said burght of Edinburgh the thrid day of Julii last,
lykwayes to this present conventioun.[26] Compeired Mathow Spens commissioner for the said burght of Rothesay and produced the forme of the electioun of thair magistrattis and counsell at Michaelmes last, quhiche being
considerit, the present commissioneris allowes heirof for this tyme, and for
caussis moveing thame dispenssis with the unlaw incurred be them of before
and ordaines them to tak [fo. 488r] preceis ordour amongst themselffis for

---

24 Kirriemuir, Angus.
25 See above, 167.
26 See above, 173.

conformeing of the electioun of thair magistrattis and counsell in all tyme cumming, conforme to the actis of parliament and burrowes.

16

The same day anent the auchteine act of the last generall conventioun of burrowes haldin at the burght of Edinburgh the thrid day of Julii last concerning the visitatioun of the Watter of Forth.[27] Compeired the commissioneris of Kirkcaldy, Dysert, and Bruntyland and produced thair diligence in visitatioun of the said Water of Forth, quhilk the burrowes acceptis for thair diligence. And ordaines the agent to pay to them the soume of fyftie tua pundis money and the same sall be allowit to him in his comptis. And also ordaines the burghes quho sall be appointit to meitt at Edinburght efter the dissolveing of this present conventioun to report the same to the lordis of counsell and to supplicat the saidis lordis for putting thair former proclamatioun maid anent the said river against the heritouris to executioun, and in causeing the customeris in Culross mak thair report of thair diligence at the making of the entrie of the tryell of the transgressouris or otherwayes to releive the burrowes of thair yeirlie visitatioun. To quhiche burrowes the present commissioneris gives full power and commissioun thairanent and for doeing quhatsumever they sall think expedient anent the premissis. And if that they sall not releive them of the foirsaid visitatioun yeirlie, gives thair full power and commissioun for appointing suche thrie burrowes as they sall think neidfull for visiteing of the said watter of new.

17

The same day anent the 19 act of the last generall conventioun of borrowes haldin at Edinburghe the fourt day of Julii last, ordaining the burght of Elgyne to have produced thair diligence to this conventioun on restrayneing of certaine inhabitantis in Germothe,[28] lyand within thair shirrefdome, usurpeing the liberties of the frie royall burrowes.[29] Compeired Robert Hardy commissioner for the said burght of Elgyne and declaired that they had chairged the saidis inhabitantis and that tua of thame hade fund cautioun to desist and the rest of them haid suffered themeselffis to be denunced rebellis and since some of them haid suspendit and relaxit, whiche the saidis commissioneris acceptis for diligence. And thairfoir the saidis commissioneris ordaines the said burght to prosecute the saidis suspensiounes againes the saidis suspenderis and to insist with captioun against the rest, and to produce thair diligence heiranent to the nixt generall conventioun of burrowes under the paine of tuentie pundis. And this to be ane heid of the nixt missive.

---

27 See above, 173–4.
28 Garmouth, at the mouth of the Spey, in Moray.
29 See above, 174.

[fo. 488v]

18

Non Julii I^m vi^c trigesimo quinto

The quhilk day the commissioneris of burrowes being conveinit haveing ressavit ane letter from the lordis of his Majesties most honorable privie counsell desyreing them to mak choyse of some discreit persones to conferre and treatt anent the matter of the tannage and for setling the same for the weill of the cuntrey and ease of the pairties interest as the said letter daittit the secound day of Julii instant beiris. For obedience quhairof the present commissioneris grantis and gives full power and commissioun to the burghes of Edinburgh, Perth, Dundy, Aberdein, Stirling, Linlythgow, Sanctandrois, Glasgow, Air, Kirkcaldy, Bruntyland, Cowper, Dumfreis, Selkirk, Anstruther Eister and Dumbartane to meitt and conveine at the burght of Edinburghe the fyfteine day of this instant with continuatioun of dayes and to treatt reassoun and conclude anent the said matter in sua far as may tend to the weill of the cuntrey and ease and good of the subjectis, with power also to the saidis burrowes and maist pairt of them conveinand to unlaw the absentis in ane unlaw of xx li. and to sitt, determine and conclude in all other thingis sall be remitted to thame be the present conventioun, and generallie all and sundrie other thingis to doe, use and exerce anent the premissis whiche the present commissioneris micht doe themselffis, firme and stable haldand and for to hald, all and quhatsumever the foirsaidis burghtis sall laufullie doe or leid to be done anent the premissis. And the saidis burghes to report thair diligence heiranent to the nixt generall conventioun of borrowes. And this to be ane heid of the nixt missive.[30]

19

The same day anent the tent act of the particular conventioun of burrowes haldin at Edinburght the tent day of November last anent the restraineing of suche as ar not admitted factouris at the staiple port of Campheir from exerceing the said office and for the restrayning of the avarice of some few quho frauchtis shippes be the grippis as at mair lenth is conteinit in the said act.[31] The present commissioneris hes remittit and remittis the same to the consideratioun of the burrowis appointit to meitt at Edinburght the fyfteine day of this instant with continuatioun of dayes, to quhome they grant and gives thair full power and commissioun for making of suche lawes, statutes and ordinances for restrayneing all prejudice this estaitt may susteine throw the saidis unlaufull deallingis, whiche the present commissioneris for themselffis and in name of thair burghes ratifies and approves the same and

---

[30] This act is noted in the Abstract of Acts of Convention, *RCRBS*, iv, 539, where the subject is given as 'tunnage' rather than 'tannage'.

[31] See above, 207–8.

obleissis them and thair burghes and inhabitantis to abyde thairat but againe calling quhatsumever. And ordaines the saidis burghes to report thair diligence heiranent to the nixt generall conventioun of burrowis. And this to be ane heid of the nixt missive.

[fo. 489r]

20

The same day anent the aucht act of the last generall conventioun of burrowes haldin at the burght of Edinburgh the secound day of Julii last, ordaining the burght of Carraill to have produced thair dilligence in writt to the said conventioun in restraineing the inhabitantis of Levin and St Monanes from usurpeing the libertie of the frie royall burrowes under the paine of tuentie pundis.[32] The present commissioneris hes thocht guid for the present that ilk burghe be againe requyred for sending thair commissioneris sufficientlie instructit with thair best advyse thairanent for restraining of the saidis inhabitantis to the said nixt conventioun. And this to be ane heid of the nixt missive.

21

The said day the saidis commissioneris of burrowes ordaines the burght of Stirling to produce thair diligence to the nixt generall conventioun of burrowes in restraining the unfrie men within thair boundis and especiallie the indwelleris of Fawkirk[33] from usurpeing the libberties of the frie royall burrowes under the paine of tuentie pundis and this to be ane heid of the nixt missive.

22

The samin day anent the 20 act of the last generall conventioun of burrowis haldin at Edinburghe the fourt day of Julii last and the sevint act of the particular conventioun haldin at the said burght the [8] day of November last anent the commissioneris then conveinit thair proceidingis with Thomas Cunynghame and James Weir, factoris in Campheir and manner of oath prescryvit be them to be gevin to all collectoris to be appointed thairefter for ingaddering the dewes of the ministeris stipend at the said port.[34] The present commissioneris haveing seine and considderit the same, they ratifie, approve and allow thairof and ordaines the said maner of oath to be administrat to all succeiding collectouris in manner contenit in the said act.

---

32 See above, 165–6.
33 Falkirk, Stirlingshire.
34 See above, 174–5, 205–6.

23

The same day anent the tuentie thrid act of the last generall conventioun
of burrowes haldin at the burght of Edinburghe the fourt day of Julii last
ordaineing the agent to uplift from the burghes of Lochmaben and Sanquhair ilkane of them the soume of tuentie pundis of unlaw for being absent
fra the said conventioun and for not sending the dewes of the missive to the
samyne.[35] The saidis burrowes ordaines the agent to insist againes the said
burghtis of Lochmaben and Sanquhair as is contenit in the said act. And if
they sall pay thair dewes resting and keip ordour in tyme cumming and pay
the expenssis of thair chairges, the burrowes dispenssis with thair unlawes.
And the said agent to report his diligence heiranent to the nixt generall
conventioun of burrowes. And this to be ane heid of the nixt missive.

[fo. 489v]

24

The same day anent the 21 act of the last generall conventioun of burrowis
haldin at the burght of Edinburghe the fourt day of Julii last, ordaining
the conservatour to intimatt to the factoris of new the act inhibiteing
them to mak rebaittis at thair awin handis and to cause them to act themselffis for obedience of the same under the paines thairin contenit, and in
speciall Thomas Cunnynghame and James Weir conforme to the ellevint
act of the particular conventioun haldin at Edinburgh the ellevint day of
November last.[36] As also anent the 13 act of the last generall conventioun
appointing Alexander Baitye factour to be collectour of the ministeris dewes
at Campheir from the first of September last till the first of Maii last, and
the comptis thairof to have beine produceit to this present conventioun
and appointing Robert Greirsoun collector from the first of Maii last till
the first of Maii nixt 1636 yeiris, and ordaineing them to give thair aithes
in manner thairinconteinit.[37] And anent the 22 and [...][38] actis of the said
last generall conventioun and 8 act of the last particular conventioun haldin
at Edinburght in November last anent the greivances of the staiple,[39] the
conservatour his dealling with the magistrattis of the said toun thairanent,
and anent the retributioun to be gevin to the conservatour for his bygaine
paines and augmentatioun of his fees mentioned in the 24 act of the said last
generall conventioun and his Majesties letter direct to the present commissioneris thairanent, and for the bygane arrieris dew to him in his office in

---

35 See above, 176.
36 See above, 175.
37 See above, 169–71.
38 Act 22 of the previous general convention appears to be the only one that specifically
    relates to grievances with the council of Veere (see above, 175–6).
39 See above, 206–7.

the haill sevinteine provinces.[40] The present commissioneris of burrowes
considdering that nather the said conservatour hes comed himselff to mak
his report anent the saidis particularis nor that the said Alexander Bautye
hes sent over his comptis quhairby ane course could have beine takin anent
the premissis, they have remitted and be thir presentis remittis the saidis
haill particularis and severall materis mentioned in the severall actis abonewrittin to be treatted reassoned and concluded be the commissioneris of
burrowes to be appointed to conveine in the conventioun appointed to be
and beginne at the burght of Edinburghe the fyfteine of this instant with
continuatioun of dayes, to whiche commissioneris and maist pairt of them
conveinand the present commissioneris grantis and gives unto them thair
full power, commissioun and authoritie to doe thairin as they sall think best
for the weill of the burrowes and that als frielie in all respectis and be all
thingis as the present commissioneris micht doe themeselffis. And quhatso-
ever they sall doe and conclude thairanent the present commissioneris for
thame selffis and in name of thair burghtis ratifies and approves the samyne
and obleissis them to abyde thairat but againe calling or contradictioun
quhatsomever. As also grants and gives unto them full power and commissioun for electing and cheising of ane new collectour for uplifting the saidis
dewes from the first of Maii 1636 yeiris to the first of Maii thairefter 1637
yeiris. And ordaines them to signifie the same to him quhan they sall happin
to elect and to the conservatour and his deputes to the effect he may mak
faythe conforme to the ordour ordainit to be keipit in suche caices. And
the saidis burrowes to report thair diligence heiranent to the nixt generall
conventioun of burrowes. And this to be ane heid of the nixt missive.

[fo. 490r]

25

The same day anent the tuentie sext act of the last generall conventioun
of burrowes haldin at the burghe of Edinburgh the [4] day of Julii last,
ordaining the burghtis of Edinburghe, Aberdeine, Glasgow, Dysert and Kirkcaldie to uplift from certaine of thair neighbouris suche dewes as they wer
addebtit of the impost appointit for the minister of Campheire or els to
have produced the saidis persounes before the present commissioneris as at
mair lenth is contenit in the said act.[41] Compeired Johnne Sinclair ane of the
commissioneris of Edinburgh and declairit that Thomas Gray, Robert Pringill, Thomas Mairtine, Johnne Denholme, George Jarden, David Robertsoun
and James Downie in Leith hes beine this long tyme out of the cuntrey
and hes not as yitt returned. As lykwayes delyverit to Alexander Aikinheid

---

40 That is the seventeen provinces of the Netherlands, seven in the Dutch Republic and ten
    in the Spanish Netherlands. See above, 176–7.
41 See above, 177–8.

agent the soume of thrie pundis fyve shillingis Flemyngis money quhairin the rest of the neighbouris contenit in the said act wer dew. As lykwayes compeired the commissioner of the burght of Aberdeine and maid payment to the said agent of the som of fyve schillingis Fleyms dew for them. And last compeired the commissioneris of Glasgow, Kirkcaldy and Dysert and obleist thameselffis for payment of the soumes dew be thair nichtbouris mentioned in the said act to the agent betuixt and the nixt particular conventioun to be haldin at Edinburgh in this instant moneth or els to produce the saidis persounes that ordour may be taken with thame for thair neglect. Thairfore the present commissioneris ordaines the said burght of Edinburght to doe farder diligence against thair neighbouris mentioned in the said act quho hes not maid payment and to produce the same to the nixt generall conventioun of burrowes. And ordanes the agent to send over to Robert Greir, present collector of the said impost, the moneyis ressavit be him presentlie thairof and quhat he sall ressave at the nixt particular conventioun if any sall be payit to him and the said Robert to be chairged thairwith in his accomptis. And the saidis burghes and agent to report thair diligence heiranent to the nixt generall conventioun of burrowes. And this to be ane heid of the nixt missive.

26

{Aganes affixing be privat men of thair names on publict workis within burgh done upone publict charges}
The same day anent the 49 act of the last generall conventioun of burrowes haldin att Edinburgh the fyft day of Julii last 1634 yeiris inhibiteing privat men from affixeing thair names upoun publict workis done upoun publict chairges, the present commissioneris recommendis the farder executioun of the said act to the counsell of ilk burght.[42] And farder becaus they understand that in some burghes some privat persounes hes so far presumed upoun the publict that thair former deidis does breid no small distcontent amongst the rest of thair neighbouris to the great prejudice of the publict good. Thairfore the present commissioneris hes thoucht good to recomend the ordour taking in suche caices to the counsell of ilk burght that convenientlie in peace and quyetnes the said prejudice be takin away that they have ane caire to execute the said act *quoad pr[e]terita*[43] with als great quyetnes as they can, as they will be answerable to the burrowes. And ilk burght to report thair diligence heiranent to the nixt generall conventioun of burrowes. And this to be ane heid of the nixt missive.

---

[42] See above, 190–91.
[43] Although the edge of the page is damaged, this seems to be the Latin phrase *quoad preterita/ praeterita* meaning 'as far as it was in the past'.

[fo. 490v]

27

Decimo Julii I^m vi^c trigesimo quinto

{Irving Ramfrew contra Kilmarnock and other burghis of Barronie}

The quhilk day the saidis commissioneris being conveinit anent the 15 act of the last generall conventioun of burrowes haldin at the burght of Edinburgh the thrid day of Julii last and the 6 act of the particular conventioun haldin at Edinburgh the 7 of November last quhairby umquhile Mr James Cockburne was elected for prosecutioun of the actioun intentit and ordainit to be intentit be the burghes of Irving and Ramfrew against the haill unfriemen within thair boundis upoun the expenssis of the burrowes, for whiche cause thair was ordainit to be borrowit be the agent the soume of tua thowsand merkis as at mair lenth is conteinit in the saidis actis.[44] Compeired the agent and declaired that he haid advanced the said soume upoun thair said commissioner his dischairge and that thair was obteinit thrie severall sentences against the unfriemen within Ramfrew ordaineing them to find cautioun [in the] sum [of] x ls.[45] and other thrie of the lyke nature against the unfrie men within Irving. Thairfoir the saidis commissioneris allowes of thair said umquhile commissioner his diligence and ordaines the said soume with the interest thairof to be allowed in the agent his comptis. And becaus they understand that thair is no sentence recovered against the inhabitantis of Kilmarnok and some other unfriemen within thair boundis, and that sundrie of the saidis persounes against quhom the saidis sentences ar recovered, both within the boundis of Irving and Ramfrew, hes of new suspendit and being willing both for ane generall preparative to the rest of the burrowes, as also for compleitlie perfytting quhat hes alreaddie beine begun. Thairfoir they have thocht meitt that contraventiounes sall be persewed upoun the burrowes chairges againes the saids contraveneris and if any of them hes suspendit of new that the samyne be discussed and that the saidis inhabitantis of Kilmarnoche, and uther unfrie people within the liberties of Irving quho hes beine chairged, be lykwayes restrained and persewit upoun thair chairges. And to this effect they have maid choise of Robert Stewart, merchand in Linlythgow for prosecuteing of the saidis actiounes with advyse of Johnne Sinclair, deane of gild of Edinburgh, and Mr Alexander Guthrie, thair clerk. And for the better furtherance hes ordainit and ordaines the agent to concurre with them and to borrow upoun interest the soume of two thowsand merkis to be imployed to the effect foirsaid and with advyce foirsaid, whiche the present commissioneris

---

44 See above, 171–2, 203–5, although neither act mentions Kilmarnock.

45 This says 'sum x^lb' although it probably ought to say 'in x^lb', as 'ls' is not the normal abbreviation for pounds. Also, the phrase should probably say 'in the sum of', rather than just 'sum'.

in name of thair burghes and haill remanent burrowes bindis and obleissis
them to refound with the interest thairof to the said agent. As also ordaines
the burghes of Irving and Ramfrew to attend thair said commissioner being
requyred be him to raise letters be advyse of the said commissioner and to
chairge the saidis persounes and to furnische probatioun and utheris richtis
to him for prosecuteing the saidis actiounes. And if neid sall be to grant unto
him speciall power and procuratorie for that effect under the paine of ane
hundreth pundis ilk [fo. 491r] burghe. And declaires that, inrespect of the
povertie of Ramfrew, that the commissioneris will have consideratioun of
thair chairges and expenssis. And the saidis burrowes and commissioner to
report thair diligence heiranent. And this to be ane heid of the nixt missive.

28
{Commission for altering the generall stent roll of the Burrowis}
The same day anent the 4 act of the last generall conventioun of burrowes
haldin at Edinburgh in Julii last anent the alteratioun of the taxt roll and
manner and forme thairof,[46] the present commissioneris haveing weyed and
considderit that since the same wes last sett and aggried upoun, many burghtis
hes fallin in great decay and povertie and some few otheris hes increassed
in power and riches. Thairfore they have all in ane voyce aggreid consentit
and ordainit and be thir presentis aggries consentis and ordaynes that the
present stent roll of ane hundreth pundis as the samyne standis, quhiche is
the proportionable squaire quhairby all commoun burdenis imposed or to
be imposed upoun them is sett and reullit, sall be altered and changed allo-
weing thairto for the ingathering thairof the soume of [...] to be conteinit
in the said stent by and attour the said soume of ane hundreth pundis and
thair taxatiounes and impositiounes to be levied of them and ilkane of
them according thairto. And for this effect they have agried, appointed and
ordainit and be thir presentis aggries, appointis and ordaines the burghtis
of Perth, Dundie, Aberdeine, Stirling, Aire, Jedburght, Couper, Bruntyland,
Hadingtoun and Dumbartane, and ilkane of them, to direct and commissioner to the said burght of Edinburgh with ample and sufficient power and
commissioun for setting of the said taxt roll to meitt and conveine at the said
burght with tua to be appointed be the said burght of Edinburgh instructed
in lykmanner, the tuentie day of November nixt with continuatioun of
dayes under the pane of ane hundreth pundis to be upliftit of ilk burght
that sall failyie. To which persounes and maist pairt of them conveinand, the
present commissioneris ilkane of them for thair awin burghtis and inhabitantis thairof and in name and behalf of the haill remanent burrowes of this

---

[46]   This is an error and should refer to the 14th act of the general convention at Edinburgh in
July 1634, see above, 171.

kingdome submittis themeselffis to be extentit and suche ane proportionable pairt of the said soume of ane hundreth pundis to be imposed upoun them conforme to whiche proportioun of the said soume of ane hundreth pundis and allowance forsaid all taxatiounes and uther impositiounes sall be heirefter uplifted of eache one of the saidis burrowes. And grantis and geives unto them full power and commissioun for setting of the said stent roll in manner abonewrittin. Lykas the present commissioneris, in name of thair saidis burghtis and inhabitantis thairof and haill remanent burrowes as said is, bindis and obleissis them and thair saidis burghtis as said is to obey fullfill and obtemper the saidis [fo. 491v] persounes thair sentence and determinatioun and in all taxatiounes and other impositiounes to pay thair pairt of the same conforme to the said proportioun and that but any contradictioun or againe calling quhatsumever. And to the effect that it may appeir that the samyne sall be sett without feid or favour of any particularitie, the present commissioneris ordaines the saidis persounes to compeir befor the provest, baillies and counsell of Edinburgh and to accept upoun them the said chairge for setting of the said stent roll and to mak faith that they sall proceid thairintill without any kynd of partiallitie quhatsumever and sall sett the samyne as haiffing God and good conscience before thair eyes, quhiche being done that the saidis persounes sall incontinent thairefter meitt and conveine and sett doun the stent roll in manner foirsaid. Quhiche roll being so sett, the present commissioneris geives full power and commissioun to the burght of Edinburgh to devyde the haill burdenis layed upoun the estait of burrowes accordinglie thairto. And ordaines thair generall clerk to give furth the same to the collectour generall and thair deputtis under his hand. And ordaines the burghe of Edinburgh, some convenient tyme before be thair missive letters, to requyre the saidis ten burrowes out of whiche the saidis persounes extentaris ar to be takin for meitting at thair said burght the said day under the paine foirsaid. As also ordaines ilk commissioner present to intimat the said appointed alteratioun to thair burrowes at thair home cumming. And the saidis burrowes to report thair diligence heiranent to the nixt generall conventioun of burrowes. And this to be ane heid of the nixt missive.[47]

29

The same day anent the 28 act of the last generall conventioun of burrowes anent ane agent at court,[48] the present commissioneris of burrowes being advysed thairwith hes thocht guid and ordainit that Hary Alexander, sonne to the earle of Stirling, sall be remunerat for his bygane service and attend-

---

47   This act is noted in the Abstract of Acts of Convention, *RCRBS*, iv, 539. This meeting seems to have taken place in October. The tax roll was altered but no revised roll seems to survive: see the discussion of this in the Introduction 23–5.

48   See above 180.

ance of thair effairis at court and thairfor hes ordainit the soume of ane hundreth pundis sterling to be payit to him. And ordaines that ilk burght be requyred for sending thair pairt thairof to the nixt generall conventioun of burrowes under the usuall paines conforme to the taxt roll. And becaus they have many effairis yitt in dependance, hes thocht good that the said Harie Alexander sall for ane yeir farder attend the saidis imploymentis upoun the lyk remuneratioun. And for this effect they ordaine the clerk in thair names to writt to him and to desire the continuance of his service and attendance upoun thair effairis and to advert to all thingis may concerne them and sua far as he can to prevene thair hurt if any sall be intendit, at the leist to give trew and tymeous notice thairof. For the quhiche they sall be cairfull to recompence his paines. And ordaines this to be ane heid of the nixt missive.[49]

[fo. 492r]

30

The same day quhairas the commissioneris taking to thair consideratioun the evident appeirance of the ruyne of the kingdome in all tred and money occasioned be the laite Englishe trade, thairfore they ordane the commissioneris appointed to meitt at Edinburgh the fyfteine of this instant to tak the same to thair serious consideratiounes and to interceid with the lordis of his Majesties counsell that they wald deall with his Majestie that that trade may be so moderated that thair be no more permitted thairof nor may be answerable to the worth of the wairis transportit in Ingland and so vertew may be heir advanced and money be brocht in into the cuntrey and keiped thairin. To which burrowes the present commissioneris geives thair full power and commissioun for setling of the said mater and doeing of all and sindrie other thingis thairanent as the present commissioneris micht doe themselffis, *promitten de rato*[50] etc. And the saidis burrowes to report thair diligence heiranent tothe nixt generall conventioun of burrowes. And this to be ane heid of the nixt missive.

31

The same day anent the 31 act of the last generall conventioun of burrowes haldin at the burght of Edinburgh the fyft day of Julii last, ordaineing the burght of Linlythgow to be requyred for sending with thair commissioner to this present conventioun the forme of the electioun of thair counsell and magistrattis at Michaelmes authenticklie subscrivit under the paine of tuentie pundis.[51] Compeired Robert Stewart commissioner for the said

---

[49] This act is noted in the Abstract of Acts of Convention, *RCRBS*, iv, 539.

[50] This literally means 'promising concerning firm/fixed'. It denotes an undertaking to abide by whatever is decided by the person or persons delegated.

[51] See above, 181–2.

burght of Linlythgow and produced the forme of the electioun of thair magistrattis and counsell with thair institutioun of the gildrie of thair burght. Quhiche being considderit be the present commissioneris togither with the said commissioneris awin declaratioun and explanatioun, they allowe thairof and ordaines them to conforme themeselffis in thair said electioun to the actis of parliament and burrowes in all tyme cumming.

32

The same day anent the 35 act of the last generall conventioun of burrowes haldin at the burght of Edinburght the fyft day of Julii last, ordaining the burght of Innernes to produce to this present conventioun the forme of the electioun of thair magistrattis and counsell at Michaelmes last and to conforme thameselffis in thair said electioun to the actis of parliament and burrowes under the paine of tuentie pundis.[52] Compeired Johnne Cuthbert, commissioner of the said burght of Innernes and produced the forme of thair said electioun at Michaelmes last, quhiche the saidis burrowes acceptis for diligence and ordaines them to conforme themselffis in thair said electioun to the actis of parliament and burrowes in all tyme heirefter.

[fo. 492v]
33

The same day anent the 45 act of the last generall conventioun of burrowes haldin at the burght of Edinburght the fyft day of Julii last, ordaineing the burght of Linlythgow to have produced thair diligence to this present conventioun in restraining the persounes mentioned in the said act, indwelleris in the Quenisferrie, from usurpeing the libertie of the frie royall burghtis. Compeired Robert Stewart commissioner of the said burght and declaired that the said burght hade chairged the saidis persounes and that they hade suspendit, whiche the burrowes acceptis for diligence at this tyme and ordaines the said burght to produce farder diligence to the nixt generall conventioun of burrowes in procureing the saidis suspensiounes discussed, under the paine of tuentie pundis. And this to be ane heid of the nixt missive.

34

The same day anent the supplicatioun gevin in be the present commissioner of Dumfermeling for the unlawes upliftit af thair burght be the agent at command of the burrowes and mentioned in diveris heidis of the present missive, the present commissioneris considdering and pitieing the puire estaite of the said burght and upoun hope of reformatioun of the abuises in

---

52   See above, 183.

electioun of thair provest, hes remitted and remittis the saidis unlawes upliftit
be the said agent as said is and ordaines the same to be redelyverit to thair
said commissioner, quhairanent thir presentis sall be to him ane warrand. As
also ordaines the said burght in thair aprocheing electioun to chainge thair
provest and mak of suche onlie as ar capable be the actis of parliament and
burrowes under the paine of ane hundreth pundis. Lykas the said commissioner in name of the said burght obleissis them to fulfill the same under
the said paine and to produce the forme of thair said electioun of thair
magistrattis and counsell at Michaelmes nixt and to conforme themeselffis
to the actis of parliament and burrowes at the nixt generall conventioun of
burrowes under the paine of fourtie pundis. And this to be ane heid of the
nixt missive.

35

The same day anent the nynt act of the particular conventioun of burrowes
haldin at the burght of Edinburgh the tent day of November last, ordaineing the burght of Edinburght to sett doun suche articles, patentis, lawes
and suche other thingis as they sall think meit concerning the erecting of
companies for the weill manageing of trade and for the advantage of the
native commodities. Considering the good redoundis [fo. 493r] to these
cities quhair trade is ordourlie reullit and confusioun takin away, the present
commissioneris remittes the same to the commissioneris to be conveinit
at Edinburght the fyfteine of this instant with continuatioun of dayes, to
quhom the present commissioneris gives full power and commissioun for
setting doun of the saidis lawes, articles and patentis as they sall think neidfull
and ordaines the saidis burghtis to report thair diligence heiranent to the
nixt generall conventioun of burrowes. And this to be ane heid of the nixt
missive.

36

The same day anent the fyfteine act of the last particular conventioun of
burrowes haldin at Edinburgh the ellevint day of November last, ordaineing
the burght of Wigtoun to be warnit for productioun of the electioun of
thair magistrattis and counsell at Michaelmes last to this present conventioun
to be seine and considderit be them. Compeirand the commissioner of the
said burght of Wigtoun and produced the forme of the electioun of thair
magistrattis and counsell at Michaelmes last, whiche being seine and considderit be the present commissioneris they fand them to have done wrong in
electing of the earle of Galloway to be thair provest and thair minister and
commisser[53] to be upoun thair counsell, and thairfore to have incurrit the

---

53 The judge in the commissary court of the shire. It was wholly irregular for a minister to
    serve on a burgh council.

unlaw of tuentie pundis contenit in the said act.Yit upoun hope of amendement they superceid the uplifting thairof to the nixt generall conventioun
and ordaines the said burght in thair nixt electioun at Michaelmes nixt to
mak choyse of none to be thair magistrattis or upoun thair counsell but
suche as be the lawes of the kingome is capable thairof, viz merchandis and
craftismen dwelling with them and beiring all portable chairges under the
paine of ane hundreth pundis. Lykwayes thair commissioner compeirand
obleissis him and his said burght for doeing thairof under the said paine and
produce the forme of thair said electioun of thair magistratis and counsell
and to conforme themselffis thairin to the actis of parliament and burrowes,
under the paine of fourtie pundis. And this to be ane heid of the nixt missive.

37

The same day anent the severall heidis of the missive mentioned in the
27 act of the last generall conventioun of burrowes haldin at Edinburgh
the [4] day of Julii last and in diveris uther actis in the subsequent particular conventiounes. Compeired Alexander Aikinheid, agent, and produced
the patent of correctioun houssis under his Majesties great seall, togither
with the proclamatioun forbidding bleaching with lyme, with the double
of the chartour of associatioun under the directour of the chancellarie his
hand, and last produced the act of counsell anent the ordour takin with
the plaiding. Which being all seine and considderit be the saidis burrowes,
they ordaine ilk commissioner to recommend to [fo. 493v] thair burrowes
at thair homecumeing the erecting of correctioun houssis for banischeing
of vyce and idlenes and inbringing of vertew, and delyverit to the commissioner of Aberdeine the act anent the plaiding whiche they recommended
to be publisched be them and to sie the said ordour tak effect, and last they
ordaine ilk burght to have ane caire that no linning within thair boundis
be bleitched with lyme conforme to the said proclamatioun. And the saidis
burrowes to report thair diligence in intimatting and observeing of the
premissis to the nixt generall conventioun of burrowes. And this to be ane
heid of the nixt missive.[54]

38

Undecimo Julii I^m vi^c trigesimo quinto
The quhilk day the commissioneris of burrowes being convenit anent the 30
act of the last generall conventioun of burrowes haldin at the burght of Edinburgh the fourt day of Julii last quhairby commissioun was gevin to certaine
commissioneris for taking course for removeing the new impositiounes in
France imposed upoun merchandis traffiqueing thither far contrair to the

54   This act is noted in the Abstract of Acts of Convention, *RCRBS*, iv, 539.

auncient liberties of this kingdome, and anent the 4 act of the particular conventioun haldin at the said burght of Edinburght the nyn of Julii last, quhairby Johnne Trotter merchand in Edinburght was elected commissioner for the whole burrowes for passing to his Majestie our soverane lord and to the Frenche king for procureing ane ease of the saidis impositiounes and fore renovatioun of the auntient liberties of this kingdome within the province of Normandy, as at mair lenth is conteinit in the saidis actis. Compeired the said Johnne Trotter and gave in his report of his haill proceidingis in the said matter in writt, quhairby he declaired that conforme to the commissioun gevin to him he hade past to our soveraigne lord the kingis Majestie and conforme to thair desyr hade procured ane letter to the Frenche king with ane other to his Majesties agentis resident thair and thairefter passed to the said kingdome of France, quhair efter the delyverie of the foirsaidis letters to the Frenche king he gave in his petitioun anent the foirsaid new impositiounes whiche was fund be the counsell of France to be ane mater of finances. And efter a long tedious and chargeable attendance at leist in the moneth of [...] lastbypast, he obteinit his answer whiche was delyverit to him be two arrests of counsell. Be the ane quhairof the counsell ordainit that the fermer generall sould verifie within thrie monethis thairefter by titillis and witnessis quhat customes war payed be the Scottis merchandis since the yeir of God 1580 unto [fo. 494r] this present whiche day fallis furth into this present moneth. And be the other they hade ordainit that quhairas thair was payit of before of custome for everie hundreth weicht of Scottish wooll importit unto Normandie the soume of fyftie sous,[55] that from the daitt of the arreist thair sould be no hier custome takin than the soume of tuentie fyve sous Frenche. And quhairas of before thair was takin fyve sous for everie Scottish hyde importit thither, that thairefter thair sould be onlie takin tua sous and sex denneiris as the said arrestis beiris. Whiche first arrest he caused intimat to the said fermer generall and procured ane mandament upoun the other arrest directt to the court Desayes in Rowen in Normandie,[56] whiche being presentit to the president of the said court, the said arrest was verified in thair register, whiche thairefter he caused be insert Maister de Ports bureau generall of Normandie in Rowen in thair registeres, the extracts and collatiounes quhairof he caused intimat to the customeris in New Heavin[57] and registrat the same in the customehous of Deip,[58] whiche haill writtis he lykwayes produced togither with ane compt of his debursementis in the said voyage, extending in the haill to the soume of four thousand ane hundreth thriescoir thretteine frankis four sous Frenche

---

[55] A *sou* (from Latin *solidus*) was one twentieth of a French pound.
[56] Presumably the court d'essaies.
[57] Le Havre, founded as a new port by Francois I[er] at the mouth of the Seine.
[58] Dieppe in Normandy was the premier French port in the seventeenth century.

money. Quhiche all being considderit be the present commissioneris of burrowes, they ratifie and approve and allowe of the said Johnne his proceidingis in the saidis purposes and gives him hairtlie thankis for his paynes and labouris takin thairin. And as to the farder prosecutioun of the first arrest and repayment to the said Johnne of the soumes of money debursit be him in manner abonewrittin, with the interest thairof, the present commissioneris in respect of the schortnes of the present tyme, hes thocht guid to remitt and remittes the same to the commissioneris of burrowes to be conveinit at Edinburght the fifteine of this instant, to whiche commissioneris they give full power and commissioun for prosecuteing of the said pretendit persute and first arrest if they sall think neidfull and expedient, as also for taking course for refounding the soumes abonewrittin, interestis thairof and quhat sall be farder neidfull for uplifting thairof conforme to the former actis maid thairanent, and generallie all and sundrie thingis to doe, use and exerce anent the premissis, quhiche the present commissioneris micht doe themselffis. Lykas the present commissioneris for themselffis and thair burghtis obleissis them to abyde thairat but contradictioun or againe calling quhatsumever. And the saidis burrowes to report thair diligence heiranent. And this to be ane heid of the nixt missive.[59]

39

The same day anent the supplicatioun gevin in to the burrowes at the last generall conventioun of burrowes haldin at Edinburgh in Julii last be the burght of Anstruther Eister craveing thair helpe for building of ane churche within the said toun, for giving answer quhairunto ilk burght wes requyret for sending thair commissioneris sufficientlie instructed to this present conventioun, and quhairwith [fo. 494v] the present commissioneris being rypelie advysed and consideddering the manifold necessities that that toun hes bein so long subject to for laik of ane churche and the diligence of the inhabitantis for building of ane churche and founding of ane ministrie within themselffis, and that they ar so meane of themeselffis that they have no power to accomplische so good ane work without some guid and considerable helpe, thairfoir they have grantit and gevin and be thir presentis grantis and gevis to the said burght of Anstruther Eister the soume of thrie thowsand merkis and ordaines ilk burght to send thair pairt thairof to the nixt generall conventioun of burrowes conforme to the taxt roll under the paine of xx li. ilk burght and that by and attour the payment of thair pairt of the said principall soume. And this to be ane heid of the nixt missive.

59   This act is noted in the Abstract of Acts of Convention, *RCRBS*, iv, 539.

40

The same day quhairas the burrowes being petitioned in name of Mr Alexander Jaffray in Aberdeine, cautioner for Johnne Burnett, factour in Campheir, inrespect that the said Johnne hes provin bankrupt and that he hes beine forced to pay great soumes of money for him to dischairge him of his said cautionrie, with the which the burrowes being advysed, they have thocht guid and ordainit that the said Johnne sall be dischairged of his said office of factorie and to this effect ordaines the conservatour with all diligence to doe the same according to the ordour. And also dischairges the said Mr Alexander Jaffray of his said cautionrie for my[60] imployment the said Johnne sall ressave fra the daitt of thir presentis. And ordaines ilk commissioner present to intimat this dischairge to thair neighouris and inhibite thame from imploying the said Johnne heirefter. And the saidis burghtis and conservatour to report thair diligence heiranent to the nixt generall conventioun of burrowes. And this to be ane heid of the nixt missive.[61]

41

The same day the saidis commissioneris ordaines the burght of Forres to produce the forme of the electioun of thair magistrattis and counsell at Michaelmes last to the nixt generall conventioun of burrowes to be seine and considderit be them and to proceid thairin conforme to the actis of parliament and burrowes under the paine of ane hundreth pundis. And this to be ane heid of the nixt missive.

42

The same day ordaines the burght of Elgyne to cause all thair friemen dwelling outwith thair burght aither mak thair residence with them or to dischairge them of the liberties of thair burght and to report thair diligence heiranent to the nixt generall conventioun of burrowes under the paine of xx li. And this to be ane heid of the nixt missive.

[fo. 495r]

43

The same day the saidis commissioneris of burrowes ordaines ilk burght to be requyred for sending thair commissioneris sufficientlie instructed to the nixt generall conventioun to give answer to the supplicatioun gevin in be the commissioner of the burght of Pettinweyme craveing helpe to thair herberie quhairby thair toun subsistes. And this to be ane heid of the nixt missive.

---

[60] Almost certainly a copyist's error for 'any'.
[61] This act is noted in the Abstract of Acts of Convention, *RCRBS*, iv, 539.

44

The same day the saidis commissioneris of burrowes grantis and geives
licence to the burghtis of Lauder, Brechin and Rothesay to abyde and
remaine fra all generall conventiounes of burrowes for the space of thrie
yeiris upoun the conditiounes and provisiounes following: provyding the
samyne be not extendit to parliamentis nor quhair the saidis burghes ar cited
for any particular cause; and also provyding the saidis burrowes send with
the commissioneris of thair nixt adjacent burghtis thair severall ratificatioun
and approbatiounes authenticklie subscryvit of all thingis to be done yeirlie
at the saidis generall conventiounes with all soumes that they sould pay to
the burrowes conforme to the missive; and that they bestow the expenssis
that they sould have bestowit upoun thair commissioneris upoun commoun
warkis and be accomptable thairof to the burrowes at the expyreing of the
saidis yeiris.

45

The same day quhairas the commissioneris of burrowes haveing of befor
grantit ane voluntar contributioun for repaireing the herberie of Northberwick, thairfoir ordaines all suche burrowes as hes not as yitt contributit
thairto to send quhat they may be moved in charitie to the nixt generall
conventioun of burrowes. And this to be ane heid of the nixt missive.

46

The same day forsameikle as the accomptis of Alexander Aikinheid, agent,
of his debursementis in the burrowes effaires since the last generall conventioun of burrowes being hard, seine, fitted, calculat and allowed be the saidis
commissioneris, they find the same to extend to the soume of twa thousand and four hundreth pundis. And thairfoir they ordaine ilk burght to be
requyred for sending thair pairt thairof to the nixt generall conventioun of
burrowes with thair commissioneris, conforme to the taxt roll under the
paine of tuentie pundis lik burght, by and attour the payment of thair pairt
of the saidis principall soume. And this to be ane heid of the nixt missive.

[fo. 495v]

47

The same day whairas the commissioneris resenting the greatt and infinite
guid micht redound to this kingdome in generall and to thair estate in
particular of the fischingis (whiche God as it wer hes bestowed in ane peculiar manner on this kingdome) wer preserved to the full, and ane blissing
not interrupted be the unlawfull and fraudfull dealling of the people quho
ar imployed that way, for the whiche caussis many guid and laudable actis
hes beine maid be the commissioneris whiche hes never as yitt takin ane
desyred effect. For the quhilk caussis the present commissioneris grantis and

geivis full power and commissioun to the burrowes appointed to conveine
at Edinburgh efter the dissolveing of this present conventioun for reviseing
of the saidis lawes and quhat sall be fund defective for supplyeing thairof and
taking suche course for causeing the same be put to executioun as they sall
think neidfull for the guid of the fisching, and for setting doun new lawes
and ordinances thairanent if the same sall seime to them requisite, ratifieing
and approveing, lykas they be thir presentis ratifies and approves, all and
quhatsomever the saidis burrowes sall doe in the premissis. And obleissis
them and thair burrowes to abyde thairat and to fulfill the same. And the said
burghes to report thair diligence heiranent to the nixt generall conventioun
of burrowes. And this to be ane heid of the nixt missive.

48
The same day unlawes the burghes of Culane, Nairne and Galloway eache
one of them in the soume of tuentie pundis money for not sending and
making payment of thair dewes of the last missive and for being absent fra
this present convention being lauchfullie warnit thairto as was presentlie
verified. And ordaines the agent to uplift the same from them and to be
chairged with them in his accomptis. And to produce his diligence heiranent
to the nixt generall conventioun of burrowes. As also ordaines the said agent
to chairge the saidis burrowes for thair bygane dewes. And this to be ane
heid of the nixt missive.

49
The same day, whairas it haveing pleased the commissioneris of burrowes
to grant to Alexander McCaitney for his yeirlie paines in thair effairis the
soume of threttie pundis, the present commissioneris consideddering his paines
daylie to grow, thairfoir they have convertit the said soume to ane hundreth
merkis yeirlie dureing thair will, and ordaines ilk burght to be requyred
yeirlie for sending thair pairt of the said soume with thair commissioneris
to the nixt conventioun conforme to the taxt roll. And this to be ane heid
of the nixt missive.

[fo. 496r]
50
The same day the saidis commissioneris ordaines the burghe of Kirkcudbright to produce thair diligence to the nixt generall conventioun of
burrowes in prosecuteing the actioun intentit be them against the Lord
Kirkcudbright and utheris persounes for recovering of certaine landis under
the paine of xx li. And this to be ane heid of the nixt missive.

51
The same day the present commissioneris dissolves this present conventioun

and appointis thair nixt generall conventioun to be and beginne at the burght of Glasgow the [...] day of Julii nixtocum 1636 yeiris. And ordaines the said burght to direct the generall missive to the remanent [burrowes] and to requyre them for conveining at the said burght conforme to the ordour etc.[62]

<hr />

62   The rest of the recto is blank.

Particular Convention at Edinburgh, July 1635

[fo. 496v]
In the particular conventioun of burrowes haldin at the burght of Edinburght the fyfteine day of Julii the yeir of God I^m vi^c and threttie fyve yeiris be the commissioneris of burrowes underwrittin be vertew of ane commissioun gevin to them be the last generall conventioun of burrowes haldin at the burght of Perth the nynt day of Julii instant.

Edinburght	Johnne Sinclair, James Leslie
Perth	Andro Gray
Dundie	Thomas Mudy
Aberdeine	Mr Mathew Lumsdeane
Stirling	Johnne Johnnestoun
Linlythgow	Robert Stewart
Sanctandrois[1]	
Glasgow	Gabriell Cunynghame
Aire	George Massoun
Kirkcaldie	Johnne Williamesoun
Bruntyland	Captaine Andro Watsoun
Couper	Robert Patersoun
Dumfreis	Mr Johnne Corsane
Selkirk	
Anstruther Eister	Robert Alexander
Dumbartane	Johnne Semple

1
{Electioun moderator}
The same day the saidis commissioneris of burrowes electis Johnne Sinclair, merchand and first in commissioun for the burght of Edinburght, to be moderator dureing this present conventioun, quha compeirand and acceptand the same in and upoun him and gave his aith *de fideli administratione*.[2]

Decimo septimo Julii I^m vi^c trigesimo quinto

[2]
The quhilk day the commissioneris of burrowes being conveinit anent the 38 act of the last generall conventioun of burrowes haldin at the burght

---

of Perth the ellevint day of Julii instant anent the resort of Johnne Trotter, younger, merchant commissioner for the burrowes towardis the Frenche king his proceidingis for ratifieing of the priviledges of this kingdome and procureing ane dischairge of the new impositiounes and anent the expenssis debursit be him in the said voyage and refounding thairof,[3] quhairanent the said Johnne compeirand maid report of his proceidingis [fo. 497r] in manner conteinit in the said act and his expenssis wer fund to extend to the soume of four thowsand ane hundreth thriescoir threttein frankis and four sous Frenche money. For refounding quhairof, commissioun was gevin to the present commissioneris as at mair lenth is conteinit in the said act, quhairwith the present commissioneris being now ryplie advysed they have thocht guid that the same sall be payit to him at home within this cuntrey and thairfoir they find the same to extend to the soume of aucht thowsand merkis usuall money of this realme, and ordaines the burght of Edinburght to pay to him the same soume of aucht thowsand merkis at the feist and terme of Mertimes nixt and for repayment to them of the same back againe, the present commissioneris hes ordainit and ordaines the impost following to be upliftit of all guidis exportit to and fra any portis within the provinces of Normandie and Picardie within the kingdome of France in manner following ay and quhill the said burght of Edinburght be sufficientlie refoundit of the said soume of aucht thowsand merkis with the interest thairof from the fyftein day of August nixt, viz: all guidis transportit out of France be Scottis merchandis to pay ane of the hundreth. And the guidis importit thither to pay in manner following, viz: ilk barrell of herring, tua schillingis; ilk hundreth weicht of talloun, fyve schillingis; ilk hundreth weicht of butter, fyve schillingis; ilk hundreth elne of plaiding, tua schillingis; ilk hundreth elne of cairseys,[4] tua schillingis; ilk hundreth weicht of wooll, tuentie schillingis; ilk barrell of salmond, thrie schillingis; ilk hundreth skynnes, fyve schillingis; ilk hundreth coalles,[5] fyve schillingis; ilk hyde auchteine pennyes. For payment of quhilk impost the saidis commissioneris for themselffis and haveand commissioun as said is, obleissis them and thair burghts and haill remanent burghtis of this kingdome to uplift the samyne of thair neighbouris that sall transport any guidis from the saidis portis of Normandie or Picardie or import thither any of the saidis guidis particularlie abonewrittin, and sall mak just, trew compt, reckoning and payment thairof

---

3 See above, 230–31.
4 Kersey – a coarse woollen cloth named after the village of Kersey in Suffolk.
5 It seems likely that a 'hundreth of coallis' was one hundredweight or something even greater than that. The *Oxford English Dictionary* identifies a 'hundred' of lime as '25 bushels or an hundred pecks': 'hundred, n. and adj.', OED Online, Oxford University Press, November 2010: http://www.oed.com/view/Entry/89464?redirectFrom=hundred (accessed 3 February 2011).

to the burght of Edinburgh or any haveand power from them at ilk generall conventioun ay and quhill the said soume of aucht thousand merkis with the interest thairof be sufficientlie refoundit to them, allowing onlie to the collector to be appointed be ilk burght for ingaddering of the said impost, two of ilk hundreth for the soumes collected be them for thair paines in uplifting thairof. And incaice of failyie, the saidis commissioneris for them-selffis and thair burghts obleissis them to be answerable for thair inhabitantis that sall be dew in any pairt of the said impost for double of suche dewtie as they sould have payit. And becaus that by the arrest procured be the said Johne Trotter, the fermeris of the custome in France wer ordainit to verifie within thrie monethis thairefter by titillis and witnessis what customes was payit be Scottish merchandis for goodis exportit out of France since the yeir 1580 to the daitt of the said arrest, quhilk day is now past. Thairfore the present commissioneris gives full power and commissioun to the burght of Edinburght to appoint some of thair neighbouris quham they may best trust and quho sall have first occasioun to goe to the said kingdome [fo. 497v] of France to interceid with Captaine Seytoun and to try quhat probatioun was used be the saidis fermeris the said day and if the said dyet is desertit, to wakin the said proces be advyse of the said Captaine Seytoun. And if ane monethis stay or tua may conclude the mater, to doe thair best for perfytting the said proces. And quhat sall be payit be them for writtis, the commissioneris does promeis to repay the samyne and to recompence thair travellis and paines for the said space. As also ordaines the said burght to writt to the said Captaine Seyttoun and to returne him thankis for his bygane concurrance with thair said commissioner and to desyre the continuance of his farder favour in the said matter. And last ordaines ilk burght that sall have any inhabitantis dew into the said impost to send with thair commis-sioneris to the nixt generall conventioun compt with payment of thair pairt of the same under the paine of xl li. by and attour thair pairt of the said impost and failyie abonementionat from the said fyfteine day of August nixt to the nixt generall conventioun of burrowes. And the said burght of Edinburgh lykwayes to report thair diligence heiranent to the nixt generall conventioun of imploying thair neighbouris as said is. And this to be ane heid of the nixt missive.[6]

Decimo octavo Julii I^m vi^c trigesimo quinto
[3]
The quhilk day the commissioneris of burrowes being conveinit anent the 22 act of the last generall conventioun of burrowes haldin at Perth the nynt of this instant and anent thair proceidingis with Thomas Cunynghame and

6   This act is noted in the Abstract of Acts of Convention, *RCRBS*, iv, 540.

James Weir factoris in Campheir and manner of oath prescryvit be them to be gevin be all collectoris thairefter for ingathering of the dewes of the ministeris stipend at the said port conforme to the sevint act of the particular conventioun haldin at the burght of Edinburgh 8 of November last.[7] The saidis commissioneris ordaines the conservator to intimat the same of new againe and caus the haill factoris act themselffis conforme thairto, and to report his diligence heiranent to the nixt generall conventioun of burrowes. And this to be ane heid of the nixt missive.

[4]
The same day anent the 10 act of the particular conventioun of borrowes haldin at the burght of Edinburgh the ellevint day of November last, anent the inhibiteing of unlaufull exercise of factorie,[8] the commissioneris hes declairit and declaires that althoche it be laufull to merchandis to imploy thair neighbour or partiner who is goeing beyond sea as factor for them for any guidis goeing with thair said neighbour or partiner, that it sall not be laufull to any who is not laufullie admittit factor to ressave any guidis whiche ar not thair awin proper guidis thairefter sent in any other shipe. And ordaines the conservator being present not to suffer suche doeing heirefter and ordaines ilk burght to intimat this present act to thair neighbouris at thair homecumming and to report thair diligence heiranent to the nixt generall conventioun of burrowes. And this to be ane heid of the nixt missive.[9]

[fo. 498r]
Vigesimo primo Julii I^m vi^c trigesimo quinto
[5]
The quhilk day the commissioneris of burrowis being conveinit, quhairas the conservator being bund to the burrowes for serving of the merchandis throughe the haill sevintein provinces of the Low Cuntreyis, and understanding that some persounes does not mak payment to him of suche dewes as ar ordainit be the burrowes for this honorable intertainement in the discharge of his office, thairfoir they ordaine all these that sall heirefter send ony coalles or other guidis to Holland or any pairt within the said sevinteine provinces, to mak guid and thankfull payment to him of his dewes or to any who sall have power from him for uplifting thairof conforme as they doe in Zeland, under the paine of payment of the double thairof. And ordaines ilk burght to intimat thir presentis to thair neighbouris at thair homecumming that none pretend ignorance. And to report thair diligence heiranent

---

7   See above, 220.
8   See above, 207–8.
9   This act is noted in the Abstract of Acts of Convention, *RCRBS*, iv, 540.

to the nixt generall conventioun of burrowes. And this to be ane heid of the nixt missive.[10]

[6]

The same day anent the 24 act of the last generall conventioun of burrowes haldin at the burght of Perth the nynt of this instant, ordaining the present commissioneris to tak to thair considderatioun the augmentatioun craved be the conservator of his dewes in respect of the great raittes all thingis ar risin within the Low Cuntreyis and of his diverse oft imploymentis quhairthrow he is drawin away for the merchandis adoes, and giving commissioun to them for doeing thairof as they sould think meitt, as at mair lenth is conteinit in the said act maid thairanent.[11] Whairwith the present commissioneris being advysit and understanding be the report of thair neighbouris his diligence in all thair imploymentis and readynes to concurre with them in all thair demandis, thairfoir for his farder incouragement to continew both in serveing of the particular merchandis that sall stand in neid of his assistance in these sevinteine provinces, as also for serving of the burrowes in suche thingis as they sall think neidfull for the generall in so far as he can, the saidis commissioneris hes grantit, gevin and disponit and be thir presentis grantis, geives and dispones to the said conservatour by and attour the first dewtie of fyfteine stuires Fleymis money and augmentatioun of thrie stuires grantit at Edinburgh the 27 Julii 1631, the soume of sex stuires farder making upe in haill the soume of tuentie four stuires money foirsaid to be levied of ilk seck of goodes to be transportit from Scotland to any pairt within the said sevinteine provinces in manner following, viz: auchteine stuires be the goodes and sex be the schipe. As also ordaines all suche merchandis quho comes over not having ane seck of goodes to pay fyve schillingis Fleymis *toties quoties*, provyding alwayes that he hes not sent over ane seck of goodes within sex monethis before, to indure dureing the burrowes will alanerlie. It is alwayes declared that in respect of the dewties imposed upoun coall [fo. 498v] that the same sall stand as of before and to be frie of any of the saidis augmentatiounes. And ordaines the merchandis and skipperis readylie to answer the said conservator and suche as sall have power from him for uplifting of the dewes abonewrittin. And incaice of refuisall or not thankfull payment, ordaines the said conservator to caus poynd or distreinyie for the same.[12]

[7]

The same day anent the 24 act of the last generall conventioun of burrowes

---

10   This act is noted in the Abstract of Acts of Convention, *RCRBS*, iv, 540.
11   See above, 221–2.
12   This act is noted in the Abstract of Acts of Convention, *RCRBS*, iv, 540.

haldin at the burghe of Perthe the nynt of this instant concerning the greivances of the staiple and commissioun gevin to the conservatour for dealling
with the magistrattis of the toun of Campheir thairanent, compeired the said
conservatour and declaired that he hade delt with the saidis magistrattis bot
did find no reall dealling with them but as of before.[13] Thairfoir the saidis
commissioneris ordaines the said conservatour to deale with them of new
and not onlie for taking away the former greivances but also for renewing
of the contract past betuixt the burrowes and them. And if he sall find them
to goe on as they have done thir diverse yeiris bygane, in that caice they
ordaine the said conservatour to deale with the tounes of Middilburghe and
Rotterdame and to try quhat conditiounes may be expectit at thair handis
and to advertise the burrowes thairof to the end suche farder commissioun
may be gevin for establischeing of the same within some of the saidis tounes
as is requisite and to report his diligence heiranent to the nixt generall
conventioun of burrowes. And this to be ane heid of the nixt missive.

[8]
The same day whairas the commissioneris understanding that the merchandis
and skipperis resorting to Flussing,[14] Middilburghe, Rotterdame and diverse
utheris pairtis in the Low Cuntreyis ar greatlie urged be brokkeris, quhom
they imploy for doeing thair effaires, for remeid quhairof they inhibite and
dischairge all merchandis or skipperis frome imploying any to be brokkeris
for them in the saidis places bot suche as sall first obleis thameselff in all
questiounes whiche may aryse betuixt them and thair merchandis to answer
before the conservatour and to underly his sentence and determinatioun
under the paine of tuentie pundis *toties quoties*. And ordaines ilk burght to
intimat this present act to thair neighbouris at thair homecumming. And
to report thair diligence heiranent to the nixt generall conventioun of
burrowes. And this to be ane heid of the nixt missive.[15]

Vigesimo secundo Julii I[m] vi[c] trigesimo quinto

[9]
The quhilk day the commissioneris of burrowes being conveinit anent that
pairt of the 24 act of the last generall conventioun of burrowes haldin at
the burght of Perthe the nynt of this instant [fo. 499r] concerning the
commissioun gevin to the present commissioneris for heiring and fitting
of Alexander Bautye, factor in Campheir and laite collectour of the impost
appointed for defraying of the ministeris stipend of the port of Campheir,

---

13   See above, 221–2.
14   Vlissingen, or Flushing, in Zeeland.
15   This act is noted in the Abstract of Acts of Convention, *RCRBS*, iv, 540.

his comptis of intromissioun with the said impost and for appointing of ane new collector as at mair lenth is contenit in the said act.[16] And the saidis commissioneris haveing seine, hard, fittit and collationat the said Alexander his accomptis of the said impost with the verificatiounes thairof produced, they fund him to have upliftit from the 6 of October 1634 inclusive till the last of Apryle 1635 also inclusive the soume of fourscoir nyne pundis sexteine schillingis aucht greitt Fleymis money quhilk differeis from the compt gevin up be him inrespect thair is not so muche payit be Robert Greirsone be tuentie thrie seck of goodes as is conteinit in the subscryvit minute of the said Robert his resaittis furth of Johnne Lichtounes schipe, extending to thrie schillingis aucht greitt; as also thair is omittit out of Johnne Urquhartis schipe thrie hundreth coalles extending to four schillingis sex gritt; and last thair is of wrang layed tua schillingis tua great and ane orque.[17] And they find the compter to have debursed conforme to the severall dischairge produced, the soume of ane hundreth thriescoir auchteine pundis, ane gritt money foirsaid. Whiche soume they ordaine Robert Greirsoun present collector of the said impost to pay to the said Alexander Bautye and the same sall be allowed to him in his comptis. And ordainis ane missive letter to be direct in thair names to the said Robert to this effect for sending home his comptis of his intromissioun with the said impost from the first of Maii last to the first of Maii nixt in the yeir of God 1636 yeiris with the verificatiounes thairof as usuall is. And for collecting of the said impost they have elected, nominate and appointed and be thir presentis electis, nominatis and appointes Richard Weir factour at the said port and that fra the first of Maii 1636 till the first of Maii 1637 and ordaines him to compeir before the conservatour or his deputtis and thair in ane fenced court and to mak faith *de fideli administratione*[18] and declaratioun in manner conteinit in the 7 act of the last particular conventioun of burrowes haldin at the burght of Edinburght in November last the aucht day thairof. And ordaines him to send home his comptis to the nixt generall conventioun of burrowes to be haldin in the moneth of Julii 1637 yeiris whairever the same sall happin to be. As also ordaines the said Richard Weir to send hom his comptis with the verificatiounes thairof under the skipper, factor or merchandis handis of his haill ressaittis with thair names that sall not mak payment of thair dewes or sall pas by the said staple port with staple guidis with thair schippes, quantitie of goodes and all [fo. 499v] other circumstances requisite. And ordaines the conservatour and his deputtis to caus the said Richard Weir mak faith in manner abonewrittin and put the said sevint act of the said

16 See above, 221–2.
17 A Flemish coin worth two doits.
18 Literally, 'concerning faithful administration', i.e. he was promising to carry out his duties with diligence.

particular conventioun of burrowes haldin at the said burght of Edinburght the aucht day of November last to full executioun in the haill heidis thairof. And becaus the saidis commissioneris hes fund be the said Alexander Bautye his saidis comptis that the persounes underwrittin hes not maid payment of thair dewes, viz Johnne Younger in Edinburghe the 28 of October last not haveing ane seck of guidis, Johnne Cowane skipper in Dysert at Middilburght from France in October 1634, Williame Trissilie skipper in Dundye at Flussing in December last not having ane seck of goodes, Johnne Ure merchand in Glasgow not haveing ane seck of guidis in December last, ane merchand in Dysert callit Gaii at Flussing and maid mercatt of plaidis and other commodities in Apryle last 1635, Robert Hoddome merchand in Edinburgh not haveing ane seck of guidis, George Hoddome merchand in Edinburght and not haveing ane seck of guidis, and Johnne Coupland not haveing ane seck of goodis in Maii 1635, 26 November 1634, Robert Allane skipper in Dysert being in the Yland[19] with 800 coallis, whiche persounes they ordaine the burghes to quhom they apperteine to conveine them befor them and to cause them mak faith and pay the double of what they sould have payit thair or els to put them under cautioun to compeir before the commissioneris of burrowes to be conveinit in Julii 1636 to answer for the caussis foirsaidis under the paine of xl li. ilk persoun. And the saidis burrowes conservatour and collectour to report thair diligence anent the premissis. And this to be ane heid of the nixt missive.

Vigesimo quarto Julii I^m vi^c trigesimo quinto

[10]
The quhilk day the commissioneris of burrowes being conveinit, forsameikle as the present commissioneris haveing, conforme to the commissioun gevin to them at the last generall conventioun, apointed ane impost for repayment of Johnne Trotter younger his chairges in the mater of the new impositiounes in France,[20] and haveing ordainit ilk burght to collect the same amongst thair neighbouris dew thairin and to apoint collectoris for that effect, and least thair sould be ane fraud committit thairin, thairfoir ordaines ilk burght to send with thair comptis ane testificat from thair burght that the said collector hes gevin his aith upoun the veritie of the saidis comptis that nothing is omittit furth thairof that sould have beine upliftit be him. And ordaines ilk commissioner to intimat the same to thair burght at thair homecumming. And the saidis burghtis to report thair diligence heiranent

---

19   The island of Walcheren, in Zeeland.
20   See above, 230–32.

to the nixt generall conventioun of burrowes. And this to be ane heid of the nixt missive.

[fo. 500r]

[11]

The same day anent the visitatioun of the Water of Forth, the present commissioneris haveing, conforme to the commissioun gevin to them be the last generall conventioun, gevin in thair diligence who last visited the said water to the lordis of counsell.[21] Thairfore ordaines the commissioneris quho sall be conveinit in October nixt anent the taxt roll to supplicat the saidis lordis for conveining befor them the heritoris and coquet keiper of Culros for trying of thair diligence in executeing the proclamatioun maid anent the casting out of ballast in the said water, to whiche burrowes the present commissioneris geives thair full power and commissioun for doeing thairof and, if they sall think neidfull, for apppointing of new visiteris conforme as hes beine done of before. And ordaines the saidis burrowes to report thair diligence heiranent to the nixt generall conventioun of burrowes. And this to be ane heid of the nixt missive.

[12]

The same day anent the 47 act of the last generall conventioun of burrowes haldin at the burght of Perth the ellevint of this instant, whairby commissioun was gevin to the present commissioneris for reviseing the actis of burrowes maid anent the fischingis for supplieing of the defectis thairof and ading of new, as at mair lenth is conteinit in the said act,[22] the saidis commissioneris to the effect the same may be solidlie advysedlie done, hes ordainit the burrowes that ar to direct thair commissioneris hither to convein in October nixt anent the taxt roll send them sufficientlie instructed anent the ordour and good governing of the fischingis, and with them the burghtis of Glasgow, Anstruther Eister and Craill. Lykwayes to send thair commissioneris sufficientlie instructed in the said mater of fisching, to whiche burrowes the present commissioneris geives thair full power and commissioun for doeing and performeing quhatsomever they micht doe themselffis. And obleissis them and thair burghtis and haill remanent burrowes to abyde thairat. And ordaines the saidis burrowes to be requyrit to the said effect in dew tyme under the paine of fourtie pundis ilk burght to be payit to the burrowes incaice of absence. And the saidis burrowes to report thair diligence anent the premissis to the nixt generall conventioun of burrowes. And this to be ane heid of the nixt missive.

---

[21] See above, 218.
[22] See above, 234–5.

[13]

The same day the present commissioneris resenting that they haveing ressavit diverse letters from his Majestie for rescinding of Robert Buchanes patent of the perill, yitt the same hes never [fo. 500v] ressavit ane desyred answer. Thairfore ordaines ane new letter to be procured to the said effect in the maist strick termes can be obtenit. And ordaines the burghes appointed to meitt in this citie in October nixt to insist with the lordis thairanent. Whairanent they give them thair full power and commissioun. And the saidis commissioneris to report thair diligence heiranent to the nixt generall conventioun of burrowes. And this to be ane heid of the nixt missive.

[14]

The same day the saidis commissioneris unlawes the burght of St Androis for not keiping of this present conventioun in ane unlaw of tuentie pundis and ordaines them to send the same with thair commissioner to the nixt generall conventioun of burrowes and to be requyrit for that effect. And ordaines the same to be remembrit in the nixt missive.

Particular Convention at Edinburgh, January 1636

[fo. 502r][1]
In the particular conventioun of borrowis haldin at the burgh of Edinburgh the 18 day of Januarii the yeir of God 1636 yeiris be the commissioners of borrowis underwrittin, be vertew of tuo missive letters direct to theme frome the said burght of Edinburgh, daittit the 8 and 16 dayes of December last, and producit thair commissiounes as follows:

Edinburgh	Johnne Sincler, Williame Carnegie
Perth	
Dundye	James Simpsoun
Abirdeyne	George Moresoun
Stirling	James Fotheringhame
Lynlithgow	George Bell
Sanctandroes[2]	Williame Jeddie
Glasgow	Patrick Bell
Aire	Johnne Kennedye
Montrose	Johnne Betay
Bruntyland[3]	George Gardin
Kirkcaldye	Johnne Williamesoun
Dysart	Andro Ranye
Culross	Gilbert Gourlay
Anstruther Eister	Robert Alexander
Craill	Patrik Huntar
Dumbartan	
Irrving	James Blair
Dumbar	George Purves
Kinghorne	Merteyne Lochore

1
The same day electis Johnne Sinclare, first in commissioun for the burgh of Edinburgh, to be moderator during this present conventioun, quha comperiand accepted and gave his oath *in communi forma*.[4]

---

[1] This folio is preceded by a blank one, also labelled '502'. The foliation sequence starts with 502, jumps to 505, then 503 (the cover-sheet for this record, the verso of which is blank), and there seems to be no 504, yet there is no missing text.

[2] St Andrews.

[3] Burntisland.

[4] Literally, in the usual way, normally expressed as taking the oath *de fideli administratione*, 'concerning faithful administration', i.e. he was promising to carry out the duties of moderator with diligence.

Vigesimo secundo Januarii 1636

[2]

The quhilk day the commissioneris of borrowis being conveinit have considderit the mater of the fischings componit be Sir James Lockhairt, as also that mater of the lichtes craived to be erected upone the Yle of the May within the Firth of Lowthean, and finding [fo. 502v] his Majestie to have bein oft informed be the urgers in the saids maters, thairfore thei have thocht guid that his Majestie sall first be informed in the particulars be sum frome theme, and least in the meane tyme thai sould suffer any prejudice thairfore hes thocht fitt and ordainit that ane appellatioun be maid to his Majestie in the saids maters and instrumentis to be taiken therupon.

Penultimo Januarii 1636

[3]

The quhilk day the commissioneris of borrowis being convenit haif according to the 2 act of this present conventioun appealed to his Majestie in the maters of the project of the fischings proposit be Sir James Lokhart and mater of the lichtes craived to be erected upone the Yle of the May within the Firth of Lawthean[5] which appellatioun wer admittit be the[6] lordis of commissioun and the commissioneris finding it now necessar that his Majestie be informed anent the ivell and hard consequence of the saids maters and how prejudiciall the same may not onlie be to the estaittes bot also the whole kingdome, thairfore they have elected nominat and chosen and be thir presentis electis nominattis and cheyses Maister Alexander Guthrie, thair generall clerk, commissioner for theme to pas to his Majestie and for theme and in name of the whole burrowis of this kingdome to represent to his Majestie thair just greivances in the saids maters and in all thir maters concerning the borrowis or that sall occure during his being at court, conforme to the instructiounes to be givin to him thairanent and humblie to beg his Majesties favour in the saids maters and friedome frome suchlyik projects. And grantis and gives unto thair said commissioner thair full powar and commissioun theranent and to mak such offers and conditiounes to his Majestie theranent as salbe givin to him in his instructiounes. And for setting doun of the saids instructiounes and offers they have nominat and apointed Johnne Sincler, commissioner for Edinburgh, George Moresoun, commissioner for Abirdein, Patrik Bell, commissioner for the burgh of Glasgow and Robert Alexander, commissioner for the

---

5   The Firth of Forth.
6   The phrase 'be the' is repeated here, at the end of one line and the beginning of the next.

burgh of Anstruther Eister, unto the which persounes the saids commissioneris grantis and gives thair full powar and commissioun, and for theme selffis and thair burghis and in name of the whole burghis of this present kingdome ratifies and approves quhatsumevir the saids personis and thair saids commissioners sall doe anent the premissis. And obleissis theme to abyid and remayne therat but contradictioun or agane calling quhatsumever and to ratifie thair saids proceidings at thair nixt generall conventioun. And for defraying of the saids commissioners charges they ordaine the burgh of Edinburgh to advance the same to him and quhatsumevir soumes of money salbe advancit or debursit be him they obleis theme and thair saidis burghis and whole remanent borrowis [fo. 505r] to refound, content and pay the same bak againe to the said burgh of Edinburgh with the interrest thairof frome the tyme of advancement thairof. And ordanes the said Mr Alexander to report his diligence and proceidings in the saids maters at his returne, and ilk burgh to be warnit for sending thair commissioners sufficientlie instructed for ratiefieing and approving of the premissis and refounding of the saids soumes to the nixt generall conventioun of borrowis. And this to be ane heid of the nixt missive.[7]

[4]

The same day the saids commissioneris understanding that the burgh of Glasgow was of intentioun to intend actioun against the burgh of Ramfrew [for] exacting of late certan customes upone the River of Clyde quhairof they wer nevir in possessioun of before and being willing according to the actis of borrowis that the same sould first be hard before themeselffes and taken away, thairfore thai ordayne the burgh of Ramfrew to be requyrit for sending of thair commissioners sufficientlie instructed with thair richtes for answering to the said complent to the nixt generall conventioun of borrowis under the payne of xl lb. and ilk burgh to be requyrit for sending thair commissioners sufficientlie instructed for decyding of the said complent. And this to be ane heid of the nixt missive.

[5]

The same day foresamikle as the commissioneris haveing fund be the late disturbance fallin out in the toun of Abirdeyne in the electioun of ther magistrattis[8] what evill may redound interlie to the said burgh bot also what dangerous consequence the proceidings in the saids maters may deale upon the rest of the estaitt, thairfore thai ordayne the said burgh to send thair

7   This act is noted in the Abstract of Acts of Convention, *RCRBS*, iv, 540.
8   For a discussion of what happened in Aberdeen, see Introduction 18 and G. DesBrisay, "'The civill warrs did overrun all": Aberdeen 1630–1690', in E.P. Dennison, D. Ditchburn & M. Lynch (eds.), *Aberdeen Before 1800: A New History* (East Linton, 2002), 238–66, at 240–43.

commissioneris sufficientlie instructed to the nixt generall conventioun of borrowes under the payne of tuentie pundis for proposing such overtouris as may best tent to the quyett of the said burgh in tyme cuming with the maner of ther ordiner electioun of magistrattis and counsall as hes bein sett doun unto theme and to heir and sie sic ordour to be taiken anent thair saids electiounes in all tyme cuming as must be maist agrieabill for intertyneing of peace amongs theme and taking away of all contraversie. And ilk burgh to be requyrit lyikwayes for sending thair commissioners sufficientlie instructed anent the premissis to the nixt generall conventioun of borrowis under the payne of xx lb. And this to be ane heid of the nixt missive.

[fo. 505v]
[6]
The same day foresamikle as the commissioneris being supplicat anent thair help for building of ane key and herberie at Portpatrik conform to ane warrand givin be the lordis of his Majesties most honorabill privie counsell be recommendatioun frome his Majestie. Thairfore the saids commissioners ordanes ilk burgh to be requyrit for sending thair commissioneris sufficien-tlie instructed to the nixt generall conventioun of borrowis for giving answer to the said supplicatioun and anent the expediencie of the said herberie. And this to be ane heid of the nixt missive.

[7]
The same day unlawis the burgh of Perth in the soume of xx lb. for being absent frome this present conventioun, they being laufullie warnit thairto be George Ramsay, post, quha verifiet the same. Thairfore ordanis theme to send the said unlaw with thair commissioner to the nixt generall conven-tioun of borrowis under the lyik payne. And this to be ane heid of the nixt missive.

[fo. 503r]
Actis of the particular conventioun of burrowis haldin at Edinburghe in Januar 1636[9]

---

9   This is written twice on an otherwise blank sheet of paper, which would have been the covering sheet or title page for the preceding record.

General Convention at Glasgow, July 1636

[fo. 507r]

In the generall conventioune of borrowis haldin at the burgh of Glasgow the fyft day of Julii the yeir of God I^m vi^c thrittie sex yeiris be the commissioneris of borrowis underwrittin and producit thair commissiounes as followes, viz:

Edinburgh	Sir Johne Sinclare of Stevinsone, knicht, and Williame Carnegye
Perth	Andro Wilsoun
Dundye	James Sympsone
Aberdeine	Mathow Lumbsdaill
Stirling	James Fotheringhame
Lynlithgow	Williame Hamiltoune
St Androis	Johne Lepar
Glasgow	Patrik Bell, Coleine Campbell
Aire	Robert Gordoune
Haddingtoune	Mr George Gray
Dysart	Alexander Sympsoun
Kirkcaldye	Johne Williamesoun
Montrose	Johne Gairdin
Coupar	Robert Petersoun
Anstruther Eister	Thomas Mairteine
Dumfreis	Mr Johne Corsane
Innernes[1]	
Bruntyland[2]	Williame Meklejohne
Innerkeything[3]	Mark Kingglassie
Kinghorne	Walter Duncane
Brichen	
Irving	Allane Dunlope
Jedburgh	Alexander Kirktoun
Kirkcudbricht	Williame Glendinning
Wigtoune	Johne Murdoche
Pettinweyme	James Richardsoun
Dumfermeling[4]	Mr Patrik Auchinleck

---

1   Inverness.
2   Burntisland.
3   Inverkeithing.
4   Dunfermline.

Anstruther Wester	be exemptione and ratificatioune producit be [the agent]
Selkirk	Williame Scott
Dumbar	George Kirkwood
[fo. 507v]	
Dumbartane	Johne Sempill
Ramfrew[5]	Johne Spreull
Lanerik[6]	Gedione Jack
Aberbrothock[7]	
Elgyne	Mr Johne Hay
Peblis	James Williamesoun
Caraill[8]	Thomas Wood
Thayne[9]	
Culros	Gilbert Gourlay
Bamff	
Quhythorne[10]	
Forfar	
Rothesay	Johne Makilcryist
Nairne	
Forres	be exemptioune and ratificatioune produicit be the agent
Rutherglen	be exemptioune and ratificatioune produicit be the agent
Northberwik	Johne Muire
Culane	
Lauder	be exemptioune and ratificatioune produicit be the agent
Kilraynie	
Annand	
Lochmaben	
Sanquhaire	
Galloway[11]	be exemptioune and ratificatioune produicit be Kirkcudbricht

---

5   Renfrew.
6   Lanark.
7   Arbroath.
8   Crail.
9   Tain.
10 Whithorn.
11 New Galloway.

1

The same day electis Patrik Bell, first in commissioune for the burght of Glasgow, to be moderator duiring this present conventioune, quha compeirand, accepted the said office in and upone him and gave his aith *de fideli administratione*.[12]

2

The same day the saidis commissioneris being convenit, forsamekle as the burgh of Innernes hes directit to this present conventioun Thomas Fraser sone to Andrew Fraser commissar quhome they find not to be of the qualitie of ane commissioner prescryvit be the actis of borrowis, and also his commissioune informall, wanting the seill of thair burgh and uther informalities. Thairfor they find the said burght to be absent and unlawis theme in ane unlaw of twentie pundis and ordainis the agent to uplift the same and to produce his diligence thairanent to the nixt generall conventioune of borrowis. And this to be ane heid of the nixt missive.

3

The same day the saidis commissioneris appoynts the houris of meitting to be and begyin at nyne houris in the morning and to last till twelff houris at noone and efternoone [fo. 508r] at twa houris till sax a cloak at nicht and sic as ar absent at the calling of the rollis to pay ane unlaw of sex schillings. And they that passe out of the hous without leive to pay ane unlaw as said is. And they that passis fra this present conventioune befor the dissolveing thairof to pay ane unlaw as absentis. And that nane speik unrequyrit without leive askit and gevin, or intermixe thair reassouning with thair votting under the payne of ane unlaw of sex schillingis *toties quoties*.[13]

4

The same day anent the tent act of the last generall conventioune of borrowis haldin at the burght of Perth the sevint day of Julii last, dischargeing portage and prohibiting thair nichtbouris frome being partineris with unfrie skipperis conforme to the former actis maid thairanent.[14] The present commissioneris ordainis ilk commissioner present to intimat the samyne of new to thair borrowis at thair home cumming and to sie the samyne keiped and to report thair diligence in putting the samyne to dew executioune to the nixt generall conventioune of borrowis. And this to be ane heid of the nixt missive.

---

[12] Literally, 'concerning faithful administration', i.e. he was promising to carry out the duties of moderator with diligence.
[13] As often as it shall happen, i.e. for each offence.
[14] See above, 215.

5

The same day anent the ellevint act of the last generall conventioune of borrowis haldin at the burght of Perth the aucht day of Julii last concerning Wedderburnes gramer.[15] The present commissioneris ordainis ilk burght to conveyne thair scoolmaisteris befor theme And to injoyne theme the teatching of the said grammer under the payne of depryveatioune. And ordainis ilk burght to report thair diligence heiranent to the nixt generall conventioune of borrowis. And this to be ane heid of the nixt missive.

6

The same day anent that pairt of the threttie sevint act of the last generall conventioune of borrowis haldin at the burght of Perth the tent day of Julii last concerning the bleitcheing of lynning with lyme.[16] The present commissioneris finding how prejudiciall the same is to that commoditie, thairfor ordainis ilk burght to trye quhat bleitcheris ar neir to thair boundis and to caus theme to be conveynit befor the justice of peice and to sie the act of counsell maid thairanent putt to executioune againis the contraveneris. And anent that pairt of the said act concerning the erecting of correctioun houssis, the saidis commissioneris recommendis the samyne of new to the haill borrowis. And als anent the last pairt of the said act concerning the burght of Aberdeine to intimatt the act of counsell anent presenting of plaiding to the mercatts in foldis, compeired the commissioner of the said burght of Aberdeine and produicit the said act [fo. 508v] laufullie intimat and publisched and maid report that the samyne had not takin effect, to the great prejudice of the merchant tredderis with the said wair. For which caus the present commissioneris, and for the better executioune of the said act, strictlie inhibitis and dischairges the quhole burgessis of this kingdome thair factouris and doers frome buyeing any plaiding in the commoune mercatts of this kingdome bot such as salbe presentit in foldis under the payne of twentie pundis. And ordainis ilk commissioner present to intimat the same to thair burgh at thair homecuming and ilk burght to intimat the same laufullie to thair nichtbouris that none pretend ignorance. As also ordainis the burght of Aberdeine by some of thair nichtbouris deputt for that effect, to attend the saids mercatts and to tak up the names of such as sall contraveine the same, and to send thair names to the burghtis quhairunto they doe apperteine. And the said burght to punische theme conforme to the tennour of the said act. And such burghtis as salbe fund remiss and negligent to incur ane unlaw of fourtie pundis. And the said burght of Aberdein and remanent

---

15 See above, 216.
16 See above, 230.

burghtis to report thair diligence anent the premissis to the nixt generall conventioun of borrowis. And this to be ane heid of the nixt missive.[17]

7

The same day anent the fourt act of the last generall conventioune of borrowis haldin at the burght of Perth the sevint day of Julii last orday-neing the burght of Kirkcudbricht to produce thair diligence anent thair nichtbouris of Monigoff[18] to this present conventione.[19] Compeired the commissioner of the said burght and produicit letters of horning raisit and execute against Hew Meinyies merchand in Monigoff, Andro Makmillen thair, Robert Goode thair and Johne Maknacht, chairgeing theme and everie ane of theme to cum and find sufficient cawtioune and souertie actit in the buikis of counsell and sessioune befor the lordis thairof that they sall desist and ceis frome useing any tred of merchandice or usurpeing the liberties or priveledges of anie[20] the frie royall burrowis unles they and everie ane of theme becum frie burgessis and actuall residentis within some of the saids frie borrowis and pay taxt and stent with theme and to leive of all sort of regraitterie hurtfull or prejudiciall to the saidis frie borrowis, conforme to the act of parliament maid thairanent with the saidis persones denunciatioune, whiche the saidis borrowis acceptis for diligence at this tyme. And ordainis the said burght of Kirkcudbricht to produce farder dili-gence in taking and apprehending of the saidis persones ay and quhill they find cautioune to desist frome usurpeing the liberties of the saidis frie royall borrowis under the payne of twentie pundis to the nixt generall conven-tioune of borrowis. And this to be ane heid of the nixt missive.

[fo. 509r]

8

The same day anent the fyft act of the last generall conventioune of borrowis haldin at the burght of Perth the sevint day of Julii last ordaineing the burght of Dumfermeling to produce thair diligence to this present conventioune in causing James Dawling in the Quenisferrie mak his actuall residence with theme or in depryveing him of thair liberties.[21] Compeired the commis-sioner of the said burght and producit ane act of thair court declaireing his residence, which the saidis commissioneris acceptis for diligence and ordainis the said burght iff he sall heirefter remove frome the said toune to the Quenisferrie to persew him for his residence or to depryve him.

17 This act is noted in the Abstract of Acts of Convention, RCRBS, iv, 540.
18 Minnigaff, near Newton Stewart, Wigtownshire.
19 See above, 213.
20 This word is inserted above the line with a caret.
21 See above, 213–14.

9

The same day anent the sevint act of the last generall conventioune of borrowis haldin at the burght of Perth the sevint day of Julii last,[22] the present commissioneris of borrowis ordainis the burght of Linlithgow to produce farder diligence againis David Wilsoun, Samuell Wilsoun, Edward Litle, James Hill, Peter Logye in prosecuting the suspensiounes raisit be theme againis the said burght and obtyneing the same discussit ay and quhill they find sufficient cautioune to desist frome usurpeing the liberties of the frie royall borrowis under the payne of twentie pundis, and to report thair diligence heiranent to the nixt generall conventioune of borrowis. And this to be ane heid of the nixt missive.

10

The same day compeired the commissioner of the burght of Ramfrew and for obedience of the nynt act of the last generall conventioune of borrowis haldin at the burght of Perth the sevint day of Julii last,[23] and produicit ane act of thair court depryving Hendrie Kelso in the Largis thair alledgit burges of the liberties of thair burght, which the borrowis acceptis for diligence.

11

The same day the saidis commissioneris ordainit the burght of Ramfrew to produce thair diligence in causing Johne Mitchell and Patrik Watsoun in Greinnock ayther mak thair residence with them betuixt and Mertymes nixt or in depryveing theme of the liberties of thair burght under the payne of twentie pundis and to report thair diligence heiranent to the nixt generall conventioune of borrowis. And this to be ane heid of the nixt missive.

Sexto Julii I^m vi^c trigesimo sexto

12

The quhilk day the commissioneris of borrowis being conveynit unlawis the burght of Innernes in the soume of fourtie pundis for not produceing thair diligence [fo. 509v] in restrayneing of certane unfrie persones mentionat in the twelt act of the last generall conventioune of borrowis haldin at the burght of Perth the aucht day of Julii last[24] and ordainis the agent to uplift the same and to be chairgit thairwith in his compts and to produce his diligence in uplifting thairof to the nixt generall conventioune. And ordainis the said burght of Innernes to produce the lyk diligence as they sould have produicit at this tyme against the saidis persones to the nixt generall

22 See above, 214.
23 See above, 215.
24 See above, 216.

conventione of borrowis under the payne of fourtie pundis. And this to be
ane heid of the nixt missive.

13

The same day anent the threttie fourt act of the last generall conventioune of borrowis haldin at the burght of Perth the tent day of Julii last,[25]
compeired the commissioner of the burght of Dumfermeling and produice
the forme of the electioune of thair magistrattis at Michaelmes last, which
being seine and considderit, they find them to have omitted the electioune
of ane provest, with the whiche the borrowis for caussis schawen to theme
dispenssis at this tyme and ordainis theme at Michaelmes nixt to mak choyce
of ane provest qualified, conforme to the actis of parliament and borrowis,
under the payne of ane hundreth pundis and to produce the forme thairof
to the nixt generall conventioune under the payne of twentie pundis.[26] And
this to be ane heid of the nixt missive.

14

The same day anent the sexteint act of the last generall conventioune of
borrowis haldin at the burght of Perth the aucht day of Julii last concerning
the visitatione of Forth,[27] the present commissioneris understanding be thair
former visitationes and the daylie report of thair nichtbouris useing tred
above the Queinsferrie that the said river is licklie be tyme to be stoped.
Thairfor ordainis the agent in thair names to acquant the lordis of his Majesties most honorable privie counsell with the forsaidis evellis and to supplicat
theme to put thair proclamatioune maid thairanent to executioune against
the contraveneris that the samyne may be keiped heirefter and to report his
diligence heiranent to the nixt generall conventioune of borrowis. And this
to be ane heid of the nixt missive.

[fo. 510r]
15

The same day anent the sevinteine act of the last generall conventioun of
borrowis haldin at the burght of Perth the last day of Julii last ordaineing the
burght of Elgyne to prosecute the suspensiones againis certane inhabitants
in Germoth[28] and to insist with captioune against the rest.[29] Compeired the

---

25 See above, 228–9.
26 For reasons which are not clear, a number of parliamentary burghs in Fife had no provost:
    see MacDonald, *Burghs and Parliament*, 39.
27 See above, 218.
28 Garmouth, at the mouth of the Spey, in Moray.
29 See above, 218.

commissioner of Elgyne and declared his burghtis proceidings in the said mater, and producit the severall decreittis obteynit be theme agains the saidis persones, which the present commissioneris accepts for diligence.

16

The same day anent the threttine act of the last generall conventioune of borrowis haldin at the burght of Perth the aucht day of Julii last ordaineing the burght of Forfar to prosecut thair former letters raisit and execute at thair instance against the inhabitantis of Killimuire[30] to this present conventioune.[31] The present commissioneris ordainis the said burght of Forfar to produce such lyk diligence againis the saidis inhabitantis of Killimuire as they sould have done at this tyme to the nixt generall conventioune under the payne of fourtie pundis. And this to be ane heid of the nixt missive.

17

The same day anent the twentie ane act of the last generall conventioune of borrowis haldin at the burght of Perth the nynt day of Julii last ordaineing the burght of Stirling to have producit to this conventioune thair diligence in restrayning the unfriemen within thair bundis and especiallie the indwelleris of Falkirk frome usurpeing the liberties of the frie royall borrowis under the payne of twentie pundis,[32] the present commissioneris ordainis the said burght of Stirling to produce siclyk diligence against thair unfriemen and inhabitantis of Falkirk as they sould have producit at this tyme under the payne of twentie pundis. And this to be ane heid of the nixt missive.

18

The same day anent the threttie saxt act of the last generall conventioune of borrowis haldin at the burght of Perth the tent day of Julii last,[33] compeired the commissioner of the burgh of Wigtoune and produced the forme of the electioune of thair magistrattis at Michaelmes last, which being sene and considderit be the present commissioneris they accept the same for diligence and ordaine theme in all tyme cumming to conforme themeselffis in thair electioune to the actis of parliament and borrowis.

19

The same day anent the threttie fyft act of the last generall conventioune of borrowis haldin at the burght of Perth the tent day of Julii last [fo. 510v] and sevint act of the particular conventioune haldin at Edinburgh the last day of

---

30 Kirriemuir, Angus.
31 See above, 217.
32 See above, 220.
33 See above, 229–30.

October last, concerning the mannaging of tred and electing of companies and for trying the quantitie of goods transported to Ingland frome Scotland and frome Scotland to Ingland.[34] The present commissioneris finding the saidis maitteris to be of great consequence so that the same cannot be suddenlie resolved and yitt to tend to the advancement of tred and manufactories, thairfor they appoynt and ordaine the burght of Edinburght to mak choyce of two or thrie of the most experienced men of trede among theme the burght of Perth, Dundie, Aberdeine, Glasgow, Air and Dumfreis eache on of theme (on)[35] for consulting anent the premissis and to send theme with thair best advyis to meitt and conveyne at the said burght of Edinburght the auchteine day of October nixt with continuatioune of dayis, and ordainis theme to trye and advyis anent the best overtures can cum to thair knawledge in the said mater and to sett doune the samyne, and iff neid beis to appoynt new dyetts of meitting and to report thair diligence heiranent to the nixt generall conventioune of borrowis. And the said burght of Edinburght to adverteis the rest and to requyre theme under the payne of twentie pundis ilk burght. And this to be ane heid of the nixt missive.

20

The same day anent the fourtie act of the last generall conventioune of borrowis haldin at the burght of Perth the ellevint day of Julii last,[36] compeired the agent and producit ane missive letter frome the burght of Forres with the forme of the electioune of thair magistrattis at Michaelmes last, whairwith the present commissioneris being advysit hes thocht guid to continue the said mater and in the meyne tyme they ordaine the burghts of Aberdeine and Elgyne to trye the trew estaitt of the said burght and conditioune of the persounes choisen and to report the same to the nixt generall conventioune of borrowis that efter tryell the borrowis may tak suche course anent the establischeing of magistrattis amongst theme as salbe most expedient. And this to be remembrit in the nixt missive.

21

The same day anent the fyftie act of the last generall conventioune of borrowis haldin at the burght of Perth the ellevint day of Julii last ordaineing the burght of Kirkcudbricht and utheris for recoverie of certane thair landis,[37] compeired the commissioner of the said burght and produced thair

---

[34] See above, 229. The second part of this phrase should, of course, read 'and to Scotland frome Ingland'.

[35] This means that Edinburgh is to choose one from each of these burghs, although that would inevitably mean that more than 'two or three' would be chosen.

[36] This should be the 41st act, not the 40th. See above, 233.

[37] See above, 235.

diligence consisting onlie in wakining the said actione, and thairfor finds theme to have done no diligence and to have incured the unlaw of xx lib. quhairwith for the present they dispens and ordains theme to produce farder and better diligence in the said actione betuixt and the nixt generall conventione of borrowis under the payne of i^c lib. And this to be ane heid of the nixt missive.

[fo. 511r]

22

The same day anent the nynt act of the particular conventione of borrowis haldin at the burght of Edinburght the twentie fourt day of Julii last ordaineing the burghts of Edinburght and Dysart to produce the persones of thair burghtis mentionat in the said act or the doubill of such dewis as they sould have payit in the Low Cuntries,[38] compeired the commissioneris of the saidis burghtis and obleissit theme in name of thair burghtis to exact the same fra the saidis persounes and to delyver the same to the agent betuixt and the auchteine of October nixt, and ordainis the agent to send the same to Richard Weir and he to be chairgit thairwith in his compts. And the saidis burghtis and agent to report thair diligence heiranent and this to be ane heid of the nixt missive.

23

The same day the commissioneris of borrowis understanding that the burghts of Dumfermeling, Kirkcudbricht and Wigtoune haveing beine erected with commoune landis and ane competent commoune guid, and yitt throch negligence of the magistrattis thair landis and rentis ar not put to the hiest availl and best proffeitt. Thairfor they ordaine the saidis burghtis to send with thair commissioneris to the nixt generall conventioune of borrowis ane perfyte rentall of thair commoune landis and commoune guid under the subscriptioune of thair magistrattis with the present estaitt thairof under the payne of fourtie pundis ilk burght. And appoyntis to trye the estaitt of the landis and rentis of Dumfermeling, the burghtis of Lynlithgow, Culros and Bruntyland, the estaitt of the landis and rentis of Wigtoune, Dumfreis and Kirkcudbricht, and ordaines the saidis burghtis to send with thair commissioneris to the nixt generall conventioune thair diligence under thair commissioneris handis under the payne of twentie pundis. And this to be remembrit in the nixt missive.

24

The same day anent that pairt of the particular conventioune of borrowis

---

haldin at Edinburght in October last[39] quhairby ilk burght wer requyred to send thair commissioneris sufficientlie instructed with thair best advyis anent ane solide course in the governament of the borrowis and electioune of thair magistrattis, the present commissioneris finding it necessar that advyis be taikin for ane constant counsell in ilk burght [or] ane yeirlie chaynge of magistratts.[40] Thairfoir ordainis the commissioneris that sall conveyne at Edinburgh the auchteine of October nixt to tak that mater to thair serious consideratioune and quhat they sall find efter mature deliberatioune to tend most to the guid of the borrowis, to sett doune the samyn in writt [fo. 511v] and to report the same to the nixt generall conventioun and ilk burgh lykwayis to be requyrit to send thair commissioneris sufficientlie instructed with thair best advyis and setting doune ane constant and solid course thairanent and this to be ane heid of the nixt missive. As lykwayis the burght of Edinburght in thair missive to be direct for conveyning the saidis commissioneris the auchteine day of October to remember the same.[41]

25

The same day anent the fyft act of the particular conventioune of borrowis haldin at the burght of Edinburght in Januarii last concerning the burght of Aberdeine,[42] compeired the commissioner of the said burght and maid report of the maner of thair yeirlie electioune of thair magistrattis and counsell with thair present estaitt of the said mater, which being hard the present commissioneris efter consideratioune, for caussis moveing thame hes accepted for diligence and anent the overtouris concerning thair peice in tyme cuming thair said commissioner procured certaine articles which the said commissioneris hes reduced to the heidis following: first, the condiscending upone the qualitie of ane counsellour within burght or magistrat; secundlie, the limitting of the tyme of ane provest; thridlie, the age of provest, baillies, deyne of gild and thesaurer; fourtlie, that non with swordis or pistollis repair to the counsell hous; fyftlie, anent the affinitie and consanguinitie of office men and counsellouris; sextlie, anent the provest two vottis and the tyme of the giving of the same.[43] Which materis the saidis commissioneris ordainis these that ar appoyntit to meitt at Edinburght the auchteine day of October nixt to tak to thair consideratioune and sett doune thair advyis thairanent to be reported to the nixt generall conventioune. As also ilk burght to be requyred for sending thair commissioneris sufficientlie instructed thairanent

---

[39] This confirms that a particular convention did meet, in October rather than November.
[40] See Introduction 25–6 for a discussion of this issue.
[41] This act is noted in the Abstract of Acts of Convention, *RCRBS*, iv, 540.
[42] See above, 249–50.
[43] This may refer to the right of the provest to have a casting vote, unusually in the form of an additional vote, if the votes were tied.

with thair best advyssis, and in the meane tyme ordainis the said burght
to proceid according to thair accustomed maner in thair nixt electione till
farder ordour be taiken thairanent. And the same to be remembrit in the
nixt missive.

26

The same day anent the supplicatioune gevin to the borrowis be the burght
of Pettinweyme at the last generall conventioune of borrowis haldin at the
burght of Perth in Julii last craveing thair help for reparatione of thair
harberie within thair said burght quhairunto ilk burght wes requyrit for
sending thair commissioneris sufficientlie instructed to this present conventioune and whairwith the present commissioneris being ryplie advysit and
considering the necessitie of [fo. 512r] the said harberie and that they ar
so meane of theme selffis that they ar not able to accomplisch the same
without help. Thairfor they have grantit and gevin and be thir presents grants
and gives to the said burght of Pettinweyme the soume of aucht hundreth
pundis and ordains ilk burght to send thair pairt thairof to the nixt generall
conventioun of borrowis conforme to the taxt roll under the payne of
twentie pundis ilk burght and that by and attour thair pairt of the payment
of the said principall soume. And this to be ane heid of the nixt missive.

27

The same day anent the supplicatioune gevin in to the borrowis be the
burgh of Peblis at the particular conventioune of borrowis haldin at Edinburgh the ellevint day of October last craiveing help to the reparatioune of
thair briggis over Tweid quhairunto ilk burght wes requyrit for sending thair
commissioneris sufficientlie instructed to this present conventioune to give
answer, and the saidis commissioneris being ryplie advysit and considering
the necessitie of the saidis briggs and the meane estaitt of the said burght,
thairfor they have grantit and gevin and be thir presentis grants and gives
the said burght of Peblis the soume of aucht hundreth markis and ordainis
ilk burght to send thair pairt thairof to the nixt generall conventioune of
borrowis conforme to the taxt roll, under the payne of twentie pundis ilk
burgh and that by an attour the payment of thair pairt of the said principall
soume. And this to be ane heid of the nixt missive.

28

Octavo Julii I^m vi^c trigesimo sexto
The quhilk day the commissioneris of borrowis being conveynit anent the
nynt act of the particular conventioune of borrowis haldin at the burght
of Edinburght the twentie twa day of Julii last ordaineing Robert Greirsoun late collectour of the impost appoynted for defraying of the minister
stipend at Campheir to produce his comptis of his intromissioun to this

present conventioun as at mair lenth is conteynit in the said act.[44] The said
Robert Greirsoun haveing sent home his comptis and the samyne being
hard, seine, fitted and calculat and allowit with the certificatiounes thairof
lykwayis sent home be him, the said Robert his intromissioun with the said
inpost frome the twuentie thrid of Maii 1635 inclusive till the first of Maii
1636 lastbypast exclusive is found to extend to the soume of twa hundreth
thriescoir auchteine pundis aucht schillings four pennyes gritt Fleymis and
his dischairge conteyning his debursementis to the minister and utheris
conforme to his warrandis and severall dischairges producit is found to
extend to the soume of thrie hundreth sevine pundis sexteine schillings
nyne gritt Fleymis money. Sua the borrowis is fund to be restand awand to
the said compter [fo. 512v] the soume of threttie aucht pundis aucht schillings fyve gritt Fleymis money, quhairin the dischairge exceidis the chairge
and becaus the said compter hes exonerit himselff with nyne last of leid ure
in Harye Greg his schip in Leyith, sex last of leid ure in Niniane Boner in
Leyith his schip, extending to sevinetine seck of guidis,[45] the dewtyes quhairof
seames to be ommitted throw his neglect. Thairfor ordainis the conservatour
to conveyne the said Robert befor him and giff he sall find the ommis-
sioun to proceid of his neglect to caus him pay the dewtyes thairof to the
present collectour and do justice to him against such as hes brocht over the
said lead ure and the said present collectour to be chairgeit thairwith in his
comptis and the conservatour to acquant the borrowis with his proceiding
thairanent. And siclyk becaus the said Robert hes omittit furth of his compts
and nocht upliftit from the particular persones underwrittin the dewis for
thair coallis, viz: in Dysart Andro Reanye, twelff hundreth coallis, James
Guthrie thair for ten thousand coallis at on tyme and als mutche at uther
tymes, James Sympsoune thair, nyne hundreth coallis, Johne Reanye thair for
twelff hundreth coallis, Thomas Wilsoune thair aucht hundreth coallis, Johne
Cowan thair ane thousand coallis, in Kirkcaldye Francis Hutchesoun for
aucht hundreth coallis, Johne Wyse thair sexteine hundreth coallis, Thomas
Quhyte thair twelff hundreth, Robert Quhyte thair twelff hundrethe collis,
James Broune thair fyfteine hundreth coallis, David Duncane thair for ane
thousand coallis; in Anstruther Williame Blak for aucht hundreth coallis at
one tyme and als much at ane uther tyme; in Bruntyland Captane James
Orrok for sexteine hundreth collis. Thairfor ordainis the conservatour to
trye his diligence in craiveing the saidis persounes and iff he hes beine in
Campheir in requyreing ane pand[46] of theme and iff he doe not qualifie
sufficient diligence to caus him pay for the same, and for such as he hes

[44] See above, 242–3.
[45] As there are fifteen lasts (barrels) of lead ore, it is unclear how that is equivalent to seventeen
sacks of goods.
[46] i.e. monetary pledge.

usit diligence against nowayis to be trublit. As also ordainis the burghtis to quhome the saidis persounes does apperteine to put theme under cautioune under the payne of fourtie pundis ilk persone for compeirance befor the commissioneris in the nixt generall conventioune under the payne of fourtie pundis ilk burght or payment of the double of such soumes as thair inhabitantis sould have payit in the Low Cuntries. And becaus the borrowis ar fund restand to the compter the soume quhairin his dischairge exceidis his chairge, thairfor they ordaine the conservatour to trye [the] collectour his diligence in sutting payment of the saidis persones quha past away unpaying thair dewis, and to report the same to the commissioneris appoynted to conveyne at Edinburght in October nixt. And iff be the said report the said collectour [fo. 513r] salbe fund to have done diligence, in that caice ordainis the saidis borrowis to giff warrand to the present collectour for paying of the said rest according to the said report, and in the meane tyme suspendis the payment of the said rest and ordainis the conservatour to be advertised heirof. And for collecting of the said impost, they have elected, nominat and appoynted and be thir presents electis, nominatts, appoynts and ordainis Patrik Suittie factour at the said port to be collectour, and that fra the first of Maii 1637 till the first of Maii 1638. And ordainis him to compeir befor the conservatour or his deputts and that in ane fencit court to mak faith *de fideli administratione*[47] and declaratioune in maner conteynit in the sevint act of the particular conventioune of borrowis haldin at the burght of Edinburgh the aucht day of November the yeir of God I^m vi^c and threttie four yeiris, and ordainis him to send home his compts to the generall conventioune of borrowis to be haldin in the moneth of Julii I^m vi^c threttie aucht yeiris wherever the samyne sall happen to be. As also ordainis the said Patrik Suittie to send home his compts with the verrificatiounes thairof under the skipper, factour, or merchandis handis of his haill resaits with thair names that sall mak payment of thair dewis or sall pas by the staiple port with staiple guidis, with thair schippis, quantitie of guidis and all uther circumstances requisite, and ordainis the conservatour or his deputtis to caus the said Patrik Suittie mak faith in maner abonewrittin and put the said sevint act of the said paricular conventioune of borrowis haldin at the said burght of Edinburght the aucht day of November I^m vi^c threttie four yeiris forsaid to full executioune in the haill heidis thairof. And the saidis commissioneris of borrowis ordainis the said conservatour and collectour to report his diligence heiranent to the nixt generall conventioune of borrowis. And this to be ane heid of the nixt missive.

---

[47] Literally, 'concerning faithful administration', i.e. he was promising to carry out his duties with diligence.

29

The same day the saidis commissioneris of borrowis being conveynit anent
the twentie fyft act of the last generall conventioune of borrowis haldin at
the burght of Perth the [9] day of Julii last,[48] compeired the commissioneris
of Edinburght, Glasgow, Kirkcaldye and Dysart and obleissed theme selffis
in name of thair saidis burght to mak payment for thair nichtbouris of
suche soumes as they wer dew for the ministeris stipend at Campheir to the
commissioneris to be conveynit at Edinburght in October nixt conforme
to the said act. And siclyk comperied the commissioneris of the said burght
of Edinburght, Glasgow and Dysart and obleissed themeselffis in name of
thair saidis burghtis [fo. 513v] to mak payment of suche soumes as thair
nichtbouris ar dew for the caussis forsaidis, conforme to the nynt act of the
particular conventioune haldin at Edinburght the twentie fourt of Januarii
last to the saidis commissioneris, which being payit the present commissioneris ordainis the same to be delyverit to the agent, to send the same over to
the present collectour with the money he did formerlie ressave, conforme
to the twentie fyft act of the said conventioune haldin at Perth and the
said collectour to be chairgit thairwith in his compt, and the burghtis and
agent to report thair diligence heiranent to the nixt generall conventioun
of borrowis under the payne of twentie pundis ilk burght. And this to be
ane heid of the nixt missive.

30

The same day ordainis the burght of Ramfrew to caus James Maknair,
James Andersoun, Johne Stevin and Johne Rowan in Govane ather to mak
thair actuall residence with theme or in depryveing theme of thair liberties
betuixt and the nixt generall conventioune of borrowes under the payne of
twentie pundis. And this to be ane heid of the nixt missive.

31

The same day the saidis commissioneris hes thocht guid and expedient
that Harye Alexander, sone to the erle of Stirling, sall continue in attend-
ence thair service and effaires at court for ane yeir to cum. And for his
bygaine service since the last conventioune grants unto him the soume
of ane hundreth pundis sterling. And ordainis ilk burght to be requyrit
for sending with thair commissioneris thair pairt thairof, conforme to the
taxt roll, to the nixt generall conventioune of borrowis under the payne of
twentie pundis and that by and attour the payment of the said principall
soume. And ordainis thair clark in thair names to wrytt to the said Harye
for attending thair said service and, as occasioune offeris, to acquant theme

---

[48] See above, 222–3.

or the burght of Edinburght with quhat sall cum to his knowledge may concerne theme. And for his service to cum, the present commissioneris promises to remunerat the same. And this to be ane heid of the nixt missive. As also ordainis ane letter to be writtin to him in name of the burght of Glasgow to assist and concur with theme in quhat they have adoe.

32

The same day the saidis commissioneris of borrowis understanding that the lynning claith of this kingdome is becum on of the greatest commodities thairof which is mutch prejudged in the saill thairof [fo. 514r] in foranye pairts throch the uncertaintie of the treid yairof. Thairfor the present commissioneris recommendis the said mater to the burghtis to be convynit at Edinburght in October nixt and ordainis theme to supplicat the lordis of counsell for commanding that the whole lynning claith be wrocht in no les nor ane elne of breid which salbe brocht and presentit to the mercat and the saidis burghtis to report thair diligence heiranent to the nixt generall conventioune of borrowis. And this to be ane heid of the nixt missive.

33

The same day anent the supplicatioune gevin in for the reparatione of the brig of Larbard over the River of Carrin,[49] the present commissioneris ordainis ilk burght to be requyrit for sending thair commissioneris sufficientlie instructed for giveing answer thair[to] to the nixt generall conventione of borrowis. And this to be ane heid of the nixt missive.

34

The same day the present commissioneris understanding be ane missiv letter direct frome the conservatour of the gritt nomber of merchandis that does pas daylie by the staiple port with staiple waires to the gritt prejudice of the staiple. Thairfor they ordaine the burghtis of Edinburght, Lynlithgow and Monros to produce the persones underwrittin, viz: Edinburght, Thomas Glaidstanes, James Lichtbodye, Robert Salmound, Johne Hirstoune and James Wilsoune in Leyth; the burght of Lynlithgow, Thomas Uddard, Patrik Bell, George Bell, Alexander Mylne, elder; the burght of Monros, David Sewair, Andro Gilbert, Alexander Andersoun, James Smyth, Johne Tailyeour, James Mylne and Thomas Ranye, before the conventioune to be convenit at Edinburght the auchteine of October nixt with continewatioun of dayis to answer for thair passing by the staiple port with staiple waires within thir twa yeiris bygaine. And for this effect ordainis the saidis burghtis to put the saidis persones under cautioune for compeirance the said day under the

---

49   The bridge of Larbert over the river Carron, near Falkirk, Stirlingshire.

payne of ane hundreth pundis ilk persone. And to the effect some ordour may be taikin with theme, the present commissioneris grants and gives full power and commissioun to the commissioneris to be conveynit at Edinburght the tyme forsaid for sitting and cognosceing upone the forsaidis persones thair particular failyies and transgressiounis and, being fand giltye, for punischeing of theme conforme to the lawis and actis of burrowis. And ordainis the burgh of Edinburght by thair letter to requyre the saidis burghis for produceing the saidis persones the said day under the payne of twa hundreth pundis. And the said borrowis to report thair diligence heiranent to the nixt generall conventioune of borrowis. And this to be ane heid of the nixt missive.

[fo. 514v]

35

The same day whairas the present commissioneris being informed that some meanes hes beine usit at the staiple port for darthing of victuall cumming to this cuntrie in tyme of necessitie and fearing the lyke dearth this subsequent yeir, thairfor they ordaine the conservatour to have ane cair of the staiple port and iff he hes fund any or sall find any subject to the natioune to transgress in this kind, to tak course with theme according to equitie and lawis of the kingdome. As also to tak heid anent the mariage of factouris and to sie that the lawis maid thairanent be keipit and observed. And the said conservatour to report his diligence heiranent to the particular conventioune of borrowis to be conveynit at Edinburght in October nixt.

36

The same day anent the twentie sevint act of the last generall conventioune of borrowis haldin at the burght of Perth the tent day of Julii last, concerning the prosecutioune of the actiounes intentit be the burghtis of Ramfrew and Irving against the unfrie tredderis and the borrowing of twa thousand markis to that effect mentionat in the said act.[50] Compeired Robert Stewart, merchand in Linlithgow, commissioner chosen for prosecutting the saidis actiounes, and Alexander Aikinheid, agent, and maid report of thair proceidings in the said mater and producit thair particular debursements. Which being seine and considderrit togither with the allowance of the annualrent of the said soumes frome Witsonday 1635 till Witsonday lastbypast 1636 and frome Witsonday last till Witsonday nixt, thair is fund resting *de claro*[51] in the agents handis the soume of twa hundreth thriscoir pundis. And thairfor the present commissioneris ordainis the saidis Robert Stewart and agent

---

50 See above, 224–5.
51 Clear, i.e. not yet spent or accounted for.

be advyis conteynit in the said act to prosecute the saidis materis to the
finall decisioun thairof. And ordainis the agent to borrow such soumes of
money as salbe requisit upon ordinarie proffeit. And for repayment thairof,
the saidis commissioneris for themeselffis and in name of thair burghtis
bundis and obleissis theme. As also ordainis ilk burght to send thair pairt of
the said two thousand markis with thair commissioneris to the nixt generall
conventioune of borrowis under the payne of twentie pundis ilk burght by
and attour the payment of thair pairt of the said principall soume. And the
said Robert with the said agent to produce thair diligence heiranent to the
nixt generall conventioune of borrowis. And this to be ane heid of the nixt
missive.

37
The same day anent the secund act of the particular conventione of borrowis
haldin at Edinburght the 17 day of Julii last ordaineing ilk burght to send
with thair commissioneris to this present conventioune the soumes of money
dew for Johne Trotter chairges, commissioner direct to Fraunce anent the
liberties of this kingdome in Piccardie and Normandie.[52] Compeirit onlie
the commissioneris of Edinburght, [fo. 515r] Dundye and Aberdeyne and
produicit thair collectouris comptis of thair intromissioune with the impost
grantit for defraying the saidis comissioneris chairges, which is fund to
extend frome the first of August last to the first of Julii instant to the soume
of ellevin hundreth fourscoir ane pundis fourtine schillings Scotts money.
And becaus it is fund that the burghtis of Monrose and Innernes hes done
no diligence in uplifting of the dewis frome thair nichtbouris and inhabitantis, they find theme to have incurrit the unlaw conteynit in the said
act. Bot for caussis moveing theme, the present commissioneris dispenssis
thairwith and ordainis the saidis burghtis to send over ane compt under thair
collectouris handis of the said impost dew since the said first of August last
to the commissioneris to be conveynit at Edinburght in October nixt under
the payne of ane hundreth pundis ilk burght, togither with ane declaratioune gevin upon the verritie thairof and thair collectouris aith under the
magistrattis handis. And ordainis the saidis commissioneris to mak upe ane
perfyte compt of the haill last yeiris dewis and to deduce the same of the
soumes of money advancit be the burght of Edinburght in the said mater
and annualrent thairof. And last ordainis the saidis burghtis and all utheris
interrest in the said mater to send with thair commissioneris ane perfyte
compt of thair collectouris intromissioune with the saidis dewtyes frome the
first of this instant to the first of Julii nixtocum under the payne conteynit
in the said former act, with ane attestatioune under the magistrattis handis

52 See above, 237–9.

of the collectouris aiths gevein upone the saidis compts with payment of the samyn. And the burght of Edinburght to requyre the saidis burghtis of Innernes and Monrose to that effect under the payne forsaid. And this to be ane heid of the nixt missive. As lykways ordainis the burght of Edinburght to conveyne befor theme Johne Dowgall thair burges who hes transported salmound and uther merchandice frome Speymouth and to uplift frome him his pairt of the said impost since the said first of August last and to contein the same in thair compts.

38

The same day anent the mater of the lichts craived to be erected upone the Ile of the May and mater of overtouris proponit be Sir James Lokhart anent the fischeing and commissiounis gevin to Mr Alexander Guthrie for pasing to his Majestie thairanent and certane uther particularis conteynit in his instructiounes, compeired the said Mr Alexander and maid his report and declaired how his Majestie wes pleassed to wryt to the lordis of sessioune for administratting of justice into the mater of the actiounes depending betuix the burghtis royall and speciallie Ramfrew and Irving and that he had remitted the said mater of fischeing to the committie appoynted to that effect; as also had grantit ane signature for erecting of the saidis lichts bot had writtin to the lordis of exchekquher for staying thairof till the borrowis wer hard. The saidis commissioneris [fo. 515v] recommendis to the burght of Edinburght the prosecutioune of the said mater and to use all lawfull meanes for stayeing of the same and quhen neid salbe to conveyne such borrowis as they sall think most interrest in the said mater. And for the said Mr Alexander his chairges in the said voyage they find the same to extend to the soume of four thousand sex hundreth pundis, which they ordaine to be repayit to the burght of Edinburght with the interrest thairof in maner following, viz: the one half thairof with ane yeiris interrest at the nixt conventioune and the uther half with ane yeiris interrest of the same to be payit the conventioune followeing. And for this effect ordainis ilk burght to be requyrit for sending thair pairt thairof conforme to the taxt roll to the nixt generall conventioune of borrowis under the payne of twentie pundis ilk burght and that by and attour the payment of thair pairt of the said principall soume. And this to be ane heid of the nixt missive.[53]

39

The same day anent the fourtie sevin act of the last generall conventioune of borrowis haldin at the burght of Perth and 7 act of the particular conventioune haldin at Edinburgh in October last concerning the setting doune

[53] This act is noted in the Abstract of Acts of Convention, RCRBS, iv, 540.

of ane solid course anent the fischeing and regulating of the same.[54] The
present commissioneris ordainis ilk burght whome the same does concerne
to put the acts maid anent the forme and sufficiencie of the barrellis and
maid anent the deschairgeing of peild hering and sufficient and loyall paking
to executioune and ordainis the burghts to be conveynit at Edinburgh in
October nixt to sett doune the haill acts maid thairanent and such uthir
as they sall think farder expedient in ane act to be intimat to the nixt
generall conventioune with thair best advyis anent the haill executioune of
the samyne in tyme cumming and, iff occasioune offer, that the samyne be
urged befor the said tyme, ordainis the burght of Edinburgh to conveyne
such as salbe thocht to theme most expert in that tred and to tak course
thairanent and to requyre theme for that effect to cum instructed with thair
commissioneris. And the same burght and burghtis to report thair diligence
heiranent. And this to be ane heid of the nixt missive.

40

The same day anent the sext act of the particular conventioune of borrowis
haldin at Edinburght the penult day of Januarii last concerning ane help
to the building of ane harberie at Portpatrik.[55] The present commissioneris
understanding the necessitie of the said harberie for all his Majesties kingdomes ar content to giff thairto the soume of tua thousand markis to be
payit in maner and upone the conditiounes following, viz: the soume of
ane thousand merkis [fo. 516r] the nixt conventioune following the begynning of the said work and the uthir at the compleitting thairof. And thairfor
ordainis ilk burght to be requyrit to send with thair commissioneris thair
pairt of the said soume conforme to the taxt roll to the nixt generall conventioune of borrowis. And ordainis in the meane tyme the burghtis of Air and
Irving to visite the said harberie that iff ane reall begynning be maid the
said soume may be delyverit. And the saidis burghtis to report thair diligence
heiranent to the nixt generall conventioune of borrowis. And this to be ane
heid of the nixt missive.

41

Nono Julii I[m] vi[c] trigesimo sexto
The quhilk day the commissioneris of borrowis being conveynit and it
being universallie regraitted that the Monnondayis mercatt in Edinburgh
and Glasgow does draw the inhabitantis of diveris utheris borrowis to travell
upone the Sabboth day to the prophanatioune of the said day.[56] Thairfor

---

54 See above, 234–5.
55 See above, 250.
56 Although the church had sought to eradicate Monday markets in the later sixteenth century,
    no civil legislation was passed until after the covenanting revolution: see *RPS*, 1640/6/74.

the saidis commissioneris recommendis seriouslie to the saidis burghtis the alteratione of the said mercatt day to some uthir competent day in the weik according as efter deliberatioune they sall think meitt. And ordainis the present commissioneris of the saidis burghtis to remember thair burghtis heirof and the burghtis to report thair proceiding heiranent to the nixt generall conventioune of borrowis. And this to be ane heid of the nixt missive.

42

The same day the saidis commissioneris haveing seine, futtit, calculat and allowed the compts of the agents debursements since the last generall conventioune in thair publict effairis, they find the same togither with the annuelrent thairof bygaine and till the nixt conventioune to extend to the soume of fyve hundreth twentie aucht pundis threttine schilling four pennyes. And thairfor ordainis ilk burght to be requyrit for sending thair pairt thairof to the nixt generall conventioune of borrowis with thair commissioner conforme to the taxt roll under the payne of xx lib. ilk burght, by and attour the payment of thair pairt of the said principall soume. And this to be ane heid of the nixt missive.

43

The same day the present commissioneris haveing hard the lawfull excuses of the burghtis of Perth and St Androis for being absent frome certane particular conventiounes since the last generall conventioune, they dispens with thair unlawis incurrit be theme for the caussis forsaid and dischairges the agent of the same for ever.

[44]

The same day the saidis commissioneris of borrowis grantis and gives licence to the burghtis of Elgyne, Kilranie, Wigtoune and Quhithorne to abyd and remayne fra all generall conventioune of borrowis for the space followeing, viz: the burght of Elgyne for thrie yeiris fra all conventiounes besouth Tay; Kilranie for thrie yeiris; Wigtoune frome benorth Forth for thrie yeiris; and Quhithorne for thrie yeiris, upone the conditiounes and provisiounes underwrittin. Providing the samyne be not extendit to parliaments nor quhair the saidis burghtis ar citat for ane particular caus. As also provyding the saidis burghtis send with the commissioneris of thair nixt ajacent borrowis thair severall ratificatioune and approbatioune autenticklie subscrivit of all things to be done yeirlie at the saidis generall conventiounes, with all soumes that they sall pay to the borrowis conforme to the missive, and that they bestow the expenssis that they suld have bestowit upone their commissioneris upone commoune warkis and be comptable to the borrowis thairof at the expyreing of the saidis yeiris.

[fo. 516v]

45

The same day the commissioneris understanding that the burghs in thair last generall conventioune had recommendit the herberie of Northberwek as ane verie necessar and cheritable worke to the borrowis and understanding that some hes contribute thairto and that thair restis manie as yitt who hes not payit thair cheritie thairto, thairfore the present commissioneris recommendis the same of new and ordainis such burghis as hes not yitt contribut thairto to send thair charitie with thair commissioneris to the nixt generall conventioun of borrowis. And this to be ane heid of the nixt missive.

46

The same day anent the supplicatioune given in be the burght of Rothesay craiveing help for making ane herberie and repairing the damage done be the watter running through thair toun. The present commissioneris ordainis ilk burgh to be requyrit for sending thair commissioneris sufficientlie instructed to give answer to the said supplicatioun to the nixt generall conventioun. As also ordainis the said burgh to send ane perfyt rentall of the whole commoun landis which does or did appertein to thair burgh with thair declaratioun when anie pairt thairof was sett out and to whome under the payne of xx lib. As also the burghis of Aire, Irrvyng and Dumbartane to trye the estaitt of the said toun and the saids borrowis to report thair diligence heiranent to the nixt generall conventioun. And this to be ane heid of the nixt missive.

47

The same day anent the supplicatioun givin in be the burgh of Lanerick craiveing help to the building of ane brig over the Watter of Mouse[57] neir to thair toun. The present commissioneris ordaine ilk burgh to be requyrit for sending thair commissioneris sufficientlie instructed for giving answer thairto to the nixt generall conventioun of borrowis. And this to be ane heid of the nixt missive.

48

The same [day] ordainis the agent to give George Ramsay post the soume of fyftie sax pundis for buying ane joup[58] and ane stand of cloathes to be worne in thair service and the said soume salbe allowit to him in his comptis.

[57] A tributary of the Clyde which runs to the north of Lanark.
[58] A jacket or short coat; cf. French 'jupe' which now means simply 'skirt' but in the seventeenth century could mean a piece of clothing covering the whole body.

49

The same day ordainis the burgh of Wigtoun to produce ane perfyte rentall of thair commoun landis and commoun guid with thair diligence in recovering the same to the nixt generall conventioun of borrowis under the payne of twentie pundis and ordainis the agent to concur and help them so far as he can. And this to be ane heid of the nixt missive.

50

Compeirit the commissioner of the burgh of Glasgow and verifiet the citatioun of the whole borrowis to this present conventioun be George Ramsay, post.

51

The same day the saids commissioneris unlawis the burght of Innernes for not sending the dewis of the missive to this present conventioun in the soume of xx lb. and the agent to uplift the same frome theme and to produce his diligence in uplifting thairof to the nixt generall conventioun of borrowis. And this to be ane heid of the nixt missive.

[fo. 517r]
52

The same day unlawis the burgh of Tayne in the soume of twentie pundis for being absent fra this present conventioun and ordainis the agent to uplift the same frome theme and to produce his diligence in uplifting the same frome theme to the nixt generall conventioun of borrowis. And this to be ane heid of the nixt missive.

[53]

The same day the present commissioneris of borrowis dissolve this present conventioun and affixes and apointes thair nixt generall conventioun of borrowis to be and begin at the burgh of Abirdein the [...] day of Julii nixtocum 1637 yeires with continuatioun of dayis and ordainis the said burgh to direct the generall missive to the haill remanent borrowis to requyre theme for conve[n]ing at the said burgh for that effect.[59]

---

[59] The volume ends immediately after fo. 517, save for two blank folios which form part of a more modern binding. Ironically, the first year for which Aberdeen has no records is a year in which the convention met at Aberdeen.

General Convention at Edinburgh, July 1647[1]

[p. 63]
At Bruntiland decimo sexto augusti 1647[2]

{C. Watsone report, the actis of burrowis}
Compeirit Captane Andro Watsone, commissioner at the last generall conventioun of burrouis hauldin at Edinburgh the fyft day of Julii last, and maid report of his commissioun and producit the extract of the whole actis quhairof the tennor followis:[3]

In the generall conventioun of burrouis hauldin at the burghe of Edinburgh the sext of Julii 1647 yeiris be the commissioneris of burrouis thair conveined who compeirand producit thair commissionis as followis:

[p. 64]

Edinburgh	Archibald Tod, Archibald Sydserff, Robert Meikiljone
Perth	Robert Arnot provest, Johne Elder clerk
Dundie	Sir Alexander Wedderburne
Abirdein	
Stirling	Johne Short
Linlithgow	George Bell
St Androis	James Robertsone
Glasgow	George Porterfeild
Air	Gilbert Richard
Haddingtoun	Richard Chaiplane
Dysert	
Kirkcaldie	James Law
Monros[4]	James Peddie
Couper	George Jamesone
Anstruther Eister	Alexander Blak
Dumfreis	Johne Johnstoun
Innernes[5]	Johne Forbes

---

1   National Archives of Scotland, Burntisland Council Minutes, B9/12/9, pp. 64–87. There is a running head of '1647' on every page that contains the records of the convention of royal burghs.
2   There follows a sederunt of the burgh council, and a list of absentees, which have been omitted here.
3   An act of the burgh council, recording the decision to copy the acts of the convention into its minute book.
4   Montrose.
5   Inverness.

Bruntiland	Capitane Andro Watsone
Innerkething[6]	Marke Kinglassie
Kingorne	George Gourley
Brechen	
Irving	Allane Dunlope
Jedburghe	Robert Rutherfuird
Kirkcudbright	Williame Glendinning
Wigtoun	Adame McGie
Pittinweym	Williame Steinsone
Dunfermling	Williame Walker
Anstruther Wester	Piter Thomsone
Selkrig[7]	Thomas Scott
Dumbartan	Johne Simple
Ranfrow[8]	Robert Hall
Dunbare	Williame Purves
Lanrik[9]	Gideon Jack
Abirbrothok[10]	Johne Auchterlonie
Elgin	Mr Johne Hay
Pibles[11]	Patrick Thomsone
Caraill[12]	Andro Daw
Tayn	Mr Thomas Ros
Culros	Mr Robert Gourlay
Bamf	
Quhythorne[13]	
[p. 65]	
Forfar	Williame Hunter
Rothesay	Walter Stewart
Nirne[14]	Johne Ros
Forres	Mr Williame Dunbare
Rutherglen	Be exemptioun and ratificatioun producit be Glasgow
North Berwick	Be exemptioun and Ratificatioun producit be
Haddingtown	
Cullen	
Lauder	Johne Edmistoun

---

6   Inverkeithing.
7   Selkirk.
8   Renfrew.
9   Lanark.
10 Arbroath.
11 Peebles.
12 Crail.
13 Whithorn.
14 Nairn.

Kilrenie	Be exemptioun and ratificatioun producit be the agent
Annand	
Lochmaber[15]	
Sanquhar	
Galloway[16]	
Dingwall	
Quenisferrie[17]	Johne Pantoun
Dornoch	

1

The same day electis Archibald Tod, first in commissioun for the burghe of Edinburgh, to be moderatour during the present conventioun, quha compeirand acceptit the said office in and upon him and gave his aith *de fideli administratione*.[18]

2

The same day appointis the hour of meitting to be and begine daylie at eight houres in the morning except on the preaching dayis in the which ten houres is appointed and to continow till tuelff houres at noon and afternoone to begin at tua houres and to last till sex houres at night, and such as ar absent at the calling of the rollis to pay sex shillingis of unlaw and they that passes frome this present convention befoir the disolving thairof to pey ane unlaw as absentis and that nane speak unrequyrit without leive askit or gevin nor intermix thair reasoning with thair vottis under the paine of sex shillingis *toties quoties*.[19]

3

The same day ordinis the burghe of Pearthe to produce thair diligence in writt in restraining and punishing unfrie traderis and in speciall Johne Drumond, indueller in Dumblaine, and Andro Lamb, ane chope keiper in the said towne of Dumblaine, for usurping the liberties of the royall burrous [p. 66] under the pane of tuentie pundis. And this to be ane heid of the nixt missive.

4

The same day the commissioneris of burrouis ordinis the burghe of Monros

---

15 Lochmaben.
16 New Galloway.
17 South Queensferry.
18 Literally, 'concerning faithful administration', i.e. he was promising to carry out the duties of moderator with diligence.
19 As often as it shall happen, i.e. for each offence.

to produce thair diligence to the nixt generall conventioun of burrouis against unfrie tradderis within thair liberties and boundis speciallie in the towne of Stainhyve[20] under the paine of tuentie pundis. And this to be an heid of the nixt missive

5

The same day ordinis the burghe of Irving to produce thair diligence against unfrie tradderis in Kirmarnok, Lairgs[21] and uther places within thair boundis and liberties to the nixt generall conventioun of burrowis under the paine of tuentie pundis. And this to be ane heid of the nixt missive.

Septimo Julii 1647

6

The same day anent the sext act of the last generall conventioun of burrouis hauldin at the burghe of Perth the sevint of Julii 1647[22] yeiris ordining the burghe of Wigtoun to produce to this present conventioun the decreit arbitrall betuix them and the earle of Galloway and to report thair diligence in the prosecutioun thairof under the paine of 20 lib. The present commissioneris findes them to have contraveined the said act in all poyntis and therfoir unlawis them in the said sowme of 20 lib. for their bygane contraventioun and ordinis them to produce the said decreit arbitrall togidder with thair diligence to the nixt generall conventioun under the paine of 40 lib. And this to be ane heid of the nixt missive

7

The same day anent the eight act of the said last generall conventioun of burrouis ordining the agent with advyce and concurrance of the commissioneris present for the tyme to use diligence in obteining ane act of parliament against the dilapidatioun of commoun landis of burrouis. The present commissioneris finding that the agentis have done thair diligence and that nevirtheles the said act was not obteined, thairfoir ordinis the said agent to continow and insist in his diligence for obteining the said act of parliament at the nixt doune sitting thairof. And this to be ane heid of the nixt missive.

8

The same day anent the [ ][23] act of the last generall conventioun of burrouis ordining the burghe of Stirling with concurrance of the agent, togidder with the assistance of the burghis of Irving and Ranfrow, to insist in prosecuting

---

20 Stonehaven, Kincardineshire.
21 Kilmarnock and Largs, Ayrshire.
22 This is obviously an error; the convention at Perth met in 1646.
23 There is no space in the MS but the number of the act ought to have been inserted here.

the suspentiones reasit be certane unfrie traderis against the said burght of Stirling. The present commissioneris finding the saidis suspensionis not as yit to be discussed ordinis the said burgh [p. 67] of Stirling with concurrance and assistance foirsaid to insist in prosecuting and discussing the saidis suspensiones against the unfrie traderis and to report thair diligence heiranent to the nixt generall conventioun of burrowis. And this to be ane heid of the nixt missive.

9

The same day anent the tent act of the last generall conventioun of burrouis ordining the burghe of Rothsay to produce the rentall of their commoun landis and the burghis of Glasgow and Dumbartane and Irving to send thair commissioneris to meit and convein at the said burghe of Rothesay at ane certane day betuix and Michaelmes nixt thaireftir to take upe ane rentall of the commoun landis pertining to the said burghe, togidder with the maner of the outgeving of the same whither in few rentall or in take, the persones names outgeveris thairof, the tyme quhen the samyn was gevin out, togidder with the present rate and state thairof, and ordining the said burghe of Rothesay to produce unto the saidis commissioneris thair originall chartour to be sein and considderit be them to the effect the same may be drawen to the best availl and hiest rate, and ordining the said burghe of Glasgow to have appointit the said day and to have adverteised the saidis burghis thairof. The present commissioneris finding the samyn to be neglectit be the said towne of Rothesay in the not productioun of the said rentall to this present conventioun, unlawis the said burghe in the sowme of fourtie pundis for their bygane contraventioun and ordinis them to produce exact diligence to the nixt generall conventioun under the paine of fyve hundreth merkis and dispenses with the said burghe of Glasgow in not advertising and conveaning of the saidis burghes in reguard of their troubles and deficulties at that tyme, and ordinis them to produce thair diligence in advertising and conveining the saidis burghes to the effect foirsaid under the paine of ane hundreth punds. And the saidis burghis of Air, Dumbartane and Irving to observe thair pairt of the said act under the paine of fourtie punds ilk burghe. And this [to] be ane heid of the nixt missive.

10

The same day anent the 17 and tuentie thrie actis of the last generall conventioun ordining the burghe of Lanerk to produce thair rentall of thair commoun landis weill imployed with the present estate thairof under thair oathes and to content and pay to the agent the sowme of 20 lib. for thair former contraventioun and to repone David Mount thair burges to all libertie he haid befoir the conventioun of burrowis haulden at the said burghe of Lanerk, and ordining the said burghe of Lanerk to make intimatioun thairof at thair mercat croce under the paine [p. 68] of ane hundreth pundis and discharging of the said burghe frome seiking either act or band frome the said David Mount, and to produce thair diligence thairanent to this present conventioun as the said act at lenth beares, and lykwayes ordining the said burghe of Lanerik to produce to this present conventioun thair diligence in rouping of the saidis landis with the rest of thair commoun good, and ordining the burghes of Glasgow and Peibles to be present at the rouping of the said commoun good, and ordining the said burghe of Lanrik to proceid in the electioun of thair magistratis at the terme of Michaelmes last bypast conforme to the actis of parliament and burrouis maid thairanent, and to report thair diligence anent the haill premissis to this present conventioun as the said 23 act mair fullie beares. The present commissioneris finding the said burghe of Lanerik to have contraveined the saidis actis be not productioun of their rentall unlawis them in the sowme of twentie pundis to be peyit be[24] the agent, and ordinis them to produce to the nixt generall conventioun thair said rentall and to produce ane sufficient testificat under the said David Mount his hand that he is reponed to his said fridomes and burgeshipe and that no act nor band to the contrair thairof is keiped abone his head, and to report thair diligence in the haill remanent articles and heidis of the saidis [17] and 23 acts respective to the said nixt generall conventioun under the paine off fourtie pundis to be payed to the burrowis. And this to be ane heid of the nixt missive.

11

The same day anent the tuentie fourth act of the last generall conventioun of burrowis ordining the burghe of Forfar to produce ane prefyte rentall of thair commoun landis weill imployed to this present conventioun as the said act beares. The present commissioneris finding the neglect thairof to be greatumlie prejudiciall to the said burghe ordinis them to produce the great chartour of thair commoun land to the nixt generall conventioun off burrouis to be by them cognosced under the paine of fourtie pundis, and ordinis the burghis of Dundie, Monros and Aberdein at ane certaine day to mak ane visitatioun of the saidis landis and the burghe of Dundie to appoint the tyme and to give advertisment to the uther burghes for that effect, and recommendis to the saidis burghes to try the forme of the electioun of the majistratis of the said burghe of Forfar and to report thair diligence in the premisses to the said nixt generall conventioun of burrowis under the paine of twentie pund ilk burghe to be payit to the agent. And this to be ane heid of the nixt missive.

---

24   This should be 'to'.

12

The same day anent the 38 act of the said last generall conventioun of burrouis ordining the burghes of Dunfreis and Selkrig to send thair commissioneris to the burghe of Lochmaben for visiting of the said burghe and trying [p. 69] of thair commoun landis. The saidis burghis having reportit thair diligence, the present commissioneris ordinis the same to be continowed as ane heid of the nixt missive, and that Johne Kennedie of [Halleaths][25] ballie and Johne Hendersone late commissioner to the parliament or aither of them compeir to the nixt generall conventioun and bring with them the great chartour of thair burghe to be cognosced be the commissioneris of the burrowis under the paine of 20 lib. And this to be ane heid of the nixt missive.

13

The same day the commissioneris present ordinis the burghe of Abirbrothok[26] to produce to the nixt generall conventioun thair great chartour quhairby thair mylne and uther landis may be redeimit to thair commoun good under the paine of 20 lib. And this to be ane heid of the nixt missive.

14

The same day anent the first act of the particulare conventioun of burrouis hauldin at the burghe of Edinburgh the 23 Julii 1646 ordining the burghe of Glasgow to produce to this generall conventioun the persones following to witt Williame Hyndshaw, Robert Alexander, Charles McLane, John Looke,[27] Charles Gray and Niniane Paterson actit[28] the conventioun hauldin at the burgh of Dunbartane, and ordining the burghe of Linlithgow to produce James Adie, James Craufurd and Johne Andro, and ordining the burghe of Air to produce Robert Boyd, and the burghe of Kirkcaldie to produce Niniane Mure, and the burghe of Quenisferrie to produce David Ramsay and Thomas Spittill, all of them for transporting of steple wair to unfrie pairtis as the said act beares. The present commissioneris unlaus the burghe Glasgow and Kirkcaldie ilk of them in the sowme of fourtie pundis for contraveining the said act and ordinis both the said burghes to produce the pairties contraveineris respective to the nixt particulare conventioun of burrowis to abyd thair censure under the paine of ane hundreth pundis ilk burghe. And this to be ane heid of the nixt missive.

---

25 See Young, *Parliaments of Scotland*, i, 388–9.
26 Arbroath.
27 It is possible that this is 'Cooke' but see G.F. Black, *The Surnames of Scotland* (Edinburgh, 1993), 443 which shows the name 'Looke' in Glasgow in the sixteenth and seventeenth centuries, and see act 38 below.
28 This should probably be 'at'.

15

The same day forsameikill as the present commissioneris of burrowis representing the manie prejudices they sustine throw the increas of unfrie people
[p. 70] and for the frequent use of the frimen in losseing, loading and
traffequeing at unfrie places quhilk evills doeth fall out in dafault of the not
executioun of the actis of parliaments and actis of burrowis formerlie maid
against unfrie traderis and friemen resorting and trading in unfrie places and
especiallie the act of parliament maid in anno 1592[29] and actis of burrouis
maid at Dumbartane 1643 and at Perth in anno 1646. Therfoir they have
apppointit nominat and electit and deputit the persones underwrittin for
executing the saidis actis of parliament and burrowis maid anent transgressores thairof viz: Johne Binnie merchand burges of Edinburgh and Johne
Semple of Dumbartane with the proveist or in his absence ane of the ballies
of the said burghe quhair they meitt quho is appointit to joyne with them
as supernumerarie to which thrie or any tua of them being ane quorum
this commissioun is grantit against all such transgressores as duell or reseid
besouth the reaver of Tey;[30] and Mr Johne Hay provest of Elgin and James
Peddie merchand in Monros to take ordor with the transgressores dwelling
benorth Tey. To which persones the commissioneris presentlie conveined
for themselffis and in name of the haill burrowis of this kingdome gives full
power and commissioun to the effect foirsaid with power to them to uplift
the unlawis incurred be the saidis transgressores to make accompt thairof to
the nixt generall conventioun of burrowis, and appointis the places of trying
and punissing of such offenderis to be such burghis of ilk shyre quhair the
offenderis doe most frequentlie reside or quhair the saidis commissioneris in
thair discretioun sall think most fitting and convenient for the advancment
of the busines. And the proveist of the said burghe, or in his absence ane of
the ballies, to be supernumerarie with the saidis commissioneris and to assist
and concure with them in trying and punishing of the saidis offenderis by
imprisoning the saidis persones till they sall underley and fulfill the sentance
givin out against them or quhat els the saidis commissioneris sall desyre to
be done for the effect foirsaid. Provyding alwayis, lykas it is heirby provydit
and speciallie declaired, that this present commissioun is and sall be without
prejudice to everie burghe to use thair diligence and liberties in trying and
punishing the offenderis within thair boundis, so being the same be done
and execut befoir the foirsaidis commissioneris be entred in executing thair
commissioun in ilk shyre and burghe respective. And ordinis this commissioun to last and indure to the nixt generall conventioun of burrowes and

29 *RPS*, 1592/4/96.
30 The Tay.

the saidis commissioneris then to report thair diligence. And this to be ane
heid of the nixt missive.

Octavo Julii 1647

16

The same day the commissioneris of burrowis presentlie conveaned taking
to thair consideratioun [p. 71] the great losse and prejudice that the wholl
kingdome, bot speciallie the estate of burrowis, is lyk to susteine by the
great aboundance of clipped money and light money[31] latlie brought in
into the samyn and lyke to be brought more and more in without ane
remedie be provydit. The saidis commissioneris haveing this day supplicat
the lordis of privie counsell for ane remeid aganist the saidis prejudices and
the saidis lordis taking the samyn to thair consideratioun hes appointit ane
committie of thair awne number to joyne with such of the burrowis as the
present commissioneris sall think maist meit to appoynt for laying doun the
best coursses and remedies aganist the foirsaidis eivills. Thairfoir the saidis
commissioneris nominats the persones following to joyne with the saidis
lordis viz: James Rucheid for Edinburgh, Sir Allexander Wederburne for
Dundie, George Porterfield for Glasgow, George Bell for Linlithgow, Gilbert
Richard for Air, Johne Semple for the burghe of Dumbartane and Mr Johne
Hay for the burghe of Elgin to meit and convein with the saidis lordis of
privie counsell for setting doun solid and effectuall courses for preveining
the said imminent evillis and to report thair diligence heiranent. And this to
be ane heid of the nixt missive

17

The same day appointis the personis following to reveise the agentis comptis
viz: George Pearsone and James Fentoun for Edinburgh, Robert Davidsone
for Dundie, James Peddie for Monros, Alexander Black for Anstruther Eister
and Mr William Dunbare for Forres and to report.

18

The same day anent the supplicatioun gevin in be Mr William Arnot,
sone laufull to umquhill James Arnot merchand burges of Edinburgh,
late maister of the conserjarie hous at the steiple port off Campheir, for
being preferred to the said chairge in place of his said umquhill father. The
present commissioneris consideering the qualificatioun of the said maister
William findis the desyre of the said supplicatioun reasonabill and theirfoir
admittis and ressavis him maister of the said conserjarie hous during thair

---

31 Clipped money = coin which had been trimmed as a way of obtaining precious metals
    while trying to maintain its face value. Light money was probably coin which did not
    appear to be clipped but contained insufficient metal.

will and pleasure, will[32] provisioun he obey and fulfill all injunctionis sett doun to any preceiding masteris of the said hous or heirefter to be sett doun be the commissioneris of burrowis in thair generall and particulare conventionis, and the said maister Williame to enjoy all priviledgis and injunctionis belonging to the said place, who compeirand acceptit in and upoun him the said office and gave his aith *de fidelie administratione*[33] and obleidges him for obeying of the saidis injunctionis formerlie sett doun to the saidis maisters and especiallie the [...] injunctioun sett doun to [...]call[34] at the tyme [p. 72] of his admissioun for provyding ane honest and sufficient dyet to the merchandis and skipperis resorting to the said port with beiff, muttoun and strong Inglishe beir, deseart and uther honest necessares. For the whilk caussis the saidis commissioneris finding in regaird of the change of wyne that the allowance of eight stuires[35] then prescryvit for ilk maill[36] not to be a competent allowance at this tyme. Therfoir they allow the said Mr Williame tuelff stuires for ilk maill, he provyding the tables sufficientlie as said is. And for the said Mr Williame his obeying and fulfilling the saidis injunctionis sett doun or to be sett doun and for doing his duties as said is in the said place Mr Samuell Johnstoun of Sheynes, Mr Henrie Foules and Mr Alexander Kynneir are become cautioneris and souerties for him, whome the said Mr Williame obleidges him to releive of all damnage and expenssis which they may sustein or incurr through thair becoming cautioneris as said is. And ordinis thair clerk to writt to the toun of Campheir and to the conservator for entering him to the said hous in thair names and ordinis ilk burghe to be advertized for causing thair inhabitantis resort thither to keip thair dyit at the said hous and to be requyred for sending ther commissioneris sufficientlie instructit with thair advyse and with such uther injunctionis as salbe neidfull to be enjoyned to the maister of the said hous and the saidis burrowis and the said Mr Williame Arnot to report thair diligence to the nixt generall conventioun. And this to be ane heid of the nixt missive. Sic subscribitur Mr William Arnot, Mr Samuell Johnstoun, Henrie Foules, Mr Alexander Kynneir.

19

The same day ordinis the agent to warne Alexander Downie and [...][37] cautioneris for umquhill Robert Greirsone sometyme factor at Campheir

---

32 This should be 'with'.
33 Literally, 'concerning faithful administration', i.e. he was promising to carry out his duties with diligence.
34 Presumably this is the name of a former master of the conciergery house, although it has proved impossible to identify him. For a set of regulations, however, see *RCRBS*, ii, 428–31.
35 A stuiver was a Flemish coin worth one twentieth of a guilder.
36 Presumably this is 'meal'.
37 Although one name is implied, there is sufficient space for two.

to compeir to the nixt generall conventioun of burrowis for answering to
the complaint gevin in against the said umquill Robert be Alexander Lock-
hart and to report his diligence heiranent to the nixt generall conventioun,
quhairanent thir presentis salbe to him ane sufficient warrand. And this to
be ane heid of the nixt missive.

20
The same day anent the supplicatione gevin in be the burgh of Jedburgh
craving help for reparatioun of kirk and calsies, continues the same to be
ane heid of the nixt missive.

[p. 73]
21
The same day anent the report maid be the burgis of Edinburgh, Stirling, Air
and Quenisferrie of the convenience of the reparatioun of the harberie of
Blacknes conforme to the supplicatioun given in be the burgh of Linlithgow
for that effect, continowis the same also to be ane heid of the nixt missive.

22
The same day anent the supplicatioun gevin in be the burghe of Couper
for reparatioun of thair towbuith, continowis the same also to be ane heid
of the nixt missive.

23
The same day anent the supplicatioun gevin in be the burghe of Kirkcaldie for reparatioun of thair harberie and for ane licence frome the present
commissioneris of burrowis to them for releif of thair present pressing burdingis to make use of thair commoun mure and unlaboured landis belonging
to them by setting the same out either in few, long takes or uther wayis.[38]
The saidis commissioners continowis the first pairt of the said supplicatioun to be ane heid of the nixt missive and ordinis Sir Alexander Wedderburne for Dundie, Captane Andro Watsone for the burghe of Bruntiland,
Mr Robert Cunninghame for the burghe Kingorne and David Symsone for
the burghe of Dysert or any thrie of them to meit and convein at the said
burght of Kircaldie and to make inspectioun of the said unlaboured landis
and give thair best advyse and assistance for setting out the same or any pairt
thairof to the hiest and best availl and the burghe of Kirkcaldie to be the
conveiner of them, under the paine of tuentie pundis ilk burghe. And this
to be ane heid of the nixt missive.

---

[38] This seems to mean 'in feu, long tacks (i.e. leases) or otherwise', rather than 'in a few long
     tacks', hence a comma has been inserted to clarify the sense.

24

The same day anent the supplicatioun gevin in be James Cunninghame merchand burges of Edinburgh craving the reversioun of the place of the conserjarie hous at the staple port of Campheir in caice of the desertioun of that place or deceis of the said Mr William Arnot now admittit to the said place. The present commissioneris agries and consentis to the desyre of the said James his supplicatioun and that in caice foirsaid, the said James sall be presentit to the said place als frilie in all repsectis as ane uther who possessed the same befoir.

[p. 74]

25

The same day the present commissioneris taking to thair consideratioun the great losse and prejudice which the haill burrowis of this kindome have heirtofoir susteined and are lyke daylie mair and mair to sustein by such of thair factoris at the steiple of Campheir who aither be thair awne misguiding or uther accidentis fall in decay of thair estate becomes unable to give sufficient compt reckning and payment to the merchandis who imploy and intrust them with thair estates, the whilk danger and prejudice is cheiflie occationed be the neglect of the burrowis in not taking heid frome tyme to tyme of the sufficiencie of the saidis factoris thair cautioneris and be not obleidging the saidis factoris to be lyable in thair awne persones to the lawis of this kingdome provydit against evill debteris, such as hoirning poynding and captioun. For remeid quhairof the saidis present commissioneris ordinis that the saidis haill factoris present and to come sall inact themselffis at the said staple port of Campheir or quhairsoever els they salhappen to be to be lyable in thair personis meins and estate to the lawis of this kingdome in the same maner as the samen wold strick against them if they wer heir residing in this kingdome and for the saidis merchandis farder securitie ordinis that ilk factor sall inact and obleidge himselff that if the commissioneris of burrows sall find thair cautioneris either to be deceased or insufficient that at the end of ilk thrie yeiris they sall be obedient to renew thair souerties being requyrit thairto and that the present factoris be actit for that effect presentlie to the conservator. And ordinis thair clerk to writt heiranent to the conservator and that he may immediately inact all the saidis factoris accordinglie and the said conservator and clerk to report thair diligence to the nixt generall conventioun of burrowis. And this to be ane heid of the nixt missive.

26

The same day anent the 11, 12, 13 and 14 actis of the last particulare conventioun of burrouis hauldin at Edinburgh the 14 of November 1646 concerning the proces intentit be Gilbert Lawder and Thomas Cranstoun, ballies of the burghe of Lawder, againes George Hair, Alexander Wilkinsone, Alexander Hog, Alexander and Thomas Murrayis, George Woodheart, Johne Allan, Charles Brysone, Johne Scott and Richard Allane, inhabitantis of the said burghe, for ane ryot committed be the saidis inhabitantis against the saidis magistratis. The present commissioneris having cairfullie perused the proces betuix the saidis pairties at the said late particulare conventioun and now againe having hard the report of ane new committee of thair awne number who wer appointit to examine farder the haill particularis of the said busines, they find the ryot committit be the saidis inhabitantis defenderis [p. 75] to have bein most insolent, incompatible, tending to the ovirthrow and casting louse of all magistracie and government within burghe and thairfoir ordinis the said Alexander Wilkinsone, Alexander Hog, George Hair, Alexander Murray [...][39] and Johne Allane presentlie convened and compeirand befoir them to pas to warde and thairin to remaine till thair farder censure. Quhilk being done the saidis commissioneris efter farder consideratioun of ane new bill givin be the saidis prisoneris unlawes Alexander Wilkinsone in the sowme of tua hundreth pundis money of this realme, the said Alexander Hog in the sowme of ane hundreth pundis and the said George Hair in the sowme of fourtie pundis, quhilk they ordaine to be presentlie peyit to the agent befoir thair persones be releeved out of prisone, and the said agent to be chairgit thairwith in his accompt. And the said Alexander Murray and Johne Allan thair personis to be keipit in prisone till farder deliberatioun. And that nane of the saidis haill prisoneris be releeved of ther imprisonment till they procure the saidis ballies whome they have offendit to interceid for them. And appointis the burghis of Hadingtoun, Jedburghe and Selkrig to meit at the said burghe of Lauder upoun ane certaine day and thair to take exact notice of their government of the said burghe and to labour for ane reconciliatioun and settling of all business betuix the saidis pairties and the burghe of Lauder to be the conveiner, and to report to the nixt generall conventioun of burrowis. And this to be ane heid of the nixt missive.

Nono Julij 1647

27

The quhilk day anent the seavinth act of the said last generall conventioun of burrowis hauldin at the burghe of Pearth in Julij 1646 ordining Johne Irving late ballie of Dumfreis to content and pay to the agent the sowme of ane hundreth pundis for his contumacie in not compeiring befoir the said conventioun and ordining him to make satisfactioun to Johne Cuninghame

---

39   There is a space here sufficient for two names, so it would appear that at least three of those named above were judged not to have been involved. That the specific punishments list only the same five as are named in the second list might even suggest that only five were found to have misbehaved.

late ballie of the said burghe of the wrong done to him in presence of the counsell of the said burghe betuix and Michaelmes nixt thairefter under the paine to be declaired incapable of magistracie within the said burghe thairefter. The commissioneris present having imprisoned the said Johne Irving with[in] the tolbuith of Edinburgh and taking to thair serious consideratioun the humble supplicatioun of the said Johne Irving and that he had givin satisfactioun [p. 76] to the pairtie offendit by craving him pardoun for his offence and contenting for his chairges, lykas in the presence of the haill conventioun he did againe desyre pardoun frome the pairtie offendit and each of them taking utheris by the hand promising heirefter evir to keip heartie friendshipe and leive ane with uther as brethren, and that the said Johne Irving did also desyre pardoun of the offence done be him to the haill burrowis as being ane scandalous and evill exemple of abusing magistracie. Theirfor the present commissioneris remittis and dischairges the said Johne Irving of any penaltie or uther censure quhatsumevir quhairunto he was lyable to the burrowis or to the pairtie offendit especiallie be these tua actis (to witt) the 7 act of the said last generall conventioun hauldin at Pearth in Julij 1626 and the 6 act of the conventioun of burrowis hauldin at Lanerick in Julij 1645.

28

The same day the present commissioneris taking to considderatioun that severall of the burrowis who wer heighted at the alteratioun of the taxt roll at the last generall conventioun hauldin at Perth did compleine of thair inhabilitie to undergoe thair proportioun thairof, quhilk taxt roll nevirtheles be the lawis and customes of burrowis could not be changed till the full and compleit ending of thrie yeiris efter the altering thairof. The saidis commissioneris for remeid of the saidis grievances and being willing to give all just satisfactioun to the saidis compleineris unanimuslie condiscendis to dispence at this present with the said law and custome in regaird of the great dificulties and changes of these tymes and ordinis ilk burghe to send thair commissioneris sufficientlie instructit to the nixt generall conventioun anent the alteratioun of the said taxt roll. And in the meanetyme that letteris of hoirning be direct be the agent aganes all such burrowis as have not payit thair proportionis of the publict dewes and that frome hence furth the pairties not paying be lyable to him in payment of annualrent for the same during the not payment thairof and the agent to report his diligence heiranent. And this to be ane heid of the nixt missive.

29

The same day anent the tenth act of the particulare conventioun of burrowes hauldin at Edinburgh in November 1646 anent the supplicatioun givin in be Johne Forbes in name of the burghe of Innernes craving (in regaird of thair great sufferingis) to be eximed frome payment [p. 77] of any publict dewes and anent ane new supplicatioun for ane voluntar contributioun for reparatioun of thair church, brig[40] and harborie The present commissioneris declairis that thair cane no exemptioun be grantit frome payment of the publict dewis and ordinis the same to be peyed and as for the voluntare contributioun, they continow the samyn to the nixt generall conventioun of burrowes, recommending in the meane tyme to the said burghe the reparatioun of the said brig in sic maner as the same doe not altogidder decay. And this to be ane heid of the nixt missive.

30

The same [day] anent the sext act of the said particulare conventioun ordining Frances Forbes nominat and chosin to be proveist of the burghe of Forres, Johne Wachester, Johne Layng, Coline Hay and Mr William Dumbare ellectit ballies and Thomas Warrand ellectit clerk to accept of and exerceise thair said severall offices, and anent the supplicatioun presentlie gevin in be the said Mr William Dumbare to the burrowis against severall unrulie and oppressing gentilmen thair nighbouris who intrude thamselfis upoun the magistracie of the said burghe and have so minaced and threatned the saidis magistratis as they cannot peaceablie exerce thair saidis offices without remeid be provydit, and also craving in name of the said burghe ane exemptioun frome payment of anie publict dewes and ane exemptioun frome sending commissioneris to the generall or particulare conventiounis of burrowes togidder with some relieff and support for releiff of thair present burdingis. The present commissioneris for repressing the insolencies of the saidis troblsome nighbouris ordinis the burghe of Edinburgh, Linlithgow and Haatoun,[41] and such utheris of thair number for the present as salhappen to be in toun with the agent, to concurre with the said Mr William Dumbare, compleiner, for purchasing of letteris frome the lordis of his Majesties privie counsell or frome the committee of estatis against the saidis defenderis quhairby they may be brought to condigne punishment. And for the better settling of thair magistracie appointis Johne Forbes for

---

40 There is a mark in the MS which looks like a hyphen between these two words but, since Inverness had only one bridge across the river Ness, it seems most likely that the mark was intended to act as a comma.

41 Probably a mistranscription of Haddington. The word is hard to discern partly because of the downstroke of an 'h' from the line above interfering with what seems to be an inital 'H' followed by what looks like the letter 'a' twice, although there is a dot above the second 'a'. The word is split between two lines, the last four letters being 'toun'. Haddington ('Hadingtoun') seems most likely, given its proximity to the other two in this list, while the three are also the head burghs of the three divisions of Lothian (Linlithgowshire, or West Lothian; the shire of Edinburgh Principal, or Midlothian; and the constabulary of Haddington, or East Lothian, each of which elected its own commissioners to parliament).

the burghe of Innernes, Mr Johne Hay for Elgin, Gilbert Mair for Bamff and Johne Ros for Nairne under the paine of 20 lib. ilk burghe to convein at the said burghe off Forres on Wednisday immediatlie befoir Michaelmes nixt and thair to give thair best advyce concurrance and assistance for settling the mag[ist]racie thairof upoun merchandis and tradismen within the said burghe conforme to the lawis and constitutionis of the burrowis secluding thairfra all such gentilmen [p. 78] who violentlie wold intrude themselfis thairin and grantis to the said burghe for the space of thrie yeiris nixtto-come [ane][42] exemptioun frome compeiring be ther commissioneris to anie generall or particular conventiones of burrowis provyding alwayis they than fullie content and pey thair proportioun of all publict dewis and anent thair releiff craved of thair burdingis continowis the same to the nixt conventioun of burrowis. And this to be ane heid of the nixt missive.

31
Exemptioun burgh of Cullen for thair paying thair publict dewis.[43]

32
The same day anent the 25 act of the said last generall conventioun ordining the actis of parliament anent measuris of victuall and peis of bread against foirstalleris and regrateris and that ilk burghe produce in writt thair exact diligence heiranent under the paine of 20 lib. ilk burghe as at lenth is conteined in the said act. Continewis the same to be ane heid of the nixt missive.

33
The same day anent Quhythorne thair exemption continoued to the nixt conventioun.[44]

34
The same day anent the fyft act of the last generall conventioun of burrowis ordining the burghis of Edinburgh, Glasgow and Air to concurre and assist the agent and the commissioneris of the burghes of Irving and Ranfrew in proscecuting and discussing of the suspentionis reasit be unfrie traderis against them till the finall dicisioun thairof. The present commissioneris continowis the same to be ane heid of the nixt missive.

---

[42] This is an ampersand, suggesting that the copyist misinterpreted 'ane' in the original as 'and'.
[43] This and a number of the following entries have clearly been abbreviated, probably to save effort in copying acts which deal with routine issues.
[44] An abbreviated entry.

35

The same day the present commissioneris understanding that quhairas [be]
the 3 act of the last generall conventioun of burrowis at Perth in Julij last it
was statute and ordinit that they sould be unanimous and continow in thair
voycing in parliament and conventionis of estatis that the said unanimitie
of voycing hes bein by some mistaken and interpret to ane sinistrous sense.
Thairfoir they have thought fitt heirby to declair thair ingenuous and true
meaning, sense and intent thairin and that [p. 79] the said unanimitie of
voicing was and is onlie meanit in matteris concerning the priviledge and
liberties of burrowis, not limiting anie of their neighbouris in the friedome
of thair voice conforme to thair conscience and knowledge in any uther
publict or private busines quhatsumevir as becomes all frie memberis of
parliament of [anie][45] estate. They declair that they naither had nor have any
uther meaning or intentioun thairintill bot as is abone exprest.

Decimo Julij 1647

36

The whilk day compeirit Alexander Wilkisone, Alexander Hog, George
Hair, Alexander Murray and Johne Allane inhabitantis of the burghe of
Lauder and conforme to ane act of this present conventioun did confes and
acknowledge thair wrong and injurie done be them to the magistratis of the
said burghe to the evill exemple of utheris to committ the lyke quhairfor
they wer presentlie unlawed and the saidis personis compeirand actit themselffis of thair awne consentis for thair good behaviour not to comitt the
lyke heirefter bot sall carrie themselfis deutifullie and honestlie to thair
magistratis in all tyme coming under the paine of 500 merkis ilk persone
toties quoties[46] and to be declaired [...][47] of any place within the said burghe.
And siclyke that they sall compeir befoir the commissioneris appointit to
meitt at the said burghe of Lauder and acknowledge the said wrong done
to thair magistrats in presence of the counsell of the said burghe, and the
burghe of Lauder to convein the saidis commissioneris so appointit betuix
and the first of September nixt. And this to be ane heid of the nixt missive.
Sic subscribitur Alexander Wilkisone, Alexander Hog, George Hair, Alexander Murray, Johne Allane.

37

The same day anent the fyft act of the particulare conventioun of burrowis
hauldin at Edinburgh in Julij 1646 quhairin the commissioneris then

---

45   There is no space in the MS but the sense requires this insertion.
46   As often as it shall happen, i.e. for each offence.
47   The missing word(s) probably convey the sense of being banned from holding office and
     may have been 'incapable of holding'.

conveined repelled ane declinator gevin in be James Weir in name of Thomas Cuninghame, James Eillies and himself, factoris, in the actioun perseuit be Walter Ranken, merchand in Dundie, against them and ordining the saidis defenderis to compeir personallie to the nixt meitting and particulare conventioun to be hauldin at Edinburgh the fourth [of November][48] 1646 yeiris with certificatioun to them gif [p. 80] they failyie that that said complaint sould be haulden as confest, as at lenth is continit in the said act. Lykas the commissioneris conveined in the said conventioun at Edinburgh the fourth of November last, the said Walter Ranke[n] compeired and was desyrous to insist in his proces bot upon certaine letteris and excusses sent to the saidis commissioneris then conveined be the conservator and factoris and they being most willing to deall most favorablie with them in thair absence did accept the saidis excuses in satisfactioun for ther absence at that tyme. Lykas they be thair saidis letteris straittlie chairged them for their personall compeirance to this present generall conventioun. Theirfoir the saidis commissioneris then conveined did desist frome deceiding and determining of the said caus till this present generall conventioun to the effect that they being personallie present might be hard and sua the caus might be equitablie decydit, lykas the said compleiner at the dounsitting of this present conventioun generall desyrit that his proces might be discust and justice efter so long and many dayes might not be farder delayit. The present commissioneris, out of the respect they carie to the defenderis being absent and being informed that long agoe they wer shipped and upon thair voyage, delay the hearing of the said matter till it might appear quhither or not the defenderis sould at all compeir befor the dessolveing of this present conventioun. And now this being the last day of this present conventioun and that thair is no appeirance of the saidis defenderis thair coming to this countrie to compeir as said is, thairfoir the present commissioneris have fund it necessar to consider and debait the laufulnes and consequens of the said declinator and efter long debait and serious consideratioun findis the foirsaid declinator to be unlawfull and of dangerous consequens and ordinis in all tymecoming that na factour henc[e]furth sall take upoun him to declyne the judgement of the burrowis in anie caus betuix any Scottis merchand or Scottis skipper and thene upon anie pretence or pretext quhatsumever, and that all the present factoris do furthwith enact themselffis thairto under the paine of deprivatioun of thair places and that all factoris that salbe admittit heirefter sall particularlie enact themselffis heirto befoir thair admissioun. As for the materiall pairt of the proces, the said Walter Ranken having provine the verificatioun of the warning usit against the defender be Mr Alexander Guthrie our generall clerk, and Johne Scrymgeor merchand burges of Dundie and the saidis defendantis not compeirand, the saidis present commissioneris grantis to the said perseuer the benefite of the certificatioun continit in the said act halding the saidis defenderis as [p. 81] confest quhairupon the said Walter Rankit [sic] askit instrumentis, and decernes conforme to the tennor of the supplicatioun and ordinis ane decreit to be gevin out be the clerk heirupoun in forme as effeiris, quhairanent thir presentis sall be his warrant.

38

The same day anent the first act of the said particular conventioun of burrowis haulden at Edinburgh in Julij 1646 quhairby Williame Hyndshaw, Niniane Patersone, Robert Alexander, Charles McClane, John Cooke[49] and Charles Gray wer ordinit to be producit be the magistratis of the burghe of Glasgow to this present conventioun under the paine of 40 lib. Compeirit George Porterfeild, commissioner for the burghe of Glasgow, Niniane Patersone, Robert Alexander, Johne Cook, and Charles Gray whome after examinatioun the saidis commissioneris sentenceth as followis viz: assoilyies the burghe inregaird of the commissioneris diligence and the said Robert Alexander inregaird of his aith, and unlawis Ninian Patersone, Charles Gray and Johne Cooke ilkane of them in the sowme of 20 lib. to be presentlie payit to the agent, and ordinis the said Johne Cooke for his irreverend speiches to be incarcerat in the towbuith of Edinburgh for the space of 48 houres, and ordinis the said toun of Glasgow to produce the said William Hyndshaw and Charles McClane befoir the nixt conventioun of burrowis to answer for thair contraventioun under the paine of 40 lib. for ilk persone. And this to be ane heid of the nixt missive.

39

The same day anent the supplicatioun gevin in be Gilbert Richard commissioner of the burghe of Air anent the wrongous imprisonment of Johne McLetchie ane of thair burgesses be the ballie of Irving within thair towbuith of Irving and in caus[ing] him subscryve ane act and fund Adame Cuninghame burges of Irving cautioner for the sowme of tua hundreth pundis for the alleadgit breaking of thair liberties, for the quhilk sowme the said Adame Cuninghame his cautioner hes intentit actioun against the said Johne McLetchie befoir the lordis of sessioun, that thairfoir the present commissioneris wold ordaine the burghe of Irving to caus the said David [sic] Cuninghame desist frome his persute befoir the lordis of sessioun and to take up his proces and exhibit the same to the nixt generall conventioun

---

49   The initial letter could be an 'L' (see act 11 above, where the name is clearly written with an initial 'L'), yet it is clearly a 'c' in at least one of the later occurrences in *this* act. Perhaps the copyist was unsure about the name that he was confronted with.

of [p. 82] burrowis. The saidis commissioneris finding the desyre of the said supplicatioun reasonable and Adame Dunlop commissioner for the said burghe of Irving voluntarlie consentit thairto and promitted to caus the said Adame Cuninghame to desist frome any farder persute against the said compleiner till the nixt generall conventioun of burrowis. And this to be ane heid of the nixt missive and bothe the saidis pairties to sent thair commissioneris instructit to prosecut the said complaint and Air to answer thairto and to produce thair right of the road of Fairlie.

40

The same day anent the supplicatioun gevin in be the burghe of Lochmaben craving help for building ane towbuith and anent the agentis concurrance with them anent the intendit reductioun of such persones thair rights who possesse thair commoun landis and that ane letter may be writtin to my Lord Queinisberrie for granting ane perambulatioun of marches betuix his lordshippis tenents and them. The saidis present commissioneris ordinis thair generall clerk to writt the generall Queinisberrie[50] anent the said perambulatioun and also ordinis thair agent to concurre with them anent the intenting of the said reductioun, and the said clerk and agent to produce ther diligence heiranent to the nixt generall conventioun, and continowis the help for thair wairdhous to the said nixt generall conventioun. And this to be ane heid of the nixt missive.

41

The same day forsamekill as the estates of parliament at the last sessioun of the last triennial parliament did grant and give to the royall burrowis ane assignement of fyftein thousand pundis sterling, by and attour tuentie thousand pundis formerlie grantit, being in all the sowme of threttie fyve thousand pundis sterling to be receaved out of the brotherlie assistance frome the honourable[51] of the parliament of England and that in pairt of and towardis the reparatioun of the burrowis losses be sea and land. The present commissioneris understanding perfytlie and taking to thair serious consideratioun the heavie conditioun of all the particulare burghis within this kingdome and how necessar it wer they paid some supplie, that also that businesse in such consequens in so dangerous tymes ar oftentymes miscaried

---

50   James Douglas, 2nd earl of Queensberry, was not yet in favour with the Covenanting regime at this point. He had joined the royalist uprising under James Graham, 1st Marquis of Montrose in 1645 (which perhaps explains his apparent militarly rank) and was imprisoned, being released only in March 1647, having paid a hefty fine (*RPS*, 1646/11/391). He was leading a Covenanting regiment in the summer of 1645 as a 'colonel' (*RPS*, 1645/7/24/79) but may have been made a general by Montrose.

51   There must be something missing here but it is not clear what. It could be 'houses' or 'members'.

for laik of cairfull and handsome convoyance and knowing perfytlie the
fidellitie and abilities of the persones underwrittin have thairfoir thought
fitt to make choise lykas they be thir presentis appointis, nominatis and
chooses Archibald Sydserff, [p. 83] Sir Alexander Wederburne and Johne
Short to be thair commissioneris factores and doeris for the spidie and
cairfull going about the procureing be all fair and possibill means payment
of the said sowme of thrittie fyve thousand pundis sterling. And for the
better enabling them in that imployment gives them or anie tua of them
full and ample power be them selffis, or such utheris as they sall pleas to
intrust and send with thair orderis, to uplift and ressave the said sowme or
anie pairt thairof, to grant recompence, allowences, fies or rebaitmentis at
thair discretioun for procuring of the samyn in sic maner and forme as if it
wer their owne particulare busines quhilk salbe discomptit of the money to
be received and the remander thairof is to be keiped be them till the nixt
generall conventioun of burrowis and they to make compt thairof at that
tyme and of their diligence quhairanent thir presentis salbe unto them ane
sufficient warrand. And this to be ane heid of the nixt missive. And with
power to them or anie whome they sall appointt to receive the said money
and give dischairges thairupoun.

42

Dispensatioun for Lanerick of thair unlaw of 20 lib. for not produceing their
rightis to the agent ordining the agent to concure with them in the persute
against the possessouris of their commoun landis. Heid nixt missive.[52]

43

Dispensatioun for Wigtoun with 20 lib. of unlaw dew be the sext act of this
conventioun.[53]

44

Exemptioun burghe of Nairne poynding thair dues.[54]

45

The same day anent the supplicatioun gevin in be John Aslowan against
Thomas Cuninghame conservator for underselling of certaine merchand
guidis. The present commissioneris ordinis the said conservator to be warnit
to the nixt generall conventioun of burrowes to answer to the said complaint.
And this to be ane heid of the nixt missive.

---

52 This suggests an abbreviated act.
53 An abbreviated act.
54 An abbreviated act.

46

The second [sic] day anent the supplicatioun givin in be the burghes of Air, Anstruther Eister, Abirbrothok against the agent for not payment of certaine sowmes [p. 84] ordanit be the burrowis to be payit be them. The present commissioneris ordinis the said agent to be vigilant and cairfulll in seiking in the publict deues and furth of the readiest thairof to pey the saidis burghes and the saidis burghes to give in to the nixt generall conventioun of burrowis ane perfyt accompt of all such moneyis so be them received and how the same hes bein imployed and the agentt to report his diligence heiranent. And this to be ane heid of the nixt missive.

47

Grantis exemptioun to the burghe of Bamff and remittis the payment of the publict deues. To be ane heid of the nixt missive.[55]

48

Grantis exemptioun to the burghe of Taine poynding thair publict dewes.[56]

49

The same day anent the supplicatioun gevin in be the burghe of Lanerick craving ane supplie for repairing thair kirkis, towbuith and calsies, the present commissioneris continowes the same to be ane heid of the nixt missive.

50

The same day anent the supplicatioun gevin in be the burgh of Lauder for some proportioun of the fynes quhairin Alexander Wilkinsone, Alexander Hog and George Hair wer adjudgit conforme to the [26] act [of] this present conventioun towardis the reparatioun of thair towbuith. The present commissioneris ordinis the agent to ressave thair haill fynes extending to the sowme of thrie hundreth and fourtie pundis and furth thairof to give the said burghe the sowme of tua hundreth pundis and the samyn sall be allowed to him in his accomptis and to be chairged in his accomptis with the rest of the saidis fynes and the said burghe to give ane accompt to the nixt generall conventioun of burrowes how the samyn is imployed. And this to be ane heid of the nixt missive.

51

The same day anent the supplicatioun givin in be the sex ordinare messeris for ane recompence for thair service at the last sessioun of parliament. The

---

55   Probably an abbreviated act.
56   An abbreviated act.

present commissioneris ordinis [the agent][57] to pey to ilk ane of them the sowme of ten merkis and the samyn salbe allowit to him in his accomptis.

[p. 85]

52

The same day anent the supplicatioun givin in be the burght of Monros craving supplie towardis the reparatioun of their herberie. The present commissioneris continowis the same to be ane heid of the nixt missive and ordinis the burghes above mentionat[58] to visit the said harborie and to report their diligence heiranent.

53

The same day the comptis of Johne Ramsay being fitted and calculat, wee under subscriveris findis Johne Ramsays dischairge to extend to the sowme of 3611 lib. 11s. 10d. and his recept to extend to the sowme of 3066 lib. 13s. 4d., so we find the compter superexpendit in the sowme of 544 lib. 18s. 8d., quhilk sowme with the sowme of 43 lib. 10s as for the annualrent thairof fra the date therof to the [...] day of Junij nixt 1648 extending in the haill to the sowme of 588 lib. 6s. 8d. the burrowis wilbe resting to him and thairfoir ordinis ilk burghe to send thair pairtis thairof to the nixt generall conventioun of burrowis conforme to the taxt roll.

54

The same day anent the supplicatioun givin in be the burghe of Rosemarkie[59] desyring the samyn to be enrolled amongis the number of the royall burrowis. The present commissioneris continowis the samyn to be ane heid of the nixt missive and this to be without prejudice to the liberties of the burghe of Innernes.

55

The same day anent the 25 act of the generall conventioun hauldin at the burghe of Lanerick in Julij 1645 ordining the burghis of Edinburgh, Perth, Dundie, Abirdein, St Androis, Monros, Elgin, Irving and all uther burghis that had trad in Piccardie and Normandie in France to produce to the nixt generall conventioun of burrowis ane perfyte accompt of all goodis transportit to and fra Piccardie and Normandie be the burghe of Aberdein frome the yeir of God 1637 and be the rest of the saidis burghis frome the yeir of

---

57 There is no space in the MS but the sense requires this insertion.
58 This might indicate an abbreviation of the act, since there are evidently no other burghs mentioned in this act nor is there an earlier act relating to Montrose harbour.
59 Resistance from Inverness meant that Rosemarkie (combined with nearby Fortrose) was not enrolled by the convention until 1660: Pryde, *The Burghs of Scotland*, no. 64.

God 1642. The present commissioneris ordinis the same to continow to be
ane heid of the nixt missive.

[p. 86]

56

The same day anent the second act of the last particulare conventioun
of burrowis haulden at Edinburgh in Aprill 1647 yeiris concerning ane
complaint given in be severall merchandis of the great prejudice they sustein
throw the great infringment of breaking of our ancient priviledges and
liberties within the kingdome of France by augmenting of our customes and
laying of heavie impositionis upoun our countriemen in the name of strangeris. The present commissioneris appointis Johne Trotter, James Rucheid,
Sir Alexander Wederburne, Johne Short, Johne Forbes, Johne Semple and
Gilbert Richard to speak and conferre with Monsieur Montrule the French
agent thairanent and procure frome him such letteris in recomendatioun of
the merchandis in France and with power to them for themselffis and in
name and behalf of the haill burrowis to direct the saidis letteris to Thomas
Thomsdrie in Rowan[60] as they sall think good and to desyre him to prosce-
cute the samyn that the natioun may not longer suffer as they presentlie doe
and the chairges deburset be him sall be rembursed them.

57

Reffuissis to give exemptioun to Rothesay and continowis their unlaw
adjudgit in a former act to the nixt generall conventioun. Heid nixt missive.[61]

58

The same day the commissioneris appointis the proveist of Edinburgh
Archibald Sydserff, Sir Alexander Wedderburne, Johne Short, Gilbert Rid
and William Thomsone to go in name of the haill royall burrowis to the
lord Register[62] and to give him humble and heartie thankis for his lordshippis manie favouris and services done to them, and the agent to delyver
such moneyis to them as they sall think most fitt for ane recompence to
his lordship and his service, quhilk moneyis sall be allowed to the agent in
his accomptis.

59

The same day anent the supplicatioun givin in be Johne Johnstoun in name
and behalf of the burghe of Dumfreis craving that the commissioneris of

---

60 Rouen, capital of Normandy.
61 This suggests an abbreviation of the original record.
62 The clerk register (Sir Alexander Gibson of Durie) was in charge of the records of
   government and was principal clerk to both parliament and the privy council.

burrowis presentlie conveined wold grant to the said burghe thair consent
for impetrating frome his majestie ane grant and gift of the imposts usuallie
collectit at the bridge for upholding thairof for the space of 19 yeiris. Quhilk
desyre the present commissioneris findis most reasonable and gives thair
consent thairto according [p. 87] to the tennor of the former act grantit to
that effect.

60

The same day the present commissioneris desolves this present conventioun
and affixis the nixt generall conventioun to begin at Burntiland the first
Tuyisday being the [...] day of Julij with continowatioun of dayes and ordinis
thair clerk to direct the generall missive to the said burghe and ordinis them
to warne the saidis haill burrowes for conveining at the said burghe at the
foirsaid tyme. Sic subscribitur.[63]

---

63   The name of the signatory, the clerk to the convention of burghs, is not recorded here but,
     as is shown in the next record, he was still clerk in August 1647. The office was given to
     Mr Andrew Ker in 1649 (*RCRBS*, iii, 338), with the last recorded appointment before that
     having been in 1610, when Alexander Guthrie was appointed joint clerk with his father,
     also Alexander. Burntisland council minutes recommence immediately after this entry.

Act of a Particular Convention of Burghs
at Edinburgh, 7 August 1647[1]

[exterior]
The conservatoris overturis

[interior]
In the particular conventione of borrowes haldin at the burght of Edinburgh the sevint day of August I^m vi^c fourtie sevin yeiris be the commissioneris thair conveind anent the remonstrances given in be the conservator of the necessitie of some new actis to be maid at the nixt generall conventione of borrowes for reforming of all former and avoyding of all future abusses at the said stapleport and for the better regulating of the same. Thairfor the saidis commissioneris ordaines ilk burght to be requyred for sending of thair commissioneris sufficientlie instructit with thair best advyse to the nixt conventione of burrowes to be haldin at Bruntreland the first Tuysday of Julii nixt with continowatione of dayes for seting doune certane actis and statutis for that effect, and speciallie for taking to thair consideratione the particullaris following, sett downe be the said conservator in his remonstrance, viz: First that all maisteris of schippis be straitlie bund and inacted to tak na staple wairis aboord bot such as ar directed to the staple port, and that he or thei upon thair arrayvell at any uther place within the Low Cuntries sall be obleidged to send or have guid securitie for sending of all the staple wairis thither without delay or reteining any pairt thairof, and to report ane nott or testificatt under the hand of the conservator, his deputt or clerk verefieing the same, under the payne and unlaw of fyve hundrethe merkis scottis for everie voyage at quhat tyme or place soever he or they sall be interpond and convicted.

2. That all merchandis and burgessis within this kingdome be inhibited and forbiden to schip or laidin any staple wairis into Duch schippis or any uther straingeris vessellis, bot upon sufficient securitie given in be them to the magistratis of the burght quhair they reseid that such guidis ar by them intendit unto na uther place and that they sall not be offered, vented nor sold bot at the staple port and to returne ane certificate thairof in name and under the payne and unlaw as before expressed.

3. That upon complaint of the conservator or his deputtis upon ane merchand skipper or utheris who have brokin the staple and hes escaped his hand and punhischment in the Law Cuntries, the pairtie offender sall be cited befoir

---

1 ACA, Press 18, Bundle 88. This act is written on one side of a single piece of paper.

the burrowes and thair make present satisfactione for his fault to the rigour and find sufficient cautione and be referred bak to the conservator.

4. That all merchandis and factoris at the staple port be discharged from selling any staple wairis to any persone or persones who sall be knowen or proven to have brought or caused to be brought for thair use directlie or indirectlie any playdes, skinnes or hydis, cairsayes or any uther sort of Scottis staple wairis ather at Roterdame, Amsterdame or any uther place within the sevinteine provinces by the staple port, under the payne of ane unlaw of twentie pundis grit Fleymis money for everie thyme they sall transgress.

5. That they be lykwayes inhibited under the payne and unlaw foirsaid to sell any staple wairis to any Dutch burgesses, merchandis or factoris to be laid up for thair awin use or in commissione and for the use of any persone or persones who sall be knawin to be ane treader or byer of staple wairis in uther places nor at the staple port directlie nor indirectlie.

6. That some trustie persones be ordaind to tak notice of the staple wairis shipped at Leith especialie of skines, fast and louse, and that he or they delyver ane nott under thair handis to the skipper specifieing the markis and number of everie cord of skins (especialie such as ar brokin up) and of hydis and uther staple wairis according to thair equalitie, and that the skipper in absence of the said appoynted persones be straitlie injoyned to tak no guidis aboord that so the multitude of such pleyis at the staple port may be eschewed.

7. That in caice that any guidis be dampnified or inlaicking in any schip the factoris or pairtie interessed be informed to give notice thairof to the conservator within four dayes efter the unleidening of the said schip, or els to have actione against the skipper.

8. That the factoris be injoynd in thair awen persones or speciall servandis in thair absence to attend upon the livering and loading of schippis and that the skipperis or thair clerk be tyed to doe the same.

9. That na merchandis or thair servandis or any persone quhatsumever not being laufullie admittit sall be suffered to pay the factor in bying or selling any staple wairis but what belongis to themselffis and for thair owin and maisteris accompt to the end that the factoris may better attend upon thair calling and not be constraned to play the merchand or thift[2] utherwayes for thair leiving contrair thair aith and act of burrowes.

10. That the factoris be injoyned to meit at certane sett tymes especialie in October and Februar or upon any sudden alteratioun or fear of change in presence of the conservator to draw up ane commone informatione tuiching the pryces of all staple commodities and appeirances of the mercat that so uniformallie they may give noticed and trew advertisment to thair

---

2   i.e. to absent onself.

merchandis in tyme according to the said right and prescript, to which they ought to be tyed under ane certane penaltie and not to be suffered everie ane to writ of the esteate of the mercat at Randomes and oftintymes much above the reat for drawing imployment to themselffis to the grit prejudice of merchandis who efterwardis findis the fruit thairof.

11. That all skipperis cumming to the staple port with staple wairis be injoyned and obleidged to have ane formall chartor parttie for the pryce of thair conditioned fraucht subscrivit be ane competent nomber of his merchandis frauchteris to the end that all questiones arraysing ordinarlie upon the different writting of merchandis to thair factoris may be avoyded.

12. That the skipper immediatlie upon thair arrayvell at the staple port delyver thair coquettis to the conservator or his clerk to the end that the entres in the custome hous thair of all staple wairis may be maid be the conservator clerk and if na uther persone or persones be suffered to writt the same that so all disordor and inconvenientis arraysing thairfra may be prevented and eschewed.

13. That the merchandis assignementis upon the factoris and the factoris nottis and promeis for accompt of thair merchandis may be absolut payment to the merchandis and indwelleris in the Law Cuntries and especialie at the staple port and uther townes within the Ylle Walker, and that all factoris and merchandis be inhibited to bargaine with any in the said ylland that will not consent to the premissis.

14. That the conservator grant na warrandis of arreistment upon any persones guidis or moneyes unles the pairtie arreister find sufficient cautione to persew his actione in tyme convenient befoir the conservator court, and incaice of failyie or that efter the proces be intended, heard or discussed he be fund in the wrong to pay all cost, skaith, dampnage, interest, costis and expenssis of the said inocent defender.

15. That some course be takin for preventing straingeris shippis to incroach upon ony sea tread especialie these of the Low Cuntries who inregairde of thair pace with Spaine will ingross all to themselffis with thair grit floytis and saill our schippis clein out of the watteris, and thairfoir it is necessar to raise sum new dewties and impositionis upon all Duchis and utheris straingeris schippis cumming into or goeing fra any port of this kingdome with any coallis to pay so much besydis everie chalder.

16. That na factor nor privileidgit persone or persones residenteris at the staple port salbe cited personallie to compeir befoir the burrowes at the instance of any merchant or indweller in Scotland unles the pairtie compleiner first hath fund and put in sufficient cautione and surtie for all lawfull chairges expenssis and dampnages of the pairtie cited at the discratione and modificatione of the burrowes incaice he be fund inocent and absolved.

17. To consider of the many inconvenientis and prejudices which must of necessitie follow upon the lait act of burrowes quhairby it is ordained

and declaired that the factoris and utheris of the natione in all caussis and materis quhatsumever betuixt them and any subject of the kingdome salbe lyable and obleidged to compeir and answer upon any complaint befoir the burrowis whom they ar to acknowledge thair onlie judges and not to declyne from them.

18. To tak unto serious consideratione the grit discredite which redoundis to our natione in generall and how prejudiciall it is to all merchandis and especialie to young begineris trafequeris in the Low Cuntries that efter the deceise of such persones in this kingdome as ar knawen responsablie, yit thair airis and executoris think na schame to defraud the creditoris in the Netherlandis and force them to ane compositione and quytting of ane pairt of the sowme befoir they will enter in any termes of any aggriement for payment with them, which grit abuse and hurtfull cheating must be in tyme luiked to crosched.

19. To reasone upon the motione of the magistratis of Campheir concerning coallis and uther commodities of this kingdome to be declared staple wairis and to considder of the reasones pro et contra mentioned in my missive letters writtin to the burrowes thairanent in December 1645 and whither or not I sall chirrisch the said motione of the magistratis at Campheir.

20. To tak notice that thair was thrie yeiris since ane cord of skins landit at Campheir without any letter or commissione to any factor, quhairfoir I ordaind Robert Greirsone to resseave and sell the same and be comptable thaifoir untill such tyme as the rycht awner should appeair, and I did giff adverteisment to the lordis commissioneris of burrowes in Julii 1645 becaus yit thair is none cum to lay clame to the said cord of skynis or frie money thairof which amountis to thriescoir pundis Flymes, whairfoir I desyre the wholl commissioneris of the wholl burghtis respective to inquyre for the right proprietare of the same and examine him about the mark, number, tyme of schipping and in quhat ship and at quhat port they war leadit, and upon certificatione thairof I sall caus the frie money to be payit or answerit to him or to any having his ordor and sufficient prooffis to the effect foirsaid.

21. To dispose upon the halff of fourtie fyve lib. fyfteine schillinges Fleimis money for the burrowes use seased upon by me in March last and deteined under confiscatione for a pairt of the pryce of certane staple guidis sent to Roterdame and sold be ane merchant in Edinburght thair.

Which haill articles abovewrittin ar remitted to be considerit upon be the generall conventione, and the clerk to report his diligence heiranent to the nixt generall conventione. And this to be ane heid of the nixt missive.

Extract furth of the register of the actis of the burrrowes be me Mr Alexander Guthrie, generall clerk to the saidis burrowis witnessing heirto this my signe and subscriptione manuell. AG

MISSIVES FOR
GENERAL CONVENTIONS

Missive for the General Convention of 1641
at Linlithgow[1]

[exterior]
To the richt honorabill our loving friendis and nichtbouris, the provest, balleis and counsall off the brugh off Aberdene

[1st page]
Rycht honorabill our loving brethren efter our hertlie comendatioun, quhairas the commissioneris of burrowes of this realme in thair last generall conventioun haldin at the burgh of [Irving][2] appointit the nixt generall conventioun to be and begine at this our burght of Linlithgow the fifth day of Julij nixtocum this instant yeir of God I^m vi^c and fourtie ane yeiris with continuatioun of dayis for treating upon the common effairis and [...] continewed heidis and articlis following to be resolved, determined and concluded thairin

{1 Your commission satisfeis this article}
First that ilk burgh send thair commissioners sufficientlie instructit with

---

1   ACA, Press 18, Bundle 88. This is written on a single piece of paper, folded once to make four pages. Some of the text is very faded and difficult to read, and some has been lost completely as a result of damage to the edges of the paper. There are marginal numbers and some annotations in a darker ink. Although the numbers are sequential, not every item is numbered, so the numbers probably refer to items in the written instructions given to the burgh's commissioner to take with him, a common practice for conventions of both burghs and parliaments. This bundle also contains examples of some of these letters and there are others published in L.B. Taylor (ed.), *Aberdeen Council Letters*, 6 vols. (Aberdeen, 1942–61): see, for example, vol. i, 160–64, from 1618. Although of considerable interest, none is reproduced here because they are not records of the convention of royal burghs but of the burgh of Aberdeen.
2   Although this is too faded to read, the general convention of burghs of 1640 met at Irvine (see, for example, Burntisland Council Minutes, NAS, B9/12/7, fo. 99r; Glasgow Council Minutes, GCA, C1/1/10, 26 June 1640).

thair commissiones subs[crivit be thair] magistrateis and common clerk, testefieing thair commissioners to be men fearing god and [of the true] religione presently in publict professed and allowed be the lawis of this realme [...] suspitione in the contrair, expert in the commone effaires of burrowes, burgesses and ind[welleris] in thair burcht, bearing all portable charges with thair nychtbouris within the same and [...] such thay may tyne or win in all thair causes under the paine of twenttie pundis [...] to be payit to the burrowes.

{2} Item that ilk burght send with thair commissioner thair diligence in intimating to thair nychtbouris the fourttie twa act of the last generall conventioun of burrowes [... at the] burght of Stirling the tent day of August 1638 yeiris anent thair ratificatioun of [the cove]nant of the cuntrie and in fulfilling and obeying of the same in all the heidis, claus[is and ...] thairof, under the paine of twenttie pundis ilk burght, conforme to the 5 act of the [last] conventioun haldin at the burght of Irving.

{3} Item that ilk burght send with thair commissioneris more exact diligence in wreate in re[...] and punisching thair outland burgesses, forstallers, regraitters, sellers without tickats [...] men usurping thair liberties and intimating to thair nychtbouris that that report is n[ot] ressavit verballie but in wreat allanerlie under the paine of twenttie pundis ilk burgh conforme to the tent act of the said last generall conventioune.

{4}Item that ilk burght send with thair commissioneris thair diligence in intimating and executing the 18 act of the said last generall conventioun discharging portage and dischairging all frauchting of schippis but with provisione expresslie to be conteined in thair chairtour pairtie that na marienar sall have portage thairin under the paine of fourttie pundis and that the burgh fund guiltie in not executing this act to pay ane hundreth lib. under the paine of twenttie lib. conforme to the said 18 act of the said last generall conventioune.

{5}Item that ilk burgh send thair commissioners sufficientlie instructit with thair best advys for suppressing of unfreemen and taking away the [cau]sis and wayes which doeth occasione thair increase under the paine of twentie pund ilk burgh conforme to the 30 act of the said last generall conventioun.

Item the burgh of Linlithgow to produce thair diligence in chargeing of new inhabitantis of Borrowstounnes and certaine uther places thairabout mentionat in the 3 act of the last generall conventioun of borrowis haldin at the burgh of Drumfermeling togither with the particular satisfactiones ressavit be them if any persones befor chargit with thair names, under the paine of twenttie pundis conforme to the 6 act of the said last generall conventioune.

Item the burghe of Glasgow to procure ane attestatioune in wreat of the residence of Williame Fergasone with them befor Michaelmes last or ane act of thair court depryving him of thair libertie under the paine of fourttie pundis conforme to the 7 act of the said last generall conventioun.

{6}Item ilk burght to report thair diligence in intimating to thair nychtbouris the elevint act of the said last generall conventioune anent the suspending of the conservatour his dewis, as also the burghis of Edinburgh, Peirth, Dundie, Aberdein, Linlithgow, St Andrewis, Glasgow and Haddingtone in meitting at the burgh of Edinburgh efter the dissolving of the last generall conventioune and prosecuting the deprivatioune desyrit to be intendit againes the said conservatour conforme to the elevint act of the said last generall conventioune.

Item the burgh of Aberbrothock to produce thair diligence in causing of Thomas Ir[...] indweller at Arbillot,[3] Johnne Johnstone at the kirk of Carmyllie[4] and such utheris that dwellis w[ithin the] parochines of Panbryd[5] and Henderkellir[6] find cautioune for desisting from usurping [the liberties of] the frie royall burrowis and in prosecuting such suspentiouns as hes bein rasit be thame [...] under the paine of twenttie punds conform to the 12 act of the said last generall con[ventioune of burrowes].

Item the burghe of Forris to produce thair diligence in causing of Williame Leith indweller [in ...] in Murray to find cautioun to desist from usurping the liberties of the frie burrowis under the [paine of twent]tie lib. conforme to the 13 act of the said last generall conventioune.

Item the burgh of Stirling to produce thair diligence in prosecuting and discussing the s[uspensioun] raised be certaine inhabitantis of Faulkirk and uther thair unfriemen under the paine of 20 [lib. conforme] to the 14 act of the said last generall conventioune.

Item the agent to produce his diligence with the burgh of Wigtone by the advyse of the burght of Dundie anent the said burghis evidenttis with the

---

3   The parish of Arbirlot lies immediately to the west of Arbroath, Angus.
4   The parish of Carmyllie lies between Arbroath and Forfar, Angus.
5   The parish of Panbride lies immediately to the east of Carnoustie, Angus.
6   The parish of Inverkeilor lies on the coast between Arbroath and Montrose, Angus.

laweris advyse anent thair redres conforme to the 15 act of the said last generall conventioune.

Item the agent to report his diligence in uplifting fra the burght of Montrose the two unlawes [incur]red be theme conteined in the 16 act to the said generall conventioun as also in uplifting ane unlaw of [ane] hundreth pundis quhairin the said burght wes decernit conforme to the 21 act of the said generall conventioun.

Item the commissioneris that conveined at Edinburgh in November last to report thair diligence in proceeding in the matteris committit to them and conteined in the 17 act of the last generall conventioun, conforme to the same.

Item the burgh of Edinburgh to report thair diligence in requyring the haill burrowis for meitting before parliament in November last conforme to the 19 act of the said last generall conventioune.

Item the agent to report his diligence in uplifting from the burght of Innernes the unlaw [due] be thame conforme to the 22 act of the said last generall conventioune.

[2nd page]
Item Richard Cowpland in Haddingtoun to produce Samuel Wallace in Campheir his purgatioune of forstalling of victuall in the Law Countries in tyme of dearth in this cuntrie under his hand and aith befor the minister under the paine of ane hundreth pundis conforme to the 28 act of the said last generall conventioune.

Item the burghis of Linlithgow and Culross to produce thair diligence in trying if any indwelleris within this cuntrie be pairtinars with any Duchmen resorting to this cuntrie and cullering thair schipps under the name of Scottis schipps under the paine of 20 lib. conforme to the 24 act of the said last generall conventioun.

Item James Giles merchand in Edinburgh, Robert Peittersone merchand in Cowper and Thomas Ward pewderer in Edinburgh to produce to the nixt generall conventioun of burrowes James Eles, Thomas [Cu]nnynghame and James Weir, factor in Campheir to answer conforme to the 26 act of the last generall conventioune haldine at the burgh of Drumfermling under the paines thairin conteined conforme to the 25 act to the last generall conventioune.

[Item the] burghis of Glasgow, Dumbartane and Irving to report thair diligence in meitting at the burgh [of] Rothesay and trying of the estate of
the said burghe thair commone landis and how the same ar set fourth [in
tacks and for] how long and the said burght of Glasgow thair dilligence
in conveining the utheris conforme to the 26 act of the said last generall
conventioun.

[Item the] agent to report his diligence in prosecuting the actionis intendit
be the burrowis of [...][7] and Ramthrow[8] againes thair unfrie men conforme
to the 27 act of the said last generall conventioun.

[Item the] burghis of Edinburgh, Peirth, Dundie, Aberdein and Eglen[9] to
report thair diligence in [meeti]ng at the burghis of Innernes befor Michaelmes last, with thair diligence in setling the contraversies [in th]e said
burgh conform to the 28 act of the said last generall conventioun.

[Item] the agent to produce his diligence in concurring with the burgh of
Dumbarton contra the burgh of Glasgow conforme to the 29 act of the said
last generall conventioun.

{8} Item the burghs of Edinburgh, Dundie, Aberdein, Montrose, Innernes
and Eglene to produce thair accomptis and payment of the impost that all
goodis transported to and frome Piccardie and Normandie in France from
the first of Julie 1638 to the first of Julii nixt and the burght of Edinburgh
to charge themeselves in thair accomptis with the dewis restand be Williame
Dick and John Dowgall in anno 1637 conforme to the 44 act of the last
generall conventioune haldin at he burght of Dunfermling conforme to the
threttie twa act of the said last generall conventioune.

Item the burgh of Linlithgow to produce thair diligence in prosecuting
the reductione of the errection of the Queinisferrie with certificatioun
contained in the 33 act of the last generall conventioun and ilk burght
to send thair commissioners sufficientlie instructit in maner to the effect
contained in the said act.

Item the burgh of Linlithgow to produce thair diligence against the persones
mentioned in the 7 act of the last generall conventioun halding at Aberdein
the 4 of Julii 1637 in causing thame mak thair residence with thame or
depryving thame of thair liberties and in restraining tham from usurping the

7   Likely to be Dumbarton and/or Rutherglen.
8   Renfrew.
9   Elgin.

liberties of the frie royall borrowis under the paine of ane hundreth pundis conforme to the 34 act of the said last generall conventioune.

Item the agent to produce suchlyk diligence againes such unfree men mentioned in the 55 act of the last general conventioun haldin at the burgh of Stirling the sevint of August 1638 yeiris as he sould have produced to the commissioners conveined at Edinburgh in August 1639 yeiris.

Item the agent to produce his diligence in uplifting from Peiter Lair and James Reid his cautionar the soume of ane hundreth pundis conforme to the 37 act of the said last generall conventioun.

Item the agent to produce his diligence in uplifting from the burghe of Dumfermling the twa severall unlaws quhairin they wer decerned conforme to the 38 act of the said last generall conventioun.

Item the said burgh of Dumfermeling to produce thair diligence in putting thair commone landis to ane heicher availl then they ar at for the present under the paine of twa hundreth poundis conforme to the said 38 act of the said last generall conventioune.

Item the burgh of Ramthrow to produce thair farder diligence in taking and aprehending of Johne Mitchell and Patrik Watsone in Greinock under the paine of twenttie pundis conforme to the 40 act of the said last generall conventioun.

[Item] Thomas Muirheid to produce his accomptis of the impost grantit for defraying [the] ministeris stipend at Campheir upon the first of Maii 1640 yeiris togither with the [certifica]tiounis thairof and attestatioun of his acceptatioun and giving oath in maner contained [in the] act of elec-tioun conforme to the 43 act of the said last generall conventioun [and the …] act of the last generall conventioun haldin at Dumfermeling and Andro Lowthian and Arch[ibald] Pattene, Andro Muirheid, Johne Denholme and Alexander Muir his cautioneris to produce the said Thomas with his accomptis to the nixt generall conventioun in maner foirsaid conforme to the same.

Item Robert Griersone to produce his accomptis of his intromissioun with the said impost from the first of Maii 1640 to the first of Maii 1641 in this instant yeir of God with the certificatiounes thairof and attestatioun of his compeirance and making faith in maner conteined in his act of electione conforme to the said 43 act of the said last generall conventioun.

Item the burgh of Dingwall and Alexander Bane thair commissionar to produce the said burghis band and to the effect conteined in the 44 act of the said last generall conventioune.

Item Johne Semple in Dumbartone and Henrie Miller in Kirkaldie, cautioneris for the said Alexander Bane to produce the said towne of Dingwallis band conforme and to the effect contained in the said 44 act of the said last generall convention.

Item the burgh of Irving to send with thair commissioners ane trew relatioun of [3rd page] the estate of thair burgh, the number of craftis and craftismen thairin and maner of government of the same. As also the craftismen of the said burgh to send ane cled with power frome them[10] anent the supplicatiounes givin in be them at the last generall conventioun conforme and to the effect contained in the 45 act of the said last generall conventioun.

Item the agent to produce his diligence in uplifting the unlawes incurred be the burghes of Bruntayland,[11] Brichene, Selkirk, Aberbrothick,[12] Taine, Culross, Bamffe, Forfar, Nairne, Forres, Cullene, Annan and Lochmabane conforme to the 49 act of the said last generall conventioune.

Item the agent to produce his diligence in uplifting of the unlawes incurred be the burghis of Kirkaldie, Innerkeything, Wigtoun, Aberbrothock, Elgen, Taine [...] Whytthorne, Forfar, Nairne, Forres, Ruglein,[13] Sanchair, Cullen, Annan, Kilrenn[ie, Loch]mabene, Galloway[14] for being absent from the conventioun haldin at Edinburgh [...] last conforme to the 12 act of the said conventioun.

Item the burghe of Dumfermeling to produce the forme of the elect[ioun of thair] magistrates at Michaelmes last and to have proceided thairintill conforme [to the actis] of the borrowis maid anent thair electioune conforme to the 13 act of the said [conventioun] haldin at Edinburgh in November last.

{9} Item the agent to produce his diligence in uplifting the unlawes incurred b[e the] burghes of Dundie, Aberdein, Montrose, Peibbles and Jedburghe for being absent from the [conventioun] haldin at Edinburgh in

---

10   i.e. to send a person clad with power (empowered).
11   Burntisland.
12   Arbroath.
13   Rutherglen.
14   New Galloway.

Januarii last: and sicklyk his diligence in uplifting the unlawis incurred be the burghes of Linlithgow, St Androwes, Cowpar, Dumfermeling, Culross, Bruntailand, Kirkaldie, Dysart, Caraill and Dumbar for depairtting befor the dissolving of the said conventioune.

{10 disassent}[15] Item ilk burgh to send thair commissioners sufficientlie instructit to give answer to the supplicatioun givin in be the burght of Wigtone craving helpe for putting up thair bell and belhous and repairing of thair streitis and bridge, and the burghis of Dumfreice Kilcubright and Whithorne sall report thair diligence in visiting of the said towne with thair opinione anent the necessitie of the saidis work conforme to the 47 act of the said last conventioun.

{11 disassent} Item to the supplicatioun givin in be the burght of Irving craving help to the reparatioun of thair bridge and utheris necessar common work within thair burght conforme to the 51 act of the said last generall conventioun.

{12} Item ilk burgh to send with thair commissioners thair pairt of the sowmes of money underwrittin conforme to the taxt roll, viz: of the sowme of twa thousand merkis with ane yeiris interest for thair commissionaris chairges that past to Newcastell conforme to the 20 act of the last generall conventioun. Item of the sowme of ane thousand pundis granttit for support of the towne of Kirkcubricht ilk burght that hes not payit the same conforme to the 31 act of the last generall conventioun and 9 and 10 acts of the particular conventiouns haldin at Edinburgh in Januarii last. Item of the sowme of four hundreth pundis grantit to the burght of Dumbar conforme to the 39 act of the last generall conventioun. Item of the sowme of ane hundreth and thrie scoir 3 lib. vi s. iiii d. restand to the agent conforme to the 46 act of the said last generall conventione. Item of the sowme of ane hundreth merks granttit to Alexander Macaitnay; with your pairt of the clerk and agent fees under the paine of twenttie pundis ilk burgh for ilk severall faillie by and attour thair pairt of the said severall sowmes conforme to the said severall actis maid thairanent.

Thairfoir we earnestlie intreat and desyr your wisdomes to send your commissionars sufficientlie instructit in the haill premissis and for keipping of the [said] conventioun as ye tender the weall of the estate of the burrowes and [under the] paine of twenttie pundis incais ye failyie. Sua

---

[15] This is a note instructing Aberdeen's commissioner to vote against any support for Wigtown and the same instruction is repeated in the next item.

resting till farder [occasioun] we bid yow heartillie fairwell from our burght
of Linlithgow the […] day of Apryll 1641 yeiris.

Your loving friends and [neighbouris] the provest, baillies and [counsall] of
the burght of Linlithgow, [subscrivit] be Robert Ker our [commoun clerk]
at our command
Robert K[er]

Missive for the General Convention of 1643
at Dumbarton[1]

[Exterior]
To the rycht honorabill and our loving bretherein the proveist baillies and counsall of the burgh of Abirdein.

[1ˢᵗ page]
Rycht honorabill and loving bretherein efter our heartilie commendatioun, quhairas the commissionaris of the burrowis of this realme in thair last generall conventioun holden at the burght of Dundie hes appointed thair nixt generall conventioun to be and begin at this our burght of Dumbartan the 4 day of Julii nixt in this instant yeir of God 1643 yeires, with continuatioun of dayes, for treating upon the commoun affaires and als continued the headis and articles following to be reassouned examined and concludit thairin.

1 First that ilke burght send thair commissionar sufficientlie instructed with thair commissiounis under thair commoun seale and subscriptiounis of thair magistratis or commoun clerke testifeing thair commissiounaris to be men fearing God, of the trew religioun presently and publiklie professet and allowet be the lawes of this realme without any suspicioun in the contrair, expert in the commoun affaires of the burrowes, burgesses and indwellaris within thair burght, bearing all portable chairges with thair neighbouris within the same and that thei ar suche as may tyn or win in all thair causes under the paine of 20 lb. ilke burghe to be payet to the burrowes.

2 Item ilke burght to report thair diligence in writ in intimating the 4 act of the last generall conventioun of burrowes, ordaining all reportes to be maid that the same be done in suche ample maner that it may evidentlie appear that thair burghe hes gotten present knowledge of quhat was ordained to be reported conform to the tenour of the said act under the paine of 20 lb. ilke burghe to be payet to the burrowes.

3 Item ilke burghe to report thair diligence in writ in intimating the 6 act of the last generall conventioun dischairging burgesses from buying any forrain wair from any unfree men not burghesses of some of thair owine burghes with the knowledge of the burght to quhom thei pertaine under

---

1   ACA, Press 18, Bundle 70. This is a single sheet, folded once to make four pages. Unlike in the 1641 missive, each item is numbered consecutively.

the paines contained in the said act. As also in intimating that uther pairt of the said act dischairging all burgesses from recaving or admitting any quho ar not actuall resideris and indwellaris with them to be burgesses within thair burghes under the pain of ane 100 poundis. Dischairging also the proveist, bailyies, deane of gild or any of the counsall to vot thairto under the paine of 20 poundis ilke persone conform to the said 6 act under the paine of 20 lb. ilke burghe to be payet to the burrowes.

4 Item ilke burghe to send with thair commissionaris thair exact diligence in writ in taking notice of thair outland burgesses and depriving them of thair liberties and causing them find cautioun for desisting thairfra and if any sall be found undeprived or not under cautioun to incurr the unlaw of 20 lb. and that under the paine of 20 lb. ilke burghe conform to the said 7 act of the said generall conventioun.

5 Item the burghes that mett at Edinburgh efter the dissolving of the last generall conventioun to report thair diligence in supplicatting the lordis of counsall and sessioun anent the suspensioun betuixt the burghes of Glasgow and Dumbritan[2] conform to the 8 act of the said last generall conventioun.

6 Item the burghes that mett at Edinburgh efter the dissolving of the said last generall conventioun to report thair diligence and proceidinges in remeading of the new impositiounis laid upon Scottische goodis imported in the province of Normandie and Piccardie in Fraunce conform to the 9 act of the said last generall conventioun.

7 Item ilke burghe to send with thair commissionaris thair diligence in intimating the 10 act of the said last generall conventioun ordaining all burgesses that sall transport themselves furthe of the countrie *animo remanendi*[3] and sall tread within this cuntrie to be holden as unfree men and in putting the actes of parliament in executioun against them as unfree men conform to the said act under the paine of 20 lb. ilke burghe to be payet to the burrowes.

8 Item ilke burghe to send with thair commissionaris thair diligence in writ in intimating the 11 act of the said last generall conventioun ordaining the commissionar failyeing to report the diligence prescribed in the missive to incurr the unlaw of 20 lb. and that for ilk article and ordaines the commissionar reporter to pass to waird till the said unlaw be payet, as also ordaining the said act to be read in the beginning of the conventioun.

---

2 Dumbarton.
3 Intending to remain (abroad).

9 Item ilke burghe to send with thair commissionaris thair resolutioun anent quhat libertie or priviledge the freemen of eache burght hes with the free men of uther burghes or within the samen in buying or selling of forrain or hamel[4] wair conform to the 21 act of the said last generall conventioun.

10 Item the commissionaris that convened at Edinburgh the 16 of Julii last report thair diligence in conveining the most expert maisteris and marineris of this kingdome and devising of the remedies for preventing the ivellis and prejudice daylie occurring through the insolencie of marineris conform to the 56 act of the said last generall conventioun, 4 act of the particular conventioun holden at Edinburgh the 19 of Julii 1642.

11 Item the saidis commissionaris conveined at Edinburgh the 16 day of Julii last to report thair diligence in setting downe ane remeadie for suppressing that ivell of burgesses separating from thair magistrattis and supplicating uther judges in materis concerning the burght conform to the 57 act of the said last generall conventioun.

12 Item the commissionaris conveined at Edinburgh 14 of Julii last to report thair diligence in taking course for supplicatting his Majestie for remeading the exorbitant custom taken of the subjectis be the king of Denmarke in the Sound[5] conform to the 67 act of the said last generall conventioun and 9 act of the particular conventioun holden at Edinburgh the 22 of Julii last.

13 Item ilke burghe to send thair commissionar sufficientlie instructed for taking course for the readie executioun of the act of parliament maid against the importing of strong wateris within this kingdome[6] and under paine of escheit thairof conform to the 2 act of the particular conventioun holden at Edinburgh the 16 of Julii last.

14 Item ilke burght to send with thair commissionaris thair advice for ane setled course for remeading the entrense of unfree men and ivellis thereby growing and for prosecuting of the saidis remeadies conform to the 3 act of the particular conventioun holden at Edinburgh the 16 of December last.

15 Item ilke burght to send with thair commissionaris thair advice for

---

4   i.e. domestic.
5   The Øresund between Zealand in Denmark and Scania which is now in Sweden but was Danish until 1658.
6   An act banning the importation of alcoholic spirits was passed in November 1641: *RPS*, 1641/8/212.

setling ane constant and uniform water mett[7] throught the whole king-dome conform to the 3 act of the said particular conventioun holden at Edinburgh 16 of Julii last.

16 Item ilke burght to send thair commissionaris sufficientlie instructed for ordaining that it may be statut and ordanit through the whole burrowes of this kingdome that the inhabitantis of ilke burght be governed in all materis concerning the burght be the ordinar magistratis and counsall thairof and that thei be dischairged from putting with thair handis to any writtinges without thair consent under the paine of deprivatioun conform to the 6 act of the particular conventioun holden at Edinburgh the 20 Julii last.

17 Item the burghes that mett at Edinburgh the 20 of December last to report thair diligence anent the patent of the searchearie[8] obtained be Mr John Drummond conform to the 4 act of the said particular conventioun haldin at Edinburgh the 21 of December last and 5 and 8 actes of the particular conventioun holden at Edinburgh the 20 Januar last.

18 Item the agent to produce his diligence in uplifting from the burght of Innernes the unlaw incurred be them conform thairto.

19 Item the burght of Forres to produce thair diligence in prosecuting the suspensioun raisit at the instance of William Leeche of Torneway[9] against them under the paine of 20 lb. conform to the 12 act of the said last generall conventioun.

20 Item the burght of Wigtoun to report thair diligence in producing of the burghes that mett at Edinburgh efter the dissolving of the last generall conventioun thair principall chartour and the saidis burghes to report thair diligence in trying of the event of the said burght of Wigtounis actioun against the earle of Galloway conform to the 13 act of the said last generall conventioun.

21 Item the burgh of Stirling to produce suche like diligence against their unfree men and especiallie against the inhabitantis of Fawkirk[10] as thei sould have producet at the said last generall conventioun under the paine of 20 lb. conform to the 14 act of the said last generall conventioun.

---

7   A measurement for goods (especially grain and salt) that were transported by sea.
8   Searchers were customs inspectors.
9   Probably Darnaway, south-west of Forres, Moray.
10 Falkirk, Stirlingshire.

22 Item the burghes that mett at Edinburgh efter the dissolving of the last generall conventioun to report thair diligence in supplicatting the lordis of his majesties counsall anent the Dutche shippes resorting to this kingdome and collouring themselves under name of natives thairof conform to the 15 act of the said last generall conventioun and that ilke burght send thair advice thairanent conform to the 11 act of the particular conventioun holden at Edinburgh the 22 of Julii last.

[2ⁿᵈ page]
23 Item the burghtes of Aberdein, Air, Innernes and Montrois to report thair diligence in producing to the burghe of Edinburgh the 16 of August last thair accomptis of the impost of all goodis transported to or from Piccardie or Normandie in France under the paine of 20 lb. ilke burghe from the first of Julii 1638 to the first of Julii 1642 conform to the 16 act of the said last generall conventioun. And all uther brughtes quhome the said mater does concern to produce thair accomptis of the said impost with payment since the said tyme.

24 Item the burght of Lithgow[11] to produce thair diligence in persecuting of the suspensioun raisit be certan of thair unfree men against them conform to the 18 act of the said last generall conventioun.

25 Item the burght of Renfrew to produce thair diligence in taking and apprehending John Mitchell and Patrike Watsoun in Greinocke under the paine of 20 lb. conform to the 19 act of the last generall conventioun.

26 Item the agent to produce his diligence in prosecuting of the suspensioun raisit be William Bruce, William Andersoun and John Milne in Clackmannan, Patrike Chalmberis and William Horn in Alloway[12] conform to the 20 act of the said last generall conventioun.

27 Item the burght of Rothsay to report thair diligence in producing thair rytes and evidentis concerning thair commoun landis that some course may be taken for thair good under the paine of 20 lb. conform to the 22 act of the said last generall conventioun.

28 Item the agent to produce his diligence in recaving fra certan burrowes suche sowmes of money quhiche thei war addebtit to the preceiding agent mentiouned in the 23 act of the said last generall conventioun and in

---

11   Linlithgow.
12   Alloa, Clackmannanshire, not Alloway, Ayrshire.

recaving from him suche writes as he had concerning the burrowes conform to the said act.

29 Item the agent to report his diligence in sending David Drummond the sowmes geven in be the brughes of Carcadie and Petenweemes[13] for John Maistertoun and William Ritchisoun thair dewes in the yland[14] conform to the 27 act of the last generall conventioun.

30 Item the agent to report his diligence ayther in prosecuting or defending the burght of Dumbartanis rychtes against the burght of Glasgow conform to the 28 act of the said last generall conventioun.

31 Item the burght of Dumfermling to report thair diligence in putting thair commoun landis at ane heighe and greater availe at Martimes last under the paine of 20 lb. conform to the 30 act of the said last generall conventioun.

32 Item the agent to produce his diligence in prosecuting the actiounis intendit be the burghtes [of] Renfrew and Irwin to the finall decisioun thairof against their unfree men conform to the 31 act of the said last generall conventioun.

33 Item the clerke to report his diligence in notifieing to Thomas Muirhead factour in Camphir of quhat sowmes he was found resting to the burghtes at the said last generall conventioun, and to David Drummond how he was ordainet to uplift the same from him and to pay the minister that quhilk was restand him of his stipend conform to the 32 act of the said last general conventioun.

34 Item the agent to produce his diligence in uplifting from the burght of Montrois the sowme of ane 100 pound quhairin thei war adjudged in the said last generall conventioun. As also the said burght of Montrois to produce to the said nixt generall conventioun the form of the electioun of thair magistratis and counsall at Michaelmes last conform to the actes of parliament and burrowes and to produce the samen under the paine of 200 pound conform to the 35 act of the said last general conventioun.

35 Item the commissionaris that conveined at Edinburgh efter the dissolving of the last generall conventioun to report thair diligence in consulting with expert laweris how far the burrowes mycht proceid in the mater of the

13 Kirkcaldy and Pittenweem.
14 The island of Walcheren, in Zeeland.

conservatorie without offence to his Majestie or his prerogative with their proceidingis anent the procuring of the said place conform to the 37 act of the said last generall conventioun.

36 Item the burght of Edinburgh to produce [...] Bell, Robert Trottar, the burght of Glasgow to produce John Alcorne and John Patersone burgesses thair for transporting staple goods by the staple port in anno 1641 and 1642 under the pain of 29 lb. ilk burght conform to the 39 act of the said last general conventioun.

37 Item the burghtes that conveined at Edinburgh efter the dissolving of the said generall conventioun to report thair diligence in supplicatting the lordis of secreit counsall for letters for putting the 8 act of King James 6 his 20[15] parliament to executioun anent the qualitie of magistratis within burght against the burght of Innernes conform to the 40 act of the said last generall conventioun.

38 Item the burght of Carcubrycht[16] to produce thair diligence in compleating the worke of their bulworke to the nixt generall conventioun conform to the 41 act of the said generall conventioun.

39 Item the brughtes conveined at Edinburgh the 14 of Julii last to report thair diligence anent thair proceidingis of severall bussinesses intrusted to them conform to the 42 act of the said generall conventioun last.

40 Item the agent to report his diligence in uplifting from the burght of Innernes quhairin thei wer adjudged for depairting from the parliament and conventioun of burrowes conform to the 46 act of the said last generall conventioun.[17]

41 Item the burghes appointed for deviding the 4000 pound sterling obtained from England for outreiking of the shippis thair in the tyme of the lait troubles to report thair diligence and proceidingis thairanent with thair diligence in supplicating the lordis of those commoun burdingis anent thair uther loses. As also for repayment of the money advanced be the burrowes to the

---

15 RPS, 1609/4/27.The act was the eighth piece of public (and therefore published) legislation passed by the 1609 parliament.
16 Kirkcudbright.
17 The commissioner from Inverness was Mr Walter Ross, who had already been punished by his burgh for failing to be a diligent commissioner: see MacDonald, Burghs and Parliament, 56.

factoris conform to the 48 and 58 actes of the said last generall conventioun and 3 act of the particular holden at Edinburgh in Februar last.

42 Item the agent to report his diligence in uplifting from the burght of Rothsay the sowme of 40 lb. quhairin thei war adjudged conform to the 41 act of the said last generall conventioun.

43 Item ilke burght to report thair diligence in intimating to their neighbouris the act dischairging thair inhabitantis resorting to any uther place than the consergerie house at the staple port conform to the 53 act of the said generall conventioun.

44 Item thair clerke to report his diligence anent the writing to the minister and sessioun of the Scottis kirk at Camphir in taking upon them the payment of the ministeris dewes and collecting of the impost to that effect conform to the 54 act of the last generall conventioun.

45 Item the commissionaris conveined at Edinburgh efter the dissolveing of the generall conventioun to report thair diligence and proceidinges anent the complaint of the burght of Renfrew against the laird of Barscuib for incrotching upon thair wateris conform to the 60 act of the said last generall conventioun of burrowes.

46 Item the burght of Air to produce thair diligence in staying of John Malcolme, John Bynnie and John McMurrane in Mynniboll,[18] Quintin Dub and Andro Wrycht, Hew Mellintoun from usurping the liberties of free royall burrowes and if thei have decreites against them alreadie to produce thair diligence in prosecuting the actiounis of contraventiounis thairupon conform to the 62 act of the said last generall conventioun.

47 Item the clerke to report his diligence in writing to Patrik Synting factor at Camphir for uplifting the impost granted for defraying the ministeris stipend thair conform to the 65 act of the said last generall conventioun.

48 Item ilke burght to send thair commissionaris sufficientlie instructed for taking course for remeading the ivilles sustined throughe forstalleris and reducing of the mercattes to the dew dyattes and ordouris contained in evrie manis rychtes and actes of parliament conform to the 5 act of the said particular conventioun holden at Edinburgh the 19 of Julii last.

18 Maybole, Ayrshire.

49 Item the agent to produce his diligence in uplifting from the burght of Glasgow the sowme of 20 lb. quhairin thei war adjudged for thair commissionaris depairting befoir the dissolving of the particular conventioun holden at Edinburgh in Julii last.

[3rd page]
50 Item the burghes following to produce thair diligence in passing throughe the coalheughes of both the sides of the Water of Forth and in trying the price of the sayle and maner thairof wither be dailes, cartes, chaulders be loadis, weght or quhat each of the saids missours does contain in weght, or peckes, viz: the brughes of Lithgow and Queensferrie to try the heughes of Borrowstounness, Bonhard, Carrin, Kinglassi, Elphingstoun, Airth, Alloway, Kennet, Tulliallan, Valifield, Culrose, Torriburn, Lymekills, Innerkesting;[19] the burghes of Carcadie[20] and Dysert, the coalheughes of Dysert and Weemes; and the burcht of Haddingtoun the coalheughes of Elphinstoun, Falsyde, Trannent and Cockennie[21] conform to the 3 act of the particular conventioun holden at Edinburgh the 13 of Januar last and 2 act of the particular conventioun holden at Edinburgh in Februar last.

51 Item ilke burght to send thair commissionaris sufficientlie instructed for deciding of the complaint of the burght of Carcubrycht[22] against the burght of Wigtoun for recaving of Hew Minyies,[23] Andro McMillan and Robert Gib, indwellaris in Monygeff[24] to be thair burgesses, thei being under chairge at the instance of Carcubrycht, and the said burght of Wigtoun to send thair commissionaris sufficientlie instructit to answer thairto under the paine of 40 lb. conform to the 63 act of the said last generall conventioun.

52 Item ilke burght to send thair commissioneris sufficientlie instructed anent the altering of the taxt roll conform to the 64 act of the said last generall conventioun.

53 Item ilke burght to send thair commissionaris sufficientlie instructed for geving ane answer to the supplicatiounis following, viz: the supplica-

19 Bo'ness, Bonhard, Carron, Elphinstone and Airth are all on the south side of the Forth. Kinglassie, Alloa, Kennet, Tulliallan, Valleyfield, Culross, Torryburn, Limekilns and Inverkeithing are all on the north side of the Firth of Forth. The identification of 'Innerkesting' as Inverkeithing is only tentative and it is not clear why Kirkcaldy and Dysart were identified separately as (implicitly royal) burghs when both Culross and Inverkeithing were also royal burghs.

20 Kirkcaldy.

21 Elphinstone, Faside, Tranent and Cockenzie in East Lothian.

22 Kirkcudbright.

23 Menzies.

24 Minnigaff, near Newton Stewart, Wigtownshire.

tioun gevin in be the burghe of Arbroth for helping to repair thair harberie conform to the 58 act of the said general conventioun; of the burghe of Air for helpe to the reparatioun of thair harberie conform to the 61 act of the said last generall conventioun; of the burghe of Anstruther Ester craving help to thair harberie conform to the 43 act of the generall conventioun.

54 Item ilke burghe to send with thair commissioneris thair partes of the sowmes of money underwritten conform to the taxt roll, viz: the sowme of 396 pound 11 s 8d addebtit to Allexander Aikenhead for his bygane accompts; and of the soume of 300 merks granted to him conform to the 23 act of the said last generall conventioun and under the paines thairin contained.

55 Item with the soume of 400 merkes graunted to the burght of Irving for to helpe to the suppleing of thair bridge conform to the 49 act of the said last generall conventioun and under the paines thairin contained.

56 Item of the sowme of 600 merkes graunted to the burghe of Brunteilland[25] for help to the reparatioun of thair harberie conform to the 52 act of the said generall conventioun under the paines thairin contained.

57 Item with the sowme of 300 merkes graunted to the burghe of Wigtoun for ane helpe of putting up the bell and bellhouse and mending thair street and bridge conform to the 65 act of the said last generall conventioun.

58 Item with the sowme of ane 100 merkes graunted to Allexander McKaichnie with thair part of the clerke and agent fiallis under the paine of 20 lb. for ilke severall failyie by and attour thair severall partes of the said principall soumes.

Thairfoir wee earnestlie intreat and desires your worships to send your commissionaris sufficientlie instructed in the whole premisses and for keeping of the said conventioun as yow tender the weill of the estat of the burrowes, and under the paine of 20 lb. incase of failyie. So resting till farder occasioun wee bid yow hartily fairweel from our burghe of Dumbartan the sext day of Apryle 1643 yeiris.

Your loving freindis and neighbouris the provoist and bailyies of the burghe of Dumbartan subscriving be David Watsoun commoun clerk at our command.

DWatsoun

---

25 Burntisland.

Missive for the General Convention of 1648 at Burntisland[1]

[exterior]
To the richt honorabill and our loving freindis and neighbouris,
The proveist and baillies of the burgh of Abeirdeine these.

[1st page]
Richt honorabill and loving brethren and neighbouris,
Efter our heartily commandatioun, forasmeikill as the commissioners of the burrowis of this realme at their last generall conventioun haldin at the burght of Edinburgh has affixit and apointit their nixt generall conventioun to be and begin at this our burght of Brunteland the third day of Julij next with conteanewation of days for intreating of their commoun [effairis] and hes conteanewid the heads and articles following to be resolved, examined and concludid thairin.

1 First that ilk burght send thair commissioners sufficientlie instructit with thair commissiones under thair commoun sealis and subscriptions of thair magistrates or commoun clerk testefieing thair commissioneris to be men fearing God, of the trew religioun presentlie in publick professid without anie suspitioun in the contrair, subscryveris of the Covenant,[2] expert in the commoun effairis of burrowis, burgessis and indwellers within thair burght, bearing all portable charges with thair nightbouris within the samen and that they ar such as may tyn and wine in all thair caussis under the pain of 20 lib. ilk burgh to be payed to the burrowis.

2 Item that ilk burght send with thair commissioners thair exact diligence in wreat in keiping of the actis of pairliament maid anent measures of victual, pease of bread, and against all forstalleris, regraitters, sellers without tickitis and unfriemen usurping thair libertie under the pain of 20 lib. ilk burgh conforme to the 32 act of the said last generall conventioun.

3 Item, the burght of Monrose to produce thair diligence against thair unfrie treaderis within thair liberties and especialie within the toune of Stanehyve[3]

---

1   ACA, Press 18, Bundle 70. This missive consists of a single piece of paper, folded once to produce four pages.
2   This stipulation was not present in the missives for 1641 or 1643, so it must have been introduced between 1644 and 1646, as it was not enacted at the 1647 convention.
3   Stonehaven, Kincardineshire, a burgh of barony between Montrose and Aberdeen.

under the pain of 20 lib. conforme to the 4 act of the said last generall
conventioun.

4 Item the burght of Pearth to produce thair dilligence in wreatt against thair
unfrie treaders and in particular against Johne Drummound and Andrew
Lamb in Dunblane under the pain of 26 lib. conforme to the 3 act of the
said last generall conventioun.

5 Item the burght of Irvin to produce thair diligence in wreatt against unfrie
treaders in Kilmarnoch, Largis and uther unfrie places within thair boundis
under the pain of 20 lib. conforme to the 5 act of the said last generall
conventioun.

6 Item the burght of Wigtoun to produce thair decreit arbitral betwixt them
and the earle of Galloway togidder with thair diligence in the prosecutioun
thairof under the pain of 40 lib. conforme to the 6 act of the said last
generall conventioun.

7 Item the agent to produce his dilligence in obtaining the act of parliament
maid anent delapidatioun of commoun landis of burrowis to be ratified
conforme to the 7 act of the said last generall conventioun.

8 Item the burgh of Stirling with the assistance of the burghtis of Irving
and Ramfrow[4] to produce thair dilligence in discussing of the suspensions
reasid be certain of thair unfrie treaders against them conforme to the 8 act
of the said last generall conventioun.

9 Item the burght of Rothesay to produce thair diligence in producing
the rental of thair commoun landis pertaining to them and the maner of
thair outgiving thairof whether in fue rental or in take, the personis names
outgivers thairof and quhen the same was given out with the present rent
and estate thairof togidder with thair dilligence in conveaning[5] the burghtis
of Glasgow, Irving and Dumbartane befoir Michaelmes last with the saidis
burghts thair dilligence thairanent under the pain of 40 lib. ilk burght
conforme to the 9 act of the said last generall conventioun.

10 Item the burght of Lanrick[6] to produce thair dilligence in rouping of
thair commoun landis with the rest of thair commoun good with ane rentall
thairof, as also the burghtis of Glasgow and Pebles thair dilligence in being
present at the rouping of the saidis landis and the said burght of Lanrick

---

4 Renfrew.
5 The phrase 'thair burght' is written here in error.
6 Lanark.

to have proceidit in the electioun of thair magistrates at Michaelmes last conforme to the act of parliament and burrowis with ane testificat thairof under the pain of 40 lib. conforme to the 10 act of the said last generall conventioun.

11 Item the burght of Forfar to produce thair chartour of thair commoun landis and the burghtis of Dundie, Monross and Abirdein thair dilligence in visiting thair landis and the burght of Dundie in conveaning the uther burrowis under the pain of 20 lib. conforme to the 11 act of the said last generall conventioun.

12 Item the burght of Lochmaben to produce thair chartour of thair commoun landis and Jone Kennidie and Jone Hendersone to report thair dilligence anent the said chartour togidder with the present estate of the said burght under the pain of 20 lib. conforme to the 11 act of the said last generall conventioun.

13 Item the burght of Abirbrothock[7] to produce thair chartour of thair mylne and uther landis to be sein and considered be the saidis burrowis under the pain of 20 pound conforme to the 13 act of the said last generall conventioun.

14 Item the burgh of Glasgow to produce Williame Hyndshaw and Charles McLeane conforme to the 36 act of the last generall conventioun and the burght of Air to produce Robert Boyd and the burght of Lithgow[8] to produce James Adie, James Crawfurd and Johne Androw, the burght of Kircadie[9] to produce Niniane Mure, the burgh of Quenisferrie to produce David Ramsay and Thomas Spittill for transporting of staple goods to unfrie portis conforme to the 14 act of the last generall conventioun, ilk burgh under the pain of 20 lib.

15 Item Johne Binnie, merchand of Edinburgh and Johne Simple merchand in Dumbartane, James Peddie merchand in Monrose and Mr Johne Hay in Elgin to produce thair dilligence in executing the acts of parliament maid against unfrie treaderis conforme to ane commissioun gevin to them and 15 act of the said last generall conventioun.

16 Item the commissioneres that wer appointid anent the matter of clippid money and light money to produce thair diligence thairanent conforme to the 16 act of the said last generall conventioun.

---

7   Arbroath.
8   Linlithgow.
9   Kirkcaldy.

17 Item the agent to repoirt his dilligence heiranent in warning of Alexander Downie and [...] cautioners for Robert Greirsone factour at Campheir to answer at the instance of Robert and Allexander Lockhartis to the next generall conventioun conforme to the 19 act of the said last generall conventioun.

18 Item ilk burght to send thair commissioners sufficientlie instructit for remeiding the prejudices that the inhabitants of burrowis may sustain through the weaknes of the factors at Campheir or thair cautioners conforme to the 25 [act] of the said last generall conventioun.

19 Item the burghts of Jedburgh, Haddingtowne and Selkirk to report thair dilligence in meiting at the burgh of Lauder and in trying of thair governament and in labouring for reconciliatioun betwixt the members of the said burgh conforme to the 25 and 36 act of the said last generall conventioun.

20 Item ilk burgh to send thair commissioners sufficientlie instructit anent the alteratioun of the taxt roll conforme to the 28 act of the said last generall conventioun.

21 Item ilk burgh to send thair commissioners sufficientlie instructit for giving answer to the supplicatione givin in be the burgh of Innernes for contributioun for repairing of the church, harberie and bridge conforme to the 24 act of the said last generall conventioun.

[2nd page]
22 Item Johne Forbes for Innernes, Mr Johne Hay for Elgin, Gilbert Marre for Bamff, Johne Ros for Nairne to repoirt thair dilligence in concurring with the burght of Forres befoir Michaelmes next anent the setling of thair magistracie conforme to the 30 act of the said last generall conventioun.

23 Item ilk burght to send thair commissioneris sufficientlie instructit to give answer to the supplicatioun givin in be the burght of Quhythorne[10] craving exemptioun conforme to the 33 act of the said last generall conventioun.

24 Item the burghis of Air and Irving to send thair commissioneris sufficientlie instructit anent the complaint givin in be the burght of Air against the burght of Irving for incarcerating on of thair nightbouris within thair tolbuith and anent the proces intendit be the burght of Irving against the

10 Whithorn.

inhabitantis of Air conforme to the 39 act of the said last generall conventioun.

25 Item Archibald Sydserff, Sir Allexander Wedderburne and Johne Short to report thair dilligence anent the commissioun givin to them be the commissioneris of burrowis conveinid at the last generall conventioun anent the moneyis that they sould have receaved anent the reparatioun of the burrowis lossis conforme to the 41 act of the said last generall conventioun.

26 Item the agent to produce his dilligence in concurring with the burgh of Lanrick anent thair persuit against the possessoris of thair commoun landis conforme to the 42 act of the said last generall conventioun.

27 Item the agent to produce his dilligence in warning of the conservatour to the nixt generall conventioun for answering to the complaint givin in against him be Johne Asslowan conforme to the 45 act of the said last generall conventioun.

28 Item ilk burgh to send thair commissioneris sufficientlie instructit for giving answer to the supplicatioun givin in be the burght of Lanrick craving supplie for reparatioun of thair kirk, tolbuith and calsayes conforme to the 49 act of the said last generall conventioun.

29 Item the burgh of Lauder to send thair commissioner sufficientlie instructit with ane perfytt accompt anent the imploying of pairt of the fynes taking from certain of thair nightbouris and receaved be them from the agent for supleying of thair commoun workis conforme to the 50 act of the said last generall conventioun.

30 Item the burghis to send thair commissioners sufficientlie instructit to give answer to the supplicatioun givin in be the burghe of Monross anent the suppleying of thair harberie conforme to the 52 act of the said last generall conventioun.

31 Item ilk burght to send thair commissioneris sufficientlie instructit anent the inrolling of Rosemarkie among the number of the frie royall burrowis conforme to the 54 act of the said last generall conventioun.

32 Item the burghtis of Edinburgh, Pearth, Dundie, Abirdein, St Androis, Monrose, Elgin, Irving and all uther burghtis that had tread to and fra Piccardie and Normandie in Fraunce to produce ane accompt with the payment of his dewes conforme to the severall actis of burrowis maid thairanent of befoir and conforme to the 55 act of the said last generall conventioun.

33 Item ilk burght to send thair commissioneris sufficientlie instructit to give answer to the supplicatioun givin in be the burght of Jedburght craving supplie for repairing of thair kirk and calsayes conforme to the 20 act of the said last generall conventioun.

34 Item ilk burght to send thair commissioneris sufficientlie instructit to give answer to the supplicatioun givin in be the burght of Lythgow anent the reparatioun of the harberie of Blacknes[11] conforme to the 24 act of the said last generall conventioun.

35 Item ilk burght to send thair commissioneris sufficientlie instructit to give answer to the supplicatioun givin in be the burght of Couper for supplie for repairing of thair towbuith conforme to the 22 act of the said last generall conventioun.

36 Item ilk burght to send thair commissioneris sufficientlie instructit to give answer to the petitioun givin be the burght of Lochmaben craving help for bigging of ane towbuith within the said burght conforme to the 40 act of the said last generall conventioun.

37 Item ilk burght send thair commissioneris sufficientlie instructit to give answer to the supplicatioune givin in be the lairdes of Barnes and Ballogie[12] anent the establishing of salt to be staple waires conforme to the 11 act of the particular conventioun haldin at Edinburgh in August last.

38 Item the burghtis of Dundie, Bruntiland, Kinghorne and Dysert to report thair dilligence in meitting at the burght of Kirkcaldie in giving of thair best advyce in setting foorth thair commoun landis and the burgh of Kirkcaldie to be conveiner of the said burghtis and to report thair dilligence heiranent under the pain of 20 lib. ilk burght conforme to the 23 act of the said last generall conventioun.

39 Item ilk burght to send with thair commissioneris thair pairt of the soume of five hundreth fourscoir aught poundis vi s. viii d. addebtit to the agent at the fitting of his accomptis under the pain of 20 lib. ilk burght by and attour the payment of thair pairt of the said soume conforme to the taxt roll.

---

[11] Linlithgow's merchants had access to the sea via a harbour at Blackness on the Firth of Forth, north-east of the burgh.

[12] Barns is near Peebles, while Ballogie is in Aberdeenshire.

40 Item ilk burght to send with thair commissioners thair partis of the clerk and agent fies conforme to the custome with thair pairt of the soume of ane hundreth merkis for the clerkis servant George Sceyne.

Thairfor we desyre your wisdomes to send your commissioneris sufficientlie instructit for keiping of the said conventioun as you tender the weall of the estate of the burrowis under the paine of 20 lib. in caice ye failyie. So resting till farder occasioun we bid you heartily fareweall.

From our burgh of Bruntiland, the last day of March I^m vi^c xlviii yeiris

Your loving freindis and nightbouris the ballies and counsill of the burgh of Bruntisland subscryving be our commoun clerk at our command [Magnus Ait]toun[13]

---

13 Magnus Aittoun was clerk of Burntisland in 1657, see NAS, Papers of the Henderson Family of Fordell, GD172/1836.

INDEX

Newburgh 83, 135, 165
Newcastle-upon-Tyne 310
Nicolson, James, burgess of Dysart 150
Noble, James, burgess of Edinburgh 149
Normandy 21, 22, 23, 46, 160, 195, 231,
    238, 268, 296–7, 307, 313, 316, 326
North Berwick 38, 42, 150, 275
    commissioners for 81, 99–100, 130,
        163, 212, 252
    harbour of 99, 150, 184, 234, 272
Norval (Norwall), William, burgess of
    Stirling 33, 37, 39

Oatlands, Palace of 108, 109
oatmeal 112
Oliphant, James, provost of Haddington
    33, 37, 39
Orkney 117
Ormiston, Robert, burgess of
    Edinburgh 149
Orrock, James, burgess of Burntisland
    263
Osborne, John, burgess of Ayr 41, 62,
    74, 80, 106, 162, 192
Ostend 155, 184

Panbride 305
Paniter, William (or Thomas), burgess of
    Montrose 12, 33, 37, 39
Panton, John, burgess of South
    Queensferry 276
Park, Patrick, burgess of Glasgow 178,
    201
parliament 1, 2, 5, 10, 11, 12, 23, 27–8,
    60, 102, 189, 234, 271, 290, 297n,
    303n
    acts of 8, 13, 25, 27, 28, 34, 36, 43,
        51, 75, 77, 78, 85, 89–90, 108,
        141–3, 148, 149, 156, 158, 165,
        168, 172, 173, 182, 183, 204, 217,
        218, 228, 229, 230, 233, 255, 257,
        258, 277, 279, 281, 289, 313, 314,
        317, 318, 319, 323, 324
    lords of the articles 11
    macers of 73
    of 1633 2, 16–19, 25, 124–8, 136,
        138n, 141, 144, 145, 147, 159, 179,
        196, 204
    of 1646 293, 295–6, 306, 318

Paterson (or Piterson, Peterson), John,
    burgess of Glasgow 318
Paterson, Ninian, burgess of Glasgow
    280, 292
Paterson, Robert, burgess of Cupar 41,
    74, 124, 129, 153, 157, 162, 165, 192,
    211, 237, 251
Paton, Archibald, burgess of Edinburgh
    178
Paton, George, burgess of South
    Queensferry 189
pearls 47, 108, 111, 145, 179, 196, 199,
    209
Pearson, Mr David, burgess of Forfar
    81, 125, 130, 135
Pearson, George, burgess of Edinburgh
    282
Pearson, Mr James, burgess of Arbroath
    81, 130, 163
Peebles 38, 54, 60, 92, 279, 309, 327n
    commissioners for 42, 81, 107, 125,
        130, 163, 212, 252, 275
    bridges of 262
Peebles, David, master of the
    conciergery house 54
Peebles, Mr John, burgess of Irvine 41,
    129
Peddie, James, burgess of Montrose 274,
    281, 282, 324
Penman, John, burgess of Jedburgh 74,
    106
Perth 38, 70, 78, 145, 146, 150, 153, 198,
    219, 225, 247, 259, 271, 296
    commissioners for 33, 36, 37, 40,
        41, 62, 74, 106, 119, 121, 124, 129,
        179, 211, 213, 237, 251, 274
    conventions at 4, 7–8, 11–13, 24,
        33–40, 54n, 92, 97, 107, 211–36,
        237, 238, 239, 241, 242, 245, 253,
        254, 255, 256, 257, 258, 259,
        262, 265, 267, 269, 277, 281, 287,
        290
    council of 45, 156, 250
Picardy 21, 22, 23, 238, 268, 296, 307,
    313, 316, 326
Pinkerton, John, burgess of Rutherglen
    130, 163
pirates 18, 20, 126, 145, 158, 159
Pittenweem 92, 98, 109, 317